CW00495985

The Thirty-Nint

Massachusetts Volunteers

1862-1865

Alfred S. Roe

Alpha Editions

This edition published in 2023

ISBN : 9789357944229

Design and Setting By
Alpha Editions
www.alphaedis.com
Email - info@alphaedis.com

PREFACE

More than fifty years after the organization of the Thirty-ninth Regiment and its departure for the seat of war, its printed history makes its appearance. The long delay has not arisen from any lack of desire for its preparation, nor on account of want of material. For many long years it was supposed that the recital was in preparation, but the comrade to whom the task was intrusted went away into the other world before its completion, and survivors of the Regiment began to wonder if their story of long marches, fierce fighting and unspeakable suffering in Rebel prisons ever would be told. At the annual reunion of the Veteran Association in 1911 it was voted to proceed with the long cherished proposition, and a committee was appointed to carry out the proposal; after two years and a half the survivors of that committee present this volume to the patient waiters among the living veterans and to the families and descendants of those who have made the final crossing.

Readers of the book should bear in mind that it is very far from being a history of the war, nor does it discuss campaigns and battles in their entirety; on the contrary every effort has been made to describe the part borne by the Regiment in said campaigns and engagements. Long shelves in the large libraries of the country are already laden with great volumes descriptive of the War of the Rebellion as a whole and of detached portions thereof; as many more have been written of eminent individual experience, like the recollections of Grant, Sherman, Sheridan on the Union side and of Beauregard, Johnston and Longstreet among the Confederates, but the story of the great struggle will not be fully told until that of every regiment finds its way into print. Regimental histories occupy a golden mean between the comprehensiveness of the general history and the minuteness of individual records.

Massachusetts veterans can not be too grateful that the Commonwealth in its wisdom, a number of years ago, offered to assist in the preparation and publication of regimental histories by the purchase of five hundred copies of the same, under certain conditions of size and contents. In this manner and otherwise, more than one-half of the organizations of the Bay State which participated in the effort to maintain the Union have been written and it is hoped that the generosity of the Commonwealth and the courage of the veterans will continue until every regiment, battery and battalion will have been adequately described. While those who made the history are rapidly passing over the divide 'twixt life and death, and personal recollections are more difficult to obtain, yet their stories are not written so much, at this late date, from word of mouth as from letters, diaries and jottings made at the time and now are carefully preserved either by the writers or those to whom they have passed as precious legacies.

A history like this of the Thirty-ninth represents many letters written to veterans or to their surviving families in the effort to secure for transcription whatever note the soldier may have made in camp, field or prison-pen, bearing on the period in which the writer wore the blue. In several cases, through fear of losing the precious documents, friends of deceased soldiers have declined to lend them for use; of course it is too late to secure them for utility in this instance but, for the sake of other efforts in this direction, let us hope that those people possessing any written observations on the trying times of 1861-'65 will freely proffer their employment by those interested in their permanent preservation. It is a lamentable fact that many papers prepared under the fire of the enemy or, at least, in that indefinite region known as the "Front," have disappeared through the extra diligence of careful housekeepers and the general dislike of "old things lying 'round."

While many months in the earlier portions of the service of the Thirty-ninth were devoted to drill and thorough preparation, including a prolonged stay in the city of Washington, yet the call to the field, soon after Gettysburg, was so obeyed that before the seal of Appomattox was set upon the fate of the Confederacy, Colonel Davis' men had proved beyond any chance for cavil that they were of the same stuff that had rallied so readily at Concord and Lexington; had bled in the streets of Baltimore and, on the decks of the Constitution and the Monitor, had shown the world what was meant by resistance to tyranny. Its first officer was killed at the front; the third mortally wounded, and the second so severely injured that his life was long despaired of and seemingly was saved as by a miracle. At the Weldon R. R., on the 19th of August, 1864, so completely was the Regiment swept off the field, through no fault of its own, its organization was nearly lost, and the deaths in the prisons of the South of these victims exceeded those of all other Massachusetts Infantry Regiments with a single exception.

In seeking printed data for condensation in this narrative the committee was rewarded in finding in the Fourth Volume of the Printed Papers of the Massachusetts Military Historical Society a very clear and interesting description of the "Operations of the Army of the Potomac, May 7-11, 1864" by Brevet Brigadier-General Charles Lawrence Peirson, the universally loved and respected Colonel of the Thirty-ninth, and from his observations liberal abstracts have been made for the edification of readers of this history. In the same volume also are found papers by Captain Charles H. Porter, Companies D and A of the Regiment, and always so active in the councils of the Veteran Association, who discusses the "Opening of the Campaign of 1864" and the "Battle of Cold Harbor," valuable in considering the parts taken in those incidents by the Regiment in which he served. Access also has been had to typewritten papers on the part borne by the Fifth Corps in the last three days of March, '65, and "The Fifth Corps at Five Forks" also prepared by Captain Porter and which have proved of great utility in this compilation.

Naturally, the papers of General Peirson and Captain Porter are of a general character, somewhat removed from the individual, but quite the reverse is found in the well preserved accounts of company experience as presented in contributions to the Woburn Journal by Albert P. Barrett of Co. K, to the Medford Mercury by John S. Beck of "C" and in the monograph of Lieut. John H. Dusseault of Company E. Unfortunately, the spirited story, as told by the Woburn scribe, goes no further than the Mine Run campaign, leaving the reader longing for a continuation of his glowing recital; Diarist Beck returns his comrades, those who survived, to their home-town, while the Somerville chronicler, whose observations are clear and instructive up to the date of his wound and consequent invalidism is compelled to end his direct comments on that direful August day of '64 at the Weldon R. R. However, whether general or specific, extended or condensed, the readers of the history owe much to the careful annalist of those trying days of the early sixties.

Thanks are due the survivors who by their answers to circular letters rendered possible the exceedingly full roster, wherein are found the individual records whence must be drawn in coming years the facts for those seeking admission to patriotic organizations on the strength of ancestral service in preserving the Union. It is a source of regret that data could not be obtained for extending the descriptive list of every name in the Regiment. Especially are thanks due to General Peirson for his unflagging interest in the work of preparation and for his generosity in helping on the undertaking. The committee representing the Veteran Association is entitled to the thanks of all concerned for its careful attention to details, for the time given to rehearsals of the story as it progressed and for its unfailing willingness and promptness in assisting in every possible manner. At the same time it is impossible to suppress the regrets that inevitably rise over the seemingly untimely deaths of comrades Brown and Whittaker. Possibly no one had been more prominent than the first named in laying out the work and securing data for the story, but he was called away in the very midst of the preparation; Comrade Whittaker entered into the scheme with all the zeal and ardor so characteristic of his intense nature, and died, as it were, pen in hand, inditing the story of the terrible opening of The Battle Summer as he remembered it.

Thanks also should be rendered to the Brothers Mentzer and Mitchell of "A" for anecdotes and incidents; to Geo. V. Shedd and Edward H. Lewis of "B" for the use of their diaries; to the family of the late John S. Beck of "C" for the loan of his well preserved diary, and to M. F. Roberts for other Company C facts; to the widow of Captain C. H. Porter, "D" and "A," for the use of his scrapbook, manuscripts and other data; to Lieut. J. H. Dusseault, "E," for his accurate and interesting account of the Somerville Company; to the family of John E. Horton for his painstaking diary; and to Ex-mayor Edward Glines, Somerville, for the use of the carefully kept diary of his brother Frederick A.; to Lieut. Jas. E. Seaver, secretary of the Old Colony Historical Society, Taunton, for valuable data concerning Company F, its officers and men; to Lieut. Chas. H. Chapman and Sergt. J. H. Prouty, "G," for facts concerning that company; to George Monk, "H," for his brother Robert's diary; to Lieut. H. F. Felch, W. H. Garfield and the Hon. H. C. Mulligan, son of Lieut. Simon Mulligan, for facts pertaining to Company I; and to the family of A. P. Barrett, "K," for the scrapbook having his letters to the Woburn Journal; George E. Fowle, Abijah Thompson and Capt. E. F. Wyer (Fifth M. V. M.) for Company K data and incidents; to all those whose journals and recollections rendered possible the unexcelled accounts of prison experiences. Finally, all concerned unite in thanks to the ever efficient and courteous corps of officers and assistants in the office of the adjutant-general at the State House for favors there extended.

Worcester, December, 1913 ALFRED S. ROE.

BATTLES IN WHICH THE THIRTY-NINTH BORE A PART

1863

MINE RUN, November 28

1864

WILDERNESS, May 5-7
SPOTTSYLVANIA (Alsop's Farm and Laurel Hill), May 8-18
NORTH ANNA RIVER, May 23
COLD HARBOR, June 1-11
PETERSBURG, June 17-August 17
WELDON R. R., August 18-19

1865

HATCHER'S RUN or DABNEY'S MILLS, February 6
GRAVELLY RUN or WHITE OAK ROAD, March 31
FIVE FORKS, April 1

SURRENDER AT APPOMATTOX,
April 9

IN THE BEGINNING

While patriotism never flagged for a moment, and the determination to maintain the Union at all hazards was still as strong as ever, it must be confessed that the midsummer military outlook in 1862 was not altogether inspiring for the Nation. Whatever hopes had been raised by the success of Burnside in North Carolina, by Grant's campaign in Tennessee, and through the occupation of New Orleans by the combined forces of Butler and Farragut, they had been more than offset by the failure of McClellan's efforts on the peninsula and the unfruitful outcome of Halleck's movement against Corinth. An army that had displayed prodigies of valor from Fair Oaks to Malvern Hill, now catching its breath on the banks of the James River, and an enemy leisurely departing from the depot which Halleck had thought thoroughly invested, were bitter morsels for Northern people who had been led to expect the capture of Richmond and a like fate for the rebel forces which had fallen back from Shiloh.

The slopes of Malvern were still red with the blood of fallen heroes when President Lincoln, on the 4th of July, 1862, startled the nation with a call for three hundred thousand additional troops. The land was rapidly becoming one vast armed camp; Massachusetts already had sent nearly or quite fifty thousand men into the army and navy, out of her population of less than one and a half million people, but before the year was done, the aggregate was swollen to more than eighty thousand. Out of the great number called for, the assignment to Massachusetts was fifteen thousand and, on the seventh of the month, Governor Andrew formally presented the demand to the people of the Commonwealth. Hitherto, there had been no regular apportionment, each division of the state having been ready and anxious to aid in filling whatever quota might be required. In this case there was a clear statement of what each city and town, from Abington to Yarmouth would be expected to do.

Concerning the number called for, the president in a private telegram to Governor Morgan of New York said, "It was thought safest to mark high enough. I should not want the half of 300,000 new troops if I could have them now. If I had 50,000 additional troops here now, I believe I could substantially close the war in two weeks. But time is everything; and if I get 50,000 new men in a month I shall have lost 20,000 old ones during the same month, having gained only 30,000 with the difference between old and new troops still against me. The quicker you send, the less you will have to send. Time is everything, please act in view of this." All this time, it must be remembered, Governor Andrew, in a mild way, was criticising the National Administration for its failure to liberate the slaves and for not imposing upon them many of the hardships borne by the regularly enlisted men.

Nor were the needs of the Government satisfied with the demand of July 4th, however large it may have seemed, for, while the entire loyal North was putting forth every possible effort to secure the required enlistments there came from Washington, on the 4th of August, another call for troops, this time also demanding three hundred thousand men, just as though there were a never-ending source of supply. This call was accompanied by the possibility of a draft, that most dreaded of all methods for securing reinforcements, provided the volunteers did not appear within a certain limited period; the apportionment, 19,080 men, it will be observed was more than a fourth larger than that in the preceding call, an excess explained on the basis that the total number, 34,080, bore the same proportion to the 600,000, the sum of the two calls, that the free population of Massachusetts did to the free population in the states that had shown themselves loyal to the Union, and were supporting the Government in the struggle.

A very prominent question in the emergency was just how should the newly enlisted men be placed; should they be added to regiments already in the field or should new organizations be made for their reception? Excellent arguments were offered on both sides; the question had been discussed from the very moment that battles or disease had begun making gaps in the ranks. When Mayor Isaac Davis, after the disastrous engagement of Ball's Bluff, telegraphed to Colonel Charles Devens, of the Fifteenth Massachusetts Infantry, asking what Worcester could do for the regiment, the subsequently distinguished officer replied, "Send us three hundred and ten men to fill our gaps; also a blanket and a pair of mittens for each of us; that will do for the present." The good mayor found it much easier to supply the woolen requirements than the men, who, for certain reasons, were unwilling to enter an old regiment where promotion would inevitably go to those who had been in the ranks longest, and soldiering without the possibilities of promotion is dull business.

Those who have considered carefully the subject of war, its progress and development, have, in many cases, taken occasion to censure some of the Northern States, and especially Massachusetts, forgetful of the fact that local feelings and a confidence in leaders whom the men know go a long way in imparting confidence to the citizen soldier. Governor John A. Andrew would have filled the old regiments, rather than form new ones, and to the newly formed organizations he would have given experienced officers instead of those elected by the men, but the latter would not have it so. In this connection that great man is said to have exclaimed, "Julius Caesar himself couldn't raise a company for an old regiment as long as there is a shoemaker left to make a captain of." The town system, so prominent a feature in New England life, had much to do with the fellow-feeling in companies and when these different companies, representing as many townships, all belonged to the same county, seemingly little was left to be desired in the background of the organization.

The numbering of Massachusetts Infantry organizations had already mounted to thirty before the call of the President in July, 1862. Recruiting was very active, notwithstanding the horrors of war, so graphically set forth in the daily press. Meetings to stimulate enlistments were held throughout the Commonwealth, becoming a daily occurrence in the City of Boston, where her historic buildings and public places resounded with eloquence in behalf of the Union and its preservation. Points of rendezvous were provided at Pittsfield, Worcester, Lynnfield, Readville, and other places for regiments, while Camp Cameron at North Cambridge was reserved for recruits to the older organizations. Within two months from the issuing of Governor Andrew's Order Number 26[B], dated July 7th, more than four thousand men had been enlisted and sent forward to old regiments, nine new ones had been raised and equipped, and eight of them had been sent forward to strengthen the hands of the Government. So diligently had the governor and his assistants labored, the dreaded draft was averted and, long before the first snowfall, the last of the great demand upon Massachusetts for the sons whom she had reared for other purposes, had gone southward, gun in hand, following the flag.

Sometimes regiments were raised by officers commissioned for this purpose; in other cases companies were raised in cities or large towns which, when full, were sent forward to the nearest rendezvous and, when a sufficient number had been thus assembled, the regimental organization followed. Many towns could not furnish men enough for a company, so the men went forward in squads or individually and these recruits either pieced out some company, not quite filled, or were thrown together to constitute a new company, this being the case with Company G of the Thirty-ninth, which had no central source like those of the others. Lynnfield had been designated as the point to which should be sent all Eastern Massachusetts volunteers for new regiments, while to North Cambridge, Camp Cameron, were forwarded the men who had enlisted in old organizations. These two points were to receive the three years' soldiers from the counties of Barnstable, Bristol, Dukes, Essex, Middlesex, Nantucket, Norfolk, Plymouth and Suffolk. Already in Camp Edwin M. Stanton, Lynnfield, usually called Camp Stanton, were the Thirty-fifth and the Thirty-eighth Regiments in process of formation and along with the Thirty-ninth in reporting there was the Fortieth; later came the Forty-first, the last of the three years' regiments under the July call.

LYNNFIELD

Several of the companies constituting the Thirty-ninth, had left their respective towns under the belief that they were to join the Thirty-fifth, but that organization and also the Thirty-eighth were so far completed, that the numerals "39" became the designation of the regiment, whose story is progressing here. Lynnfield had been a rendezvous, already, for the Seventeenth, Nineteenth, Twenty-second and Twenty-third regiments and, however satisfactory it may have proved for those bodies, it was clearly inadequate to the demands of the several thousand men to congregate here during July and August. Placed on a branch railroad, it was difficult of access and did not have space for the formation of a regimental line; so rapidly did the volunteers report, they found only scant comforts in their rendezvous. While only thirteen miles from Boston and being nearer still to Lynn, the rush of recruits to the rendezvous sadly tried the resources of the commissary, and made many a boy wish he were elsewhere. Says one observer, "No preparation had been made for our reception; finally however, tents were found for a portion of the company and we passed the first night in camp in anything but a peaceful frame of mind or body. Quite a number of the men left camp for home, or found quarters elsewhere. Rations, too, were conspicuously absent and for a time we depended on outside sources for our supply." Time, and patience however, relieved many of these distresses. The companies as they reached camp were known only by the name of the town whence they came, or that of the officer who was in command. Their designation by letters of the alphabet came later. Herewith follows a brief account of the several companies, their respective beginnings, their organization and time of reporting at Camp Stanton.

COMPANY A

SOUTH DANVERS, since 1868 PEABODY.

The allotment of this town on account of the call for troops was seventy-five. An enthusiastic meeting was held July 11, in the Town Hall, over which B. C. Perkins presided and at which the Rev. Mr. Barber and others spoke. A committee on resolutions was appointed consisting of Messrs. F. Poole, Lewis Allen, John D. Poore, Alfred McKenzie and Dr. George Osborne. A committee of nine members was also appointed who were to assist or supervise enlistments. On the 21st, the anniversary of the Battle of Bull Run, a special town meeting was held at which it was voted to pay one hundred and fifty dollars' bounty to each volunteer. Speeches were numerous and a committee of forty citizens was appointed, five for each school district, to co-operate with that of nine men already in existence. One-fourth of the quota had been raised in two days. It was voted to borrow twelve thousand dollars, and a committee was appointed to secure the money on time at six per cent.; on the 25th, Friday, a great open air meeting was held in the town square, a platform having been erected in front of the Warren Bank Building. Isaac Hardy presided and spoke as did others. On the next day, Saturday, the recruits, accompanied by about one hundred citizens, under the direction of Roberts S. Daniels, Jr., and having a brass band, marched from the recruiting station to Lynnfield, distant several miles away, an exacting experience for raw recruits on a hot July day. Among those witnessing the departure was one who, fifty years before, had been a prisoner in Dartmoor. All of these newly enlisted men supposed that they were going into the Thirty-fifth Regiment. July 31st, an adjourned town-meeting was held in which it was announced that Eben Sutton, a public spirited citizen, had volunteered to take the entire loan at five and one half per cent., an act that was greeted with great applause by all present. Captain, George S. Nelson; first Lieutenant, Henry W. Moulton; second lieutenant, George H. Wiley; all of South Danvers.

COMPANY B.

Recruiting began early in Roxbury and on the 10th, there was a special meeting of both branches of the City Government, at which it was voted to give seventy-five dollars to each recruit in addition to whatever the General Government might offer. It was also voted to appropriate thirty thousand dollars for expenses, and the treasurer was directed to borrow. Roxbury's quota was three hundred and eighty-nine; Saturday night, to inspirit enlistments, a public meeting was held in Institute Hall at which Mayor William Gaston (subsequently governor) presided and numerous and eloquent speeches were made, and the previous action of the City Government was publicly endorsed. July 17th, the bounty was raised to one hundred dollars, and on the 19th a brass band concert was given in front of Institute Hall, with an address by the Hon. John C. Park. August 7, the Company, numbering sixty-nine men, under the command of Captain Graham, escorted by the militia of the city, paraded and all were entertained by Colonel Hodges of the Horse Guards in Bacon's Hall, where Judge Russell spoke. Sunday, the 10th, the Company attended service in the first Universalist Church; on the 11th, again escorted by the Horse Guards, the Company paraded through the principal streets to Bacon's Hall where speeches were made by several persons, including Private George F. Moses, of the Company, the latter being filled to its maximum. It was on the 15th of August that the Company assembled and through lines of friends and relatives, at a little before noon, started for Boston, whence it took train for Lynnfield, arriving at about three o'clock, p. m. Captain, William W. Graham; first lieutenant, William T. Spear; second lieutenant, Julius M. Swain.

COMPANY C.

Medford's popular company, the Lawrence Light Guard, had already distinguished itself in the Fifth M. V. M., under the first call for troops, and was enjoying something akin to dignified ease when the president's call for three hundred thousand men placed new responsibilities upon all the cities and towns, Medford having to raise eighty-eight men as her quota. Though the selectmen, acting under the governor's orders, did their best as recruiting officers, and though there was an offer of seventy-five dollars' bounty, voted by the town, and though on the 21st of July the offer was increased to one hundred dollars, the eligible men did not seem disposed to enlist until, on the 29th of the month, the selectmen addressed a letter to the Light Guard, asking its members to step to the front and assist in filling the requisition. The request was complied with at once and, on the 14th of August, the company was complete with its complement of one hundred and one men, including many who had served under the earlier demand. Mustered in on the 14th, it left Medford for Lynnfield on the 25th of August under most auspicious circumstances, these including religious exercises, speeches and the presence of thousands of sympathetic people. The commissioned officers, all of whom had been out with Colonel Lawrence, were captain, John Hutchins; first lieutenant, Perry Coleman; second lieutenant, Isaac F. R. Hosea.

COMPANY D.

The quota of Quincy was one hundred and five men; and to secure this number of new soldiers the first meeting was held in the Town Hall, July 12th; a special one, called by the selectmen, and the crowd was so great that the hall would not hold it. Chief Justice Bigelow, presided and spoke, being followed by Josiah Quincy, Jr., John Quincy Adams and others; it was voted to offer a bounty of seventy-five dollars, and patriotic resolutions were adopted. At a meeting held July 21st, it was voted to raise the bounty to one hundred and twenty-five dollars. The third meeting was held July 29th, with William S. Morton presiding; addresses were made by Lieut. Colonel Henry Walker of Quincy, Lieut. Colonel Guiney of the Ninth Regiment, and by one of the recruits, Charles H. Porter, son of Whitcomb Porter, whose remarks were of a very enthusiastic character, Captain Spear receiving numerous compliments. By the 2nd of August, ninety-six men had been secured, the recruiting being done by a town committee. Monday, the 4th of August, "Good-bye" was said to the Company; line was formed at the Town Hall under escort of Niagara Hose Company, Captain Newcomb; an address was given by Lieut. Colonel Walker, and a collation was served in Lyceum Hall. Thence by horse cars, accompanied by the firemen and a band, the soldiers went to and through Boston, and so on by steam to Lynnfield, reaching that place at about two p. m. There had been one hundred and twelve enlistments in the company, but some had been rejected. On the 22nd, the town generously voted to pay the recruits one dollar per day for the time spent in drilling. This same day the company came home on a furlough, and on the next night, that of Saturday, the men assembled in the Town Hall and presented Captain Spear with a sword, costing fifty dollars, and to First Sergeant John Nichols, a sash and belt. It was a noisily enthusiastic meeting, so much so that very little of the speaking could be heard. Sunday, the 24th, beheld a part of the Company at service in the Universalist Church in the morning and, in the afternoon, Lieutenant McLaughlin, U. S. A., came out from Boston and mustered the Company into the United States service. Monday, the 25th, the men returned to camp, all save three, who were apprehended as deserters and sent after their fellows, everyone proving himself a good soldier afterwards; they were just a trifle dilatory in keeping up. Captain, Edward A. Spear; first lieutenant, William G. Sheen; second lieutenant, Charles H. Porter.

COMPANY E.

SOMERVILLE.

For the apportionment of fifteen thousand men to the Commonwealth, Somerville had to raise ninety-two men and this she succeeded in doing within the months of July and August. The aggregate bounty paid each enlisted man was one hundred and twenty-five dollars, one hundred dollars coming from the town, the remainder from private subscription.

The selectmen, acting as agents, had recommended three men as commissioned officers of the projected company, and these, all of whom had seen service in the Somerville Company of the Fifth Regiment, M. V. M., in its three months' tour of duty, applied themselves diligently to their task. Camp was pitched on Prospect Hill and the flagstaff, erected there and then, remained until the digging down of the hill some fifteen years later; this occupation if possible added to the fame of the spot on which Israel Putnam had intrenched himself after falling back from Bunker Hill. The stay on elevated and breezy Prospect was far from tedious, the nearness of home supplies more than compensating for any hardships incident to camp duties. Mustered into the U. S. service, August 12, the Company remained here until September 2nd, when it proceeded to Boxford, there to join the other companies which were to constitute the Thirty-ninth Regiment, having had no taste of the stay in Lynnfield, the rendezvous of the other companies. The Commissioned officers were captain, Fred R. Kinsley; first lieutenant, Joseph J. Giles; second lieutenant, Willard C. Kinsley. All of the officers had been commissioned in the Thirty-eighth Regiment, Captain Kinsley and Lieutenant Giles, August 14th, and Lieutenant Kinsley, August 8th, but the assignment of the company to the Thirty-ninth Regiment compelled the transferal of the officers.

CAPTAIN FREDERICK R. KINSLEY
B'v't Major and Colonel

COMPANY F.

Work for the formation of what was to be Company F did not begin until the 5th day of August, when a meeting of the sub-committee of the military committee was held to consider the raising of a new company, Captain Presbry, one of the selectmen, presiding, with T. Gordon, secretary. Joseph J. Cooper was authorized to raise a company under the conditions as stated in a letter of the Adjutant General, dated July 29, '64, and the general order of the War Department, Number Seventy-five. The *Taunton Gazette* comments that the lieutenancies will be offered to Isaac D. Paul and John D. Reed, both men of integrity, and "it is believed that the company will be speedily filled and that it will be one of the most creditable of those provided by Taunton." The record for the 6th of August was that Captain Cooper had opened a recruiting office in Templar Hall Building, and had secured about a dozen names. By the 7th, the total had risen to twenty-four men; the 8th saw thirty-six names enrolled and, on the 11th, the tide had risen to forty-seven good and true patriots. The 13th beheld the citizens assembled in town meeting, wherein it was voted to increase the bounty to two hundred dollars, thus adding a stimulus which resulted in filling the company to the maximum. The 18th was a day of memories for the good old town, since on this date the new company departed for the rendezvous at Lynnfield. The largest assemblage of people that the town had seen since the leaving of the Seventh Regiment, early in the war, was out at seven o'clock in the morning to witness the going of the new soldiers. They formed on the green, whence they were escorted by the Light Guard, with music by the Bridgewater Brass Band, to the railroad station. Followed by the enthusiastic cheering of the populace, the men were borne away to new scenes and experiences. Five days later or on the 23rd, the men had a furlough home for twenty-four hours, returning to camp on the 24th. Of course, Company F moved with the other companies in the transfer to Boxford, where on the 3rd of September, a noteworthy incident took place. The men of Taunton's company were drawn up in front of their tents when George Childs, Esq., in behalf of Taunton citizens, presented Captain Cooper and Lieutenants Paul and Reed with elegantly mounted revolvers, each officer responding in a very happy manner. Captain, Joseph J. Cooper; first lieutenant, Isaac D. Paul; second lieutenant, John D. Reed.

COMPANY G.

BOSTON, HINGHAM, SCITUATE AND THE SOUTH SHORE.

From information furnished chiefly by Lieut. J. H. Prouty it seems that Hingham was about as liberal a contributor to Company G as any single place, having thirty-seven men in the ranks of "G" and another in "D." It was the only company in the regiment that started without some local head or centre. When the call came, Hingham took action at once, and on the 5th held a town meeting at four o'clock p. m., with Captain John Stephenson presiding; it was voted to raise five thousand dollars to aid the families of volunteers as state aid, and a thousand more to be distributed under the direction of the selectmen. July 11th brought the people together again, in the evening of Friday, to take action towards filling the town's quota of fifty-one men; Luther Stephenson presided and several patriotic addresses were given; it was voted to pay seventy-five dollars bounty to every man enlisting, a committee of twelve was appointed to co-operate with the selectmen in securing enlistments. This committee met on the 15th, organized, heard a deal of eloquent speaking and voted to recommend to the townspeople that a bounty of one hundred dollars be paid to every volunteer. The Town accepted, July 19th, the recommendation of the citizens' committee. On the same evening, a number of volunteers put down their names. An adjourned war meeting was held on the 22nd, and a large committee of ladies was chosen to help forward the filling of the quota. The next meeting, August 6th, was on the call of the ladies and was largely attended; August 15th, the town voted to make the bounty for each volunteer two hundred dollars. The thirty-seven Hingham men who went into Company G were not all new to service, for two, at least, had gone out with the Lincoln Light Infantry in the Fourth Regiment in 1861, on the first call for troops. The volunteers expected to go with the Thirty third Massachusetts; next with the Thirty-fifth, but finally fetched up with the Thirty-ninth. They had no officers. The governor commissioned, as captain, Ezra J. Trull, better known as "Jack" Trull, who had been a corporal in the Thirteenth Massachusetts, and he was assigned to the command of "G." Though only nineteen years old, he was one of the best drilled officers in the regiment and his active, stirring nature kept his company in excellent shape. He was a Boston man, as was the first lieutenant, C. W. Thompson; the second lieutenant, C. Henry Chapman, was from Cambridge. First and last, more than thirty cities and towns contributed to the roll of the company.

COMPANY H.

Early action was taken in Dorchester towards raising the town's quota of one hundred and thirty-seven men. On the 15th of July, the citizens convened at the town hall with James H. Upham, moderator, and they started proceedings by the singing of patriotic songs. It was voted to pay all recruits one hundred dollars, and to borrow fourteen thousand dollars for such purpose. The selectmen were empowered to carry out the expressed will of the meeting and the same board was directed to see to the securing of enlistments, by the appointment of a "suitable person" to raise a military company as a part of the town's quota. The Hall had been plentifully bedecked with flags, some one hundred in number, among them there being one that had been borne in the Revolution. Besides, there were curios and relics to excite the curiosity and patriotism of all beholders, the display being the work of Frederick F. Hassam, who received the enthusiastic thanks of the meeting for his thoughtfulness and action. On the 19th there was a great meeting on Meeting House Hill, with artillery company firing sixty-eight guns and the Hon. Marshall P. Wilder presiding; of the event the *Boston Journal* says: "Shoulder Arms! Forward, March!" The Company left Dorchester Wednesday, August 13, receiving a parting salute from Captain Harris' Battery; in Boston there was a short parade with refreshments, 1.30 p. m., at John Preston's chocolate establishment on State Street. A hearty escort was given by the selectmen, many citizens, and Fire Engine Company Number 5, and all kept step to music afforded by a brass band. From Boston, cars on the Boston and Maine Railroad bore the men, one hundred and thirty-seven in number, to Lynnfield. Captain, Charles N. Hunt; first lieutenant, Robert Rhodes; second lieutenant, Robert Williams.

COMPANY I.

Natick was expected to provide one hundred and three men, or just a company, and this she set about doing through a meeting in the evening of July 17th, in School House Hall, over which the Hon. J. W. Bacon presided. To report a plan of action, the following committee was appointed: Leonard Winch, John J. Perry and E. P. Fay. Another meeting on the 25th voted to pay volunteers one hundred and fifty dollars each, and a committee of fifteen was appointed to assist the recruiting officers. Monday, July 28th, brought out a great meeting which was addressed by United States Senator Henry Wilson, Capt. Ephraim H. Brigham and others. By August 1st, matters had reached ignition pitch with a great meeting in the Town Hall, Captain Brigham presiding; there were eloquent speeches, but the one which excited the most admiration was that of Benning Hall, Jr., the village expressman, who on this occasion made his first public address, chiefly to his comrades, of whom twenty-two had put down their names. The fourth public meeting was held August 4th, in School House Hall, Lieut. Simon Mulligan in the chair, and it was voted to act at once, and to talk afterwards. Then followed "a scene such as few people ever witness" when forty-seven men marched up and signed the roll amid waving hats and handkerchiefs, the very best men in the grand old town. The Hon. Henry Wilson was present and spoke, as did Edward Choate, G. L. Sawin, H. B. Moore, C. B. Phillips and B. Hill, Jr. In one week Natick had raised one hundred and twenty-seven men for her company, twenty-four more than necessary. It was Saturday, August 9, that, escorted by the Victor and Union Fire Company, and crowds of citizens, the Natick newly enlisted men set forth for their rendezvous. After a brief parade in Boston, Lynnfield was sought in the afternoon, where the reception was not just what the would-be soldiers expected. So many recruits had reported there was no room for the Natick people, who had to hire a building outside for use until the departure of a regiment gave them access to the regular quarters. Captain, Ephraim H. Brigham; first lieutenant, Simon Mulligan; second lieutenant, William H. Brown.

COMPANY K.

Woburn's assignment was ninety-eight men and it came at a time when recruiting was dull. Still the selectmen, in obedience to State House orders, called a meeting of Union loving citizens in the Town Hall, on the evening of Saturday, the 12th of July. The response was large and enthusiastic; it was voted to give every volunteer a bounty of one hundred dollars and a committee of fifteen was appointed to forward enlistments. It was further voted to call a town meeting on the 24th of the month for the purpose of carrying out the provisions of this popular gathering. Thirty-three men had enlisted or put down their   Aug., '62   names before the excitement began or the offer of bounty was made, and these men became "the immortal thirty-three" in company annals. Recruiting began on the 15th, and was very slow, though the office was open day and evening. At the town meeting, it was voted to give a bounty of one hundred and twenty-five dollars, and enlistments thereupon increased. Under the encouragement of a grand rally and a banquet in upper Lyceum Hall in the evening of the 24th, followed by a march through the streets accompanied by a brass band and speeches by prominent citizens, the roll of enlistments reached fifty names. Subsequent rallies and parades resulted in the securing of considerably more than the required number by the 1st of August. On the 5th of the month, after a collation in Lyceum Hall, escorted by the Fire Department, the company departed for the rendezvous, Camp Stanton, in Lynnfield, having the following commissioned officers: captain, John I. Richardson; first lieutenant, Luke R. Tidd; second lieutenant, Luther F. Wyman.

Life at a rendezvous camp is much the same, wherever found. The change from the untrammeled habits of home to the restrained conditions of military life is seldom made without friction on the part of the newly enlisted men, and if there were a lack of quarters, an insufficiency of food, and if the latter were of indifferent quality, they were only features to be expected wherever and whenever inexperienced citizens undertake the transforming act of becoming soldiers. However disagreeable some of the conditions at Camp Stanton may have been, nothing was encountered there that would not have been laughed at, when two years later the men were passing through the exactions of the "Battle Summer" or later still, when they realized the horrors of Salisbury and Andersonville. Nor were the days of Lynnfield altogether disagreeable to the recruits, for were there not the visits of home friends who always came laden with the best of goodies for the "boys," and passes for brief trips to the homes themselves? Besides every day had its round of duties, such as guard, the policing of the camp and the early induction to drill, even before the giving out of uniform and arms.

Col. Edward F. Jones, who had won distinction in the earlier months of the war as commander of the Sixth Regiment, and later had been assigned to the colonelcy of the Twenty-sixth Infantry, was in command of the camp and occasionally the newly made soldiers repined at the rigor of his commands, quite uncalled for to their undisciplined minds. Nothing, however, better exhibited the adaptability of the American soldier than the speed with which the material from school, shop and farm, caught the step, learned the manual and responded to the command of superior officers. In the case of the companies that were to constitute the Thirty-ninth Regiment, they arrived after the most of the desirable quarters had been taken by the men of the Thirty-fifth and the Thirty-eighth Regiments. The first named departed for the front on the 22nd of August; on the 24th, the Thirty-eighth took train for the South and as colonel went Timothy Ingraham who originally had been commissioned as the leader of the Thirty-ninth; a Captain in the Third Infantry during the three months' service, he had been lieutenant colonel in the Eighteenth Infantry and there were feelings of regret when the New Bedford officer was transferred to the earlier numbered organization.

BOXFORD

The limitations of Lynnfield finally became so apparent that the authorities determined to seek a new location and officers were directed to investigate, the result being that Boxford, still further away from Boston (twenty-eight miles) was selected. Here were the grounds that had been used as a musterfield by the Second Brigade, Second Division ⸢Sept. 1, '62⸥ of the State Militia and, on this extended plain by the side of a beautiful pond of water, it was determined to pitch the new camp. Orders were given for the cooking of three days' rations and on the 28th, by special trains the troops were transferred from Lynnfield to Boxford. It is possible that had the nearness of the day of starting for the front been known the trouble of removal had been avoided. Colonel Jones still commanded the camp which continued to be called "Stanton" and the commandant's rules were quite as rigid as ever. On the 29th, some of the soldiers were gladdened by the receipt from the State of twenty-five dollars' bounty and they soon found ways enough for disposing of it, though many of them had signed allotment papers, agreeing to have a portion of their pay reserved for friends at home.

Camp life during the week's stay in Boxford had its share of variation such as came from short trips away, the visits of friends, the receiving of uniforms, arms and equipments and the presentation of gifts to officers and men. Sept. 1st brought Col. P. Stearns Davis, the new commander of the Thirty-ninth Regiment. A brigadier general in the militia, he had been one of the most efficient of those assisting Governor Andrew in organizing and forwarding regiments, and the governor parted from the officer with regret; he succeeded Colonel Jones in the command of the Camp. Company officers were remembered by their friends, both those in the ranks and outside; on the 29th of August, his company gave to Captain Richardson of "K" a set of equipments and on the 1st of September, when on leave of absence in Woburn, Lieutenants Tidd and Wyman were presented by citizens with swords and sashes. Sept. 2nd, Company E, from Somerville, appeared in camp, the very last to report. On the 3rd, the commissioned officers of Company F, Taunton, were given revolvers by their fellow townsmen, of whom there was a goodly number present, their representative being George Childs, Esq. On this day also Springfield rifles were placed in the men's hands, accoutrements following on the 4th, so that they began to feel like real soldiers. On the 3rd also appeared Lieutenant Ladd, U. S. A., who began paying out one month's pay in advance. During these days the ladies of Woburn made and presented to the Woburn Company (K) a National flag, Miss Henrietta M. Young making the address of presentation and Lieutenant Tidd receiving, though the acceptance speech, in the absence of the captain, was made by Lieutenant Wyman. The flag was returned to Woburn to be retained there until the return of the company from its three years' term of service.

BOXFORD TO WASHINGTON.

On Friday, the 5th, came the regimental colors and orders to prepare three days' rations against the expected departure of the Thirty-ninth on the following day, and the same day saw the first dress-parade of the regiment under the command of Colonel Davis, also the efforts of embryo soldiers as they tried to pack into a knapsack two or three times as much as it would hold. When the active campaigning began, they were to learn some of the wisdom of Socrates when he exclaimed, "How many things there are that I do not need." Breaking camp on the morning of the 6th was a spirited affair and, after an early breakfast, line was formed and the men marched to the station not far from 8 o'clock a. m. Here came a lesson in delay that was to be repeated many times as the years moved on. Boston was sighted between 1 and 2 p. m. and, speedily disembarking, the regiment took its way through the city to the Boston and Worcester station. The day was extremely hot, the men had overloaded their knapsacks, hence many suffered badly, some having to fall out, though all reached the station in time for the train. Company E, Somerville, held the right of the line and "C" Medford, the left,

so that double-quick, with the Medford men, was the order | Sept. 6, '62 |

occasionally which, considering the heat, was a trying test. Of the march through Washington Street, the *Boston Journal* has this comment, "The men appeared hardy, robust and of excellent fighting material and were evidently superior in drill to many of the new regiments."

Though the crowds were great and friends by the hundred, not to say thousands, were there to say "Good-bye," the greetings and partings were had in passing, as the quickstep was kept through the city. At the station, the regiment was soon entrained for Worcester, as its next step on its southern way. There was no lack of interest in the departure by people all along the route to Worcester, and there the good citizens were not slow in supplying food, somewhat more appetizing than the rations borne in the haversacks; said rations in many cases became useless through the taste imparted by the recently painted receptacles, the traces of turpentine working through. One veteran relates, at this late day, his anguish over the spoiling of a quantity of fresh mother's made doughnuts. Thence, via the Norwich route, the way was southward, the first train reaching Groton, Connecticut, the summer terminus, about 10.30 in the evening. As the soldier-laden train was in two sections, there was a somewhat prolonged wait here for the arrival of the second part. However, sometime between 10.30 and midnight the steamer "City of New York" proceeded on its way to the great city, along the Sound, over which had passed so many New England men and boys on their Union-preserving mission. Though there was ample space on the soft side of the respective decks for the soldiers to lie down, there was altogether too much novelty for them to encamp at once. While the majority secured some sleep during the passage, there were those who watched the night through and were ready to greet the dawn and to experience the sensations of an early approach to the mightiest city of the Western Continent. Those who saw that sunrise and the course through East River and the final round-up at the Jersey City landing never forgot it; besides, the morning sights included a view of the "Great Eastern", the famous British steamship, then the greatest in the world and the wonder of all beholders.

Sunday morning at 8 o'clock, the steamer was docked at Jersey City and soon afterward the regiment was again embarked on a train for the trip through New Jersey and, though it was Sunday and, presumably, many people were at church, there seemed to be no lack of generous citizens, ready to supply the most luscious of fruit and to prove that whatever fun might be had at the expense of the state's being a "foreign country" the hearts of the people were all right. The day itself was in that delightful early fall, when Dame Nature does her best to outdo her June wonders, and the hearts of the Massachusetts travellers were all aglow as they saw the possibilities of the Garden State and when, having been ferried across the Delaware River, Philadelphia was reached, every man was in splendid appetite for the lavish lunch that the ladies of the City of Brotherly Love had prepared for them in the Cooper Refreshment Rooms. Few Eastern soldiers failed at some time in their experience to test the hospitality of William Penn's great city and that veteran is yet to be found who does not wax eloquent over the spread there afforded, and that was his without money and without price.

The march through Philadelphia was an enjoyable one, the people being in such evident sympathy with the men, who at every step were going further from their own homes and loved ones. When the station was reached, whence they were to start for Baltimore, there was a considerable halt during which the Massachusetts boys had a fine chance to make the acquaintances of certain of the fair daughters of the Keystone State and addresses were exchanged which, in subsequent months, afforded pleasure to both man and maiden, as letters passed between those in the field and the loyal dwellers on the banks of the Schuylkill. The ride southward, according to some of the chroniclers, was not   Sept. 7, '62   as enjoyable as the previous portions had

been; indeed one careful writer says, "Here the comfort of our journey ceased for we were put aboard cattle cars, with rough and hard seats"; in most cases, no seats at all; yet the time would come when that writer would be delighted to ride standing, on platform cars even, if thereby he could the sooner gain his destination. Wilmington, Delaware, reached at midnight or thereabouts, was the first stop and, notwithstanding the lateness of the hour there was a modified repetition of the Philadelphia reception, every one being anxious to contribute to the well being of the "boys in blue." Among those in waiting were former dwellers in the Bay State who were delighted to grasp the hands of men just from the old home.

The crossing of the Susquehanna River from Perryville, Delaware, to Havre-de-Grace was a source of great interest to these tyros of travel, and whole trains of cars, run aboard great ferryboats at once, for a trip over the river to the Maryland town opposite, excited not a little wonder, if not admiration. On reaching the further side of the river, the usual waiting was experienced and, though it was in the dead of night, those young soldiers were too full of life to allow the time to waste and in their search for mischief they discovered that the place abounded in geese and, long after midnight, these representatives of staid and sober New England awoke not alone the squawking fowls but the people as well and, over and through the gullied ways of this first bit of "Maryland, My Maryland" that they had encountered, these men, on fierce battle bent, pursued these poor feathered bipeds, though what they were to accomplish by a complete round-up, they had not the least notion. However, from any such test they were happily saved by the appearance on the scene of Colonel Davis who, apprised by the noise of the need of his presence, admonished his valiant followers to cease harrying the birds; nor were the mischievous fellows sorry, for they had gone about as far as they could and not have their fun changed into serious fault.

The regiment had reached the region where constant watch was kept over stations, railroad bridges and all points where it might be easy to obstruct transportation; hence the sight of dimly seen figures performing sentinel duty as the train swept along was not a little interesting to the men who were, as rapidly as possible, advancing from the abode of peace and plenty to that of privation and danger. Dawn of the 8th brought with it the entrance of Baltimore by the latest Massachusetts organization and, as the men marched through the silent streets in the early morning, many of them contrasted the reception accorded them in the unquestionably loyal city of Philadelphia, and that in the Monument City, which a year and five months before had caused the first bloodshed in the Civil War. A substantial breakfast was served at the Union refreshment rooms, though nothing like the generous spread made the day before by the ladies of the city on the Schuylkill. Several regiments, like the Thirty-ninth on their way South, were found waiting orders and transportation and the situation was somewhat emphasized by the sudden and serious illness of a number of soldiers, the rumor gaining circulation that they had been poisoned. Fortunately before the irate soldiers could begin retaliatory measures against the people, it was decided that the ailment was simply *cholera morbus*, occasioned by injudicious eating of green fruit obtained in transit.

Ellicott's Mills, not so very far from Baltimore, towards the west, was at first announced as the destination of the regiment, but, as there was no supply of tents or wagons, the order was countermanded and cars were taken for Washington. The sight of the incomplete Capitol and other public buildings was a glad one to these Massachusetts men who, in spite of warlike intentions, were alive to all of the geographical attractions that they might encounter. Reaching the Nation's centre of activity somewhat late Sept. 9,

'62 in the afternoon there was some time in which to take cursory glances of many edifices, already familiar through picture and print. Supper and lodgings were found in the barracks, close by the Baltimore and Ohio depot, and those who did not like the fare at the barracks, and could afford the price, had the privilege of supping outside. Weariness can sleep upon a flinty bed while lazy sloth may toss upon the softest of couches, hence the floor of the so-called "Soldiers' Rest" afforded comfort for the cattle car travellers. In the morning of the 9th, it was discovered that the Tenth Vermont had arrived during the night and was encamped outside, a regiment with which the Thirty-ninth was eventually to be brigaded for a time.

POTOMAC CROSSED.

The breakfast was not of a sort to elicit any great amount of praise from the soldiers and once more those who could got their food outside, and the forenoon was passed largely in seeing the sights of the Capital. Very likely the folks at home were thinking that their boys were so much needed that they were to be ordered into battle-line at once; but all concerned were to learn that in the fiercest of wars there are many waits, and this delay in Washington was incident to finding out just where the Thirty-ninth was to report, for all knew very well they were not to halt there long. The orders came from Gen. Silas Casey in time for them to move out of the city about noon and so to take their way across the Long Bridge, the thoroughfare connection between Washington and Alexandria, then the most famous structure of its kind in America; on account of the vibrations the regular route-step was broken. The day was hot and sultry, the dust intense, made so by the constant passing of horses and men, and the newly enlisted soldiers, loaded down with their bloated knapsacks and other burdens, began to think that soldiering was no joking matter.

While thus advancing into Virginia the Thirteenth Massachusetts Infantry was encountered, the men having all of the activity and swing that come from long experience, though thinned ranks spoke volumes for the encounters they had passed through, but they were in no halting mood and with only the greetings possible in passing the Bay State men kept in motion. It was the time when the disastrous Second Bull Run had necessitated realignment, and measures were afoot which in a little more than a week were to lead up to Antietam. It was a march of seven miles which brought the dust begrimed men to the vicinity of Fort Albany, an extensive fortification situated on the estate of Gen. Robert E. Lee, the famous Virginian so prominent in the Confederate Army, a locality rapidly growing in reputation as Arlington. Though camp equipage had not as yet made its appearance, the weather was so dry and warm no trouble was found in camping without other outfit. In every direction the eye could see very little save tents and campfires, with the passing of long baggage trains, and the night air bore the strains of many bands of music, all joining in a mighty effort to keep the minds of the soldiers alert and free from the care which besets solitude and repose.

On the slopes of Arlington the morning of the 10th found the regiment, its members all alert to observe and learn the lessons of each successive day. The night had brought about great changes, for a large portion of the camps so apparent during the watches of the night had entirely disappeared; to be sure there had been some extra fires during the preceding hours when, as it appeared later, camp debris had been burned, but all of these indications were lost on the newcomers, to whom the symptoms of breaking camp were unfamiliar, and how should they know that already the fates were preparing for Antietam, the bloodiest single day's fight of the entire war? That the enemy was not very remote was currently reported and many of the young soldiers thought they might be   Sept. 12, '62   ordered into the fray at an early hour. Then too, for the first time, they saw the coming into the Union line of escaped negroes, the "contrabands" of General Butler's ruling; "strange looking beings," one of the observers remarks. The 11th day differed in no essential from its predecessor save that the arrival of tents permitted the pitching of them and the instituting of regular and strict camp orders. The proximity of great earthworks, known as forts, prompted many to visit them and thus to appreciate the efforts that had been made to render safe the nation's capital. Drills were begun, roll-calls were frequent and the first dress parade in Dixie was recorded for the Thirty-ninth on this day.

After a day of routine on the 12th, while companies were forming for battalion drill, orders came to pack up and be ready to move out. It was after dark and in the midst of a driving rain that the start was made, but through the mud and darkness the regiment proceeded with as much willingness as the circumstances would permit till, at last, after what seemed a very long time and a great distance, really the latter was only two miles, the welcome command, "halt," was heard, and as it was not followed by one to move forward the men were content, the rain having stopped, to throw themselves upon the ground and there to find the rest that ever comes to the weary whatever the conditions. The regiment was now near the outermost lines and pickets were thrown out. The next morning, 13th, revealed the location as near Fort Tillinghast, and work was immediately begun on clearing the ground for a camp, this being the third effort for this purpose made by the men and some of them hoped they might be allowed to remain long enough to see just how a real camp at the front would look. It appeared that to the Thirty-ninth had been assigned the duty of picketing the line between Forts Tillinghast and Craig. Here Sibley tents were received, the same having been left by the Sixteenth Maine on the departure of the latter for the march into Maryland. This was the introduction of the Thirty-ninth to an organization whose later history was considerably involved with that of our Massachusetts men.

The forts, which occupied almost every elevation of land, were conspicuous on every hand, and were a part of the system devised for the thorough protection of Washington. They numbered in all, including batteries, sixty-eight, and were for the most part named for distinguished officers slain in the conflict. All of them were not constructed at this time, but the record includes those that were built later as well. The total perimeter of the fortifications was thirteen miles, and the outer border thus guarded was nearly or quite equal to that of the original District of Columbia. Besides the forts there were twenty miles of rifle trenches, thirty-two miles of military roads and ninety-three unarmed batteries for field guns, with four hundred and one emplacements. In the total armament of these earthworks there were nearly a thousand cannon and mortars. Notwithstanding this formidable array, Early and his men came near getting through and into the city in July, 1864.

ON THE MARCH.

Whatever hopes of permanency may have been cherished as to the new camp they were all destroyed before the day (14th) was done. There were inspections, always a Sunday feature, the distribution of cartridges, which had a businesslike aspect, and the dispatching of three companies to the picket line only to be recalled later with orders to pack up and be ready for a long march. In addition it was ordered that knapsacks be left behind, a fact that brought up visions of forced marching and a possible encounter. To the inexperienced soldiers separation from their knapsacks was a serious matter and each man debated   Sept. 15, '62   with himself as to what he could best leave behind, the upshot of it all being that generally his blanket, tied in a roll and slung over the shoulder, was the one item deemed absolutely necessary. It was quite seven o'clock before the march began, the way being through camps and along the sides of forts until the Aqueduct Bridge, leading across the Potomac to Georgetown, was reached; the name of the bridge arising from the fact that the Chesapeake and Ohio Canal crossed here, terminating in Alexandria. Over the bridge and through Georgetown the pace was a brisk one until, after a march of possibly seven miles, a halt for the remainder of the night was ordered on a prominence back of the village of Tennallytown.

The 15th began with the soldiers at five o'clock and there was a march of fully two miles before the halt for breakfast. Apparently in the same line with our men were the Tenth Vermont and a Pennsylvania Battery and the news gradually spread through the ranks that the purpose of the speedy trip was to do picket duty along the Potomac River. To the undisciplined mind it did seem as though a less headlong pace might have been set for such an end, but it was not for the men to complain nor to reason why, but rather to plod along as rapidly as possible. Inasmuch as the heat was extreme, the roads dusty, many of the men, quite unused to the strain and wilting under the sun's rays, fell out. This day, too, the preparation of meals was entirely by the soldiers themselves, company cooks having done the work before. When a halt was ordered it was obeyed with the utmost alacrity, the men throwing themselves upon the ground with expressions of relief. When at last, after another advance, there came the orders to halt and prepare coffee, they were heard with gladness, the location being near an old mill on Waitt's Branch, this being an affluent of the Big Muddy Branch, but the night was not to be spent here, the officers deciding that it was not a defensible place, hence the march was continued in the most quiet manner possible, to the brow of a hill where camp was pitched for the night. In the light of subsequent knowledge that the enemy was many miles away, the extreme caution must have been the result of false information to those leading.

Another day, 16th, began early and the route was still up the Potomac, though the pace was not so rapid as that of yesterday. At noon dinner was eaten at Seneca Mills and then followed a stretch of about fifteen miles, leading up to Poolesville, a village by no means important in itself, yet it had been heard of frequently in Massachusetts since here, or in this locality, a year ago were encamped the Fifteenth, Nineteenth and Twentieth Regiments from the Bay State and through here had marched the Thirteenth. To Lieut. Colonel Peirson and Major Tremlett, the place must have seemed very familiar since both had been officers in the Twentieth. Not a few of the latest visitors thought that its size and appearance hardly comported with its notoriety. A sudden and violent rainstorm accompanied the entrance of the place where were found two cavalry companies on duty, who informed the inquirers that the Battle of Poolesville, shouted so loudly a few days before at Arlington, was really only a skirmish, in which the only casualty was the killing of a horse, the whole affair being one of many incidents, accompanying the movements of Stuart's Cavalry in the general advance of General Lee into Maryland. Notwithstanding the rain, weary men threw themselves upon the ground, glad to rest in any way anywhere; but long before morning the fierceness of the storm and the level character of the plain on which the men were lying, reducing the latter to something like a duck-pond, made the soldiers get up, build fires and try to dry themselves, but with indifferent success.

The day of Antietam's great battle, the 17th of September, found the regiment making coffee around fires that were larger than usual, owing to the moisture that pervaded everything, but wet or dry, there was to be no protracted Sept. 17, '62 halt here and the village, later to be quite familiar to the Thirty-ninth, was left behind as the regiment plodded along about three miles further. Turning off into some woods, camp was established, rations drawn and preparations were progressing for staying a while when orders came, directing five companies (B, C, D, G, and K) to go on picket at once. Marching about two miles further, the river was reached by the companies at Edward's Ferry. The latter is thirty-five miles from Washington and the section had been more or less mixed up with the war from the very start. Edward's Ferry was familiar on account of the Battle of Ball's Bluff, just across the Potomac, on the 21st day of October, one year before. Out in the river is Harrison's Island, a bit of land that had been seen in fancy by thousands of Northern people whose loved ones had died there. The road, traversed by the men, was the Leesburg pike, the ferry being one of the features of the way. While the country is attractive, with the historic river flowing through it, the soldiers were not there for historic studies. Posting one company at the Ferry as the extreme left, the men were strung along the river to Conrad's Ferry, five miles further up the stream. So on the banks of

Old Potomac began the duties of soldiering in a region that had already echoed to battle's din. Parallel with the Potomac, sluggishly flows the Chesapeake and Ohio Canal and along its banks many of the picket groups were posted. Five miles to be under observation by about five hundred men or, as they were posted in groups of five, there were twenty posts to the mile and, if stationed at equal intervals, each set of sentinels was responsible for sixteen rods, but other circumstances than mere distance determined the placing of men on picket. Probably no more vigilant soldiers than these of the Thirty-ninth ever watched the river and opposite shore, for the novelty of the situation and the knowledge that the rebels were within shooting distance made the responsibility great. Besides, the rumbles from distant Antietam, throughout the 17th, were calculated to waken apprehensions in the minds of men who had no means of knowing what way the fight was going.

PICKET DUTY.

Thence onward till the 23rd of the month this tour of duty continued and however irksome it may have been to many, as a rule, men preferred such service to the routine of roll-call and almost constant drill in camp. Happily for these tyros in military experience, nothing of note disturbed the general quiet of the period, though every man was on the alert for the first indication of hostile approach. The proximity of Maryland farms and well-filled larders suggested foraging and, while some of the men paid for the food which they obtained, others did not, and a considerable raid is recorded which resulted in the bringing into camp of a great variety of material, both animal and vegetable, as well as cereals and fruit. While it was new business for the majority of these well brought up young men, they speedily adapted themselves to their new conditions, and rare was the soldier who could not secure food to eat if anything of the kind were within reaching distance. It is said that bills, aggregating fifty dollars, were presented to the Colonel by suffering farmers from the afflicted locality and they were paid by someone, though the amount was later assessed upon the offending companies. Sickness made its appearance among the men, largely the result of indiscretion in eating, the abundance of all sorts of fruit inducing indulgence therein to the extent of serious stomach and bowel difficulties. Also, the individual cooking done by the men may have had a share in the disorders named, for while some of the combinations of fried pork, apples and molasses may have been very palatable, they certainly were a surprise to many of the stomachs, into which they were introduced. At the same time the lesson of self help had to be learned. Sept., '62 On the 23rd, the companies on picket were relieved by those in camp and there came a chance to receive the knapsacks left at Arlington on the 14th, and the extra clothing thus was appreciated by all to whom the coldness of Southern nights was a revelation. Shelter tents were distributed and every one speedily learned how much comfort could be found beneath them. Here too began in good earnest the school of the soldier, and four drills a day, along with roll-calls at frequent intervals, induced a degree of attention and a weariness that made many a lad seek his rest, when possible, without any prompting. The first death in the regiment came on the 27th, when Nathan Mitchell, a Bridgewater boy, Company F, twenty-one years old, passed out of this life. The funeral was held the next (Sunday) morning, an impressive lesson for the soldiers of the possibility of death in camp as well as on the battlefield.

For a number of days there followed a regular exchange of duties between camp and picket, the latter being considered preferable, as a rule, having so much less of drill and the fretful features of military life. Men learned to wash their own garments, to mend their apparel and to do many things of which, had they remained at home, they would always have been ignorant. The bi-weekly arrival of the mail was a regular event that never lost its interest, and happiness and misery were separated only by the receipt of letters or their failure. The folks at home knew this full well, and there were few boys in blue for whom some one in the distant Northland was not planning some pleasant interlude during these months of separation. Confederate prisoners, too, were not unusual, on their way under guard to Washington, and while they at first excited curiosity, the latter feeling was mingled with wonder at their lack of uniform and the general soldierly appearance which the Union soldiers maintained. Under the impression that the Maryland side was held by his people one rebel forded the Potomac, clad in citizen's garb, wearing a Pennsylvanian's knapsack which, he said, he had acquired at Manassas; he was a queer looking soldier, though he claimed to belong to the Sixth Florida Infantry. Someway, he had managed to get off the rebel route on the way back from Antietam. It was no infrequent thing for an alarm to bring the men into line at any time of night and to make them stand thus until daylight did appear. Seemingly the foe was constantly fording the Potomac above or below the portion guarded by the Thirty-ninth Regiment. In one case, the "sure rebels," who had built fires across the river, proved to be the division of General E. V. Sumner returning from a raid upon the wagon-train of General Lee.

Since reaching "Old Potomac's Shore" no more memorable day had been recorded than Sunday, October 12th, when the regular inspection was interrupted by the arrival of a courier with orders to march at once since the enemy was crossing the river at one of the upper fords, and skirmishing was already in progress. Much to the wonder of some, in spite of the urgency the inspection was finished and the rations drawn before the Thirty-ninth, in heavy marching array, started off at a double-quick, to make up for lost time. The heat of the day and the heaviness of the attire made the march exceedingly trying, but Conrad's Ferry was reached at last, knapsacks were unslung, line of battle was formed, and the approach of the enemy was awaited; but in vain, for the rapid riders of J. E. B. Stuart had already crossed at White's Ford, two miles further up the stream. Some of the hypercritical soldiers thought that if the inspection had been ended at once and the march made in light order, the Thirty-ninth might have arrived in time to interrupt the placid passage of the Potomac by the venturesome Confederates.

STUART'S RAID.

It is in place to state that the affair was the termination of one of the most picturesque incidents of the entire war.

Oct. 9, '62   On the 9th of October, Confederate General Stuart with eighteen hundred of the best mounted and most reliable men in the brigades of Wade Hampton, Fitz Hugh Lee and B. H. Robertson started from Darksville, a place some miles above Martinsburg in the valley of the Shenandoah and, moving northward, crossed the Potomac at McCoy's Ford and reached Chambersburg, Penn., in the evening of the 10th. In the Keystone State the troopers had helped themselves to whatever they chose to take, but they had carefully refrained from molesting property on their way through Maryland. In Chambersburg and vicinity, horses and whatever might contribute to the welfare and comfort of the invaders were appropriated. The night in the Pennsylvania city was spent in drizzling rain which added not a little to the peril of the situation, for Federal authorities were astir, hoping to surround and capture the entire rebel outfit. The morning of the 11th, the horsemen turned their steps eastward, proceeding towards Gettysburg as far as Cashtown; thence the route was directly southward, through Emmitsburg, New Market, Hyattstown, etc., with only momentary halts, to the Potomac. There was no bivouac for the night, since any hour might confront the riders with a Union force to effectually block their way. Stuart had the good fortune to be guided by Capt. B. S. White, a Poolesville man and a member of his staff who knew the entire country thoroughly, so that, while the Federal forces were looking for the enemy further down the stream or at points higher up, White piloted them to the ford and saw them in safety on the other side.

It was one of the great events of military history; General Stoneman with infantry and cavalry was stationed at Poolesville, and Pleasanton was in readiness at the mouth of the Monocacy, places which the astute Confederates carefully avoided. The net results of the expedition were the destruction of public and railroad property in Chambersburg to the amount of two hundred and fifty thousand dollars; two hundred and eighty wounded and sick prisoners, paroled; thirty United States government officials and other citizens of prominence, captured and forwarded to Richmond, to be held as hostages for Confederate citizens held by the North, and more than twelve hundred horses brought away to replenish the mounts for the daring rebels. Within twenty-seven hours, the Confederates had ridden ninety miles, encumbered with artillery and captured horses, and had forced the final passage of the Potomac virtually under the very eyes of the Union forces, their only loss being two men who wandered away, and the only casualty was the wounding of one man. Not a few observers in the Union ranks wondered why things were thus, and Hooker's pertinent question, "Who ever saw a dead cavalryman?" is remembered.

An interesting postscript to the escape of Stuart and his men came about soon after when Poole and Leslie of Company K, in spite of the strict orders as to watchfulness and care, laid off their clothes, when on picket, and swam over to Harrison's Island where they found no other rebel than an old mule, feeding in solitary, but on their way back they found in the river a pair of saddle-bags that had belonged to the Chaplain of Hampton's Legion, one of Stuart's force, and evidently lost in the crossing. The contents consisted in pious tracts, a vest with Confederate buttons, needles and thread, and a hospital flag, a yellow cotton affair, which years afterward would be one of the finder's choicest relics. Leslie was always very sorry that those tracts were not distributed among the Johnnies, for he thought they needed them badly.

The same rain that had made the rebel raid all the more difficult rendered the return of our men to camp very uncomfortable, but they had learned something of what might be expected of them. Besides, during the evening they acquired a bit of military knowledge from certain troops under Gen. D. B. Birney of the Corps, lately commanded by Gen. Phil Kearney. They too had come in a hurry from Hall's Hill and found themselves too late for the game.

Oct. 14, '62 It had been a hard day and the men were tired and hungry; flocking over to the camp of the Thirty-ninth, they were cordially received and the Massachusetts men generously gave what they could to the comfort of the weary soldiers, receiving in payment many thanks and some pretty large stories of the fights in which the older soldiers had been. One of the latter's first acts was to build great fires, using therefor the fence rails, hitherto untouched by the Bay State lads, this being in conformity with orders, but the experienced campaigners cared not a copper for rules, but speedily laid hold on the combustible matter and lighted roaring fires that astonished the lately arrived. Such desecration was not to be tamely endured by those who strictly interpreted the law, so the colonel of the Thirty-ninth undertook to stay the hands of the wet and muddy soldiers and thus to save the fences, but the veterans of the Peninsula, Groveton and Antietam were not to be diverted by mere language, and the conflagration continued till long lengths of zigzag fence had disappeared.

MOVING AGAIN

Tuesday, the 14th of October, saw the regiment again in line, and marching something like eight miles towards Washington to Seneca Landing, camping there for the night. The land was low and wet near the canal, and in the morning all turned out as wet as if they had been in the rain, so dense was the fog that overspread the locality. By morning's light, a new camping-place was found on a high hill, half a mile to the rear, where camp was once more pitched, the Sibley tents having arrived; the location was the same that was occupied by the Second Massachusetts Infantry in the winter of 1861 and 2; the Landing, about twenty-five miles from Washington, was at the mouth of Seneca Creek and was a depot of supplies for the army. A noteworthy arrival of mail is chronicled for this place, since in the maneuvers of the last few days, a large quantity of such matter had accumulated at Poolesville and it is recorded that fully eight bushels of letters and papers were distributed among the men, hungry for news from home. Hitherto, the Thirty-ninth had acted in an independent capacity, but on Friday, the 17th, orders were promulgated, organizing a brigade, to be under the command of Brigadier Gen. Cuvier Grover and to consist of the Thirty-ninth, the Tenth Vermont, the Fourteenth New Hampshire and the Twenty-third Maine along with a battery and certain cavalry, the same being an independent brigade, though under the ultimate command of General Heintzelman, who was in charge of the defenses of Washington, the duties being similar to those hitherto performed.

During these days, while there were drills, inspections and other camp duties, the enlisted man had time, or he took it, to visit neighboring farms, to quiz the natives, to sample the products of the land and in many ways to prove his derivation from Yankeedom. The men found the negroes glad to see them and ready to hurrah for the flag, while suspicion was generally harbored that professions of loyalty on the part of slave-owners were not particularly sincere. Target shoots were indulged in, a practice of which there should have been more throughout the army; Sunday, the 19th, was remarked as quite uneventful, since there were only inspections and dress parade, and no alarm of any sort. October 20th orders came to pack up, and a removal to the mouth of Muddy Branch was made, possibly three miles nearer Washington, where the old routine was continued. As the name of the stream would indicate, the locality was still very unhealthy, being low and damp, but the duties were less arduous when on picket, through there being less posts and less hours of duty. Illicit traffic with the enemy had to be strictly watched and prevented.

On the 21st, a long stretch of embankment on the canal breaking away, a detachment of five men from each company was made to proceed to the scene, some three miles down the stream, and to repair the same, an employment hardly contemplated when they enlisted. However, they succeeded in stopping the crevasse and permitting the renewal of transportation. Though comparatively near the base of supplies, provisions at times were scarce and hardtack and water seemed scant rations for men accustomed to more generous fare. If, under such circumstances, soldiers foraged occasionally, sometimes paying for what they got, more often not, why, it was only a part of the game that the North and the South were playing; and to prove themselves rapidly progressing, October 24th, ostensibly in retaliation for excessive charges, a raid was made on the regimental sutler,[C] mulcting his assets to the amount, so said, of about eighty dollars.

The section guarded by the Thirty-ninth and the other regiments of the brigade, being on the canal and river, was one pretty thoroughly traversed by the Union soldiers and those who kept diaries made many interesting entries. There was a constant passing of boats on the canal and all roads led to Washington. Negroes on their way to the Nation's Capital might be intercepted, but if the black man asserted that he was running away from his master, he would have been a rare soldier who would turn him back. One colored person, thus halted, very aged, claimed to have been a slave of General Washington and, in reply to a query, said that the Father of his Country looked very brave. Though situated on the top of a hill, the constant wet weather made the surroundings of the camp anything but agreeable, the soil being soft and sticky; to crown all misfortunes, occasionally a tent would collapse upon its occupants in the midst of rain and wind, resulting in hurried action on the part of the unfortunate fellows who may have just come in from the exactions of a prolonged tour of picket duty.

Lucky was the man on picket when the last day of October rolled round, for on this date there were inspections and waitings in line, armed cap-a-pie, sometimes at a "shoulder arms," drills, reviews and a muster for pay. Everything seemingly that could be rung into a day's work was had. Perhaps the fact that the muster for pay covered two months of service was as agreeable an exercise as the day afforded. It was during these days that at least one company, possibly more, undertook to repeat the game so nicely played by Birney's veterans when they camped near the Thirty-ninth at the time of Stuart's crossing the Potomac; in other words, representatives of the companies, under supposed proper orders and directed by sergeants, went out some distance from camp and secured a good supply of well dried fence rails for the use of the company cooks in the preparation of food. The matter was thought quite proper, until the men were ordered into line and compelled to pick up what rails had not already been chopped into firewood and to carry them back to the place where they were obtained, though in depositing them the soldiers surely raised a sign of offense before the doors of the parties making complaint. Somehow the men could not be made to appreciate the tender manner in which some in authority thought the residents should be treated.

While each day brought its regular round of duty, there was little of novelty in successive days, the soldiers gradually hardening into the restraints and exactions of camp life. The 7th of November brought the first snow fall of the season, and though only about two inches of the fleecy reminder of northern regions fell, it was enough to impart a robe of whiteness to Mother Earth and boys-in-blue had the pleasure of snow-balling while it lasted, which was scarcely more than twenty-four hours. The 9th was Sunday and it brought the regular inspections, though the rain   Nov. 11, '62   and cold prevented religious service and dress parade. The cold was severe enough to freeze liquids left by the occupants in their tents while out on duty. Monday, the 10th, marked a brigade inspection by General Grover, which the men inspected voted much easier than those made by their Colonel. This was the last appearance of General Grover in the brigade since on the 11th he was ordered to report to General N. P. Banks, who was organizing reinforcements for the Department of the Gulf. A native of Maine and a graduate of West Point, 1850, he had won honors at Williamsburg, Fair Oaks and at the Second Bull Run. As commander of a division in the Nineteenth Army Corps he will win still further laurels both in the extreme South and in the Valley of the Shenandoah. His independent brigade had grown to respect him highly.

OFFUTT'S CROSS ROADS

The departure of General Grover was followed by the assignment of Colonel Davis to the command of the brigade and the elevation of Lieut. Colonel Peirson to that of the regiment. In close connection with the foregoing, a change of location was ordered by General Heintzelman and, on the 13th, another move towards Washington was effected. Turning out long before daylight, an early breakfast was eaten and the line of march was begun before sunrise, the terminal being Offutt's Cross Roads, some twelve or more miles from Washington, the crossed roads being that from Rockville to Great Falls, and the turnpike which paralleled the river and canal, terminating at Tennallytown. There was a deal of grubbing out of stumps and other obstacles necessary in providing for a parade ground, though the site was considered better than the one just left, even if there was no adequate supply of water near. All the other regiments in the brigade were camped close by, viz.: the Tenth Vermont, the Fourteenth New Hampshire, and the Twenty-third Maine. In honor of the retiring brigade commander, the new stopping place was named Camp Grover.

In diaries of the period two quite diverse entries are found for the 15th, one stating that Colonel Davis, acting brigade commander, was thrown from his horse, though fortunately he was not seriously hurt; the other that the band of the Fourteenth New Hampshire played "Home Sweet Home" so beautifully that it made a wave of homesickness sweep over and through the brigade. A company from each regiment in the brigade was sent out by Colonel Davis to look after some of Captain White's guerrillas. A distressing accident was that of the 17th when James W. Finn of Company I, only eighteen years old, a farmer boy of Natick, fell from the containing wall of the canal-lock into the water and was drowned. During these days, the men were learning how to make their tents warmer through a system of stockading, and there was need enough of it, since cold weather had begun. Of all the regiments, there is a large representation in the hospitals, though the Thirty-ninth is better off in this respect than the others. However the best is bad enough, for on the 21st Charles H. Morrison of the Natick company passed on, followed on the 22d by Sumner P. Rollins of Somerville, a young man of eighteen years. Again on the 23rd, two more men of "I" crossed over, George L. Fogg and Francis E. Mann, and on the 25th, died Francis E. Newhall, also of Natick. Hugh Connoly of the Woburn company died November 25th. In the five weeks' stay at this point, the Tenth Vermont lost twenty-five men, their funeral marches through the camp being of almost daily occurrence.

Two and a half miles from the canal, at or near Great Falls, where begins the aqueduct which carries Washington's water supply, a considerable portion of these soldiers' duty was the guarding of the Government buildings there, including a bakery; near by was a large freestone quarry whose product was utilized in the building of the reservoir and the aqueduct itself. Considering the rain, which was Nov. 27, '62 very prevalent, and the mud which deepened on little provocation, the distance seemed to grow as the days advanced. On the 24th two companies were sent off in a hurry to intercept some of Stuart's cavalry said to be in the vicinity of Edward's Ferry; nothing came of the effort more important than the capture of two negroes. There was little going on that did not involve the colored man more or less. Even Mr. Offutt, for whom the cross roads are named, had been in the Old Capitol Prison because of his inability to render up one of his slaves when called for by General Jas. S. Wadsworth, when the latter was military governor of the District of Columbia.

November 27th was Thanksgiving Day at home, possibly the most generally observed day in New England. For several preceding days there had been a steady stream of packages from the homeland, indicative of the appreciation in which every soldier was held somewhere. Of course these boxes and bundles contained articles of comfort both for internal and external use. The approach of the day on which the Governor and State Secretary unite in "God Save the Commonwealth" brought out many expressions of wonder among the soldiers as to how the day would or could pass without something unusual in the way of food. The care and foresight of the home-army supplied the answer to the query, whether expressed or not, and though there was no general table around which the hundreds gathered, in some way it was possible for the greater portion of the men to feel that the day had its special significance even if they were far from home. Company K, which hailed from Woburn, was especially well served, and the display of boxes and other receptacles in the company street excited no little admiration, not to say envy, in the minds of some not so well provided for. It is stated that even fluids, particularly interdicted, were smuggled through some of the packages, notwithstanding the thorough search of the captain, and specimens of Northern distillations were submitted to that officer's approval. From that date, "canned tomatoes" acquired a new distinction. There was a release from the greater part of camp duties and the time thus secured was devoted to baseball, football and the other diversions so easily devised by the American youth.

A feature of the Thanksgiving spread, possibly not wholly understood at the time, came out subsequently when the "boys" learned how much work their pleasure had cost others. C. F. Whitney of Company I was serving as wagoner, and the night before the 27th, soon after "Taps," he was aroused by the wagon-master with the statement that there was no hardbread for the men, that the morrow brought Thanksgiving; he ordered Whitney to proceed to the Canal Locks, about three miles away, and with the commissary sergeant get a load of 'tack. Having worked hard all day, Whitney naturally demurred, but he had to comply, so he harnessed his six mules, took in Sergeant Hilton and started on his night ride. It was after 10 o'clock, the sergeant went to sleep at once on a bed of bags in the bottom of the wagon, but no such comfort attended the driver who, in his saddle on the wheel-mule, had to look after things. About halfway to his destination, he had to pass through a stretch of always muddy road, now actually overflowing with water, so deep in places that he had to take his feet from the stirrups to keep them dry. Night work of late had fallen to Whitney's lot, hence he was sleepy to the point of actually dozing off while in the saddle, this of course, after getting through the morass, and from this semi-sleeping state he was suddenly roused with the cry of "halt," uttered seemingly by a dozen voices. With as many bayonets pointed at his breast, his first thought was of "Johnnies," but he put on a bold front and shouted, "Let the mules alone, I can handle them myself." He would not tell them where he was going neither would he give the countersign, because he had none, nor had there been any picket-line along the way before. All this time the sergeant had slept on in his cosy bed, but he was roused and proved equally ignorant of the password. It seemed that the Tenth Vermont, camped near, had just established a picket-post at the place, and the men were acting according to instructions; much to the disgust of the two men of the Thirty-ninth they were compelled to turn about and return to their camp; nor did their troubles end there for, having cared for his animals and being on the point of turning in himself, the quartermaster again informed the driver and the sergeant that they would have to go back for that load of 'tack. So back they went, mules, mud and all, and with the countersign, getting by the Green Mountain boys, they reached the canal boat which they found having a great pile of Thanksgiving boxes from the North; wisely choosing these instead of the hardbread, they took the offerings to camp, reaching the same just after reveillé, and had no trouble in unloading; and this is how the regiment got its spread for Thanksgiving.

The remainder of November and the beginning of December had no special variants from the recent routine of drill, police and picket duty, though the scribe of Company K makes mention of the formation of a "construction corps" from a portion of that company, the object being the erection and equipping of a structure which should be used as a bath-house and a barber-shop. The labor essential to the cutting down of the necessary timber, the transportation to camp and its preparation there for use, absorbed the time and attention of a large number of men, who welcomed a relief from the constant round of drill with its endless repetition of facings, pacings and flank-movements, though the work performed was by no means light. At the same time increased labor fell on those who were obliged to perform the picket, sentinel, guard and other duties which were incessant. In the night of the 14th, a party of rebel raiders surprised in Poolesville a detachment of Scott's Nine Hundred, a New York Cavalry regiment, resulting in the capture of a number of the Union soldiers, with the death of one and the wounding of others. The place being so near the earlier camps of the Thirty-ninth, on or near the Potomac, the men were not surprised at increased vigilance in the placing of pickets all along the interval between the Cross Roads and the Leesburg pike. An observer in Company B says for this day, "Buried one of our men by the name of Hiedenway (David), the first one in our company."

During these days, news from the terrible battle of Fredericksburg began to filter into the camp, at first very favorable for the Union side and then the awful truth came in all of its horrors. Our men of the Thirty-ninth had brothers and friends by the hundreds in the Bay State regiments that suffered there, the news, by no means, making easier the duties of the guardsmen along the Potomac. The weather was cold and any proposition to move from the well established camp was exceedingly unpopular, but just such intimation came in the evening of the 20th, when orders were received to be ready to march. The boy who wrote in his diary "We have just got nicely settled for winter" learned, ere he was many months older, that wars are not conducted on the basis of being comfortable. The four regiments of the brigade were in line by nine o'clock in the morning of the 21st. Fortunately the weather was fine and the start was made, with music by the band, and six of the miles were marched, before the halt was made for the preparation of dinner. As Poolesville, the destination, is about twenty miles away from the Cross Roads (Offutt's) there yet remained a deal of walking to be done. With all of their camp belongings, over the frozen ground, the distance seemed greater than it really was.

POOLESVILLE

It was after dark, 6 o'clock on the evening, when the village was reached. Once a fairly prosperous Southern town, Poolesville revealed at this time a sorry spectacle of Dec. 21, '62 the ravages of war. Many of the men had straggled, unable to keep the pace of the hard march and only about one-fifth of the entire body arrived with the colors, but the delinquents limped loyally in, though late. Accommodations for the night had to be found wherever available, the village church holding many, the schoolhouse others; many found shelter in barns and not a few sought sleep on fence rails whose native hardness was softened a bit by straw obtained from a nearby strawstack, though its complete demolition was prevented by those soldiers who had managed to burrow into it. A sergeant of Company E who kept a small quantity of "commissary" for medicinal purposes had entrusted the precious flask to the keeping of John Locke, the most likely member to be faithful to his trust. Alas, when the sergeant called for the flask he got it empty, the contents had gone to help dry the thoroughly saturated comrades of Locke, who thought the boys would never have greater need. While in the morning of the 22d, some of the regiment were detailed for picket at Edward's Ferry, more remained in the village. Some of Scott's Nine Hundred, the regiment that had suffered from White's guerrillas about a week before, chose this day as one for wreaking vengeance on certain storekeepers, one of them Jesse Higgins by name, these natives being suspected of complicity with the enemy. The goods of the merchants were thrown out regardless and the lucky soldiers who chanced to be near helped themselves to whatever they liked best, though Companies B, H and K, being at the Ferry, missed their share of the wreckage. In Poolesville were thus halted the Thirty-ninth and the Fourteenth New Hampshire; the Tenth Vermont went further up the river and the Twenty-third Maine found its post lower down.

Duty along the Potomac was not unlike that performed some weeks before, but in the interval these men had learned a deal; not only had they been drilled but they had observed that all of the people resident in the vicinity were not wholly loyal, that many of them were ready to pass the desired word along to the enemy whenever opportunity offered, and for such reasons they determined to piece out their own rations with whatever was obtainable from the citizens. Nothing that was edible and transportable was safe from the predatory hands of the men and boys who, a very few months before, had been conspicuous in their own localities for their sterling honesty and straightforwardness. War and so-called necessity worked wonderful transformations in these well reared New Englanders. If all the stories that have been told in subsequent years may be believed, the marvel is that the natives had anything left to subsist upon. December 23rd brought the camp-stores and equipage by way of the canal, and a large force was set at work cutting away trees to make ready for the new camp. The site chosen for the camp was that on which the regiment had halted at the end of its first considerable march, that from Arlington in the preceding September. A large detail of men from the several companies, not on picket, worked hard through Wednesday the 27th, to properly pitch the tents and so collect the men into camp once more.

Of course the 25th of December came to Camp Davis, the name of the new winter quarters, just as it did to the rest of the world, but signs of Christmas were painfully lacking. One youth made this record, "To-day is Christmas; four of us went out of the lines and got a Christmas dinner and had it charged to Uncle Sam." Furnishing food to Union soldiers in those parts must have been like a lottery with the chances against getting anything back. Said another observer, "Christmas day! And we would not know it by the work going on in camp; dined on salt beef, more commonly known as 'salt-horse'." The later days of the month were devoted to properly equipping the camp which, for location, was the best yet occupied except for wood and water, the latter having to be brought fully half a mile, and the former was two miles off. For Dec. 28, '62 purposes of drill the parade ground was unexcelled and was extensive enough to admit of the maneuvers of an entire division at one time. Once more the Sibley tents are stockaded and the men believe that winter quarters are really realized. In the light of later years, the occupants of that camp claim that there was no better in the entire army. Though located on a level plain, it was so well drained that no amount of rain was able to render it disagreeable underfoot, a fact which no doubt contributed to the prevailing health of the men.

On Sunday, the 28th, as the men were falling in for inspection, their eyes were gladdened by the sight of the Tenth Massachusetts Battery, subsequently known to fame as "Sleepers," approaching Camp Davis. This event is thus cheerfully alluded to in John D. Billing's excellent history of the Battery, "'How are you, Boxford?' was the greeting from the Thirty-ninth Regiment, as soon as we were recognized, and it seemed like meeting old friends to fall in with those who had been encamped with us on the soil of Massachusetts." It was a strange stroke of fortune that should bring these Boxford neighbors again so near to each other, for the battery was assigned to the brigade and found a camping place close by. This day, too, brought to the ears of many, for the first time since leaving Massachusetts, the sound of a church bell, but it was not for these soldiers, who were still perfecting themselves in the school of the soldier; lessons so well learned that the Thirty-ninth stood second to none in discipline and soldierly appearance, and better still in general health, conditions largely due to the unceasing diligence of the Colonel, with whom drill seemed to be the chief end of man, especially those wearing uniforms. Long before daylight in the morning of the 30th, an alarm brought the men into line and four companies of the Thirty-ninth with a single section of Sleeper's Battery started off towards Conrad's Ferry where, as usual, a crossing of the rebels was reported. In light marching order, over the most difficult of roads, the party hastened to the scene, as supposed, of trouble. Though there were the reaching of an island in the river by means of a boat and a certain amount of fortifying, nothing came of the affair and at 1 p. m., tired and hungry the return trip was begun, ending at 4 o'clock, with every one out of conceit with military movements. On the last day in the month the Regiment was mustered for two months' pay, always a welcome exercise.

1863

The new year was ushered in on Thursday, and the prevailing sentiment among the men is indicated by this entry in his diary by one who evidently had entertained other opinions, "The boys are rather blue on the war subject; they begin to think they will not get home in the spring." Very few soldiers had any idea of the many long and weary months before them. The first men who went out, the Three Months' Men, thought it hardly possible that it would take all of their projected term to wipe out the Rebellion, nor were the rebels any less in error in their estimate of the duration of the conflict. In the middle of the month, the same writer once more reflects thus, "Our hopes of getting home in the spring are somewhat blighted," yet he and his comrades attended strictly to duty just the same. As the month progressed, the men had full opportunity to size up and adequately estimate the village near which they were encamped. Like everything that ever fell under the blighting hand of slavery, it exhibited a lack of paint and enterprise. Poor Richard long since remarked that he who by the plow would thrive must either hold himself or drive. In the South the slave-owner did neither; superintendence was entrusted to the overseer and what work was done, the slave did. How well this was accomplished, the surroundings showed. It has been said that there were only two loyal men in the village, Mr. Metzger, the postmaster; and Dr. Brace. Under such   Jan. 2, '63   conditions there need be little wonder that the Yankee boys thought it no sin to spoil the Egyptians.

It was in the night of the 2nd that some vagrant members of Scott's Nine Hundred, that redoubtable New York cavalry body, which in December had cleaned out Higgins' store, came back to do it again. On guard was F. R. W. Hall of Company F whose brother, Eben A., was performing similar duty in a neighboring building. "Whiskey" was the battle cry of the New Yorkers and they sailed in to wreck things. At first, to oppose them, was only "A little red-headed guard" and they soon found that that *Hall* could neither be hired nor scared, though he was extremely happy to find soon at his side the brother, supposed to be in another place. Both boys were "Sons of Temperance" and they proved to the rummies that, once at least, prohibition prohibited, for the Halls managed to keep the mob out till Lieutenant Paul appeared with the reserve guard; even then the raiders did not subside, for they formed under their leader preparatory to a fight. Not having their cavalry outfit with them, they gave way to discretion, always the better part of valor; and all the more readily when Lieutenant Paul gave the order to charge, and they rapidly disappeared in the darkness. They had succeeded in smashing all of the windows, however, and almost unroofing Hall, whose gory scalp was proclaimed the first case of bloodshed for the Regiment. Though Higgins might have been a rebel, he doubtless was, the boys were set to protect and they always obeyed orders.

The 5th of January beheld the return of Colonel Davis to the Regiment, the command of the brigade devolving on Col. A. B. Jewett, of the Tenth Vermont, who after all these weeks had discovered that his commission antedated that of our Colonel just one day and there were people so uncharitable as to intimate that he had had the document redated just for this special purpose. Though there may have been those who did not altogether love Colonel Davis, because of his excessive devotion to drill, and the rigors of a soldier's life, all were as one in their admiration of his military bearing and his fitness for the head of the brigade, while his successor was notably lacking in all such characteristics. The Colonel made his first reappearance at dress parade and was greeted with a round of hearty cheers. In the evening he was honored by the Regiment's gathering round his quarters, accompanied by the band of the Fourteenth New Hampshire. The serenade prompted the officer to make a very happy speech, thanking everybody for progress in the past and urging a continuance in the same commendable direction. That the head of the Regiment was deeply interested in the welfare of his command was evident to every man.

The month was not entirely devoid of interest and the sham-battle between the battery and a portion of Scott's Nine Hundred (Eleventh New York Cavalry), on the 6th, roused the admiration of all onlookers to a high pitch; the rapid firing of the guns and the shouts of the charging cavalry gave the boys a notion of what the real thing must be, an impression rendered all the more vivid by the accidental wounding of several of the combatants, through premature discharges and too close proximity of certain ones. The endless round of all sorts of drill was rendered less irksome by the remembrance of those at home who were constantly sending choice bits of food for the delectation of their dear ones in the field and, to crown all, on the 17th, came seventeen barrels of apples for the Woburn company, right from the town that had first produced the famous Baldwin apple, and the generosity of the "K" boys was unstinted in distributing their pomological treasures among their less fortunate friends. Sunday, the 18th, some three hundred or more of the men repaired to the Presbyterian Church for religious service, expecting to hear the Chaplain, but in his stead, Private Batcheller, one of the older members of Company B, preached, a fact well illustrating the diversity of talent among American soldiers.

Jan. 20, '63

The "knapsack-drill" of January 20th has lodgement in the minds of many, the Colonel ordering that the 1 p. m. company drill be executed in heavy marching order. Considerable growling and grumbling were heard in the progress of the duty, and at its end Companies F and G gave three rousing cheers for "knapsack-drill," an act that roused the ire of the officer so that the companies were ordered on an hour's drill without cessation. At the end of the battalion-drill, the Regiment was formed in solid square and Colonel Davis very clearly explained to the men his reasons for the heavy task imposed, dwelling on his mortification at the episode of the morning. He said that whatever had been done as yet, it was only a prelude to what must follow and he desired the men to become inured to fatigue through such exercises as those of the earlier hour, concluding his words by the remark that if they would act like men, they would receive corresponding usage from him. The next three days were marked by a very severe rain storm; tents went down before it, and the sheds for the stalling of the wagon-train mules, some one hundred and thirty in number, fell in upon the animals. Covered with straw, and saturated with rain, the burden became too great and the calamity followed, luckily not to the fatal injury of any of the beasts. The 25th being Sunday, it is recorded that some of the men went to prayer meeting and that in the afternoon the Chaplain preached, though his auditors were chiefly from Company A, the one in which he had enlisted. Of the 29th and 30th, it is told that a snow storm that would have befitted Vermont or New Hampshire raged, much to the discomfort of those on guard, while others had not only to clear the company street but to free the parade ground for brigade inspection, the same coming on the afternoon of the 31st and being conducted by Col. Robert Wilson, of the Fourteenth New Hampshire, Colonel Davis acting Brigadier-General, in the absence of Colonel Jewett.

February proved to be a stormy month, severe snow storms reminding the men of the climate at home, but guard rounds had to be maintained, no matter what the weather might be. On Monday, the 2nd, a battalion of the Sixth Michigan Cavalry, Major Kenyon, appeared, and became a part of the local Union force. Armed with the very latest of breechloading carbines, they had every sign of ability to put up a good fight with whatever foe the future might develop. Very likely no event of the month gave the soldiers any more enjoyment than the coming of the paymaster on the 6th, with the money that the Regiment had been looking for so long and anxiously. "He took us all by surprise," says one writer, "coming on the grounds at 3 p. m., with his four-horse team." While a considerable part of the sum received went into the tills of local dealers and of the sutler, by far the larger part was sent home for the comfort of loved ones there, Company K sending thus fully $2300. The payment was only to the first of November, and it was the first coming of the dispenser of Uncle Sam's compensation since leaving Massachusetts. He was employed two days in passing out the money.

One of the episodes of this snowy Poolesville winter was the effort that a certain notable member of Company ——— made to get out of the army. On account of a certain grievance, real or fancied, he simulated insanity so perfectly that there was a pretty general agreement that he had lost his head. Having committed to memory the entire contents of the American First Class Reader, he would station himself in the middle of the parade ground and in the stillness of the night hours declaim from the reader; even Colonel Davis began to think his man had lost his reason. Had the soldier stopped here or had his readiness to say a good thing, regardless of consequences, been under better control, his ruse probably would have succeeded. In the system of rigid camp neatness, a barrel for night refuse was provided for every company, to be carried off   Feb., '63   each morning; to the increased astonishment of his comrades our declaimer now added fishing to his pranks and most soberly bobbed for bites in the filthy liquid. Finally Colonel Davis, after watching the performance from the tent of a company officer, approached the fisherman and asked what he was doing. "Fishing, sir," was the sober reply. "What do you expect to catch?" says the Colonel; "My discharge, sir." It was there that the man fell down, but he never could resist the temptation to make an apt reply. Plenty of hard work soon restored the orator and emulator of Izaak Walton to all of his normal senses and to becoming a model soldier.

During these days a strange rumor gained credence, viz., that the Regiment, with the Fortieth and Forty-first was to be assigned to the nine months' quota, the Government having found that the State had exceeded its three years' allotment by three regiments. If the origin of such insane propositions could be ascertained a great boon would be conferred upon humanity, since many a man found himself most grievously disappointed when the whole affair was recognized as an illusion. A great snow storm began on the 17th, and for twenty-four hours raged fiercely, changing finally into rain, which effectually removed what otherwise would have occasioned many a backache; the men counted the time well spent in checkers, cards and other camp diversions, in place of regular drill. It was a sorry time though for those on guard. The 20th brought pleasure to the quarters of Colonel Davis, for, on this day, his wife came to pay him a visit. Washington's birthday brought another old fashioned storm of wind and snow, testing fully the texture and endurance of the Sibley tents; fuel was scarce also, and, orders to the contrary notwithstanding, neighboring fence rails found their way into the fireplaces, thus giving a measure of comfort to the shivering occupants. The only official notice of the day was the firing of a salute by Sleeper's Battery, thirty-four guns, the report of which could hardly be heard above the roar of the storm.

As soon as the storm abated there was the usual heavy detail of men from the several companies for the purpose of clearing the streets and parade ground, the wisdom of such procedure had, by this time, become apparent to the men, since they could go about their several duties dry shod, while neighboring regiments plodded with wet feet through the slush and mud which followed the disappearance of the rapidly melting snow. Experience and observation are the best of teachers. A very pleasant instance of camp amenities was exhibited in this month, when First Sergeant Oscar Persons, of Company K, having been promoted to a second Lieutenancy and assigned to Company D, was presented by his late comrades with the equipments essential to his new position. The presentation was made by Lieutenant Wyman, and the recipient very happily responded. The ever obliging band of the Fourteenth New Hampshire accompanied the men on their errand of love, and discoursed music fitting to the occasion. The month ended with the bi-monthly muster for pay, the same making the Government just four months in arrears.

March will not be much, if any, improvement on the preceding month. The demand for fuel to supply heat for cooking and also for rendering the tents comfortable makes it necessary for details to go further and further from camp, and it is very fortunate that so much of the country has been allowed to grow up to forests. All men have to take their portion of the chopping exercise and in the performance of all camp duties. Possibly there was some abatement in drill on account of the weather and consequent condition of the grounds, and if the wearied soldiers were allowed a little more time in quarters, they accounted it no real loss. Pertaining to the variable character of the March weather, and illustrative of certain most admirable racial characteristics, Abijah Thompson, of "K," tells the story of a certain Irishman among the Woburn boys, the very best natured lad in the company, who was on guard duty in the midst of one of the hardest downpours of that

March 17, '63 torrential period. The weather, however, made no difference with Colonel Davis, for his regular rounds were made, rain or shine; when he neared Patrick the latter faced the officer, presented arms and said, "Good marnin, Kurnel! It's a foin mornin' this, if wan't for the rain." 'Tis said the Colonel laughed so hard he almost fell off his horse. Both February and March witnessed a steady coming into the lines of rebel soldiers, really deserters, whom it was necessary to escort down to the City of Washington. To serve on the squad which thus guarded the men-in-gray to the Capital was considered to be a privilege. Also in this month, the authorities pursuing their investigations determined that several so-called Union citizens of the vicinity were really sympathizers with the South, and for such reasons a Mr. Pleasants and Colonel Leonards were arrested and sent to the old Capital prison.

The 17th was "house cleaning" day and, the tents having been removed from the stockades and everything carried out, the spaces were carefully inspected by the surgeon, the lieut. colonel and Captain J. Henry Sleeper of the Battery; the report of the officers was very complimentary to the Regiment. Whatever the coincidence, the event had no connection with the British evacuation of Boston nor with St. Patrick's day. The two months were notable in the number of furloughs that officers and men obtained for trips back to Massachusetts, not long ones, but sufficient for a taste of home comforts and a sight of the dear ones there. The month ended with the severest storm of the season, the snow falling in great quantities, but at the period of the equinox, snow cannot be expected to remain a very great while and it departed more rapidly than it came. An observer on the spot wrote thus in his journal for the 31st, "Woke up and found the ground covered with snow; realization of the sunny South is very different from what I had fancied it."

April found the Thirty-ninth still in its Poolesville camp, that is, when its members were not out on picket and other duties, the same extending a long way up as well as down the Potomac. The weather was as variable as ever, a mixture of good, bad and indifferent, yet through it all the regiment maintained a fair condition of health. "Many jokes and sells, for it was All Fools' Day," was the entry in a certain diary for the first day of the month, and what nonsense a thousand men of military age could not devise on such an occasion, it would be difficult to imagine. The 2d was the regular New England Fast Day, and a holiday was proclaimed by the Colonel, for which he received the mental if not verbal thanks of all the "boys" who proceeded to enjoy the day to the limit. Probably as large a proportion of the regiment attended the religious services at 11 a. m., conducted by Chaplain French, as were present at similar exercises at home churches in distant Massachusetts. However this may have been, there was no failure in taking part in the races, sparring-matches and various games, or at least witnessing them. The baseball game was between the men of Sleeper's Battery and those selected from the Thirty-ninth with the honors remaining with the Infantry, though the cannoniers were supposed to be particularly skillful in the throwing of balls.

The 5th of April found the ground again covered with a heavy fall of snow, and though it departed quickly it left a deal of mud and discomfort generally. The roads and by-paths were not so well drained as the grounds of our Bay State regiment. Thanks to the careful annalist, we know that the new bakery was in working order on the 8th and that the first batch of bread was to be baked that night. Too bad that it had not come earlier or that any necessity for its coming at all existed when the entire camp was so near the army bakery of Washington. Once more rumors became current that moving day was near, and Saturday, the 11th, it was given out that seven days' rations would be drawn on Monday, the 13th, preparatory to departure. A target shoot marked this last Saturday in the Poolesville camp. Sunday was a beautiful spring day,   Apr. 11, '63   though not as quiet as the day might be elsewhere, for the bustle of preparation was evident on all sides. The ever welcome band of the New Hampshire Regiment made the time pass all the more rapidly with its vibrant melody. There were just two days more in Camp Davis and then came the change.

A RAINY MARCH

The first orders were to the effect that the whole brigade was to move, but these were so far modified that only the Thirty-ninth was to go, though the New Hampshire Regiment followed later. Washington was known to be the destination, and provost duty was understood to be the occupation. The start was made in the midst of a driving rain, a fact, however, which did not prevent the Granite State friends and those of the Battery thronging about to wish their comrades a "God-speed." It was pretty generally understood that the Thirty-ninth was selected as the first to go because of the rasping relations, as to priority of commissions,[D] existing between the respective colonels of the two regiments.

The storm did not prevent the New Hampshire band from turning out to give us a hearty send-off and there was need of it, since the general sentiment, long before the halt for the night came, was "the hardest yet." "Now came an awful march through mud and water up to our knees; many straggled behind, while others found it easier going ahead of the Regiment." A stop for dinner was made in a wood by the roadside, and by patience and care fires were made for the preparation of coffee, and then we were off again till at a distance of fourteen miles from Camp Davis, about three miles from Rockville, a very moist camping place was found in some pine woods, and such rest as saturated garments would permit was sought beneath the protecting cover of shelter-tents though many, utterly miserable in their soaked condition, preferred to stand before great fires which they had coaxed into burning. Others, more thoughtful, but less careful as to orders, had taken the opportunity to seek cover in barns and other places of refuge along the way, some even getting good lodgings in dwelling houses, all confident that they could easily overtake the Regiment after a night's rest and drying. Appreciation of Maryland villages or hamlets was at the lowest ebb, one observer charactering Dawsonville as a place of one house, a blacksmith shop and a few other tumbledown buildings, while Darnstown was considered appropriately named without further comment.

The morning of the 16th came none too soon, and many of the boys who were getting great lessons in the "school of the soldier," started off before the regimental orders to march were given at 9 o'clock, the rain continuing to fall, though not with all the emphasis and continuity of yesterday. Those who had the money and started early enough obtained excellent breakfasts in Rockville, the county seat of Montgomery County, and by far the prettiest village these blue clad wanderers had seen since passing through New Jersey, an opinion coincided with by more than one regiment in subsequent months. Here began a new experience since, thence onward to the Capital, the road was macadamized which, however much dryer it might be for the feet, soon began to make them exceedingly sore, more trying even than the muddy roads thus far encountered. While thus advancing on Washington, the headquarter's wagon was met on its way to Poolesville and, on the order of Colonel Davis, the mail belonging to the Regiment was taken out and distributed to the men, a most cheerful episode in an otherwise very dreary day.

Apr. 16, '63 Whatever the speed of the men who marched ahead of the Regiment, they were all held up by the vigilant guards at the first post of the pickets who were stationed around the entire city. This was a few miles before reaching Tenallytown and, at the post, the advance stragglers awaited the coming of the main body. Showers had been intermittent throughout the day and, after a march of sixteen miles, the drenched sons of Massachusetts were pleased to reach the above named place, practically a Maryland village, though within the confines of the District of Columbia. In or near the village was a large edifice, used as a retreat for the priests and pupils of Georgetown College during the summer season, and here the bedraggled Regiment found refuge, reaching it through the great fortifications which surrounded the city, portions of which had been seen on the Virginia side of the Potomac, the nearest forts being Reno and Gaines. That straggling was common became apparent when an entire company found ample space in a single room, whose comforts were all the more comfortable as the men heard the rain which persisted through the most of the night.

"Somewhere the sun is shining" never had a more hearty greeting than when, after so many hours of pitiless pelting, the morning of the 17th dawned clear and bright. Naturally there were orders to dry and clean up, the house grates affording opportunity for one, and our own industry accomplishing the other. It was ten o'clock when the start was made, but alas for human expectations! In vain were all of our burnishings, for the mud, Georgetown-way, was simply bottomless, and long ere the latter city was reached, the Thirty-ninth looked even worse than it did when Tenallytown was attained, though in their anxiety to retain the morning's polish, in several cases dividing fences were broken down that men might march between the street-fence and the houses, thus getting out of some of the mud. The ineffective rage of some of the protesting housewives is still remembered. But an excess of mud and water could not efface the results of months of the hardest kind of discipline and when "company front, by the right into line" was heard, it was obeyed with a readiness and unanimity that would have delighted the great Frederick and, baggage-burdened, mud-bespattered and wearied with forty-eight hours of most trying marching, the Regiment acquitted itself most admirably through the streets and avenues of Washington. At last the men realized the value of their arduous labors on the drilling-grounds of Poolesville; they believed in their Colonel and his associate officers, and when they saw their lines as an arrow straight, every one, in spite of all obstacles, keeping perfect step, best of all they believed in themselves.

WASHINGTON.

The halting place was Martindale Barracks, named thus for General John H. Martindale who, a West Pointer from New York (1835), had won distinguished honors in the Peninsular campaign and, from the preceding November, had been Military Governor of Washington. The barracks, themselves, large and roomy, were located near the "circle," so called, where Washington and New Hampshire Avenues intercept Twenty-third Street, all being to the Northwest of the White House. The men had no difficulty in recognizing the equestrian statue of Washington, by Clark Mills, which, since February, 1860, had stood as the principal figure in the Circle. The buildings to be occupied by the Thirty-ninth were new, well ventilated and lighted, having all reasonable conveniences, two stories in height, the first for officer's quarters, cooking and dining rooms, while in the second story were the best of accommodations for the men. The quarters had been occupied hitherto by one regiment only, the One Hundred and sixty-ninth New York, which having reported in Washington, in October, '62, had been doing provost duty until a few days before when Apr., '63 it was ordered to proceed southward to assist General John J. Peck in the defense of Suffolk, Virginia. The hospital, large and well equipped, won the admiration of the men though, fortunately, there were few occupants during the regiment's stay in the city.

Such were the new appointments to which the Thirty-ninth was commended, something of a change from its former rural surroundings, and a new course of duties was about to be undertaken, though hardly had the brightening up of uniforms and equipments begun ere orders came to stay proceedings, for the regiment was to proceed at once to Fortress Monroe, possibly to have a part in the Suffolk campaign. Had this order not been countermanded and the organization had followed after the One Hundred and Sixty-ninth New York, and had participated in the latter's services, while the Thirty-ninth would have had enough to do, it would have entirely escaped the Wilderness, Spottsylvania, Weldon Railroad and other experiences which make up its thrilling war history. Once more settled in their new quarters, confident that provost work in the Capital is before them for an unknown period, the men proceed to burnish up their weapons, to wash, brush and brighten their uniforms and by the time for dress parade, at the close of this first day in Washington, the closest observer could not have detected any traces of the tribulations through which the soldiers had so recently passed.

It is a life of rigid routine to which the regiment is now committed; military conventionalities in the highest degree are to be the rule for nearly three months; no more "Go as you please" when on picket, nor the free and easy conditions of the Poolesville camp for, seemingly, the eyes of the public are on every man and he must be in the stiffest form of polished brasses, dustless apparel and shiny shoes. The discipline that was thought so severe before, now becomes doubly so. Reveillé sounds at 5.30 a. m. and thence onward till 8 o'clock, save for breakfast, the detailed men are preparing for inspection, which takes place at the office of the provost marshal, Captain Todd. When on duty, the utmost punctiliousness is demanded and, if the men of the Thirty-ninth do not approach perfection, it will not be the fault of the regulations nor of the officers who direct. To such an extent are the polishing and shining of the rifles carried that some of the men are actually afraid that they will wear the barrels out by such constant attrition. When fully settled into the system of provost and other forms of duty, much of the old time drill is suspended, but there is something to do every day, as much as if the men were laboring in a shop, at the desk or on a farm.

The chief exhibition occasions are those of dress parade when distinguished people are not unlikely to appear. At such times, President Lincoln is seen, and Senator Henry Watson, that Massachusetts man of the people, is not an unusual figure. Is Colonel Davis proud of his men? Rather, how his face lights up at the immediate and perfect response to his commands, and every movement of the long line of soldiers is an effectual refutation of the stilted idea that well informed men cannot make good soldiers. Indeed the entire war was proof convincing that thinking bayonets are the most reliable. Of the satisfying spectacle of dress parade, an observer of the time comments, "So perfect and strict were the drill and personal appearance that in our line, of from eight hundred to nine hundred men, not the slightest difference could be detected in any movement from one flank to the other, as if performed by one man, and, in that test of perfect drill, 'Order arms,' though on a brick sidewalk, not one musket was behind the other, all striking with one crash, which startled the spectators, resembling a perfect volley of musketry."

It was a great change from picketing the banks of the Potomac and doing guard duty about the Poolesville region, to patrolling the thoroughfares of Washington and guarding such points as the War Department, the White House, the offices of the paymaster and quartermaster general, General Heintzelman's Headquarters, the medical Apr., '63 purveyor, the post office, the headquarters for forage, corrals for horses and mules, contraband camps, courts-martial and other places of kindred character. The men who had all of these duties to look after grew to consider Washington a paradise for officers not on duty, but quite the reverse for the enlisted man. The former could come and go at his own sweet will while the latter, if he got a pass at all, was subjected to so many conditions that more than half of the pleasure was lost.

At the same time, in one way or another, the Regiment grew to know Washington pretty well; the most of the notable points were inspected and the young men from far away homes took pleasure in seeing the evidences of real home life on every hand; said one of them, "It seems good to be in civilization once more." The 21st of April brought the New Hampshire friends of Poolesville memory and those beholding bade the Fourteenth a hearty welcome; the regiment was assigned to quarters on New York Avenue, its principal duty being the care of the Central guard house; a fact that resulted most happily when Lieut. Carroll D. Wright, subsequently colonel, was in charge, for certain inconsiderate members of Scott's Nine Hundred, having run in some of the Thirty-ninth's men, without sufficient reason, that very efficient officer released the prisoners at once, the incident being the only one in which our Massachusetts men were even temporarily under arrest in Washington. The two regiments partook of the neighborliness, so long characteristic of the states whence they had come.

Many a soldier boy made mention of the fact that on the 22nd Uncle Sam's paymaster happened around and left four months' compensation, squaring accounts to the first of March, and with "plenty of money in our pockets" even provost guards could be gay and happy. An indication of the steadiness of at least some of the men is found when a diarist writes of the city division of the Sons of Temperance and the cordial reception accorded him and the lieutenant who accompanied him; later the same writer states that a large number of soldiers were present; not all soldiers were or are dissolute. In these days the objects of interest were pretty thoroughly inspected and many a lad thought his blue coat quite in place in the President's blue room; and few items near escaped them. They even noted the cow that furnished the milk for the President's family, and some admired the equestrian Jackson, nearly opposite the White House; they threaded the mazes of the Smithsonian Institute, lingering longest over Catlin's wonderful collection of Indian faces, and one recites his pleasure at meeting Frank Brownell, the slayer of Jackson, the Mansion House murderer of Colonel Ellsworth of the New York Fire Zouaves. On the 28th the shoulder-scales that became a part of the display-uniform thereafter were dealt out, a fact that secured for the Thirty-ninth the reputation from certain ignorant fellows of being a regiment of major generals. The month ended with a general observance of the National Fast Day appointed by the President in compliance with a request of the National Senate that he set apart a day for national prayer and humiliation.

May found everybody intent on the struggle which Union and Confederate soldiers were waging on the banks of the Rappahannock. Hooker, who had been preparing since the last of January, had begun the campaign which Union-loving people were wishing would atone for the disaster of December at Fredericksburg. Again the latter name became familiar to the national ear, and these Massachusetts men in Washington believed that their fellow native of the Bay State would atone for some of the earlier misfortunes. Incidentally much extra work came to the regiment in the care of rebel prisoners, whom the Federals captured in the later days of April and the earlier ones of May. Also, it was the task of the Thirty-ninth to escort many of the captives to more or less remote points for permanent retention. Another duty was that of returning to the army at the front large relays of deserters, many of whom had returned under the general amnesty proclaimed for them, May, '63 and in visiting Fredericksburg for this purpose, the escort had a chance to see what real war meant. While following the forces in the field up to and through Chancellorsville, there was no lessening of local occupation and all articles of wearing apparel had to be kept just as bright as ever.

On the 10th much attention was attracted by the funeral procession of General A. W. Whipple, one of the victims of Chancellorsville, having been shot on the 4th, though he survived till the 7th. A native of Greenwich, Massachusetts, he was graduated at West Point, 1841, and his fellow Massachusetts soldiers felt almost a personal interest in the tokens of respect as the procession passed, including, among many other distinguished public officers, President Lincoln; the pall-bearers were eight first sergeants from the Thirty-ninth Regiment. For many years, thereafter, one of the great forts on the Virginia side of the Potomac was to bear his name. Those of the Regiment, not on other duty on the 11th and 12th, had the benefit of one of the periodical scares liable to any locality near the seat of war. Just before dress parade on the earlier date, at a quarter of six, orders came to have the Regiment ready to march to the Chain Bridge, the most northerly of the three great connections between the District and Virginia. After supper, with rubber blankets and overcoats properly slung, the men were in line, prepared for the order to advance to repel any possible rebel raid. The bridge is about five miles from the barracks and the troops reached that point soon after 10 p. m. No sign of any enemy appearing, they stacked arms by the roadside and proceeded to get what rest they could from the materials in their possession, every one taking the trip as a mild kind of lark. At an early hour of the 12th the return march was made by the men, tired and dusty, though they were quite prepared for the eight o'clock breakfast which the cooks had in readiness.

It was not all work in Washington; there were pranks by the score, and now and then one was written down in the book of someone's recollection,— witness the following: "a corporal of Company A with a guard was detailed to look after certain condemned goods some two miles out; with stripes and chevrons he was as slick and dapper a youth as ever wore a uniform. Without a cent in his pocket, and his entire party of twelve men equally lacking, he took them all to the theatre to see Maggie Mitchell play 'Little Barefoot'; he had said to the men, 'Be ready at seven o'clock, sharp, with shoes blacked and with brass scales on shoulders, the U. S. on the belts, well polished.' They obeyed and were marched off the grounds and along Pennsylvania Ave., the Corporal saluting any patrol they chanced to meet, right up to the theatre, itself; past the ticket-office, and when tickets for the company were demanded, the natty corporal threatened to arrest any one venturing to halt or impede his men, so in they went to the very best seats in the building, two dollar ones, and there he seated his squad. Never was play better enjoyed and when, at 9 o'clock or later, a lieutenant of cavalry looked the house over in search of parties without proper credentials, the corporal rose and, like a veritable Crichton, saluted; how could any officer disturb such serenity and immaculateness? He asked no questions; not a boy in the party understood the circumstances under which they were having the time of their lives, and the return was quite as successful as the going; the whole affair, a triumph of unqualified bluff and cheek."

Very likely many good veterans never knew that the Northern soldiers in Washington maintained an active Division of the Sons of Temperance, having their meetings in Odd Fellows Hall, corner of Nineteenth Street and Pennsylvania Avenue, and that, on public occasions, no branch of the order turned out more men. Several officers and men of the Thirty-ninth were deeply interested in the society, and one of them records with some evident satisfaction the fact that he had closed a rum hole and arrested the keeper,

making one less source of temptation. On the   May 24, '63   24th the boys

from New England, with eyes alert for anything savoring of home, discover the passing of the Eleventh Massachusetts Battery, the Commonwealth's only Nine Months' Artillery organization, on its way homeward. Naturally the exchange of greetings was most hearty. On meeting Major S. E. Chamberlain of the First Massachusetts Cavalry, only recently severely wounded, yet out and ready to return, an admirer writes, "If the service were made up of officers like him, more would be done towards putting down the Rebellion."

Pay-day came on the 28th, and the promptness of the Government won no end of praise from the always impecunious soldiers, a feeling that they were disposed at a later time to considerably moderate.

The crowning event of the end of the month was the joint drill of the Regiment along with the Fourteenth New Hampshire some three miles away, in the rear of Mt. Pleasant Hospital on Fourteenth Street. It was hot and dusty, there having been no rain for three weeks, but the men were put through their evolutions by Brig. General Martindale, in a manner that evidently met his approval, whatever those exercised may have thought of it. White gloves and shiny scales suffered from the heat and dust laden air, but the men bore ample testimony to the quality of the drill on the old Poolesville grounds. However, the principal honors came when the return was made, for though the route step was allowed until the heart of the city was reached, then came the display moment and, in column of companies, the Regiment wheeled into Pennsylvania Avenue with the precision of a machine, winning the applause of the crowd of officers who were occupying the piazzas of Willard's Hotel; and without music, but with the regular tramp, tramp, that drill alone can impart, the men marched to their quarters with an added notch in their appreciation of what the Thirty-ninth could do.

In the way of dust and heat, June was to be a trying month for the men who had to keep themselves in the very primmest form possible, since to be neat and speckless was deemed the highest attainment of a soldier in town. In those days there was voting by the citizens on local matters and the drift of the ballots cast on the first day of the month gave indications of a large secession spirit in the city. On the second day, the Thirty-fourth Massachusetts appeared in Washington for the performance of duties, similar to those already falling to the lot of the Thirty-ninth. Though from Worcester County and Berkshire there was the common bond of statehood, and the Thirty-fourth also prided itself no little on its discipline and well drilled ranks. One of the members of the Thirty-ninth comments on the hardness of appearance of some of the prisoners whom he had to watch over and remarks that, at the window by his beat is a girl, about eighteen years old, who is a rebel spy, and that for five months she was a corporal in the Union ranks. Of this same person, Colonel Lincoln in his story of the Thirty-fourth relates that, to curb her and keep her within bounds, one of his officers was obliged to handcuff her.

So far as the amenities of Washington life for the regiment were concerned, nothing contributed more than the evenings spent in connection with the Sons of Temperance organization, of which something might be said in addition to former items. Formed in the Poolesville camp during the preceding winter, it had been chartered by the Grand Lodge of Massachusetts and was known as Army Lodge, Number 39, and after reaching the Capital, its membership increased to about two hundred. No better indication of the moral quality of the regiment could be found. Similar organizations among the residents of the city were especially hospitable, and invitations to all sorts of entertainment were of frequent occurrence. A festival on the 12th, where not only the delicacies of the season were served, but where literary and elocutionary ability were displayed, was long memorable in regimental circles. Also long remembered was Monday, the 15th, when large details [June 15, '63] assisted in bearing to the several hospitals the grievously wounded from Chancellorsville, many of whom had been lying on the field for almost two weeks with scant attention, some having suffered the amputation of limbs at the hands of Confederate surgeons. Carried upon stretchers as gently as possible, some of them fully two miles, through the intense heat, some died on the way, many more soon after arriving. While people along the route did all that they could do to alleviate their suffering, the condition of these unfortunate men was a startling lesson to all of the awful possibilities of war.

It would be very strange if the guarding of the White House grounds did not occasion some meetings with the President. Of William S. Sumner, Company H, a second cousin of Senator Charles Sumner, the following is related: He had been stationed at a path, leading across a recently seeded lawn, the path having formed a short cut to one of the departments. Several officers had been turned back, when Sumner saw the president approaching to take the cut-off himself. He was promptly halted when the President exclaimed, "What's up, Sentry?" To this, the sentinel replied, "The grass is up, Mr. Lincoln." Looking down at his feet, the president said, "Some of it would be down, if I crossed over the lawn. I gave the order to place a sentinel here and I am just ready to be an offender." He commended the soldier for obeying his orders so strictly, even to halting the President, and Sumner was also commended by his own officers. Later when a comrade of his company had obtained a sick furlough and could not secure transportation, Sumner went with him to the White House, to present the case to Mr. Lincoln, who, remembering the incident of the hold-up at the lawn, readily wrote a line to the quartermaster which speedily brought the desired means of going home.

The campaign which was to reach its culmination at Gettysburg was well under way. Lee was headed northward and Union Governors were speeding troops towards the South to assist in driving him back. Naturally, expectation was at fever heat and every rumor simply added to the excitement. Some of the men who visited Baltimore to escort thither certain prisoners found the city with barricades in the streets and negroes working on fortifications, all under the apprehension of the coming of the rebel army. Friday, the 26th, under the tidings that the enemy was near Fort Massachusetts, north of Georgetown, the regiment was ordered to be in readiness to move at a moment's notice. Ammunition was given out and, in light marching order, the men were excitedly expectant when the order came to turn in and "snooze." As the sequel showed, had the Thirty-ninth and other regiments marched out beyond Tenallytown, a great wagon-train might have been saved, but those in command had not the power of reading the future.

How near the men came to meeting Stuart's Cavalry appeared a little later. Rumors were afloat as to some sort of disaster on the Maryland side of the Potomac and not so very far away from the District. The result was that late at night, orders were received to start at once for the scene of depredation and after a rapid march of several miles beyond the Chain Bridge, line of battle was formed at about two o'clock in the morning of the 29th. If all concerned could have known that the terrible Stuart and his men were many miles away at the time, with no thought whatever of molesting Washington or its defenders, very likely the impromptu bivouac or "In place, rest" might have been more comfortable than it really was. The event, in which any act on the part of the regiment was altogether lacking, was one more of those audacious deeds for which the Confederate Kleber was famous. Crossing the Potomac at Rowser's Ford somewhat south of Poolesville, under the most difficult circumstances, early in the morning of the 28th, he rode east to Rockville, whence a detachment, a very small one, dashing towards the District, encountered a wagon-train of one hundred and twenty-five vehicles,

June 28, '63 heavily loaded, on their way to supply the Union Army, then marching towards the north. Though Stuart was able to retain the train and to take it with him into Pennsylvania, the delays occasioned by it rendered him and his men much less efficient in the great encounter at Gettysburg than they might have been otherwise.

The resignation of General Hooker from the command of the Army of the Potomac had produced many an expression of regret among the rank and file throughout the army, but especially were regrets expressed among the men reared in Massachusetts, the boyhood's home of "Fighting Joe." With the steady progress of the rival armies northward, it was apparent that a great battle was impending, and that all available troops would be called into the fray, though the demand did not come quite as early as expected. While on the banks of the Mississippi, Vicksburg, and around the quiet Pennsylvanian city, Gettysburg, were acquiring new significance in the world's history, the capital city, Washington, was preparing for the celebration of the 4th of July, just as if that were the only matter of importance. To begin with, all guards and patrols were reduced one half in numbers, thus leaving a larger force to participate in the parade. The military escort consisted of the Second District of Columbia Volunteers, the Fourteenth New Hampshire, the Thirty-fourth and Thirty-ninth Massachusetts Regiments. The civic organizations of the city looked and marched their best; the Marine Band discoursed the kind of music for which it was famous. Added interest might have been given to the day, had news from the two great battles, just fought and won, arrived in time. They would have given the celebration the greatest cause for enthusiasm ever had by an Independence Day, not accepting the first one of all. One prosaic participant comments only this, "We marched from seven-thirty to one o'clock; the sun terribly hot." So far as the military features were concerned, the day ended at the Provost marshal's office, where all were reviewed by Generals Heintzelman and Martindale. On reaching their quarters, the soldiers were regaled with as good a dinner as their cooks were able to provide. Another loyal Bay Stater entered on his book these characteristic words, "It was very well, but nothing when compared with Boston celebrations."

Sunday, the 5th, brought to the city general Daniel E. Sickles, minus the leg which he lost on the second day of Gettysburg, out by the peach orchard. A detachment of the Thirty-ninth met the distinguished officer and escorted him to his home. Official news of the surrender of Vicksburg to General Grant was received on the 7th and loyal Washington went wild with marching columns serenading prominent officials and with the general illumination, the Martindale Barracks not accepted. President Lincoln, members of his Cabinet and Major General Halleck were called on and each one responded with an appropriate speech. On the 9th came the orders which, long expected, were not unwelcome, for, though the Washington tour of duty was free from long marches, the risk of battle and the privations of camp, there was ever the thought that the service was not strictly ideal for real soldiers, hence the willingness with which dress coats and other form of superfluous clothing were packed against their possible need in the following winter. Contents for the knapsacks were chosen with considerable more judgment than would have been used nine months before.

JOINING THE POTOMAC ARMY

It was about eight o'clock in the evening when the Regiment formed line for the last time on the parade ground and the men marched off for the Baltimore and Ohio Railroad station. The drums were beating and laughter and shouting were quite in contrast with the solemn demeanor of former passages through Washington, then intent on making and retaining a reputation for discipline and self control.

July 10, '63 At the station there was a considerable wait for the Thirty-fourth Massachusetts and two batteries which were to accompany us. Hence it was late of the ninth or, rather early in the morning of the 10th, before the start from the city was made. Seven hundred and fifty strong, a large shrinkage for the nine months of peaceful service, loaded upon freight cars, the Regiment was headed for Harper's Ferry. All sorts of items made the journey long and tedious; says one of the boys, "The locomotive came near running over a 'nigger'; the train broke in two; one of the cars ran off the track," and another observer comments on the heat and closeness of the night and cars. The ride during the day was varied with characteristic incidents of the halts where efforts were made to secure food from nearby houses; at Frederick Junction where a branch road runs up to the city, made famous by Barbara Frietchie and Whittier, other troops joined the train and the same sped on to its destination, not exactly the Ferry itself, but Sandy Hook, the Maryland village opposite.

Darkness had settled down when the train reached the point of unloading, and the debarkation was effected with every one wishing he could see the wonderful panorama that the place afforded, but before the scenery could be enjoyed there was the biggest climb before the men that they had ever undertaken. The road was only an apology for one, though its mud was deep and adhesive; following closely one's file leader was necessary, if a man would keep in the procession. Finally there came a real climb up a mountain's side with every man for himself, until there was a blessed emergence on a plateau where, mud encrusted, the men threw themselves upon the ground and slept the sleep of exhaustion. The sun of the 11th, was well up the sky, ere the wearied climbers awoke to admire the scene developed around them. It did not matter much at what time the waking came, since there were no rations and the company cooks had no facilities for cooking even were rations ready. It was not till a large detail had gone down to the railroad and brought hence the hardtack, coffee and pork, that eating could be resumed, each one becoming his own cook, though some of the soldiers declared that a twenty-four hours' fast, along with unusual exertion had made the repast the most appetising they had eaten in months.

Those thus inclined had a chance to view a landscape which had engaged the attention of Washington and Jefferson, and which in more recent times had been the observatory of John Brown, previous to the raid which, without doubt, had helped precipitate the great conflict. Down along the opposite banks of the Potomac were the blackened ruins of the great armory, where had been made so many guns, now in the hands of the enemy, and nearer the middle of the village was the fire-engine house which was to go down into history as the "John Brown Fort." At Harper's Ferry, the Shenandoah joins the Potomac, and, as a point of vantage, it had been held by both rebel and Federal. A year before, the place had been given up by Col. D. S. Miles to Stonewall Jackson, and is now in Confederate possession, though the hurried construction of a bridge across the Shenandoah indicates a disposition on the part of the men in gray to depart. The retreat of Lee from Gettysburg had involved the entire region in uncertainty, hence the ordering out of regiments from Washington, and the presence in the immediate locality of the Eighth, Forty-sixth and Fifty-first Massachusetts, nine months' regiments, which on their way home from North Carolina were shunted off into this section, along with the Thirty-ninth, forming a brigade under the command of General Henry S. Briggs, first colonel of the Tenth Infantry, also a Bay State organization.

While individuals might improve the opportunity to admire the locality and to secure whatever the vicinity afforded in the way of food, it was not a tour of observation that took these men to this elevated section, and about noon of Sunday, the 12th, came orders to move, but according July 12, '63 to traditional custom, the order was not carried out until six o'clock. The march of the preceding night had convinced many that they were too heavily laden, and there being near the camp an elderly gentleman of a most obliging nature, he consented to take charge of bundles which the men made up, and, carefully marked, left in his care, to be called for later. Of course many who relieved themselves of burdens never called for their possessions and the most of them thought the man himself would become tired of his charge; but when years afterwards, a Woburn veteran tried the experiment of writing for his package, it came back to him forthwith, a remarkable tribute to the honesty and system of the man. During the ensuing night very many, who had not thus anticipated the exactions of the march, lessened their burdens by throwing away what had become intolerable.

The roads, trod by new regiments, were always marked by just such evidence of the lessons of experience. The regiments thus starting were the Eighth, Forty-sixth, Fifty-first and Thirty-ninth Massachusetts, forming the Fourth

Provisional Brigade of the Second Division, First Army Corps; the respective commanders being Generals John Newton of the corps, John C. Robinson of the division, and Henry S. Briggs of the brigade. The Thirty-fourth, which had accompanied the Thirty-ninth from Baltimore, remained and gave the parting good word as the Thirty-ninth departed, the two organizations not to meet again until the homeward march through Richmond in 1865.

AT THE FRONT

When a brigade advances, all portions thereof do not, cannot move at once, hence it was fully nine o'clock in the evening of the 12th, before all were fully under way. It is a forced march on which the soldiers are entering, and those who are keeping the run of events will merge the 12th and 13th together, there being no good stopping place between them. As one writer expresses it, "up hill and down, so dark that we can scarcely see, all night, right up to 5 o'clock in the morning, when we halt for rest and breakfast in a belt of woods, about two miles from Boonsboro."[E] The trials of that night were long matters of reference, blankets were thrown away, so heavy did they become under the severe strain to which all were subjected. When the halt came, many threw themselves upon the ground for sleep, rather than prepare their coffee, the prime source of strength to the campaigner, and some of those who did set about breakfast getting immediately fell asleep over the task, so completely worn out were the marchers by the exactions of the night.

Nor was the end yet, since all too soon for the tired soldiers the sound of "assembly" calls them into the ranks and "forward" is again the word. To crown their discomforts, rain begins to fall and the mud to deepen, as the ranks once more press forward through Boonsboro, and thence over ways trodden by the participants in the Antietam battle of the year before, the men obey orders and, being at the right of the brigade, they pretty effectually distance their friends in the other regiments and, finding themselves practically alone, they are obliged to halt and await the coming up of the remainder of the brigade; so thorough had been the disciplinary drills on the Poolesville parade, the men of the Thirty-ninth were equal to almost any exaction. The termination of the long march was Funkstown, an insignificant Maryland village, important only as the point near which was stationed a part of the Army of the Potomac, all awaiting the word to advance against July 13, '63 Lee, whose forces had been unable to recross the Potomac, on account of the heavy rains, which had greatly swollen the waters of that important stream.

Also the name had been heard a year before, when the Battle of Antietam had for the first time given Funkstown distinction, otherwise it might have slumbered a thousand years with no signs of awakening. To the wearied men of the Thirty-ninth who, in twenty hours or less, had traversed through rain and mud from twenty-five to thirty miles of wretched roads any sort of place was agreeable for a terminal, and they were glad to hear the command "Halt," and the subsequent direction to pitch tents was equally grateful. Those that could turned in early, but those unlucky ones who had to stand guard faced their duty grimly, realizing that war was not altogether fun. A skirmish line actively engaged, out towards the lines of the enemy, gave to these inexperienced soldiers just the least foretaste of what hostile bullets meant. There was a general feeling that the morrow would bring the clash of arms, and that the days of preparation were over. Ten days after Gettysburg, the Confederates, at bay between the river and the Federals, must either fight, drown or surrender.

Lieut. Colonel Peirson who, when a member of the Twentieth Massachusetts had served on the staff of General Sedgwick, now commanding the Sixth Army Corps, naturally improved the opportunity to call upon his former leader. Our officer was received most kindly and the situation was freely discussed, the General saying that he had just returned from a conference of all the general officers, at which it was decided that it was then inexpedient to attack Lee, his force being about as large as our own and his position for defense being stronger than ours for attack. So depleted were the regiments by the great battle, so recently fought, the Thirty-ninth was as large as almost any brigade. Years later, on meeting General Meade in Boston, the decision of the conference was confirmed, the Potomac Army Commander telling Colonel Peirson that the risk involved was considered too great. Of course of this the rank and file, wondering when the orders to attack would be heard, knew nothing.

The dawn of Tuesday, the 14th, revealed an entirely different situation; the Confederates, afar from their case of supplies, impoverished as to ammunition by the demands of Gettysburg, hence in no condition to attack even if so disposed, had worked industriously all of Monday, the 13th, in constructing a pontoon bridge across the Potomac, at Falling Waters, over which they had withdrawn during the night. To the rank and file, the situation did not appeal as it did to those in command who saw in the escape of the enemy the possible results of the fierce engagement at Gettysburg vanish away. Men with guns, as they advanced, were not encountering the expected opposition and finally, when in the afternoon Williamsport was reached and still no sight of the foe, the dullest man in line realized that the fight for that day was off. One of the observers inscribes in his diary these reflections, "If we had attacked the rebels yesterday, we might have made great havoc among them, crossing the river, but, as it is, we probably will have to follow them into Virginia; pitched our tents, cooked some coffee and went to sleep." Another commentator remarks, "The Somerville (E) Company is detailed as guard at General Newton's headquarters."

History is now repeat to itself, since Lee with his army is moving up the Shenandoah Valley as he did after Antietam, while Meade and the Union army will follow the route of McClellan along the eastern side of the Blue Ridge, appearing at each one of the successive gaps through which the

Confederates might essay a passage on their return to their former stamping grounds. With what might have had been, had Meade done this or that, we have no more to do than with the events which followed Antietam, and a like dilatoriness on the part of McClellan in moving immediately on the enemy's works. Our present July 14, '63 concern is with and for the Thirty-ninth Regiment which hears the reveillé at five o'clock in the morning of the 15th, with the injunction to be ready to march in twenty minutes, a command which resulted in a start at six o'clock. The day is hot and sultry, the pace rapid and again men rid themselves of everything possible to lighten their burdens as they hasten over the dusty Maryland roads. Funkstown is again sighted, though on the right, and the battle-line of the day before is hurriedly passed. The gory field of Antietam, where so many of the blue and the gray mingled their life-blood, is also recognized and a halt is called near Antietam Creek.

One of the early incidents of the day's march was the meeting of the Sixth Corps and the First, rendering it necessary for the two bodies to pass each other at nearly right angles. The writer also notes the peculiar coincidence that this passage of the Thirty-ninth was effected through the ranks of the Thirty-seventh, a Western Massachusetts regiment; just a chance to say "Good-morning and Good-bye," all in the same breath. It was on this day's march also that the news came of the fall of Port Hudson and the bloody combats before Charleston, South Carolina. Burnside's bridge, over the Antietam, is crossed in the opposite direction from that taken by that leader a year ago and the hurried way is pursued through Keedysville to Rohersville where the camp is pitched for the night. It has been a hard day, with a record of fully twenty-five sun-broiling miles passed over, and to crown the miseries of the march, rations are scarce, in most cases entirely lacking. The story is told that a goose was appropriated on the way, with the hope that soon opportunity might be found for cooking it, but the wearied men, successively, grew tired of carrying it and its body was left for some luckier party, nearer the rear of the line, to enjoy on reaching camp. The strain must be excessive which will cause a soldier to throw away an edible luxury.

As usual, the bugle summons the men from repose at an early hour on the 17th and not a little rejoicing follows the announcement that rations are to be drawn, so that the day's exactions will begin on full stomachs. At not quite so brisk a rate as that of yesterday, the route continues through Crampton's Gap, on to a hillside near Petersville, not far from Catoctin Creek, a name often heard in stories of the locality. Berlin, a village somewhat below Harper's Ferry on the Potomac, is the name of the nearest river point, and all are pleased at the chance to pitch their shelter tents, to rest, to clean up clothing and weapons, and to realize that the soldier is not always on the march. It was at this point that the chaplain and the men who had been left in Washington rejoined the regiment. The 17th of July introduces the variation of a heavy rain, yet this does not prevent our active men from visiting neighboring regiments whose depleted condition contrasts vividly with the full ranks of the newly arrived. Says one visitor, "Some of the old regiments do not number more than our one company." On this day, obedient to orders, the Fifty-first Regiment takes its departure for the North and its muster-out, its entire tour of duty from the first of the month having been over and above the time called for by its term of enlistment.

The assembling of a great army is ever a magnificent sight, and that presented by the several corps of the Potomac Army, awaiting the laying of pontoon bridges across the Potomac for the use of this great array of humanity, forms no exception, a glorious sight even though seen through showers of rain. It is the period also of wheat-harvest and, notwithstanding the moisture, something of an idea is obtained of how the staff-of-life looks in its earlier stages. There is a deal of talk among the soldiers as to how they ought to have fought and finished Lee, many of them believing that the end of the Rebellion might have been effected at or near Williamsport. By the 18th, the bridges being in readiness, early orders are given that ⸾ July 17, '63 ⸿ all must be ready to advance at four o'clock, and for a wonder the start is only half an hour behind the appointment. The Fifth Corps and the cavalry crossed last night. The Forty-sixth Massachusetts, one of the nine months' regiments, accompanying us all the way round from Maryland Heights, is but a few rods from the river, when orders are received to fall out and proceed immediately to Baltimore and so Northward; for some reason, the Eighth Massachusetts, in the same category, still continues in line. It was in these days that certain of the regiment, thinking themselves so far from the region of military precision they might essay a little abandon of style, attempted to wear the "bell-hats," worn by some regiments, in place of the visored, regulation caps required where style was effected, but the Colonel would have none of it and to trade back was the next thing necessary.

IN VIRGINIA

Quite nine months have passed since that hurried departure from Arlington for the Maryland side of old Potomac's shore and now, on the 18th of July, the sacred soil is again trodden by Massachusetts feet as the regiment takes its way through a section that fairly captivates the eyes of these men so far from home and, after a march of possibly thirteen miles, the lovely village of Waterford is reached at about two o'clock in the afternoon. Considering the unusual beauty of the village, its marked similarity to just such assemblages of dwellings in the North, the surprise of the visitors is not so great when they learn that the place has furnished two full companies of soldiers for the Union army. After a good night's rest, at 6 a. m. of Sunday, the 19th, the regiment passed through the village, keeping step to patriotic airs, while the people displayed Union flags and cheered the passing men in blue; the scene would hardly have been different, were they in one of their own Northern towns. Through a continuation of yesterday's scenic beauties, the march is made to the village of Hamilton fifteen miles away, also a beautiful place, and here the halt is made under trees so umbrageous that tents are unnecessary, all declaring it the very best camping place yet. The neighboring fields abound in seemingly endless quantities of blackberries of which the hungry soldiers proceed to eat their fill, not only satisfying hunger but proving an excellent specific for certain ailments incident to the season. Had the officers purposely directed the army this way, they could have done nothing more opportune for the health of the men. What Northern home is ignorant of the healing qualities of blackberry cordial? Better far than many responses to the surgeon's call.

The men thought the Sunday well spent and, after a twilight devoted to reminiscenes, wherein of course home abounded, couches on mother earth were sought, hoping that sleep might be undisturbed until morn. It was well that rest was taken early for it is only two o'clock of the 20th when morning sleep is broken by the bugle call; evidently a long march is in prospect, but from characteristic delays, it is fully five o'clock before faces are again set southward, the route being through a section badly scarred by the ravages of war. About twenty miles are passed over in reaching Middleburg, a place on the Alexandria and Winchester turnpike, of some local importance, whose inhabitants are largely if not entirely secesh, and we are told that many of them, being in Pickett's Division, had suffered greatly at Gettysburg. Indeed one lady, the mistress of a large and elegantly furnished mansion, apparently one of the F. F. V.'s, who very kindly responded to the requests of the Union soldiers, when thanked most respectfully for her consideration, replied that she only wished people on the other side might have done as much for her son who was killed at Gettysburg. On the way   July 20, '63   hither, the regiment has the new experience of fording a stream, Goose Creek, from two to four feet deep and from 80 to 100 feet wide.

A heavy picket line is thrown out because of the proximity of guerrillas, who prowl around like jackals intent on mischief; and they already had captured several division staff officers who had ridden too far ahead, for the purpose of selecting proper camping grounds. The tour of picket duty was not without its compensation since an abundance of blackberries was revealed by the morning of the 21st which, with food foraged from the enemy's country, helped out the somewhat reduced rations of the haversack. In the preceding night Samuel W. Joyce, Company C, a Medford boy, had died, worn out by the exactions of the expedition, and a prayer by the chaplain is the sole service as his body is committed to the earth, since in active warfare scant time is found for burial ceremonies. The entire day is passed in this camp, thus affording a needed rest while time is found for observation, not alone of the neighboring fields, abounding in berries, but of the people among whom no men of military age are found and of the fact that Confederate money finds greater favor here than the currency of Uncle Sam, a peculiarity however that gradually disappears as the months advance.

It is two o'clock, p. m. when the command to pack up is heard, but it is nearly or quite sundown before the start is made, since the brigade is taking its turn on the left of the line; also the guarding of the wagon train is committed to the brigade and in this somewhat arduous duty the Thirty-ninth bears its part. Over roads, never conspicuous for smoothness, now worse than ever, the troops and the train pick their weary way till 3 a. m. of the 23rd, when White Plains is reached, a distance of not more than eight miles from Middleburg, but a wearying march nevertheless. It is pretty generally understood that both the rebel and the Union armies are racing for the Rappahannock, and the Federals have the inside track. The wagons are parked here, for mules must, if men do not, rest, and those guarding have the privilege of a bivouac for a short period, while the other troops have been resting a large part of the night. Repose is enjoyed for about four hours when, at seven o'clock in the morning, we are routed out and, two hours later proceed on our route to Warrenton, some thirteen miles away, getting there not far from five in the afternoon. Much to the astonishment of the wearied marchers, a dress parade is ordered, and the men go through the form, though they would much prefer to rest their tired bodies prone upon the ground.

Warrenton is one of the names which every one has heard, over and over, ever since the beginning of the war, and all conclude that it must have been a very interesting as well as beautiful place before hostilities had marred its loveliness; the county seat of Fauquier County it possesses all of the public buildings belonging to such a place and betrays evidence of thrift, enterprise and culture. Secesh to the core, the people prefer Southern currency, though they will also take that of the North. In camp on a hill to the rear of Warrenton, the 24th is spent, rations are drawn, letters written to the homeland, and a big notch made in the stick of soldierly experience. With true military routine a dress parade is had at seven o'clock, just for the sake of maintaining the regimental altogethery feeling. Early in the morning of the 25th march is resumed and continues through a dry, level country, destitute alike of shade and water, the sun all of the time giving indications of his heat rays; occasional halts do not negative the fact that it is a long and tiresome march, on account of which many a man would have been overcome by the heat had not all been thoroughly acclimated in the vigorous drills of the preceding months. Thirteen miles of desolation bring us to noon and Warrenton Junction and, best of all, to the sight of water. The stream, though small and already muddied by all sorts of animals in their efforts for drink, is none the less sought with ardor by the thirsty men, July 25, '63 who pronounce this the dryest day in all their army experience.

Here is found a depot of supplies, the communication by rail and steam with Washington being direct and regular so that commissary and quartermaster stores are replenished; near by is the whole Army of the Potomac, though there is every indication of going further on every hand and, while seemingly in direst confusion, no one appeared to get in another's way, convincing proof that some guiding power had all these different lines well in hand. What a chance to visit this and that friend in other regiments, an opportunity of which hundreds of men availed themselves, and many a meeting here was the last in this life. Making camp in a nearby grove, rest is sought, save as it is interrupted by rations-drawing, until there comes the order to fall-in once more, but by this time the men have learned that a certain amount of leeway is to be allowed in these marching orders, and they do not respond with all of their former alacrity. It is from this point that Major Tremlett, accompanied by men from several companies, goes North for the purpose of looking after recruits expected from conscripts and substitutes. The second installment of this day's march really began about 7 p. m. and continued possibly seven miles to Bealton Station, on the Orange and Alexandria Railroad. Lack of water had made the morning's route hard to bear; nothing of the sort troubled that of the evening, since a pelting rain beat upon the faces of the marchers, filled the roads with mud and made the rivulets swelling torrents. With a single exception this was the severest storm ever encountered by the Thirty-ninth, that exception being the one when crossing the Occoquan on the return of Washington after the surrender. It is one o'clock in the morning of the 26th, that the regiment, though completely saturated with rain, files into an open field, and finds such repose as it can until the light of day.

FIRST ARMY CORPS.

It was here and on this day that the Eighth M. V. M., having accompanied the Thirty-ninth in all of its wanderings from Maryland Heights, took its leave of the Potomac army and, obedient to orders, embarked at Warrenton Junction for Washington, its nine months' tour of duty being long overpast, and a happy lot of soldiers they were, with the prospect of a speedy return to their homes. Of course there were the regular details for pickets, but the most of the regiment had a chance to clean up and to rest after the exactions of the preceding night. The departure of the Eighth caused the end of the Provisional Brigade, under the command of General Briggs, the latter returning to Washington, while the Thirty-ninth became a part of the First Brigade, Second Division, First Army Corps, the division and corps being the same as before; the other members of the brigade were the Thirteenth Massachusetts, Sixteenth Maine, Ninety-fourth and One Hundred and Fourth New York, and the One Hundred and Seventh Pennsylvania, the Commander being Colonel Peter Lyle of the Ninetieth Pennsylvania regiment. The dress parade at the close of this day was signalized by a sequel to the bell crowned hats, already referred to, since a number of the men in Woburn Company (K), wearing the obnoxious headgear and otherwise grotesquely arrayed, appeared on the parade ground, exciting the risibles of all beholders and securing for themselves a command to report at the colonel's headquarters, where even his equanimity was upset and, after a hearty laugh, he let the culprits off with a reprimand and some extra policing about his tent.

The sweet sleep to which the regiment commended itself at "Taps" was interrupted at 11 p. m. by the command to "pack-up" and "fall-in" and soon afterward the Thirty-ninth was marching southward, making the best of the way alongside the railroad, not always careful to keep the middle of the road, this being one of the lapses of July 26, '63 Colonel Davis, viz., that he was willing that the men should keep their feet dry if possible. He had even excited the ire of General Briggs by insisting that, when only keeping in line was the point at issue, his men should march dry-shod, thus possibly accounting for the extra marching ability of his men. Rappahannock Station, where the Orange and Alexandria Railroad crosses the river, was the point aimed at, and very early in the morning of the 27th it was reached, and the broken slumbers of the preceding night were resumed for a brief period. The remainder of the First Brigade was here along with several thousand cavalrymen. The remaining days of July were spent in the camp established near the banks of the Rappahannock, on an elevation overlooking the river. There was nothing to disturb the general quiet of the place, though Union soldiers picketed one side of the stream, a narrow one here, and rebels the other. The railroad bridge had been destroyed and the coming of a train load of pontoons, in the evening of Wednesday, the 29th, called for a large detail of men from each company to unload them, a rather heavy task, while showers, many of them very severe, made even tent life anything but comfortable. Somewhere, in these meanderings, a character of Company G won fame for himself in the aptness of his reply to Captain Trull. As he fell in for dress parade, the Captain noticed that the private's shoes were plastered with Virginia mud, and sent him to his quarters to make them more presentable. Presently he returned with the fronts of said shoes much improved, but the after portions were as before. When asked by the irate Captain why he had not blacked the heels as well as the front of his shoes, the witty fellow replied that a good soldier never looked behind.

Lest the men through idleness might grow rusty, the last day of July was marked by a drill, and later the orders were given that at two o'clock in the next morning, August 1st, the camp should be broken and all be ready to march soon after. While the day did not bring on an engagement there was much of interest in seeing the cavalry cross the river and in beholding the disappearance of the Confederate pickets and in hearing the sounds of more or less firing beyond the hills across the stream, in the direction of Culpeper Court House. Our crossing was effected about two o'clock in the afternoon, line of battle was formed and under a blazing sun we advanced until a piece of woods was reached where every man improved the least chance possible for escape from the intense heat. After a considerable halt and consequent rest, the line fell back fully a mile, halting on the brow of a hill where trees and underbrush were cut away to favor firing of both artillery and musketry, while the fallen timber would serve as an abatis. Until the 8th of August the Regiment remained here, digging intrenchments, doing picket duty, witnessing the almost constant activities of the Cavalry, which kept the enemy stirred up, and on the 3rd it seemed as though the Confederates were really coming our way, but it proved to be only a reconnoisance in force, and the Union forces were found on the watch. Colonel Lyle having leave of absence, Colonel Davis succeeded to the command of the brigade and Lieut. Colonel Peirson to that of the regiment. For diversion, the men had berry picking and foraging generally in front of, and bathing in the Rappahannock behind their lines, and on Wednesday, the 5th, all were surprised and delighted by the appearance of Major Bell, paymaster, who left many tokens of Uncle Sam's honesty in the hands of the men, a large portion of which was speedily sent northward for the benefit of kindred there. Thursday, the 6th, was a day of national thanksgiving for the victories that had attended the Union arms and at brigade headquarters there were religious services by the chaplains of the Sixteenth Maine, the Ninety-fourth and One Hundred and Fourth New York, and by General Briggs, temporarily in command of the division. The proclamation of the President, calling for this observance, was issued July 15th, the kind heartedness and devotion of Mr. Lincoln appearing in every sentence. While the entire document might be read with profit to-day, let the following extract suffice:—

But these victories have been accorded not without sacrifices of life, limb, health and liberty, incurred by brave, loyal and patriotic citizens. Domestic affliction in every part of the country follows in the train of these fearful bereavements. It is meet and right to recognize and confess the presence of the Almighty Father and the power of His hand equally in these triumphs and in these sorrows.

That the men might participate in the spirit of the day there was a suspension of drills, though a morning inspection reminded everyone that routine constitutes a large part of a soldier's life.

Dress parade on the 7th was omitted on account of one of the severe storms with which the season was rife, accompanied by thunder and lightning and wind to the extent of blowing down the brush protection which many of the men had set up around their tents; many of the tents went down also—as one of the unfortunates records it, "most of the boys got drowned out." Saturday, the 8th, brought a change, in that orders were received about 11 a. m. to prepare dinner early in order to be ready to march, though we did really remain till after five o'clock before starting, carrying with us tent-poles and everything movable that might contribute to the comfort of the new stopping place, which proved to be across the river and very near where we were before the advance beyond the Rappahannock. Apparently, the entire brigade came back with us. Though no one was conscious of the fact at the time, here the Thirty-ninth was fated to remain with the other parts of the Potomac Army for more than a month. Though we had marched with the army all the way down from Funkstown, we had not fought at Gettysburg, nor had we participated in that trying race with Lee's forces all the way from Falmouth to the foregoing sanguinary field. Regiments had become little better than skeleton organizations; mounts for cavalry and artillery were sadly wanting and a period for recuperation and replenishing was absolutely necessary.

"Reveillé at 4.30 a. m.; splendid morning and the distant bugles and drums over hill and vale proclaim that the army is awake," such was the entry in his diary of one of the Thirty-ninth whose day was given to guard duty, in an open field exposed to the fierce rays of an almost tropical sun, while many of his comrades devote much of their daylight to procuring and placing boughs around and over their tents to render less oppressive the August heat. One wonders whether it was piety or dislike of work which prompted the following item in another diary, "Other regiments have religious services;

ours never does; had to keep at work all day"; that dress parade closed the day might be concluded without the saying. Owing to the nearness of other regiments, it is easy to compare their scanty numbers with the full ranks of the Thirty-ninth, while the Twelfth and Thirteenth turn out with scarcely a corporal's guard in numbers for several of the companies, the Thirty-ninth has five hundred men, this very day, on parade, though a shrinkage of one half is quite an item, especially when there has been no loss on the battlefield. The utility of constant drill, especially in these superheated days is not appreciated by the older regiments in the brigade, and means are usually found to sidetrack the orders of Colonel Davis, acting commander of the brigade, but the Thirty-ninth obeys them to the letter.

The round of guard and picket duty keeps everyone in active condition, particularly as there are drill and fatigue for any not otherwise employed. The picket line is across the Rappahannock, about two miles and a half towards Culpeper, not far from the early August camping ground. That there is every indication of a prolonged stay here is emphasized by the appearance of the sutler, on the 12th, who proceeds to establish his plant and to open out some

luxuries, always appetizing to the average soldier, though Aug. 12, '63

forty-six cents a pound for cheese and one dollar a bottle for syrup and preserves make a man think twice before buying. The Medford men, Company C, are somewhat exultant over the fact that Captain Hutchins, on the 13th, is in command of the Regiment, since Lieut. Colonel Peirson is in command of the picket line and Major Tremlett is in Boston. During these days many drafted men arrive and are added to certain of the older regiments, though the permanent good derived from their coming is hardly commensurate with the trouble and expense incident to their presence. America never had much use for involuntary soldiering.

The 15th, Saturday, brought orders to be ready to march at a moment's notice but, as often happened, nothing came of it. The following day there was a movement of certain troops by train to Alexandria, for what purpose no one knew, though doubtless a part of the scheme to strengthen the Carolinas and the West which, eventually, will take a considerable number of men from Meade's Army. Everyone is learning the extremes of midday heat and midnight cold and many sigh for the material thrown away on the marches southward from Antietam. Those in authority are becoming alive to the fact that sleeping on the ground is conducive to summer ailments, and the consequent order goes forth that bunks shall be constructed and the tents correspondingly elevated. No one is permitted to get homesick on account of having nothing to do. Owing to the absence of Surgeon Page, the surgeon of the One Hundred and Seventh Pennsylvania has temporary charge of the sick in this regiment, and his diligence makes an exceedingly favorable impression. During this quiet period along the Rappahannock, the railroad bridge across the river is repaired or rebuilt, the pontoons are taken up and sent away and the men are realizing what regular mails and rations mean. The latter are so full and free that an excess of coffee especially forms an excellent medium of exchange with the rebel pickets.

On the 19th, more troops returned from the south side of the river, leaving scarcely more there than the Second Brigade of the Second Division; evidently some change of lines is in prospect. One man records his opinion that the construction of an oven for the baking of beans is a sure indication of a general move of the army, activity generally following any attempt at permanency. It is in these August days that the several companies are recalling the first anniversary of their muster-in and comparing notes between now and then. Though the Regiment has not been called to face the enemy on the field of battle, the time has by no means been wasted, since the drill and discipline that Colonel Davis and other officers have insisted on have made the organization ready for almost any test that may come in its way. The 28th of the month was marked by the return of Colonel Davis to the Regiment; Colonel Lyle having resumed his position at the head of the Brigade. As a consequence, all forms of drill received an immediate impetus. It was about this time (28th) that the Pennsylvania Reserves presented General Meade with a magnificent sword, the presentation taking place some three-fourths of a mile away, and Governor Curtin of the Keystone State, General Heintzelman and other distinguished men being present. Rumor says that the blade was originally intended for General John F. Reynolds, Commander of the First Corps, killed at Gettysburg.

It was in the last week of August that the knapsacks, left by orders at Funkstown, were received by their owners, but their contents, valuable or otherwise, had already been appropriated by others; much disappointment resulted, since many a soldier had reckoned on the material, supposed to be there, for relief in the cold nights along the Rappahannock. As Government allowance for clothing was only $42 a year and the securing of sufficient apparel seemed necessary, not a few boys in the Thirty-ninth found themselves in debt to Uncle Sam instead of being   Aug. 29, '63   prospective recipients of two months' pay, one of the hardships that the men were obliged to undergo through no fault of their own. Over in the Fifth Army Corps, on the 29th, was enacted a play in real life, if such a scene could be called a play—the execution of deserters. The coming and going of recruits had become so common that examples must be made of some of the flagrant cases. Drafted men, unwilling to enter the service, had the privilege of purchasing exemption by the payment of a large sum of money, the men accepting the same and taking the place of the drafted men received the general name of substitutes. In quite too many cases these men, finding the occupation lucrative, deserted again and again, each time re-enlisting, gaining many dollars thereby, while the army received no increase. These five men, shot to death while sitting upon their coffins, afforded a salutary lesson for others, similarly inclined, to see and heed. General F. A. Walker, in his history of the Second Army Corps, says, "The shooting of a score of bad men in 1861 would literally have saved the lives of thousands of good men in 1862 and 1863." The best soldiers were those who, realizing the peril of their country, took their lives in their own hands and, as it were, offered them a willing sacrifice for the Nation's salvation; if they escaped death, that was their good fortune, their supreme devotion was nothing lessened thereby. The month ended with an inspection by Lieut. Colonel Peirson and muster for two months' pay.

In the concluding days of August, pains had been taken in rearranging the camp, resulting in well defined company streets, and thereafter much time was spent in securing boughs and placing them so as to lessen the burning heat of midday; it is an excellent trait of healthy, well meaning men that, following a brief rest, they always are disposed to enhance the possibilities of comfort. With the 3rd of September (Thursday) came a rigid inspection of equipments and clothing, conducted by General Robinson,[F] Division Commander, the event having a suspicion of greater military activity. The entire brigade with its six regiments numbers about two thousand men, of whom the Thirty-ninth constitutes more than one-fourth, our Regiment being the only one not yet exposed to the losses of battle. Another indication of aggression or apprehension is the building of defenses and the advance of the Union picket line; a like approach of the enemy brings the Blue and the Gray pretty near each other. Friday night, the 4th, was noteworthy in that boxes, which should have reached the Regiment in Washington, were announced. Of course the food, prepared by loving hands in the distant North, was long past the condition of use, but articles of apparel came in a most convenient season; had they come before leaving Washington or on the trip southward, they doubtless would have been thrown away or, at any rate, left behind in some of the cachés established on the march.

FIRST ANNIVERSARY.

Sunday, the 6th of September, set many a mind to thinking, for it was the first anniversary of the departure from Boxford, and a year before hardly an enlisted man thought the war would last so long, yet he beheld himself a mere atom in the immensity of the strife, at the moment taking breath before the next effort. One of the scribes writes in his book of innermost thoughts, "I see very few signs of   Sept. 12, '63   the end as yet." Another laments the barbarity of men and boys who, gently born and reared, will destroy needlessly the property that comes in their way, instancing a beautiful house, across the river, out towards Culpeper, whose F.F.V. owner had followed the Confederates in their falling back, and not only had the furniture, elaborate and choice, been utterly broken to pieces, but the covering of the mansion had been torn off also, so that the bare framework of the structure remained, only one of hundreds of examples that might be narrated. On this day a cavalry force, under the lead of Generals Buford, Kilpatrick and Gregg advanced across the Rappahannock and, engaging the mounted force of General J. E. B. Stuart, drove it steadily back to and through Culpeper, capturing one hundred prisoners and some of the English light guns of the enemy. Dashing along to the Rapidan, Buford and his men, encamped on the banks of that already noted stream and then made their way back, not without difficulty, to the Union side of the Rappahannock.

With the beginning of the second year's service since the start from Boxford, enters a new division of time in the camp:—Reveillé at sunrise, police-duty, fifteen minutes later; sick-call at 6 a. m.; breakfast, 7; drill, 7.30; recall, 9.30; dinner, 12.30; drill, 3 to 5; dress parade, sunset; tattoo, 8.30; taps, 9 p. m. A long-needed rain came in violent form on the 12th, doing much good, yet was not exactly comfortable for those who had their tents blown down; however, well filled springs were quite consoling in that the regular water supply had grown conspicuously low. The 12th, too, is the day which marked the departure of Longstreet from Lee's army to the relief of Bragg in Georgia and Tennessee, not to return till the battle of the Wilderness is in progress. It takes very little time for the news to reach the hither side of the Rappahannock and an immediate movement towards the south follows, the Second Corps and the Cavalry being the first to advance on the 13th, with the purpose of so engaging the attention of Lee that he will send no more troops to assist in the possible discomfiture of Rosecrans.

The 14th marked the coming of Paymaster Major Burt, and the squaring of accounts for the preceding two months, though the clothing items reduced the compensation in certain cases almost to the vanishing point. Constant activity across the river, the passing of many heavily loaded trains and their return with loads of prisoners and wounded Union soldiers indicated the rapid pushing of things in that direction, and the inevitable advance of the remaining portions of the Federal force. Early in the morning of the 16th came the expected order to be ready to march at 5 a. m. Everything was in readiness, but the start was not made until 7 o'clock and then the regiment and the entire First Corps again crossed the Rappahannock by means of pontoon bridges and advanced towards Culpeper. A considerable part of the way was over an excellent road, though the rations, extra supplies of cartridges and the recently filled knapsacks made the way a hard one. Recent experience of cold nights had taught the men the necessity of retaining their extra apparel but, if some of the unnecessary ammunition were thrown away, it was because the men soon learned that large quantities of cartridges were entirely too burdensome. Though the distance marched was only twelve miles it seemed very much longer, leading by Brandy Station, a name in a few months to become almost a household word both North and South, and in general along the line of the Orange and Alexandria Railroad. While the Second and Sixth Corps had advanced to the Rapidan, the First Corps was held in reserve, some three miles east of Culpeper.

For a little more than a week this was to be the camping place of the Thirty-ninth and with accustomed diligence there speedily followed the regular round of inspections, drills and parades, though there were many and large details for picket duty. An inspection on the 17th seemed largely for the purpose of ascertaining how generally Sept. 14, '63 or otherwise the men had retained the extra ammunition dealt out to them; how successfully delinquents were helped out by those who had retained their heavy loads was long a theme for lengthy dissertations in company circles. The location of the camp upon a rising knoll made it the sport of the winds and the distance of both wood and water was a special hardship. Even then, when water was obtained, it was found to be so hard or so impregnated with lime as to be very distasteful to New England men who had been brought up where soft water was quite the vogue. An indication of a more or less prolonged stay appeared on this, the 17th, when the regimental sutlers put in an appearance and setting up their tents were ready for business. They were not likely to follow too closely an army in motion. Also drills and inspections marked the resumption of regular soldier regimen. The weather was singularly cold for the season of the year; in strolling about the vicinity, it was easy to discover where the enemy had lately encamped.

The advent of eight days' rations on the 22d with an injunction to pack five days' portion in our knapsacks made us think that some unusual stunt was impending. A Division-drill signalized the 23rd, General Robinson conducting the same. The 24th brought the expected change, the regiment marching a few miles down the Rapidan near Raccoon Ford, occupying some portions of the camp held until this morning by the 12th Army Corps, the latter along with the Eleventh having been ordered to arrange for a transfer to the Army of the Cumberland in the Tennessee country; this move being made lest Longstreet's presence with his force should give too hard a problem for Rosecrans to solve. While the orders to Howard and Slocum, of the Eleventh and Twelfth respectively, were issued on the 24th, it was not till the 3rd of October that the great organizations reached their destination. Of far greater consequence to some of the men in the Thirty-ninth was the fact that home-boxes just arrived from Washington had to be left behind. The 25th sees the renewal of regular camp activities along with the necessary cleaning up after the departure of the Twelfth Corps. The 26th saw a large force of twenty-five men from each company, under the command of Lieut. Colonel Peirson, proceeding to the banks of the Rapidan for picket duty. It was while nearing this point that the residence of Dr. John H. Stringfellow of Kansas notoriety, then or later a Confederate Surgeon, was reached and the man himself was interviewed, who declared his undeviating secession proclivities. Though certain of these Massachusetts men would have liked to repay some of the debts due him, they concluded that he was getting his punishment as he went along, for evidently his situation in the midst of contending armies was rapidly reducing him to a condition of absolute destitution.

THE RAPIDAN.

Picketing along the Rapidan at this time was not a hardship, since by mutual consent there was no firing, and the native Yankee disposition to explore had full vent, when not actually on post, the reserve furnishing many opportunities for learning habits and conditions of the people not otherwise attainable. Relieving the Ninetieth Pennsylvania, one-half of the detail attended to extreme outpost duty, while the other part enjoyed absence of drill and inspections around the reserve camp, "Revelling in that delicious abandon, one bright spot in a soldier's life, when he can do just what he pleases." Thus it was an even turn-about during the days on the river, in these parts only a narrow stream of possibly three rods' width. Most cordial relations existed between Reb. and Fed. and the trades between the Blue and the Gray proved that no monopoly in the swapping habit was enjoyed by the Yankee. Whatever extra coffee the boys possessed proved to be as good as cash, if not better, when dealing with these   Sept. 27, '63   lads from the Southland. They even swam across the river to partake of Northern hospitality and to facilitate exchanges. The nights being cold, campfires were kindled on both sides and the alleged enemies kept as comfortable as possible, in plain sight of each other.

In the stillness of the Sunday evening (27th) the Confederates in their camp indulged in a prayer-meeting and their hymns, the same that Northern Christians were singing at that very moment in the far away churches, were plainly heard by the hostile soldiery on our side of the stream. Need there be any wonder that some listeners moralized on the absurdity of men who read the same Bible and sang the same songs, spending several years of their lives, none too long at the longest in shooting at each other? Here took place the famous exchange of song, so often told in campfires and wherever it is desirable to prove that one touch of Nature makes the whole world kin. One night the Rebs. started off on the "Bonnie Blue Flag," and when their strains had ceased, the Yanks got back at them with the "Star Spangled Banner"; next the Boys in Gray tuned up with "Maryland, My Maryland" and those in Blue naturally retorted with "The Red White and Blue"; breaking the lull that ensued, our men started John Howard Payne's immortal and universal "Home Sweet Home"; scarcely had the first note been struck before the sympathetic enemy chimed in, and Virginian woods and hillsides echoed with the tender strains clearly showing how Saxon blood remembers. On another occasion a musical exchange, beginning with "Pennyroyal," ran through the list of then popular melodies, though all sang in unison, and very naturally, too, for ending "Old Hundred." Will not coming generations wonder that men who could together sing the old songs should ever fight each other?

Monday, the 28th, ended the stay by the river's side and the detail returned to camp, coming up with it some two miles nearer than when it was left, a fact that in no way disturbed those coming back. While a large part of the Regiment was on its tour of duty, those left behind were by no means idle and they too had their observations of Confederates who apparently had heard from Chickamauga, a favorite shout of theirs across the river being, "How are you, Rosey?" In the afternoon of the 27th, the Regiment and the whole Corps again changed locations; the pickets along the river could plainly see and hear the rebels at their respective tasks; the work upon their fortifications, their drills and other occupations. Here it was that Lieut. Colonel Peirson's detachment found the Regiment on its return. A short move on the 29th, brought the Regiment out of shelling range, but in a place so heavily wooded that trees had to be felled to make camping places, and on ground so low that very little rain made it extremely moist. By building bunks, we were enabled to keep out of the mud, but we were far from comfortable and, to crown all our discomforture, though there was water everywhere, as in the case of the Ancient Mariner, we found not a drop to drink; that had to be brought from a distance. The fires for cooking and bodily comfort were maintained with difficulty, and inflamed eyes, through prevailing smoke, became the rule.

Friday, October 2d, marked a sad day in the annals of the Divisions; the forenoon had been so rainy that it seemed as though nothing could add to the discomforts of the situation, yet the prospect of a march to witness the execution of a bounty-jumper was not so inviting as it might have been under less watery conditions. It was about noon that the Regiment fell into line, and, after standing an hour under the pelting rain, thoroughly drenched it moved out and in mud and water seemingly knee-deep marched some two miles or more to the assigned rendezvous where, after many changes of position to accommodate other portions of the Division, the rain having cleared away, the band of the Sixteenth Maine playing a dirge announced the approach of the procession; the same consisting of the provost Oct. 3, '63

guard, followed by an ambulance in which rode the prisoner, sitting upon his coffin, accompanied by his chaplain. Blindfolded and kneeling upon his coffin, the firing squad, obedient to orders, discharged their weapons and the deserter of the Ninetieth Pennsylvania passed on to his reward; however gruesome the scene may have been, undoubtedly the lesson was a valuable one upon such as thought the laws of the land could be broken with impunity.

The return from the execution to a camp, practically under water, was anything but inspiring and whatever was eaten had to be taken out of the haversack, for campfires were out of the question and sleep to men soaking wet was hardly possible. The weather clearing during the night gave some chance for drying garments during Saturday, the 3rd, and Sunday began to seem endurable and adapted to letter writing, when there came orders to pack up, once at least heard with no sigh of regret. While waiting for orders to march, all ears were startled by the sound of cannonading, which proved to be an effort of the enemy to shell a Union wagon train which had driven somewhat near the rebel works. When the start was made and the new camping spot found, it proved to be an excellent one, high and dry, with plenty of wood and water, and by general consent, the site was first-class; in honor of the Surgeon-in-Chief of the First Corps, the place was known as "Camp Nordquist."

At dress parade, Oct. 7th, an order was read to the effect that men, desirous of changing from infantry regiments to light artillery batteries, could do so by sending their names through the proper channels. Much to the surprise of the officers, there was a very general response to the proposition; indeed two hundred and twenty-three men, almost one half of the effective regimental organization, had filled out papers. Colonel Davis forwarded the long list to division headquarters with his approval, but the applicants had so far overdone the matter, nothing came of it, save that General Robinson in a special order said that the service must inevitably suffer, if so many men were to go from one organization, and there the project ended. However fitting the men found Camp Nordquist, it was not theirs to remain there long, since after lights had been extinguished in the night of the 9th and the men were in the midst of their before-midnight slumbers, there came peremptory orders to pack up and be ready to march. Quickly responding, and building great fires for light and comfort, the Regiment was soon in place and prepared for the next command. It did not come until the morning of the 10th, when in obedience to it the Brigade, Division and all, started out over a by no means easy route and kept in motion until morning. Finding ourselves in the vicinity of Morton's Ford, we were ordered to cook breakfast and make ourselves as comfortable as possible.

A BACKWARD MOVE

An explanation of the event of this and subsequent days is in place here; by a singular coincidence, just as Meade was beginning to do what Lee had been expecting of him, for several weeks, the latter began a move similar to that of the year before when he had hurried Pope across the Rappahannock; in other words, he flanked Meade's right, thus making it necessary for the latter to end any southern plans that he may have formed, and to devote himself exclusively to heading off the Confederate leader. While the entire Union army is in motion our interest centres in the Regiment whose story is in progress. As originally proposed, the First Corps was to cross the Rapidan at Morton's or Raccoon Ford, co-operating with the Cavalry which was to cross the river at Germanna Ford, and to assail the Confederate right; meanwhile the Sixth Corps was to cross at a point further up the river and to attack Lee's left. An early attack was the motive for the very unseasonable start, though its purpose was largely negatived by the great fires with which the men had lighted their way through the night.

Oct. 11, '63 All day long the troops awaited the approach of Buford and his troopers before crossing, but no cavalry appeared; night approached and preparations for repose were afoot when the command came to pack up and be off. Evidently the purposes of Lee had been disclosed and an "About Face" was only preliminary to "Forward, March." The night was memorable to those concerned in its exactions, not so much for its length as on account of the difficulties encountered. Along a narrow road, infantry and artillery jostled each other, frequently the former having to take to the fields, many of them low and marshy, or to lie along the roadside while the cannon had the thoroughfare. At last the top of the hills near Mountain Creek, where the first camp south of the Rappahannock had been pitched, was gained and an unparalleled scene broke upon the vision of these sleepy and wearied soldiers. As far as the eye could reach the entire landscape was starred with campfires, and it began to look as though we were to sleep on our old campground. Every conceivable noise saluted the ear; the stroke of axes as they cut up rails for fuel, the clamor of teamsters, endeavoring to get their teams through difficult places and the incessant hum of human voices, raised for a thousand reasons. It was midnight, however, before the Thirty-ninth was ready to commit itself to sleep, and even then, not for long, since at 2 a. m. of the 11th, the call to arms was heard by the tired and sleepy men.

All may have heard the call, but all did not obey at once. Some of them had been known to ignore parental rising calls at home and, on this occasion, they were the happy, lucky ones, since six o'clock arrived and still no orders to move forward, though the right of the corps had been long on the march.

The many and rapid changes of the last thirty-six hours have brought about some hitherto unexperienced trouble. Many of the Regiment had been left on picket and one of those, performing this at present hazardous duty, records the following in his diary, "About nine (p. m.) receive orders to pack up and leave; march to our old camp and get some rations; then start again for Pony Mountain. About 3 a. m. (11th), arrive at our old campground, where we first stopped (Aug. 1) after crossing the Rappahannock, and I was just ready to lie down when we were ordered back about a mile to our Regiment." Not all, however, were so fortunate. Though under the command of that sterling veteran, Captain John Hutchins (C), owing to the darkness of the night, some of the men lost their way and thirteen were captured by closely following rebel cavalry; seven of the captives being from "E," the Somerville company, were as follows: Sergt. J. R. Hyde; Privates F. J. Oliver, Henry Howe, Joseph Whitmore, Washington Lovett, all of whom died in Andersonville; and Corp. G. W. Bean and Private J. W. Oliver; the corporal survived seventeen months of imprisonment, getting out March '65, while the private, more fortunate, was paroled after three or four months of durance; John K. Meade of "K" was also taken the same night, the event happening near Stevensburg, about six miles from the Regiment.

The soldier's time honored privilege of grumbling had free course this afternoon, since it was between 10 and 11 a. m. that the lines finally moved. The hardened campaigner understands that no one in the regiment is responsible for unseemly hours of turning out; it means just the same for shoulder straps that it does for men in the ranks; the enemy is near; exactly when or where he may appear no one knows, but all can be ready to respond immediately to the first command. The chances are that not even Colonel Davis was aware that to him and his regiment was to be entrusted a considerable part of the safety of the rear of the retreating army. Yet such was the case, and when the fact became apparent not over pleasant memories of their former experience in a similar duty were recalled; happily in this case the wagon trains had been hurried forward and the coast was comparatively clear all the way to Kelly's Ford, passing on the way all that was Oct. 2,

'63 left of the hamlet of Stevensburg. Further down the river was a pontoon-bridge over which other troops were passing but, as the enemy was near, there could be no delay and at 5 p. m., or thereabouts, the men marched through, the water being about waist deep and, in chilly October, anything but agreeable. With all possible precautions taken for defense against the closely following foe, and with great fires to dry their saturated garments, the soldiers were soon comparatively comfortable.

CAMPAIGN OF MANEUVERS.

By way of explanation of the marchings and counter-marchings in which the regiment is indulging, it should be stated that a considerable portion of October was devoted to what Wm. Swinton calls "A campaign of maneuvers." So far from reading each other's mind, it would appear that neither Lee nor Meade was accurately informed of the actual procedure of his rival for, while the Confederates were still making their way northward, but not being encountered by Meade where he expected, the latter ordered the Second, Fifth and Sixth Corps to turn about and to be ready to face Lee at or near Culpeper; the Third Corps, under French, meanwhile was at Freeman's Ford on the Rappahannock, and the First we have seen at Kelly's Ford. When the Union Commander learned that Lee had simply gone a little further west for his crossing of the Rappahannock, White Sulphur Springs, on the 12th, and was rapidly nearing Warrenton, he recalled the troops south of the river and then began the forced march to prevent Lee's distancing him completely. Thomas Nelson Page says, "Meade was a master at moving his troops and now, making a forced march that night was in Lee's rear the next morning"(13th). It was a hotly contested race as to which army should first reach Bristoe Station, thus ending any purpose that Lee might have had against Washington.

In all these movements on the great chessboard of war with its army corps, divisions and brigades, what was a single regiment among so many hundred? How much less was the individual, and it is the province of a history, such as this, to keep as near the individual as possible. Even a brigade, in such a vast array of men, was scarcely more than a pawn in the mighty game the Blue and the Gray were playing for American supremacy. Still every regiment had its part to perform in the progress of the contest, and thousands of people in the homeland were watching each and every day's doing with supreme interest, their thoughts chiefly centered on some particular organization, and to them and the members themselves there was no other body quite so important as "ours." To follow day by day, the march, bivouac and duty of the Thirty-ninth Massachusetts in this and all other campaigns in which it had a part is the office of this story.

The white frost that greeted the eyes of waking soldiers in the morning of the 12th was quite as cold as any that New England could present, and campfires never were more appreciated. A hurried breakfast was prepared and eaten when the brigade was ordered into hurriedly made rifle-pits, where the day was spent with the understanding that trouble might arise at any moment. This was the day in which Meade was looking for Lee. While there were sounds of activity elsewhere, nothing disturbed the Thirty-ninth, some even writing letters as the hours passed on. At no time in the history of the Regiment, did legs play a more important part than they did on the 13th of October; called from slumber at midnight, the advance was begun at one o'clock of the morning, and through the darkness the blue clad men were pushing forward as rapidly as possible towards Warrenton Junction, reaching it at 11 a. m., with fifteen miles to the credit of the forenoon's effort. At Bealton station on the way, at six o'clock three had been a halt, and the men naturally supposed that coffee and breakfast were in order, but, much to the disappointment Oct. 12, '63 of all, came the order to advance and that, too, without delay. When men demurred and undertook to continue their preparation of food, staff officers rushed among them and, kicking over their utensils, put out the fires, thus impressing on the hungry fellows the fact that the march was a forced one. It surely was a hurried getting-away and many a vehicle came to grief, particularly among the sutlers who had been somewhat venturesome in their coming to the front; it was even claimed that misfortunes to the outfits of the sutlers were not always unprovoked, since the removal of linchpins by mischievous boys and the consequent running off of wheels gave opportunity to fill otherwise empty haversacks.

At Warrenton Junction all preparations were made for the possible attack of the enemy, batteries being unlimbered, the Regiment formed in battle-line, though the noon hour, after the long retreat, suggested dinner to the almost famished men, but the experience of the preceding July had taught all that the locality was sadly lacking in water supply. Except those who were looking out for the rear, the troops were in active motion, all passing by at the height of speed. Great quantities of commissary stores were piled up, and these were either carried off by the soldiers themselves or loaded upon the trains and thus saved, so disappointing the enemy who had reckoned on getting to these food supplies first. After a considerable halt the march proceeded along the line of railroad past Catlett's Station to Bristoe's, reaching the latter point late in the evening and camping at about nine o'clock. On the way we had passed the great wagon trains of the Army of the Potomac, packed in one, great, solid square, with wheels chained together, the mules being secured in the centre, indicating that the danger of immediate attack from the enemy was thought to be over for the present at least, and it also seemed that the First Corps came near being in the lead. A march of nearly twenty-five miles with almost empty haversacks gave the men reason for being considerably tired.

"Not every boo is a bear" was clearly shown on this march towards Centreville when Fred, brother of Sergeant L. of "K," having permission from the colonel, undertook to secure a chicken for the sergeant whose stomach was not in accord with his regular rations. With instructions to be extremely careful, the soldier went from house to house but without success, the guards at these places telling him that he was running great risks, since the men, seen in the distance, were clearly bushwhackers. It was nightfall before he found the chicken he was after, and by the time he was making his way back, darkness settled down. He had to pass through a strip of woods where every object was distorted and even a deaf man would have heard sounds. Halfway through the woods, a real noise in the roadside bushes made his hair begin to rise, but he did not stop to investigate too closely, when the climax was reached by six or seven razorback hogs dashing across the road in front of him. The sudden change from probable guerrillas to actual swine was a relief unutterable, but the former were about and that very night carried off two men from the headquarter's wagon train. While the sergeant enjoyed his chicken broth and improved thereon, he declared the risk too great and Fred went on no more such errands.

It was a four o'clock call of the bugle, in the morning of the 14th, that summoned frost covered and sleepy soldiers from dreams to realities, but their distress was somewhat offset by the appearance of rations, of which they drew supplies for four days and thereby were better equipped for the day's progress which began at seven o'clock, as one veracious chronicler states, with the First Corps on the left and the Sixth at the right of the railroad. While these two Army Corps were thus continuing their way in relative quiet, heavy firing in the rear indicated that the Second and Fifth Corps were having something to do, the Oct. 14, '63 Second fighting the battle of Bristoe Station; General Warren having his hands full in warding off the attack of the enemy while the cavalry, on both sides, were piling up the portentous list of battles, many of them bloodless, which adorn the histories of so many mounted regiments. Centreville, so famous in the July days of 1861, was now the evident destination of the forces and crossing Bull Run, at Blackburn's Ford, the scene of the first day's fight in the memorable First Bull Run engagement, the brigade arrived at Centreville not far from noon. To build fires and to prepare a dinner, undisturbed, was the next act in this day's drama and, if tired soldiers caught a few hours sleep before the next scene, it need not be wondered at. Some of the men in the Thirty-ninth were participants in the disastrous battle of Bull Run; to them it was a case of old scenes revisited, and if they took some pride in rehearsing their experiences they did not fail of interested listeners.

But the day was by no means done; though Centreville had been reached, the enemy was still near, only a little way to the west, and picket lines must be established. Accordingly the Regiment proceeded on its somewhat confusing task, while the greater part of the division went on a reconnoisance. Apparently there was little definite knowledge of localities, since one writer observed that they reached their destination at seven o'clock and marched around till eleven, and another of Company E relates the interesting experience of trying to obey the orders to follow Bull Run until the pickets of the Sixth Corps were reached. After crossing Cub Run, three miles away, Major A. D. Leavitt of the Sixteenth Maine, division-officer of the picket, went on ahead to ascertain his whereabouts, leaving the Regiment in a field. Returning in less than an hour, he reported a rebel camp in the immediate front; in trying to retire, the line was halted by our own pickets when it appeared that we had been more than a mile beyond our own lines. On calling the roll, Sergeant Dusseault found that twelve men were missing. Major Leavitt would allow no one to go back after them but himself and he found the missing men fast asleep where we had been waiting. Bringing them all safe and sound to their own, established the reputation of the Major with the Thirty-ninth from that time on, as long as he lived. To one member of Company E, "Johnny" Locke, the memory of the Major was specially grateful, because of the latter's kindness. The young man had been suffering for days from a carbuncle on his neck; in any other place than the army, he would have been laid up completely, but here he kept going; he was one of those found by the officer and, recognizing the condition of the soldier, he kindly got down from his horse and mounted the boy in the saddle. Sidney himself could have done no more.

The dawn of the morning of the 15th did not reveal the situation with certainty to these inexperienced soldiers; they knew that they were very near the thrilling scenes of more than one and two years before, that the sound of musketry and cannon-firing in their front indicated the possibility of a third battle of Bull Run. It was theirs, however, to watch and wait in constant expectation of orders to lend a hand. One writer enlarges on the delights of persimmon-eating, the October frosts having ripened the yellow delicacy to perfection, and the various other diversions that unoccupied hours ever suggest. Though the brigade was finally rejoined and there was a movement towards Centreville with orders to pitch tents, before the same could be obeyed a long threatened rain began to fall, putting out whatever fires had been built and essentially adding to the discomforts and uncertainties of the day. Rations were drawn late at night and record is made of the giving out of a portion of whiskey as a stimulant to the wet and weary soldiers. The experiences of the 16th and 17th did not vary essentially from those of the 15th; there were picket duty, acting as reserve, the drawing of rations and all sorts of prognostications as to what the outcome of Oct. 16, '63 the expedition would be. While the cavalry of both sides kept up an exchange of compliments, very few casualties were reported from any source. That those who directed believed there was immediate danger was evident in the degree of caution constantly maintained; roll-call every two hours and constant injunctions to be ready to move at any moment.

The 18th marked the end of the Confederate effort to repeat the campaign of the preceding June and July, and that of 1862. General Lee writing to his wife on the 19th of October says:

I have returned to the Rappahannock. I did not pursue with the main army beyond Bristoe or Broad Run. Our advance went as far as Bull Run, where the enemy was entrenched, extending his right as far as Chantilly, in the yard of which he was building a redoubt. I could have thrown him farther back, but I saw no chance of bringing him to battle, and it would have only served to fatigue our troops by advancing farther. If they had been properly supplied with clothes, I would certainly have endeavored to have thrown them north of the Potomac; but thousands were barefooted, thousands with fragments of shoes, and all without overcoats, blankets or warm clothing. I could not bear to expose them to certain suffering on an uncertain issue.

From the foregoing it would seem that only the Confederate cavalry had been responsible for the Federal activity in and about the old Bull Run battlefields, and now even the horsemen were to follow the foot forces and the Union troops would again move west and southward. Ordered out and to pack up in the morning of the 19th the prospects were not improved by a severe rain storm which completely drenched both tents and apparel so that, to regular burdens, was added the weight of water absorbed by the fabrics. Starting at about eight o'clock, the route was along the Warrenton turnpike, the very road, so prominent in all accounts of the two Bull Run fields, with the sad sights of only partially covered bodies of those who had perished in the engagements; the severe rain was constantly adding to the heaviness of the way and Thoroughfare Gap, the reputed destination of the march, seemed a very long distance off. The vicinity of Haymarket on the Manassas Gap Railroad was reached about 4 p. m. and the noise ahead indicated a fear that the enemy was there in force, our artillery keeping up a vigorous shelling of what was thought to be the rebel position. Camps were made and tents pitched only to have the vexatious order "Pack up" given just as we were disposed to get a bit of rest. Rations, too, were scarce and everything combined to make the day and night particularly trying; at 3.30 p. m. or thereabouts of the 20th an advance was made through Thoroughfare Gap, though there were those who thought "No Thoroughfare," on account of the difficulties of the way, would be a better designation.

The 21st was spent in camp which was pitched on such a hilly surface that at least two bunkies had to stake a board at their feet, lest they slide from under their blankets. Every one remarked on the beauty of the locality and comments were made on the five storied flouring-mill standing in the Gap, the same being thought the finest edifice yet seen in Virginia. Notwithstanding the recent destruction of railroads on the Confederate retreat, so quickly were repairs made and so immediate the communications between the different departments that a wagon supply train came through in the afternoon and hungry men were fed once more. One man said his breakfast had consisted of half a hardtack; the same writer, his stomach being at rest, could enlarge on the beauties of the moonlight in the evening. Poetic thoughts are not prevalent in the presence of hunger. The 22d brought inspection, an indication that the officers, at least, thought us anchored for a while; the 23rd was marked by a battalion drill, another sign of permanency and, to complete the soldiers' happiness, quartermaster's stores appeared so that many defects and wants in uniform were supplied.

While every prospect was pleasing, it was not for sightseeing that these men in blue were so far from home and   Oct. 23, '63   all realized that a long stay here was out of the question, so the orders to be ready for a start at seven o'clock of the 24th surprised no one. A very heavy, cold rain had been falling during a large part of the preceding night, hence wet tents increased the burdens of travel while empty haversacks reminded the owner of an equally vacant stomach. Every day, during an active campaign, reminded all concerned of the truth of the old adage that an army, like a snake, moves upon its belly, and Oliver Twist, ever insistent on more, was reproduced in every healthy soldier in the Potomac Army. Only the few who had provided for a possible lacking of rations had anything to eat this morning, hence no time was lost in preparing breakfast. It was through a pitiless rain that the day's march, beginning early in the forenoon, was made back through Thoroughfare Gap; following the railroad as nearly as possible, luckily the grade being down rather than up; fording streams, especially Broad Run, though they could make the men no more wet than they already were from the rain; through Haymarket, Gainesville to Bristoe Station, the scene of the Second Corps' fight on the 14th. On every hand were evidences of the fierce encounter, as dead horses and the many graves of the slain. Though the most of the brigade halted here, the Thirty-ninth and the Ninety-fourth New York had not reached their limit, and they continued until Kettle Run was reached.

The special duty assigned to these two regiments was the guarding of the railroad, which had been repaired to this point and the bridge which was in process of building; all were exceedingly tired from the long day's exactions; there was no food to cook for supper but they could build big fires and dry to some extent their drenched apparel, and then seek rest and the sleep which hovers near the wet and weary. Sunday, the 25th, dawned bright and beautiful, its warmth imparting sun soon dried what the fires of the night before had failed to do and, had there only been rations for the hungry men, they might have been in a better mood for enjoyment. Ten of the clock brought inspection, as inevitable as death itself; before noon the anxiously expected rations appeared and, with them disposed of, the Regiment was ready for any duty that might be assigned. With the food also came some articles of apparel, so that long needed blankets made nights more comfortable. For eleven days or until the 5th of November, this locality, the camp having been changed a bit and more carefully laid out, became the habitat of the Thirty-ninth. It was during the night of the 25th that Lieutenant I. D. Paul of Company F came near losing his life; orders had been given to those on guard to challenge no one but to shoot at sight; only the recognition of his shoulder strap saved the popular officer's falling a victim to the very orders that he had himself given out.

Though the camp was to continue quite a while for an active campaign, the men did not know it, nor anyone else for that matter, so orders to be ready for a move were not unheard during this period of comparative rest; still the regular routine of roll-calls, drill, etc., was resumed, for absolute ease was unknown to members of the Thirty-ninth. The season being the last of October, the weather was sharp, the rains cold and need of warm clothing apparent. The 29th brought quite a rarity in the shape of a ration of "soft bread" as the soldiers always called the baker's product, in the shape of loaves, in distinction from the hard bread or the regulation hardtack, the real standby. The last day of the month was written down as the date of muster for two months' pay and the fact that food was abundant, since, being right on the railroad, by means of steam, rations came direct from Washington. On Tuesday, November 3rd, there was a brigade drill, conducted by Colonel Leonard of the Thirteenth Massachusetts, commanding the brigade, and the giving out of eight days' rations had a decided look towards a change of camps. The 4th was signalized by the arrival of boxes from home Nov. 4, '63 and many a boy's heart, as well as stomach, was made glad by evidence of home regard and recollection.

While the men regretted leaving their comparatively comfortable camp, all realized that the mutations of war demanded almost constant action, so the orders while battalion drill was in progress to get ready for a move were not entirely a surprise; besides, the many rations of the day before were a warning. Arms having been stacked, tents were pulled down and everything made ready for the start, which was about 4 p. m., and a large part of the march to Catlett's station, some seven miles away, was made after dark, hence tedious, made all the more so by the burden of extra rations and a winter outfit of clothing and tent material. Some one has characterised the march as a helter-skelter one, every man "going on his own hook," without regard to regimental formation, let alone so compact a matter as a company; each man camped down where he could do so most comfortably; "there was no roll-call that night." The next day the soldiers found their own, and the Regiment moved half a mile or so from the night's bivouac and pitched tents on a side-hill, resuming the routine of regular camp life, and entry is made of the burning of the tall grass which grew near, necessitating some energetic work on the part of the campers to extinguish, and the all too apparent exertions of the preceding twenty-four hours merited the whiskey ration which was dealt out.

That no degree of permanency had yet been attained was evident when early orders were received to be ready to march at 6.30 a. m. of the 7th, and the start was made at 7, much nearer than usual to the allotted hour, and the trend was southward, through Warrenton Junction and Elktown to the vicinity of Morristown, a few miles from the Rappahannock. Not only was the entire First Corps in motion but the same was true of the Second and Third as well, all indications pointed to a resumption of the status prior to the October Northward move. Whatever the plans or purposes, they were not carried out without provocation to firing as appeared in the sounds from the river region; later knowledge acquaints us that the noise arose from portions of the Sixth and Fifth Corps at Rappahannock Station and the Third Corps at Kelly's Ford, disputing possession with the ever present and always vigilant enemy. The distance marched varied according to the one estimating, the same ranging from fifteen to seventeen miles. In October, 4.30 a. m. is a long while before daylight, yet this was the time of waking on the 8th and, after the very essential coffee-making, the line was off soon after six o'clock. The first considerable halt was at Grove Church where were seen a large number of Confederate wounded from yesterday's engagements.

BRANDY STATION

The Rappahannock was crossed at Kelly's Ford by means of a pontoon bridge and, at 5 p. m., the Regiment was near Brandy Station, having marched ten or twelve miles; the route, where possible, was along the railroad which will be in operation to-morrow probably. Tents were pitched and large fires built and many were pleased to find not so very far away the Tenth (Sleeper's) Massachusetts Battery which we had left at Poolesville and now is connected with the First Division, Third Army Corps and which, yesterday, had borne its part in the incidents of the day. Many a handshake and "Glad to see you" signalized the meeting. The earlier part of the 9th was passed in the halting place of yesterday, some of the men improving the chance to call on friends in the Tenth Battery, but at two in the afternoon, the familiar "Pack-up" order was heard with the accompanying direction to be ready to march at four o'clock. A little before sunset, the start was made by a countermarch, recrossing the Rappahannock on the pontoon bridge and a long, wearisome, night trip followed, one of the features being the first snowstorm of the season, Oct. 10, '63 all tending to make a very tired lot of men, who were pushed along without halting to Licking Run, between Bealton and Warrenton Junction, possibly fifteen miles from the starting place, arriving a little past midnight. Very many fell out on the way quite unable to stand the pace, and those who did stick to the colors wasted no time in preparations for camp, but dropped at once and straightway fell asleep.

The morning of the 10th revealed a tired array of men and a snow-covered earth, but human nature and human bodies rally readily. After a short move further into a considerable piece of woods, camp was pitched and preparations were made for as comfortable a stay as possible, some of the men expressing the wish that they might remain a while because of the abundance of wood and water, and here they were to remain almost two weeks, though from them the fact was concealed; probably no one knew what the future would unfold. There was work for many of the men repairing the railroad, some having to go into the woods to cut sleepers, others to assist with pick and shovel. This day, the 10th, the promotion of 1st Sergeant Dusseault, Company E, was announced and he was assigned to Company H as Second Lieutenant. Within this period, drills were resumed and all else that pertained to routine and efficiency; clothing was drawn, the Regiment was paid for September and October on the 16th and 17th and by a singular coincidence the sutler made his appearance at the same time. Evidently some of the men were in arrears, as for that matter, most soldiers were wont to be. Considerable care was taken with the tents of both officers and men, the idea gaining credence that a prolonged stay might be made here, but neither army was ready, as yet, for winter quarters.

Orders to move were circulated on the 22d and at four o'clock in the forenoon of the 23rd, drowsy men were summoned from their sleep to pack-up and be ready for another change, starting from their late camp at about sunrise. On reaching Bealton, a union was effected with the remainder of the division and a few miles further, towards the Rappahannock, camp was made for the night, all realizing that cold weather was upon them and that the burdens, on the march by day, had to be heavy in order to insure any comfort for the night. Rain fell very easily during those days, and it was somewhat discouraging to have to turn out at 4 a. m. and, breakfasting at an early hour, to stand in line momentarily expecting the order, "Forward," and all the time pelted by the falling rain. After a while we were ordered to put up our tents again, a change of mind having been experienced higher up. Wednesday, the 25th, differed in no essential from its predecessor, though many of the men were wondering whether the mail, express or freight, would bring them anything from home by way of a reminder of Thanksgiving, due on the 26th. Disappointment was the lot of all, for authorities in Washington must have known of impending activity and so withheld what thoughtful friends had attempted to forward to the army; sutlers however put in an appearance, an ill-starred act, on their part, as the morrow was to show.

MINE RUN

Thanksgiving day in the North, November 26th, should be remembered as the beginning of the famous Mine Run affair, one of the greatest of the battles that were never fought. Judging from results in former years, when campaigning was undertaken at this season of the year, it would seem that winter quarters would be a better proposition for the army than another forward movement, but General Meade, feeling that the Northern public demanded some aggressive movement on his part, determined to avail himself of the withdrawal of Longstreets' Corps and the remoteness of Lee's remaining Corps, Ewell's and Hill's, from each other, and to take the offensive. Ewell's men, under the command of General Jubal A. Early, Ewell being ill, held the Confederate right, the same resting on the Rapidan Nov. 26, '63 at Morton's Ford, while Hill's forces in their dispersion extended fully twenty miles to the southwest. Meade could lead 70,000 men into the assault, while Lee's troops were rated at 50,000; the lower fords of the Rapidan were quite uncovered, Lee depending for defence on a line of fortifications extending along the left bank of Mine Run, an insignificant stream, tributary to the Rapidan and entering the same near Morton's Ford. The words of Robert Burns concerning the plans of mice and men never had better application than in the events of the following days. Had army corps crossed and attacked as projected, considering the detached, not to say scattered, condition of the enemy, it seems as though he would have been beaten in detail.

Had General French and his Third Corps started at the early hour named in the orders; had not the engineer miscalculated the width of the stream and so provided too few pontoons for the bridge which had to be pieced out with a trestle; had not the banks of the river proved too precipitous for the artillery which had to go down to Germanna Ford and even then, if the Corps had not taken a wrong road and so fallen foul of Confederate General Edward Johnson and his forces, the entire story of the war might have been very different from what is written. In brief, the expedition was scheduled to begin early in the morning of the 23rd, but was delayed by the severe rain of that and subsequent days. The orders under which the start of the 27th was made were that the Third Corps, General French, followed by the Sixth, General Sedgwick, should cross the Rapidan at Jacob's Mills; the Fifth, General Sykes, followed by the First, General Newton, was to cross at Culpeper Mine, while the Second, General Warren, was to cross by the Germanna Ford, between the other fords named. With ten days' rations carried by the men, General Meade was justifiable "in cutting loose from his base of supplies, and undertaking the feat in three columns of seizing the plank road and turnpike and, by advancing rapidly towards Orange Court House, of turning the enemy's works and compelling him to give battle on ground not previously selected or prepared."

That the expedition failed is history, its outlines have often been told in many places; our interest rests principally in what the First Corps and Thirty-ninth Regiment were doing during these days of stroke and counter stroke. General John Newton, commanding the First Corps, in his report to the Headquarters of the Army of the Potomac, tersely narrates the doings of each day from Thursday, Nov. 26th, to Thursday, Dec. 3rd, both dates inclusive. Leaving the Third Division of the Corps guarding the Orange and Alexandria Railroad from Rappahannock Station to Manassas, he advanced the other two divisions to the Culpeper Mine Ford, getting only one of them across by seven o'clock; starting at 3.30 a. m. of the 27th, he reached the rear of Robertson's Tavern a little after 7 p. m.; the Corps was roused at 3 a. m. of the 28th and put in position at the left of the Second Corps and Robertson's Tavern; about seven o'clock the corps was ordered to advance, still keeping to the left of the Second Corps; advancing in two lines through the woods to near Mine Run, the enemy was discovered in line of battle to receive us. Establishing a picket line, with a little firing of the enemy, the corps remained in position for the remainder of the day. November 29th, an attack on the enemy being contemplated on the right and left, General Newton, in the centre, commanded his own troops and some of the Fifth and Sixth Corps; at 8 a. m., agreeably to orders, cannonading began along his front, continuing a short time only; skirmishers were sent across Mine Run who performed their duties gallantly, losing in killed and wounded about forty men; under cover of the picket lodgement, four bridges were built, for later use if necessary; under advice from headquarters the pickets were withdrawn to the Federal or east bank of the Run at 3 a. m. of the 30th and an hour later fell back to Germanna Ford to cover the crossing of Nov.

26, '63 the Fifth and Sixth Corps. Dec. 1st all of the army recrosses; Dec. 2d, under orders, leaving a single brigade at Germanna, proceeded to Stevensburg with the remainder of the Corps; Dec. 3rd reached Paoli's Mills about noon and sent a brigade to Kelly's Ford.

Returning to the 26th of November and confining ourselves to the work of the Thirty-ninth we find the same awakened at an early hour and starting out before four o'clock. The Rappahannock was again crossed at the station of the same name as the river. During a brief halt on the south side of the stream, Colonel Leonard, commanding the brigade, read a telegram from headquarters, announcing the great victory of General Grant at Chattanooga and at least one soldier remarked, "That's good news to march on." With hourly halts, the extended march was not so tiresome as certain shorter though more rapid ones had proved. About 6 p. m. the Rapidan was crossed at Culpeper Mine, and ascending an elevation south of the river, a mile further along, camp was pitched for the night. Not a few commented on the change from Thanksgiving Day the year before, and still more remarked on the difference between the day at home and that passed in active campaigning; no cases of insomnia were heard of during the night, for all were tired and sleepy and "taps," if sounded, found very few waiting to obey. Eighteen miles were put down as the distance marched.

Certain men were detailed as pickets, and it was their duty to see to it that no harm befell their sleeping comrades; going on duty at ten o'clock last night, they came off at two this morning (27th) and an hour later the camp was alert with preparations to depart. Starting a little before daylight, we marched southward, passing through a part of the country very near the Chancellorsville battlefield of the preceding May and of the Wilderness, yet to be. After striking the Orange and Fredericksburg pike at eight o'clock in the morning, a halt was called and the men rested while the wagon and ambulance trains passed. The march continued till after dark, ending at Robertson's Tavern with a total distance covered of about thirty miles, from the starting point of yesterday.

The 28th of November, Saturday, brought a part of the Regiment under fire. Before daylight an advance of a mile or so was made, followed by breakfast and the use of pick and shovel in entrenching and then a still further, though brief, advance. The sound of the skirmishing comes from front and battle line is formed; Companies C and E being detailed as skirmishers, they went forward some 300 yards, the regiment remaining behind the crest of the hill. As a Company C participant wrote, "It commenced to rain very soon and we lay on our bellies and watched the Rebs.; their sharpshooters watched us closely and some were wounded. Benj. Dow of our company was shot through the leg,[G] but the boys were cool and stood their first fire like veterans; after lying thus all day, cold and wet through to the skin, we were relieved about eight o'clock and rejoined the Regiment, tired and hungry; the Rebs. are in good position and I doubt whether Meade will attack first."

The night that followed, though quiet, brought very little comfort to the men, thoroughly chilled by the rain of yesterday and, at 3 a. m. of the 29th, some of them were stirring to prepare the soldiers' solace, a cup of hot coffee. Everybody expected to storm the enemy's works at some time on this day; knapsacks were piled up that full use of all the muscles might be had. Old campaigners were writing their names and regiments on bits of paper and pinning them on their garments for identification since it seemed sure that the works could not be assailed without a terrible loss of life. A brigade of the Fifth Corps formed the first line of battle and our brigade came next;

skirmishing between the rival lines prevailed all day. Shells even came over from the Confederates, but they drew no reply from our lines. The rebels having withdrawn across the Run, the same wider than usual through having been dammed, formed the line of separation between the blue and the gray. At nightfall, to shield themselves from the cold wind, trees were cut down for a shelter, and to the mercies of the night the soldiers again commended themselves.

Sunday was the last day of the month, and it seemed impossible that the day should pass without the long impending assault; three days' rations were distributed and the men were told that they must make them last five, a pretty severe exaction from an army which we have been told moves on its stomach. The attack did not take place, but there was a deal of activity in arranging the forces for the projected advance. It was understood by the leading officers that in the early morn of the 1st of December there should be a simultaneous cannonading along the entire line to be followed by an assault by Warren and his massed forces, to be succeeded on the right by like action on the part of Sedgwick and his loyal Sixth Corps followers. The morning of the first day of winter came, but Warren did not order the assault as expected. To his practiced eye, the works erected and defended by the enemy were too strong for the attack and to his judgment Meade, himself, deferred when he had ridden to the extreme left and there saw their magnitude and strength. His messenger, who happened to be his own son, rode with breathless speed to countermand the orders of the day before and the Battle of Mine Run was not fought. At nightfall the backward movement began and at or near midnight, the Thirty-ninth with many other regiments was at the Rapidan once more.

During the last of these Mine Run days, our Lieut. Colonel Peirson was in command of the division line of pickets, being officer of the day, and his experience was interesting for, entering upon his duties, he rode a white horse, furnished him at Division Headquarters, riding just in rear of the picket line until the plentitude of the enemy's bullets compelled him to alight and to walk or crawl the rest of the way. Desiring to cross a little elevation, he took the precaution, before exposing himself, of raising his cap upon his sword and, as it was the immediate target of several rebel bullets, he concluded that a more circuitous route would be preferable. So cold was it that men, in their falsely named "shelters" were frozen to death, as they held on to their posts to which the relief did not come. On reaching the desired point and, after driving the enemy across a small stream which he later learned was not Mine Run but a tributary, with the assistance of a few pioneers he successfully bridged it for the passage of troops. In this labor he had the misfortune to fall into the water and, in a few minutes, was completely clad in icicles. Colonel Peirson was still advancing his line before reporting upon the situation, having discovered another branch of the stream which he was about to bridge, when the orders to fall back were received.

The retreat is made across the river at Germanna Ford and to the Thirty-ninth is committed the task of seeing all safely over. We see the Fifth and Sixth Corps safely across, then our own troops, including our brigade; finally the Regiment goes across, all save Companies C and F and then C is left alone; stragglers have passed over; apparently the last cavalryman is riding on the further side when the pontoons are taken up and, in the last boat, the Medford Company crosses over to join its fellows on the northern bank. The expected dash by Confederate horsemen did not take place and, chilled to the bone, the Union army after a rest of an hour proceeded to Stevensburg or near that point. Later, finding a suitable camping place, rationless and wearied, the men sought what comfort sleep might afford. Some of the soldiers find time to moralize on the outcome and they secure some satisfaction from the fact that if they did not assail the enemy, neither did the

Rebels attack the Federals. Years afterward, General Early, in Dec., '63 command in the immediate front of the line held by the First and Fifth Corps, wrote of the situation, "A direct attack from either side would have been attended with great difficulties, on account of the necessity of having to descend the slopes of Mine Run and then, after crossing that stream, to ascend the opposite slopes under the fire of artillery as well as infantry." Very few soldiers have ever been heard to criticise the wisdom of Warren's judgment or of Meade's acquiescence.

TOWARDS WINTER QUARTERS

In the forenoon of the 3rd, the Regiment marches a few miles to the vicinity of Kelly's Ford on the Rappahannock where certain log huts built by the enemy and used by them until driven out on the 7th of November by the Third Corps are occupied; a diversity of opinion as to their condition is put down by certain scribes of the period, though Company C comes up too late to get in at all. Some of the boys are very certain that winter quarters are to be right here on account of the nearness of wood and water but, meanwhile, the old duty of picketing is resumed and some of the Medford men find their line along the waters of Mountain Run. For three weeks there is little variation in daily routine: drills, inspections, parades and the regular off and on for picket and guard duty. Meantime everyone finds time to try to retain whatever heat his fire may induce, but in spite of his efforts, as one boy writes, "We suffer with the cold every night." On the 5th, came orders to move, but happily they were soon countermanded. The 6th brought the sutler again and opportunity to invest money for creature comforts at exceedingly high rates. In these days, men are able to exhibit their mechanical ability, or the want of it, in their efforts to make comfortable and presentable the cabins in which they expect to pass the winter. Drills are suspended on the 11th that more time may be given to work on the huts.

For the 12th and the 13th there are records of the arrival of boxes from the North; in one case, "The provisions are all spoiled"; in another, "All right, except the shirts and drawers which are missing." Had the latter case arisen while the men were in rebel prisons, the enemy would have had to bear the blame; it would appear that there were pilferers also among our own people. The regularity of the arrival and departure of mails affords these letter-writing soldiers no little pleasure. The weather is not so cold as that of New England at this time of the year, but it varies from bright sunshine to points away below freezing with an occasional flurry of snow, but however disagreeable it may be, all realize that it is harder still for the Confederates, since they are not so well clad as we are. It is also a time for furloughs and, on the 19th, seven men from the Thirty-ninth start on a ten days' visit to the northern homes, the time spent there to be the very happiest in their entire lives. The 21st had special mention in the diaries, in that the chaplain attended two funerals of as many men belonging to the Regiment and that Colonel Davis began a ten days' leave of absence for a trip to the Bay State. The 23rd carries the record of wintery weather, made all the more so by having the ground covered with snow, the first time in the season, also the surprise for all, in that they are ordered to have everything in readiness to move tomorrow at five o'clock in the morning. Sad looks on soldierly faces follow this announcement, "for it is such a good place to spend the winter in."

Though awakened at 3 a. m. and formed in line at 4, it was 8 a. m. before the orders to march were heard. Not a little grumbling accompanied this departure on a cold wintry day from semi-comfortable quarters for new camping places. One man's observations come down to us thus: "Why couldn't they let us sleep a while longer and then let us prepare and eat our breakfast, rather than make us stand in line on such a cold, cheerless morning?" Had all kept diaries the entries would have differed in no | Dec. | 24, '63 | essential from the foregoing. The day proved to be a good one for marching and after reaching Brandy Station, the course was along the Orange and Alexandria Railroad, through Culpeper Court House to a point possibly four miles beyond, when it was found that the Regiment had lost its bearings, thus necessitating a bivouac in a convenient stretch of woods. The burden of extra winter necessities and the frozen earth made the eighteen miles' march a trying one. Though it was "The night before Christmas" and many thoughts wandered northward to far away homes where the loved ones dwelt, there was little of the divine flavor to the night which settled down and enfolded these armed men, on the very outposts of the Union Army.

Christmas dawned as expected, but it did not seem just as it would under other circumstances; the "Merry Christmas" that passed from mouth to mouth seemed to lack some of the home fervor, yet all put the best foot forward and, determining to make the best of it, there was more than one expression of wonder as to whether "We'll be here a year hence?" Luckily, boxes from home came to cheer some of the men, a real demonstration of Santa Claus, and all the more welcome for this reason; the entire First Corps was included in this movement and the many campfires, that lit up the night, gave a gloss to what otherwise might have been cheerless; song and story made the evening pass rapidly away, and the ever melodious "taps" set these patriotic North men to slumber and the sweetest of dreams. There was an inspection in the forenoon of the 26th and orders to be ready to march in the afternoon. Starting at 3 p. m., the trip was only about two miles still nearer the Confederacy, along the railroad, halting at or near Mitchell's Station, the very last before reaching the Rapidan; here in a large field the brigade encamped in column by regiments. Rain falls on the 27th and this, coupled with the marshy character of the fields in which the Regiment is camped, makes moist beds for the men, though they try to obviate the situation by tearing boards from an unoccupied house and by the use of boughs and branches in getting the bunks off the saturated ground.

MITCHELL'S STATION

In the matter of residents, it could not be said that Mitchell's Station was exactly densely inhabited, but where was there ever a girl whom someone did not admire and, if possible, make her acquaintance? One family, with the staunchest of German names, in which the sons had gone into the rebel army, had a father, mother and three grown-up daughters. When sober, the "old man" claimed to be a good Union man; when drunk, as was sometimes the case, he was an out and out Secesh; as to the girls, it made no difference what their affiliations were; they were girls and that was enough. One evening, three officers called at headquarters and asked the privilege of calling on the Y—— girls; "Umph," exclaimed Colonel Davis, "I verily believe half the officers in the Regiment are there already, but you may go if you think it will do you any good."

With the 28th comes Sutler Pullen again and until afternoon the rain continues; the 29th does not bring the change of camping place that so many wish. During the day, Colonel T. F. McCoy (One Hundred and Seventh Penn.), commanding in the absence of Colonel Leonard, compliments the entire brigade on the cheerfulness and fortitude of the men and their endurance in marching in the cold and stormy weather; he also calls attention to the exposed position of the brigade, being the nearest the enemy and warning every one to be on the lookout constantly. On this day also was promulgated the plan to secure reenlistments of the men, with the promise of a thirty days' furlough and a large bounty. The proposition did not appear to find much favor with the Thirty-ninth, although all of the men would appreciate that month at home. The 30th brought orders to be ready to march on the morrow. December Dec. 28, '63 goes out with mud and moisture much in evidence; the camp is moved in the forenoon less than a mile, thereby finding better conveniences in a piece of woods. Major Leavitt of the Sixteenth Maine musters the Regiment for pay, and Lieut. Colonel Peirson performs a like act for the Maine soldiers. Colonel Davis gets back from his furlough, having walked from Culpeper last night in the dark and through the mud. Here, then, ends the year with its record of Gettysburg and Chattanooga, but for our Regiment, with all its preparation, marching and undeviating performance of duty, its fiery ordeal is yet to come.

1864

January 1st the day dawned bright and cold, the weather having cleared in the night; the mud and the streams have taken on the repose of winter, but, if any protection against the inclement season is to be had, the men must get to work at once and this they do, cutting down trees to fashion therefrom the primative habitations that the early settlers of all new countries have had to make. Though the men do not know it, and though there will be many rumors of departures, they may even pack up at times yet, until the last of April, Mitchell's Station will be the P. O. address of the Thirty-ninth Regiment, but winter in camp is no trifling matter with a regular routine of camp duties, besides the necessity of maintaining the utmost vigilance towards the foe. Hence the building of quarters cannot be effected in a day or week, in the meantime the ordinary shelter tent affords only slender protection against the wind and cold. It is to be a second winter's experience with our Regiment, hence the building of log huts is not an innovation; all that is needed are time, tools and material. For several months the Rapidan is to be the most generally named stream in the eastern part of the Union, for along its northern banks are to camp the several corps which make up the Army of the Potomac and, every day thousands of letters to far away homes will tell the people there what is doing down in "Old Virginny." For four months a thin line of blue will patrol its shores for more than twenty miles and equally vigilant men in gray, will keep their watch upon the south side. With the Second Corps on the extreme Union left, with headquarters near Stevensburg, the Union army stretches to the westward till it terminates with the First Corps, which will furnish infantry pickets on a line of cavalry outposts.

South of the river, the Confederates are guarding an equal distance, yet there will be very little indication of hostility, something like an armed neutrality, each line of sentinels quite content to be let alone; there is however this difference between the two armies, one has all that boundless means can supply to make its soldiers comfortable, the other wanting nearly everything that would contribute to personal enjoyment. The lack of clothing and camp outfit had become such that winter with its rigors became far more an object of fear to the enemy than any army the Yankees might send against them. Thomas Nelson Page, in his Life of General Lee, has this to say concerning the Confederates in camp along the Virginia Central Railroad:

Lee's army was in a state of such destitution that it is a wonder that the men could be kept together. Only their spirit enabled them to stand the hardships of the winter. Barefooted and hungry, they stood it throughout the long months of a Virginia winter, and when it is considered that until they joined the army many of these men had never seen snow, and that none of them had ever experienced want of adequate clothing, their resolution is a tribute to their patriotism that can never be excelled. That Lee himself endured hardships and suffered with them in their self denial was sufficient for them.... From his camp, General Lee writes to his wife on January 24, 1864, "I have had to disperse the cavalry as much as possible to obtain forage for their horses, and it is that which causes trouble. Provisions for the men, too, are very scarce, and with very light diet and light clothing, I fear they will suffer, but still they are cheerful and uncomplaining. I received a report from one division the other day in which Jan. 1, '64 it was stated that over four hundred men were barefooted and over one thousand were without blankets."

During the early January days, all the time that could be secured from regular duties was devoted to house building, and every man worked with a will, since the weather was extremely cold, the amount of clothing possessed being insufficient, in the open air, to maintain warmth; some of the men resorted to the old fashioned practice of putting a heated stone at their feet to help make them comfortable, every one thus getting a notion of what it meant to build homes in the wilderness as so many pioneers had done. Because of so many of the men in Company C having been ship carpenters when at home, a large part of the company was detailed to work on the houses, though the Woburn delegation (K) was not far behind with its thirteen men selected to use axe, saw, hammer and plane. The arrival of packages from home, from time to time, did much to lessen grumbling and the coming in of seven deserters on the 6th, barefooted and telling pitiful stories of the conditions across the Rapidan, made the Yankees more nearly comfortable just by way of contrast. With big fires burning, we were sure of one side being warm, even if the other was almost freezing. However, song and story wiled away many a long evening before trying to woo the goddess, sleep, in comfortless shelter tents. In the demands of picket, camp, regiment and brigade guard there was something in the guard-way for nearly every man, every day, so the houses did not grow any too rapidly.

Such entries in the diaries of the period as, "mudded our hut to-day," would mean little to the novice unless told that this meant the stopping of the spaces between the log cob-pile which constituted the walls of the habitation, with real old Virginia soil, properly mixed with a certain amount of water and, when plentifully applied, was warranted to stand indefinitely, keeping out the much dreaded wind. The same material judiciously mingled with sticks, staves, boards or boxes made the chimney-exit for the smoke produced in the fireplace, which was a necessary feature of every cabin.[H] Making the quarters for the squad that was to hold and occupy did not end the enlisted man's duties, for he had also to take a hand in the fabrication of similar structures for his company officers and then to do his part in behalf of the care and comfort of the Field and Staff. Nor did the chain end here, since there must be places for the retention and protection of commissary and quartermaster stores and, never to be forgotten, were all the important, superlatively useful yet ever railed at, "The good old army mules," and who should build their shelters, if not the men for whom they had drawn through so many miles the supplies which fed and clothed the soldiers?

The long delayed Thanksgiving dinner came to "C," the Medford company, on the 10th and a relay of clothing such as, "Nice flannel shirts and drawers, socks, mittens and a few caps for nights." The company received them very gratefully and the friends at home would be more than paid, could they see how thankful the men were. "We eat our dinners to-morrow," says the scribe. The details of the dinner, eaten on the 11th, are not uninteresting; remembering that twenty-two men had been discharged from the company, that some men were on detached service and that many were in the hospital, the fact, that less than forty were present for duty and the dinner will not

Jan. 10, '64   seem so strange. Owing to the limited number, the liberality of material for that feast is conspicuous; they might have called in some of their less fortunate neighbors and then have had a very large meal for themselves; the record is, "One turkey and one pudding for every four men; one half a mince pie per man with sauces for turkey and pudding, also the real old orthodox cranberry, redolent of the Cape, besides, pickles, cheese and condensed milk." The folks at home did nothing by halves and how many hours of careful and diligent labor in those northern homes did this magnificent layout represent!

Everyday life in these winter-quarter days of the Army of the Potomac are a practical illustration of the old maxim, "Eternal vigilance is the price of liberty"; for, despite the efforts given to hut building, all the men are really under arms or the next thing to it. "Men are obliged to wear their equipments twenty-four hours" and an immediate response is expected to every order. A few recruits are joining the Regiment, not exactly a pleasant season of the year in which to be broken into the routine of military life, yet the proper officers take them in charge and begin the breaking-in process. On the 12th, remains of the great Company C dinner are sent over to the sick at Culpeper, and those who are not users of the weed distribute their tobacco, also from Medford, among those who are not so abstemious. Notwithstanding all of the alert watchfulness, the enemy seems to be perfectly quiescent and, probably, perfectly willing that we should be. After a deal of policing and general slicking up, the 16th brings the monthly inspection, conducted by Lieutenant Bradley of the brigade staff. The habits of the far off homes are fixed and in the evening of Sunday, the 17th, might be heard the sound of many voices as they joined in singing the songs and hymns of childhood; "a splendid, moonlight evening."

Deserters and contrabands are frequently discovered fording the Rapidan, whose chilly waters have less terrors for the escaping parties than the tribulations left behind. In the night of the 19th the firing of the Confederate guards hastened the steps of some deserting rebels and prevented the departure of others. The cabins having been constructed and occupied, the men are now making corduroy sidewalks, by laying moderate lengths of poles side-by-side, crossways of the walk itself, and, thus, are able to get about without being lost in Virginia mud. Many a remark is heard on the admirable appearance of the camp, all agreeing that it is the best in the brigade, and some even lay that claim as against the entire Army of the Potomac. Company H and a part of "K" go out on a reconnoisance, Thursday, the 28th. Towards the end of the month, unusual stir is observed among the enemy, apparently fresh troops are replacing those long on guard, possibly through fear that all of the latter will desert; our own camp also has a spell of falling-in according to orders and, on the 29th, we packed up at 5 a. m., stacked arms and awaited further orders, sorry enough at the prospect of quitting the comfortable quarters, so recently completed. Fortunately for us, it all blew over and the Second Brigade moved instead. On this same day our eyes were gladdened by the unusual sight of a lady in camp, the same being the wife of General Maj. John Newton, commanding the First Corps, who accompanied the General and Division Commander, General Robinson, and their respective staffs, all on a tour of observation. A dull, though not stormy day closed the month with regular inspection and we see a Confederate major and three men brought in as captives by the cavalry.

February starts off full of rumors as to the future of the Regiment; one says it is to join an expedition to Texas; another sends us home to be recruited to full ranks, while still another sends us back to become a part of the Sixth Corps. Who can explain the starting of so many baseless reports? The weather, early in the month, is cold yet there are few breaks in regular routine, if parades, drills   Feb. 1, '64   and inspections can be injected between the many calls for picket duty. A hospital is in process of erection near the surgeon's quarters and it is a fine building, considering the circumstances under which it is going up. There is talk, also, of a chapel or schoolroom for the use of officers and men. The 5th of the month, late at night, came the summary orders to be ready to move early in the morning, reveillé to be at 3 a. m. The drawing of rations, etc., kept us busy until one o'clock in the next morning, hence not much sleep, but no end of grumbling. Reveillé sounded according to programme on the 6th; the men turned out, cooked their breakfasts, packed their tents and were ready to start before daylight. At seven o'clock the orders came to replace the tents and to resume regular camp life. This break in the usual calm was explained as an incident in the movement of the Second Corps to Morton's Ford, on the Rapidan, as a supplementary act to the proposed attempt of General B. F. Butler from the south against Richmond. As Butler's plan proved abortive, activity on the part of the Second Corps subsided at once and things were soon as they had been.

Sunrise, gilding the snowy tops of the Blue Ridge Mountains, awakens the sensibilities of some of the men as the 10th day of the month begins and, later in the day, the paymaster makes all happy with compensation for services rendered up to December 1st. General Robinson and staff, accompanied by ladies, also by some of the corps staff officers, rode into camp on the 12th, evidently thinking it one of the show places of the cantonment. Over the fact that the men left in camp, the Regiment being on picket, are all merged in two companies and these go on dress parade prompts one commentator to remark that he supposes if only one man were left in camp, he would have to appear at the regular time on parade. Injudicious use of the ardent was the probable reason for the advent of a Thirteenth Massachusetts' party evidently bent on mischief. Whatever they came for, the colonel cut short the career of a sergeant and a private by placing them under arrest and so returning them to their Regiment. How strange it is, that men will tolerate an evil that makes such fools of them! The evening of this day was brilliantly illuminated by great forest fires on both sides of the Rapidan. The coming of Major William Thorndike, the new surgeon, is chronicled on the 15th; Surgeon Calvin G. Page, on account of disability, had been discharged Nov. 16, 1863. The 16th is so cold that large quantities of wood are brought in from the forest for the building of fires just for the warmth thereof. The new hospital is opened and much is expected from it.

The 20th of February marked the dedication of the new chapel, whose building had taken the time and strength of the soldiers, some of them, for a number of days. Nicely decorated and appointed, the men were not a little proud of their place of worship. Chaplain French had charge of the exercises; the band of the Sixteenth Maine was present and most obligingly discoursed appropriate music. Among the people who crowded the interior were Colonel Leonard of the Thirteenth Massachusetts with his wife, Surgeon Alexander of the Sixteenth Maine and wife, with others. Compliments were dealt out to the men who had labored so zealously for the success of the project and Colonel Davis' remarks in this direction were especially happy. The next day was Sunday, and regular service was held in the new chapel. Apparently the 22nd, Washington's birthday, received no special attention. The new chapel afforded most excellent quarters for the regular meetings of the Masonic Lodge which had been one of the features of the Regiment for considerably more than a year. As far back as Offutt's Cross Roads, November 20, '62, the lodge had been instituted, under a special dispensation from the Grand Lodge of Massachusetts, Grand Master, William D. Cooledge, the document bearing date, November 13, 1862.

Feb. 22, '64

MASONIC LODGE

This original meeting was held at the regimental headquarters, Colonel Davis presiding, he having been named as Worthy Master of the Putnam Army Lodge, No. 8, thus called in compliment to the East Cambridge Lodge of which he was a member. It appears that army posts were no innovations at this date as the number of this new one would indicate. Already lodges had been formed in the Third, Sixteenth, Seventeenth, Twenty-fifth, Second and Forty-eighth Massachusetts Regiments and later dispensations were granted to the Forty-second and the Thirty-second. Aside from the Master of Putnam Lodge, Colonel P. S. Davis, the officers were Henry B. Leighton, S. W.; Capt. Geo. S. Nelson, J. W.; Capt. F. R. Kinsley, Treasurer; Lieut. Julius M. Swain, Secretary; Daniel Henry, S. D.; Perry Coleman, J. D.; Lieut. Henry F. Felch, S. S.; Lieut. Wm. T. Spear, J. S.; Lieut. Willard C. Kinsley, Marshal; and John M. Curtis, Tyler. In the distribution of officers it would seem that army rank had no place, fraternal relations being the only line of consideration. By-laws for the proper management of the lodge along with blank forms for application for membership were adopted and, though the Third Thursday of each month was named as the regular meeting date there were far more special than regular assemblings.

The second meeting of the lodge was in the Methodist chapel and when the Regiment moved back to Poolesville, the schoolhouse there was utilized, proper secrecy being gained by putting on guard, near the place of meeting, members of the order. Applications for membership came in rapidly and the record for the remainder of the calender year was twenty-three candidates admitted and seventeen meetings, $580 being received for dues and degrees. From April 6 to July 15, in front of Petersburg, after the death of Colonel Davis, there was a lapse; then the Lodge voted to bear the expense attending the return of the Colonels' remains to Massachusetts but, at the request of the family, the part of the lodge was confined to embalming and transportation to Boston, along with the expenses of Chaplain French, who accompanied the body on the sad journey to Boston. Help was given to the families of comrades who had been killed or were in hospitals or rebel prison. October 16, '64, at Fort Dushane it was voted to pay the expenses of sending the body of Lieut. Wm. T. Spear, Company B, to Roxbury, the officer having died in hospital from wounds; the same consideration was shown to the remains of Lieut. Willard C. Kinsley when he was killed. The final meeting of the lodge was in the State House Boston, January 29, 1866, with fourteen members present when it was voted that of the remaining funds, $198, $50 should go towards a portrait of Colonel Davis and the rest for relief. The officers were given the regalia that they had worn; the Bible was given to the widow of the Colonel, the square and compasses to the East Cambridge

Lodge, the remaining set to go to Brother Henry B. Leighton, the S. W. During the activities of the field, the Master, S. D., J. S. and Marshal were killed, the Treasurer and Secretary were captured. There are recorded considerably more than fifty names of those voted in, while the brother, turning in the records, says that thirty-nine took the three degrees.

MITCHELL'S STATION AND THE SCHOOL IN CAMP

Channing Whittaker, Company B

Our most ideal winter's camp before the Wilderness Campaign was that at Mitchell's Station. A more perfect parade and drill ground could not have been desired. It had abundant length and breadth. It was the smooth level top of an extensive plateau. The log cabins of the officers were in a straight row where the slope to the rear began. The log cabins of the men stretched down the Feb., '64 slope toward a veritable Eldorado of firewood and drinking water. These log cabins were very comfortable. Each accommodated eight men. The entrance from the company street was at the middle of its length. The fireplace and chimney were directly opposite the entrance. The living room was between the two. There were four bunks, two at each end with one above the other. Each bunk was long enough for a tall man to stretch out at full length with his head upon his knapsack and wide enough for two men to sleep comfortably, side by side. The cabins of the field officers had, of course, the right of the line. The chapel was more to the front and a little to the left of the cabins of the field officers. The pioneers who constructed Col. Davis' cabin and the chapel were master workmen. No keel of ship in New England shipyard had timbers hewn and dowelled into a substantial whole with more absolute perfection. I never shall forget the perfect delight of an afternoon when, convalescing from a severe attack of measles, I was detailed to report at the Colonel's quarters. Here I was received by Lieut Colonel Peirson with a smile upon his face. He showed me that the cabin was not yet dry enough for occupancy, showed me the wood which I was to burn to dry it out, showed me the charming fireplace in which I was to burn it. If I remember well its top was arched. Perhaps the arch had blocks, with a central one of keystone shape. He gave me a comfortable seat and an entertaining book to read, by an army chaplain, "The Whip, Hoe, and Sword," by George H. Hepworth. The friendly behavior of the Lieut. Colonel, the restful charm of the roomy clean interior finished in natural wood showing its grain, the blazing fire in the big fireplace with its perfect chimney, and the extreme comfort of it all, after the discomforts of the measles, filled me with agreeable sensations and with gratitude to the Lieutenant Colonel.

And the chapel! It may have been thirty by fifty feet inside. Its hewn oaken logs were perhaps twelve inches square, its roof was a fly that the Christian Commission had furnished. Its fireplace was huge, magnificent. The prayer meetings were held in it, the Freemasons used it as a lodgeroom, the Sons of Temperance had meetings there, and the regimental school for those who could neither read nor write nor cipher was held in it. I well remember the morning when Comrade John F. Locke, of Company E, and myself were detailed to report at the chapel and appointed to be the teachers of the school by Lieut. Colonel Peirson. I remember hearing the roll-call of the students of my own and of a neighboring company and the ugly mutterings, the dissatisfaction, the almost mutinous emphatic expressions of discontent of some of those whose names had been called, because they had been detailed to attend a school. I fully expected trouble. A considerable number of men were in anything but a teachable spirit. We met in the chapel, the Lieut. Colonel, the teachers, and thirty students, some of them bristling with unwillingness. But the Lieut. Colonel, who was always a gentleman, drew us all into a comfortable semi-circle about the hearth where the cheerful fire blazed. He told us of the personal benefits and advantages which it was hoped that the work in the school would bring to each student, and his manner and speech almost immediately disarmed the embryo antagonism of the others in the group. When he finally asked if there were any present who desired to be relieved from attendance at the school, not a man wished to withdraw, all were glad of the opportunity. The antagonism had melted away like a mud-puddle in the light of a July sun. And the antagonism never returned. I have taught many hundreds of students since but none who were more interested, more attentive, more constant. Each of the men learned to write his name. Seven wrote letters home before we broke camp, to the great delight of themselves and their families. Twenty-three made especially commendable progress in reading and arithmetic. Our text and copy books had been   Feb., '64   the generous gifts of Colonel Davis and his brother Robert. The Lieut. Colonel had offered a gold pen and case as a prize to the man who should gain the greatest proficiency in writing. All of the written exercises were carefully preserved from the beginning and, when the time came to award the prize, it was almost impossible to say whether it had been won by Johnny Gibbs of Company A, a brick layer, who was well along in years or by Daniel Lines, a carriage painter. For year after year the good right hand of Johnny Gibbs had clasped the small handle of a trowel. Its active exercise in that cramped position with the acrid lime sometimes in contact with it had caused its bones and cords and muscles to grow out of shape. He could no longer open it much more than enough to enter and remove a trowel handle. He could not hold a pen in usual position. There were sharp crooks made at the joints of his right thumb and forefinger when he brought them together, and there were similar crooks in his capital O's when he wrote his best. But his handwriting, though characteristic, was absolutely clear. It was perfectly easy to read. He had mastered his hand for the purposes of a writer. Despite the crooks he wrote a handsome hand. The hand of Daniel Lines had gained a wonderful cunning in the business of a carriage painter.

He could do what he would with a camels-hair brush, when making scrolls and stripes and decorations. He brought to his copy book the artistic power of a hand over which he had a complete control. From the beginning his double-reversed curves were lines of beauty. At the end his writing had almost the perfection of the copyplate. There was no possible doubt that Daniel Lines' writing was more beautiful than that of any other pupil in the school, but which had gained the greatest proficiency in writing in the school, he or Johnny Gibbs? The teachers were puzzled. They called in the Lieut. Colonel as referee. He too was in doubt and suggested that Gibbs and Lines should draw lots. The lot fell to Gibbs. On Sunday, the 21st of August, 1864, Johnny Gibbs and his teacher, John F. Locke, were taken prisoners in a battle on the Weldon Railroad. They were both very sick, together, in that fearful prison in Salisbury, North Carolina. There were no tender-hearted, white-capped, trained nurses there, to keep in extreme cleanliness the clothing of the very sick. But the gratitude, the compassion, the sympathy of the old man for his youthful teacher became too strong. Like many another soldier who has volunteered to dare almost certain death in a forlorn hope, weak Johnny Gibbs washed the soiled clothing of John Locke. Within a day, Johnny Gibbs was dead.

STILL IN CAMP.

Incessant picket duty has marked the month of February with a great variety of weather and the men are not sorry to see the 29th day, Leap Year's allotment, for they know that they are just so much nearer the end of the war and their consequent return to their homes. A spring feeling begins to be felt on both sides of the river and indications of activity are discovered among the Confederates, and at least twice recently orders have been given for the preparation of rations for the haversacks, as though some sort of a move were contemplated. On this final day of the month, the Regiment is mustered for two months' pay, while drill, inspection and parade have their accustomed places. Doubtless very few are aware of the hardening effect upon the bodies of the men this regular and constant round of discipline is having; the same will appear in the exactions of the coming months. While February is expiring thus quietly with our Regiment, in the First Corps Kilpatrick is making his famous raid towards Richmond, having started on the night of the 28th, crossing the Rapidan at Ely's Ford and, with Colonel Dahlgren's forlorn hope, is entering upon a project which will make history rapidly. To cover this attempt, a diversion of Confederate attention is made by the Sixth Corps and a cavalry force Feb. 29, '64 under Custer. Passing through the camps of the Third Corps, Sedgwick and his men move out towards Madison Court House, while Custer and his mounted force push on to Charlottesville, where, on this final February day, hostile forces are contending within sight and sound of Monticello, the home and the tomb of Jefferson.

March started off rainy and cold with usual rumors as to immediate orders for some sort of a move, but duty on the picket line continued just the same, and not a few remarked on the discomforts of those who had gone out to Madison Court House and were compelled to bivouac in the snow, into which the rain had changed. For the 2d day of the month, the return of the Sixth Corps and its cavalry accompaniment was chronicled, along with the fact that nothing had been heard from Kilpatrick. Even in wartimes, it did not always rain and the 3rd, being "a splendid day," some of the men climbed up the sides of Cedar or Slaughter Mountain for the view, and to look up traces of the fierce encounter, August 9, 1862, when the Second and Third Corps, Generals Banks and McDowell respectively, all under General John Pope, were beaten by "Stonewall" Jackson and his men. Having encamped so long under the shadow of the eminence, the trip was particularly enjoyable and there was no difficulty in locating many of the prominent features of the bloody day which served as a prelude to the still bloodier battle of Second Bull Run. A two hours' brigade drill on the 4th, under Colonel Leonard, took all available men to the extensive plains across Cedar Run. As an illustration of the degree to which neatness was carried, it should be stated that from their respective company funds pay was given to men, detailed for the purpose, who should do the company washing, hence no excuse for uncleanliness would avail thereafter.

Sunday, the 7th, marked the relief of the Second Brigade on picket, and its return by train to Culpeper, while the First Brigade took its place. An order, promulgated March 10th to the effect that all women in the camp must depart at once, was taken as a sign of increased activity and the next day saw the departure of the visiting betterhalves for their northern homes. Further indication of active campaigning appeared on the 12th when the Colonel issued an order directing the several captains to send back to Washington all dresscoats. John S. Beck, Company C, entered in his diary, the 14th, "In the evening, took the Second Degree in Army Lodge, No. 8, and Free and Accepted Masons," an unusual incident in army life; two nights later, he took his Third Degree. St. Patrick's Day, or the 17th, secured no recognition in camp, though large fires on the rebel side of the river betokened something doing there, yet the afternoon's sun, lighting up the hillside on which the Confederates were encamped, revealed their tents still in place. The 18th, in the afternoon, witnessed no end of hurry and bustle as all effects were packed, even to removing tents from the cabin roofs, and all were to be in readiness to move at once. It was the general agreement that Stuart and his lively followers were surely in the saddle. With stacked arms and expectant hearts, the next order was awaited and, at 5.30 p. m., it came, not to fall in and "Forward," but the bubble-burst words heard so often, "As you were," with a resumption of regular camp routine and duties.

The signing of pay-rolls on the 19th was a sure sign of the approach of the paymaster and the perfection of the weather gave light hearts to all, though a clergyman of the Methodist Church South, seized outside our lines for conducting certain of Stuart's men to the capture of one of our pickets may have had a leaden heart as he was dispatched on his way to Washington, there to account for his conduct; bearing the name of Garnett, he must have belonged to one of the best families of the Old Dominion. The 20th was Sunday, not usually a pay day, but were there signs of activity it was thus employed and, as the paymaster came on this date, the event was considered

a   Mar. 20, '64   pretty sure sign of a movement; so late did he begin, it was

8 p. m. before the last company was reached. Much to the disgust of all who had thought winter over and past, snow began to fall on the 22nd. By nightfall the ground was white with it, the wind blowing as in an old-fashioned "nor'-easter," so that the on 23rd there was a foot of snow lying around and all hands had to turn out and shovel the same out of the streets and from the parade ground, which was quite ready for the dress parade of the late afternoon.

To the Regiment, however, the most important event of the day was the rearrangement of the several corps constituting the Army of the Potomac, though this act had no immediate effect upon the regular life of the Thirty-ninth. The First Army Corps of the Potomac Army, commanded successively by Generals McDowell, Hooker, Reynolds and Newton, had left an excellent record through the nearly two years of its existence; the disk which, in red, white and blue, represented its several divisions, had ever been a badge of honor and now the advent of General Grant to the command of the army was to bring about various changes, among them the merging of the First Corps with the Fifth; its three divisions, reduced to two, became the Second and Fourth under Robinson and Crawford respectively while Warren, of late temporarily in command of the Second, was assigned to lead the Fifth Corps, and Newton [1] who had succeeded Reynolds at Gettysburg, was relieved. Under the same general orders, the Third Corps also was disbanded, its first and second divisions going to the Second Corps, its third division to the Sixth, and General Sykes, the Commander, to the command of the District of South Kansas. There were thus left the Second, Fifth and Sixth Corps in the Potomac Army, to which in the campaign of 1864 the Ninth Corps, under General Burnside, was to be added.

This rearrangement of army relations was not accomplished without some heart-burning and many adverse remarks. John D. Billings in his story of the Tenth Massachusetts Battery says:

"Next to the attachment men feel for their own company or regiment, comes that which they feel for their corps. All the active services that we had seen was in the Third Corps, and its earlier history and traditions from the Peninsula to Gettysburg had become a part of our pride, and we did not care to identify ourselves with any other. If such was our feeling in the matter, how much more intense must have been that of the troops longer in its membership, whose very blood and sinew were incorporated with the imperishable name it won under General Sickles."

The farewell of General Newton to the men of the First Corps bears date of March 25, 1864, and is as follows:—

"Upon relinquishing command I take occasion to express the pride and pleasure I have experienced in my connection with you, and my profound regret at our separation. Identified by its services with the history of the war, the First Corps gave at Gettysburg a crowning proof of valor and endurance, in saving from the grasp of the enemy the strong position upon which the battle was fought. The terrible losses suffered by the Corps in that conflict attest its supreme devotion to the country. Though the Corps has lost its distinctive name by the present changes, history will not be silent upon the magnitude of its services."

Mar. 26, '64 Though the Thirty-ninth had borne no part in the battle-trials of the corps, save in the premonitions at Mine Run, yet its marchings and campings, during eight months of service, had done much towards impressing upon the Regiment the character of the corps and an appreciation of the corps and an appreciation of its excellent record.

Foundation facts for the coming summer are coming fast in these days for, on the 26th of March, General U. S. Grant established his headquarters at Culpeper, a little south of those of the Army of the Potomac. For just a month, the General's name has been heard in the public ear more than usual since, on the 26th of February, the bill restoring the grade of lieutenant-general became a law; on the 1st of March, General Grant's name was sent to Congress and it was confirmed March 2nd; on the 3rd, he was ordered to Washington to receive his commission and he started the day following. March 9th, in the White House, in the presence of the President's Cabinet, his staff or such as were with him and his son, Fred, General Grant received his commission from the hands of Lincoln, with the briefest possible exchange of compliments. The Thirty-ninth Regiment knew it not, but on the 10th, the Lieutenant-general was at Brandy Station viewing some of the scenes that were to be better known by him in approaching days; the next day he was in Washington again and in the evening started back to the west. Many plans were evolved by Grant and his lieutenants before his return to Washington on the 23rd, whence he went to Culpeper as before stated. Henceforth his military record will be a part of that of the Potomac Army.

While this is strictly a story of the Thirty-ninth Massachusetts, of any happening in the camp of our near neighbors and good friends, the men of the Sixteenth Maine, passing mention is due here. Colonel Charles W. Tilden had been captured at Gettysburg and had been held prisoner in Richmond until the 10th of February, when with others he got away from Libby through General A. D. Streight's famous tunnel and on the 28th of March, at four o'clock in the afternoon, he was received by his old boys with a heartiness which only old soldiers can give to the tried and true; in the evening followed a feast in the regimental chapel, attended by the officers of the Sixteenth and the field officers of the brigade, all uniting in the most fervent expressions of respect and admiration; the history of the Sixteenth has this concerning the words of our esteemed Commander, "Colonel Davis, whose encampment is a paragon of neatness and comfort, replied in his calm and witty way to a toast complimentary to the Thirty-ninth Massachusetts." The next day several hundred men from other regiments in the brigade assembled at 9 a. m. to witness the presentation to Colonel Tilden by his regiment of a magnificent black stallion duly caparisoned; evidently the officer was greatly admired. The remainder of the day was one of diversion for the men of the Sixteenth and their friends.

The One Hundred and Seventh Pennsylvania, a member of our brigade, whose Colonel, Thos. F. McCoy, at times commanded the brigade, pretty generally enlisted in the month of February, but its re-enlistment home-going did not begin until this day; surely no April Fool's occasion for the happy men who crowded aboard the train which was to carry them hence, all intent on the happiness in store for them; the "battle summer" will be well under way before the regiment rejoins us; a considerable part of the One Hundred and Fourth New York also started away on a similar errand. On the 3rd, the Ninetieth Pennsylvania came over from the Second Brigade and occupied the camp of the One Hundred and Seventh. The general harshness of the season marked early April, rain and snow, and not till the seventh day did the weather clear up effectually and, even then, as matters shaped themselves, there were those who claimed that there was an improvement, not so much on our account as that there might be a bright day for General Grant's inspection. It was Fast Day, too, at home, but   Apr. 8, '64   we were eating all we could get. We were out early and active on the 8th, doing very thorough policing. We were in line at 11 a. m. and before noon, the hero of Vicksburg, accompanied by his staff and General Robinson, appeared, receiving three cheers from the men as he rode by us; he took a look at our camp and highly complimented its appearance. Evidently the General had heard of our camp for he went down through the company streets which were spick and span as usual. Then he went out to the picket-line and thence to the signal station on the hill, Colonel Davis going with him. Everyone was sizing him up and making some sort of a mental entry concerning him, and one man wrote this, "He has a good, resolute look." There seemed to be a general opinion that he was no great talker, but that, as a doer, he would probably be all right.

Stormy weather was resumed on the 9th and continued almost every day until the excess of water washed away bridges between us and Washington to the extent of stopping trains on the 11th, with consequent lack of mails and other inconveniences; so efficient, however, were the artificers of the army, the very next day trains resumed running and letters from home made glad the hearts of men. During these days we were packing all superfluous articles, preparatory to sending to Alexandria, at the same time all were enjoined from writing about this to the friends at home. The new management did not believe in the utmost publicity. Saddened reflections followed the departure of the sutler, on the 16th, since thereafter, it would be necessary to forego luxuries altogether. The 19th saw seven discouraged rebels come into our lines, saying that there were many more waiting a chance to get through. Notwithstanding this, we could see that the enemy was working hard on making breastworks, evidently expecting us to march directly upon them; nobody knows just what way we shall advance, but it probably will not be by the line surmised by the Confederates. Everyone felt better on account of the serenade that the band of the Sixteenth Maine favored us with in the evening of the 20th. The 21st marked the departure of thirteen men from the Thirty-ninth, transferred to the Navy, many of whom, being familiar with nautical duties, fancied that service afloat would be preferable to that ashore.

The Cavalry had been even more active, if possible, than the Infantry during the winter and General Sheridan commented on the lean and hungry look of the horses when he reached the army, but in spite of leanness, this branch was the first to move—some said it had not stopped moving,-and on the 23rd, one man wrote, "The Cavalry moved out to-day" and, could he have foreseen the service that the restless "Little Phil" was to exact from the horsemen, doubtless he had written more at length. He also entered in that same journal, "The covering of our chapel was taken off to-day, so I suppose our meetings are over." Dismantling was the order of Sunday, the 24th, and unroofed cabins lost their homelike look. The move of the 26th looked much like an abandonment of our long time camp and the beginning of active warfare, for the whole brigade, leaving the old camp behind, crossed Cedar Run and, at a point a mile away from the former stopping place, pitched its shelter tents in column by companies, the thirty-ninth Regiment being on the right. Some went back to their old quarters to bring thence boards to help out their sleeping facilities. By this change of camp, it was expected to free the men from all surplus stuff and, at the same time, to re-inure them to the hardships of active campaigning. The remaining days of April were uneventful, given to parades, inspections and drills, wherein knapsacks figured largely, thus testing the endurance of the soldiers and on the 30th, Saturday, the Regiment was mustered for two months' pay, March and April.

No month in the year among dwellers in northern regions prompts to brighter, happier thoughts than May; in distant Massachusetts, children who had sought the fragrant Apr. 30, '64 arbutus through the daylight hours, were repining that Sunday made it impracticable for them to hang May-baskets when the evening shades appeared, a pleasure deferred however only till the following night. To the men and boys, afar from familiar scenes and cherished friends, the pleasures of peace were denied, and being on the eve of departure, much of regular camp life was omitted. Their neighbors, the Sixteenth Maine, formed in hollow square and had religious services, but letter writing was the most serious employment for the men of the Thirty-ninth. Could they have known the horrors through which they were to pass before another Lord's Day returned, with what eloquence had those messages teemed which carried simply the usual words of love and fealty.

Hands that wrote tender words on this May day, ere another week had passed, were folded on soldierly breasts, asleep in battle-made graves. For nearly an entire year, with no long rest in winterquarters, no respite from the noise of combat, the men of the North and their brothers from the South are about to engage in a death grapple, and a baptism of blood awaits the tyros of the Lynnfield camp, the cadets of Edward's Ferry and Poolesville, the Capital guardians of Washington, and the admirably equipped soldiers of Colonel Davis' pride.

Though it is the 2d day of May and we are in the supposedly "Sunny South," snow is plainly visible on the tips of the Blue Ridge and where the mountains are high enough, anywhere snow may be found the whole year round. Company E, Somerville, is taking the least bit of pride to itself in that its Captain Kinsley, the senior officer of that rank, commands in the battalion-drill. Keen observers of signs are these soldier boys and, when they learn that the cars have come up for the last time, and when they hear, at dress parade, a letter of praise and patriotic prompting from General George G. Meade, all this on the 3rd, they know full well that the days of winterquarters are all but ended; certainty is added to surety when, at 10 p. m., three days' rations are issued with the not over cheerful information that they must last us six; at midnight, we are awakened and told to be ready to move in fifteen minutes. How many glances are cast towards the Rapidan, during the nearly three hours' wait before the start is made, not of apprehension but of wonder as to what the outcome will be when "brave Northmen shall the Southern meet in bold, defiant manner?" We know full well that our faces are soon to be set towards the south, that once more the stream, so often crossed and recrossed, will soon greet us again as we pass over or through it; remembering the mettle of the man who is now leading, one who never made provisions for retreat, because he never retreated, we realize that in our progress southward there will be no backward turning, that, while "few shall part where many meet," some of our numbers will survive to carry forward the Flag, and everyone had a perfect conviction of the righteousness of his cause and absolute confidence in its eventual triumph.

The main incidents of these days in early May are writing themselves deep in the hearts of America; as long as he lives will every participant, whether in blue or gray, recall the impressions that were his as he realized the immensity of the struggle that is impending. Of it, Grant has said in his Memoirs, "The capture of the Confederate capital and the army defending it was not to be accomplished without as desperate fighting as the world has ever witnessed." Lee left no memoirs but his biographer wrote, "He divined Grant's plans, and cutting the latter from the object of his desires, threw himself upon him in a contest whose fury may be gauged by the fact that the musketry fire continued in one unbroken roar for seventeen hours, and trees were shorn down by the musket balls." The outlines of the movement which began with the start of the Second Corps, at 11 p. m. of the 3rd, crossing at Ely's Ford at six o'clock in the morning of the 4th, followed at Germanna's in turn by that of the Fifth and Sixth Corps   May 4, '64   in order, have been told in hundreds of places by both tongue and pen; they form the a, b, c of 1864 military history, so we must content ourselves with the fact that when, at three o'clock of the 4th of May, the Thirty-ninth hears that ever significant command, "Forward, March!" the Second Corps, under the lead of Hancock the Superb, is nearing Ely's Ford in its all night's march; and the ever-vigilant Sixth Corps, under glorious "Uncle John" Sedgwick, is only awaiting the advance of our Fifth Corps, led by Warren, around whose head must ever wreathe the halo of Little Round Top, before following to take position at our right in the forthcoming battle-line.

JOHN C. ROBINSON
B'v't Major-General
Second Div. Fifth Corps

GOVERNEUR K. WARREN
Major-General
Fifth Corps

PETER LYLE
B'v't Brig.-General
First Brig., Second Div. Fifth Corps

THE WILDERNESS

At first our own course is northward, toward Culpeper, then we bear off to the right, passing the headquarters of the Sixth Corps, and those of the Army of the Potomac skirting the base of Pony Mountain and on to Germanna, remembered well in our Mine Run campaign. Though nominally, for several days a part of the Fifth Corps, we do not actually meet any part of the Corps itself till just before reaching the ford. We cross the river at about 11 a. m., nowhere encountering any opposition from the enemy, who evidently is endeavoring to ascertain what Grant's objective may be, catching up with the other portions of the Corps late in the afternoon. After an arduous march of considerably more than twenty miles, burdened by heavy knapsacks, filled in winter quarters, our division bivouaced near the Wilderness Tavern.[] From this point the almost countless campfires of our army could be seen, always an impressive sight, and never were the soldiers of the Potomac Army in a more impressible mood than after their long period in winter quarters. Of the troop thus in bivouac, Lieut. Porter of Company A wrote, "The men were in the best of spirits. They believed that the supreme effort to bring the rebellion to a close was being made. There were enthusiasm and determination in the minds of everyone." A year ago the word "Wilderness" was frequently heard as the events of Chancellorsville were discussed and now it is to gain even wider mention; it seems a name quite out of place in the midst of the Old Dominion, not so far from the very first settlements in British North America.

General Morris Schaff in his story of the great battle says this of the section, "What is known as the Wilderness begins near Orange Court House on the west and extends almost to Fredericksburg, twenty-five or thirty miles to the east. Its northern bounds are the Rapidan and the Rappahannock and, owing to the winding channels, its width is somewhat irregular. At Spottsylvania, its extreme southern limit, it is some ten miles wide." Considerably more than a hundred years before, there were extensive iron mines worked in this region under the directions of Alexander Spottswood, then governor of Virginia. To feed the furnaces the section was quite denuded of trees and the irregular growth of subsequent years, upon the thin soil, of low-limbed and scraggy pines, stiff and bristling chinkapins, scrub-oaks and hazel bushes gave rise to the appellation so often applied. Hooker and Chancellorsville are already involved in memories of the region and coming days will give equal associations with Grant and Meade, while the Confederates, remembering that within its mazes their own shots killed their peerless leader, Jackson, ere many hours have passed will lament a similar misfortune to Longstreet.

Within this tangled thicket, artillery will be of no avail and the vast array of thunderers will stand silent as artillerymen hear the roar of musketry; cavalry

will be equally out of the question, but within firing distance more than
two hundred thousand men will consume vast quantities of
gunpowder in their efforts to destroy each other. It is generally understood
that General Grant did not expect an encounter with Lee within the
Wilderness itself, as is evident in Meade's orders to Hancock and the Second
Corps; indeed on the 5th the latter was recalled from Chancellorsville to the
Brock Road at the left of the Fifth Corps, the Confederates having displayed
a disposition to attack much earlier than the Union Commanders had
thought probable; how Sedgwick and the Sixth Corps held the Union right,
Warren and his Fifth the centre and Hancock with the Second were at the
left are figures from the past well remembered by participant and student.
While every movement of the Union Army has a southern tendency, a
disposition to get nearer to Richmond, yet in the Wilderness all of the
fighting was along a north and south line, the enemy exhibiting an
unwillingness to be outflanked as easily as the new leader of the Potomac
Army had evidently expected.

In the morning of the 5th of May, General Richard S. Ewell commands the
Confederate left with "Stonewall" Jackson's old army or what may be left of
it; next to him, at his right, is A. P. Hill with the divisions of Wilcox, Heth,
Scales and Lane; Longstreet has not arrived as yet, the morning finding him
as far away as Gordonville, but he is making all the speed possible towards
the scene of conflict, and when he arrives his station will be on the rebel
right, his lieutenants being Anderson, Mahone, Wofford and Davis. The
intricacies of this jungle-infested region are much better known to the
Southern soldiers than to those from the North, and this knowledge is a full
compensation for any disparity in numbers known to exist. Burnside and the
Ninth Corps of the Federal forces are just crossing the Rapidan after a forced
march from Rappahannock Station and when they reach the battle line, it
will be to occupy some of the thinly covered interval between Warren and
Hancock. All of the amenities of the long winter months are now forgotten,
and war to the death is confronting every combatant, whether in blue or gray.

In coming days, these men will recount the events of May, 1864, and while
the roar of musketry will play a veritable diapason of war for them, they will
not forget how readily they dropped the musket and, grasping axe or shovel,
felled the trees and, weaving them into earth-covered breastworks,
interposed thus much protection from the cruel missiles of the enemy. If the
survivors of the Potomac Army in the battle summer had chosen to wear
subsequently as under-guards or supports of their respective Corps-badges,
whether, trefoil, Greek or Maltese Cross or shield, the semblance of musket
and shovel crossed, no one would have questioned its oppositeness.
However averse men may have been to the regular use of pick and shovel,

experience soon told them that an old fence rail, a small sapling or a shovelful of earth might ward off a hostile bullet and, lacking the intrenching tools, they were known to throw up, in an incredibly brief time, serviceable defenses, using no more effective utensils than their bayonets, case-knives and tin plates. Future archaeologists, in the Wilderness region, will have difficulty in distinguishing between the works of the Eighteenth century miners and their soldier successors more than a hundred years later. Deeply scarred was the battle-riven surface of the Old Dominion and, centuries hence, poets and historians will wax as eloquent over some of these fiercely contested places as did Charles Dickens over the bloody field of Shrewsbury where "the stream ran red, the trodden earth became a quagmire and fertile spots marked the places where heaps of men and horses lay buried indiscriminately, enriching the ground." Macaulay, too, never wrote with more brilliant pen than when he described the poppy-strewn plain of Neerwinden, "fertilized with twenty thousand corpses."

May 5, '64 If Grant had known as definitely the mind of Lee as the latter appeared to divine the intentions of the Union General, the story of the Wilderness might have been very different. The orders for the morning of the 5th were for Warren to move to Parker's store, towards the southwest; Sedgwick was to follow Warren, ranging up at his right; Hancock with the Second Corps was to advance, also towards the southwest, his left to reach to Shady Grove Church. The enemy was discovered before Warren reached Parker's store and he was ordered to attack; Getty and the Second Division of the Sixth Corps were sent to defend Warren's left flank and Wright with the First Division of the Sixth Corps was ordered up to Warren's right, and at nine o'clock Hancock was ordered to come to the support of Getty, all this happening where Grant had expected, at least had hoped for, an unopposed passage. Instead of a retreating enemy, Warren opened the great battle of the Wilderness by an attack upon a foe ready for the fray; but let the Fifth Corps Commander tell his own story:—

"Set out according to orders, 6. a. m., towards Parker's store—Crawford, Wadsworth, Robinson; enemy reported close at hand in force, and when Crawford had nearly reached Parker's, Generals Meade and Grant arrived and determined to attack the force on the road near Griffin (Warren's right division). Wadsworth was gotten into line immediately on the left of Griffin with one brigade of Crawford, Robinson in support. We attacked with this force impetuously, carried the enemy's line, but being flanked by a whole division of the enemy were compelled to fall back to our first position, leaving two guns on the road between the lines that had been advanced to take advantage of the first success. The horses were shot and the guns removed between our lines. The attack failed because Wright's (Third) division of the Sixth Corps was unable on account of the woods to get up on our right flank and meet the division (Johnson's Ewell's Corps) that had flanked us. Wright became engaged some time afterward. We lost heavily in this attack, and the thick woods caused much confusion in our lines. The enemy did not pursue us in the least. We had encountered the whole of Ewell's Corps. The enemy that moved on past Parker's along the Plank Road was Hill's corps. General Getty's division of the Sixth Corps was sent to the intersection of the Brock Road to check the column, which it did, and General Hancock was ordered up from Todd's tavern, and also engaged Hill's corps. At this time I sent Wadsworth with his division and Baxter's (Second) Brigade (Second Division) to attack Hill's left flank as he engaged Hancock. It was late when this was done, but the attack produced considerable impression. Wadsworth's men slept on their arms where night overtook them. During the night, I sent instructions to Wadsworth to form in line northeast and southwest, and go straight through, and orders were given to attack next morning at 4.30 with the whole army, Burnside being expected up by that time to take part. With the rest of my force I prepared to attack Ewell in conjunction with a part of the Sixth Corps."

During the day, General Alexander Hays, commanding a brigade in the Second Corps was killed, a contemporary of Grant at West Point, he was one of the bravest of the brave; Generals Getty and Carroll were wounded, but remained on the field. The report of General Robinson, commanding the division, does not add any essentials to the report of General Warren. Unfortunately no report of our Brigade nor of the regiments composing it are found. Comrade Beck of Company C has this to say of his observations during the day:—

"Turned out at three o'clock and started at about light; after some delay found the rebels in force; the advance forces of our Corps drove the enemy from his first line of works; we were in reserve till about 12 m., when we were ordered into line-of-battle on the right of the Plank Road; dead and wounded are in evidence and there is hot work ahead. The Rebs have a strong position across a ravine; our artillery could not be placed in position; volley after volley was fired all day from all along, both left and right; we had to lay low, the balls whistled thick around us; at six o'clock were ordered to charge but were ordered back; it would have been madness, since the enemy had a cross fire on us. We lay in line-of-battle all night; many of our wounded could not be reached, and it was awful to hear their cries; when the stretcher-bearers tried to get them, the Rebs opened a battery on them."

Readers with memories will recall that, some time after Gettysburg, Longstreet was detached from the Army of ⸏May 5, '64⸎ Lee and sent to Georgia to help the Confederates whom Rosecrans was pressing hard;

sometime before this, early in 1863, two divisions of the Ninth Corps had been withdrawn from the Potomac and dispatched to the Department of the Ohio to aid in the campaign Burnside was then projecting. Both Confederates and Federals had returned to the East; Longstreet, most remote of the rebel array, had been striving to reach the field where his chief was struggling with the Union Army and, by one of the most wonderful coincidences in all history, Burnside and his following, save two divisions, were swinging into position between Warren and Hancock, only a few minutes later than Longstreet when the latter came up to the help of Hill. Grant in his Memoirs says that Meade wished the hour of attack on the 6th to be set at 6 a. m., an hour and a half later than the orders of the night of the 5th. "Deferring to his wishes as far as I was willing, the order was modified and 5 was fixed as the hour to move." So then we come to the 6th of May and a resumption of Warren's report:—

"At precisely five o'clock the fighting began. General Wadsworth I re-enforced with Colonel Kitching, 2400 strong (an independent brigade of the Fourth Division). He fought his way entirely across the Second Corps' front to the south side of the Plank Road, and wheeling round commenced driving them up the Plank Road toward Orange Court House. The accumulating force of the enemy staggered his advance, and the line became confused in the dense woods. In the very van of the fight, General Wadsworth was killed by a bullet through his head, and General Baxter was wounded. On our right, the enemy was found to be intrenched and but little impressions could be made. I then sent another brigade to sustain General Hancock, who had now two of my divisions and one of the Sixth Corps, and was defending himself from both Hill and Longstreet. They charged and took possession of a part of his line but were driven out again. Late in the evening, the enemy turned General Sedgwick's right very unexpectedly, and threw most of his line into confusion. I sent General Crawford at double-quick, and the line was restored to him.... In most respects, the result of the day's fighting was a drawn battle."

The report of General Robinson of the Second Division repeats some of Warren's statements, at the same time mentioning the fact that he accompanied General Baxter with the Second Brigade, which went with Wadsworth of the First Division on the 5th, when all hastened to the relief of Hancock; he names Colonel Lyle, of the Ninetieth Pennsylvania as commanding the First Brigade. He also mentions the death of his Assistant Inspector General, Lieut. Colonel David Allen, Jr., of the Twelfth Massachusetts on the 5th, and mentions the charge of the First Brigade (ours) late on the 5th, when the Ninetieth Pennsylvania suffered so severely. In the afternoon of the 6th, he was ordered to send another brigade to the support of Hancock, and later still one more which he accompanied, ranging them on the right of the Second Corps. There he ordered the building of rifle-pits, while he rode to Hancock's headquarters; the latter telling him that he is ordered to attack, and requesting Robinson to join in the assault, our Division Commander returned to his command and made ready to advance, awaiting orders. Two hours later, heavy firing was heard on his left and he was visited by General D. B. Birney who stated that the enemy had broken through our lines and that Hancock was cut off. Robinson at once faced his second line about and made ready to receive attacks on his left and rear. Before any further change was effected, General Birney was summoned by Hancock, and Robinson learned that, instead of breaking through, the enemy had been repulsed. It seems a little strange that the General does not mention the death of General Wadsworth, his fellow division commander, nor the wounding of Baxter of his own command. The taking off of Wadsworth was a great calamity, representing, as he did, the vast array of citizen soldiery. Far past the age of military duty, one of the wealthiest men in the Empire State, he nevertheless threw in his services and, eventually, his life for the cause he loved.[K]

May 6, '64 Returning to the meager records of our own Regiment, we glean certain facts, as that the Brigade was advanced in the morning to nearly its former position and that it was shortly withdrawn and sent to the extreme left on the plank-road, where breastworks were thrown up under active skirmishing. Also on this day, in the various changes of position, the Fifty-sixth, Fifty-seventh, Fifty-eighth and Fifty-ninth Massachusetts Regiments were met, all of them in the Ninth Army Corps, and all of them having officers largely drawn from the older organizations of the Bay State. Private Horton of "E" says, "We lay all night in the same place, the rebels keeping up the firing. We are relieved at 4 a. m. and go back and get breakfast. Travel around almost all day; go to the left where is heavy firing; throw up some rifle-pits." Beck of "C" in effect coincides with the foregoing, though he closes the day's account with the words, "Some of the hardest fighting on record; we build intrenchments on the side of the road and sleep in them through the night; troops were passing and repassing all of the evening; we are having nice warm weather for our operations." Lieutenant Dusseault of "H" relates the incident of a false alarm, while the men were lying along the road, between that and the breastworks:—"About midnight, while the boys were trying to get a little sleep, a great racket was heard not far away, and some in their alarm thought the whole rebel army was upon us. It proved to be a stampede of our own cattle, and they came bellowing down the space between the flanks and the works, and over the prostrate forms of our men. The choice language of the startled sleepers, when they came to understand the situation, added not a little to the tumult." During the day, in one of the several charges made upon us, "A rebel prisoner, apparently wounded and just able to crawl about, on hearing the shouts of his compatriots so near, and dreading to fall into their hands, much to our amusement, jumped up a well man and ran like a deer towards our rear."

Of the charge made in the afternoon of the 5th, this story is told in the history of the Ninetieth Pennsylvania whose Colonel, Peter Lyle, was in command of the Brigade, having succeeded Colonel Leonard of the Thirteenth Massachusetts:—

"The command was formed in line-of-battle and advanced until it reached the open ground, beyond which the enemy was intrenched. The line was established behind a slight rise of ground with small trees and bushes in front, the right of the Ninetieth being separated from the rest of the Brigade which it was impossible to occupy, being raked by the enemy's artillery. We lay in this position for some time when General Griffin,[L] in command of the First Division, rode up and commanded a charge. Colonel Lyle promptly led his regiment forward and, as soon as it had cleared the shrubbery in front, and emerged upon the open field rebel batteries opened upon it with grape and canister. The order was given to double-quick and with a shout it advanced within close range of the rebel lines. When Colonel Lyle discovered that he was unsupported, he gave the orders to about-face and what was left rallied around the colors and, under a fierce fire of infantry and artillery, returned to its original position.... Out of two hundred and fifty-one men, one hundred and twenty-four were killed, wounded or captured. From some misunderstanding or not having received the same peremptory orders from General Griffin that he gave the Ninetieth the rest of the brigade did not advance any distance, leaving the Regiment entirely alone in the charge.

"In fairness to our Regiment, it should be stated that the left wing heard the orders which sent the Ninetieth forward and, responding, suffered with it. The wonder is that, in the confusion of numbers, noise and misunderstood commands, more errors May 6, '64 rather than less, are not recorded. It is not to the discredit of Colonel Lyle that he is said to have shed tears over the calamity which befell his brave followers through no fault of his."

Colonel Peirson in a paper read before the Loyal Legion also has a fling at these same guns to the following effect:—

"We also left behind two guns which were on the turnpike in front of Warren's position, which were lost by Griffin on the 5th, and were between the two armies until we retired. A brigade of Robinson's division vainly attempted a charge to retake them, but the plain was swept by canister at 350 yards, and the brigade returned with heavy loss. It was understood that the sixth Corps was to join in this attempt but General Upton, whose brigade lay on the right of Robinson, refused to move, saying, 'It is madness.' So sensitive were the enemy about the matter, they fired on our stretcher-bearers, who advanced to bring in the wounded; and the wounded were not brought in, but lay all night calling for water and help, to the great distress of their comrades."

Two such days, as were the 5th and 6th of May in the Wilderness, evidently were as much as even Grant and Lee could endure. The former is said to have remarked to Meade on the 7th, "Joe Johnston would have retreated after two such days' punishment." The losses on both sides were frightful; there was little of the spectacular which will always characterize Gettysburg, but men, in all their mortal combats, never grappled in fiercer, more determined struggles than in those of the dense and tangled Wilderness. In his Memoirs, Grant says, "More desperate fighting has not been witnessed on this continent than that of the 5th and 6th of May," and he was at Shiloh and Chattanooga; evidently the great Westerner was changing his mind as to the fighting qualities of Eastern armies. The Union force had lost 2,265 killed, 10,220 wounded, and 2,902 missing; an aggregate of 15,387. While Confederate data as to numbers are frequently questioned, the Medical and Surgical History of the War makes the Southern losses, 2,000 killed, 6,000 wounded and 3,400 missing; a total of 11,400. The Confederates also had lost Brigadier Generals Micah Jenkins and John M. Jones, both gallant officers, but their greatest personal loss was that of General Longstreet, grievously wounded on the 6th and immediately carried from the field. Thomas Nelson Page refers to the event as the fourth similar incident where, seemingly, the loss of one man ended the hope of rebel victory, as the deaths of A. S. Johnston at Shiloh, "Stonewall" Jackson at Chancellorsville, the wounding of "Joe" Johnston at Seven Pines and of Longstreet, "at the critical moment when victory hovered over his arms."

THE BATTLE OF THE WILDERNESS

By Channing Whittaker

Most of the Infantry fighting of the Wilderness, as is well known, occurred on May 5th and 6th, 1864, in almost impenetrable thickets of tangled woodland growth, a growth facilitated by warmth of climate, by a multitude of streamlets and by areas of morass. The Infantry line of battle may have been from five to seven or eight miles in length. General Grant said in his "Personal Memoirs," written just before his death, "More desperate fighting has not been witnessed on this continent than that of the 5th and 6th of May, 1864." The bloodiest battlefields of those two days were those of Caton's Run of May 5th and of the thicket bordered by the Brock and the Orange Plank Roads on May 5th and 6th. During the battle I was pretty completely occupied with what was occurring close about me and I had little knowledge of what was occurring beyond my individual eyesight. Since the war I have been too completely occupied by daily duties to seriously search the records to ascertain the contribution which the Thirty-ninth Massachusetts made to the battle as a whole. Since I received your letter I have tried to ascertain where the Regiment was and what it did with relation to the battle as a whole on those two days. It participated in the Battle of Caton's Run on May 5th and in that of the Brock and Plank Roads on May 6th, but because I am not at leisure and my sources of information are limited, I shall attempt no account of either battle as a whole.

It is only recently that I have learned of the trap which the Confederates had deliberately set for us on the morning of the 5th of May in the gully of the unwooded valley of Caton's Run, where, ambushed in the woods on the western edge, they awaited   May 5, '64   "with fingers on triggers" the initial charge of our brave men, under the orders of Grant and Meade and Warren, down the long unwooded slope, across the roughly shaped gully of a primeval forest stream and up the long and open slope beyond it; of the brutal and terrible carnage on the slopes and at and about the battery caught in the gully; and that here, where at about eight a. m. was killed Charles H. Wilson of Wrentham, Co. I, Eighteenth Massachusetts, the first Federal infantryman to fall in the campaign, were controlled and stayed the proud banners of 17,000 Confederates under Lee and Ewell, including those of Walker, commanding the famous Stonewall Brigade. The first assault in this murderous trap was made by Griffin's First Division of Warren's Fifth Corps, while our Brigade, the First of Robinson's Second Division of the Fifth Corps, was held in reserve in their rear.

What I remember of the Battle of the Wilderness after the lapse of almost fifty years is a story quickly told. Some of the things which I saw and experienced made an indelible impression upon my mind. Other events have been crowded out by intervening occurrences, and of them I have no memory.

I will now state all that I remember of what occurred within my own experience on the morning of May 5th, 1864. I suppose these things occurred during Griffin's assault through the gully, and while the Thirty-ninth was being held in reserve in Griffin's rear.

We were standing in line of battle in a grove of oaks, the largest of which were perhaps eight inches in diameter. I was in the front rank near the right of Company B. First Lieutenant Spear was in his usual place in the rear of the Company and a little to my left. Lieutenant Spear turned on his heel and momentarily vacated his place. Almost instantly a piece of a shell buried itself where he had stood. Occasional bullets passed over our heads and among the oaks. Captain W. W. Graham of Company B was at rest in front of the Company, leaning against an oak but not behind it. A raw recruit in the rear rank who had joined the Company at Mitchell's Station and who had not yet learned to await the word of command aimed his rifle at a venture and planted a bullet in Captain Graham's oak, close to his head. Orderly Sergeant Allison shook the recruit by the collar and threatened terrible things if he should fire again without orders.

I can not recall that I knew anything of Griffin's assault while it was in progress, or of the rout which followed it. I have since learned from General Robinson's report that at the close of Griffin's sanguinary assault, Griffin's Division was relieved by Robinson's First and Second Brigades, ours, the First, taking the line of battle.

I remember that the Regiment moved to a new position and that later in the day we were lying, faces down, on the grass covered slope of a ridge. Small pines branching from near the ground broke its surface. Erect, and close behind us, Lieutenant Colonel Peirson walked back and forth like a sentinel upon his beat, but with his eyes never off of his ready but prostrate men. Absolutely alert, in quiet and calm tones, he said to each restless one who sought a dangerous relief from his unbearable immobility, "That man in — — Company, lie down," or whatever would cause the man to safeguard himself. The minie balls continually showered the green pine needles and pitchy twigs upon us. No one was in such danger as the Lieutenant Colonel, but he ever walked back and forth, back and forth, speaking his words of friendly caution. Still later it was desired that we should lie nearer the top of the ridge. He said to Colonel Davis, "If you will stand here" (at the right of the line to be formed) "I will align the men on you." When we again stretched ourselves upon the slope our heads were close to its top. Later in the afternoon we were standing in line of battle on the top of the ridge. The line of battle of a Regiment on our left made an angle of less than 180 with our own. For a moment I had a clear, distinct view of its front brilliantly lighted by the rays of the declining sun. I saw Colonel "Dick" Coulter on his prancing horse in front of them. The vision though momentary was changeful, unsteady, as if the men were staggering, falling. Our Brigade charged down the western slope. A Battery was in the gully at the foot of the slope, and neither the Federals nor the Confederates could touch it. The Brigade did not reach the Battery but returned to the ridge. The cries of the wounded on the slope were heart breaking. They called for help, for water. I was told, "General Grant says, 'Let no well man risk himself for his companion. He will need the help of all well men to-morrow.'" There was a call for volunteers to act as skirmishers on the slope toward the battery. I volunteered without any personal request that I should do so. I was located some distance down the slope and walked back and forth upon a "beat," like a camp guard. Then I had a genuine surprise. While I walked and watched with fear in my heart, the sun not having yet gone down, Lieutenant Colonel Peirson came sauntering along the skirmish line as if he was enjoying a pleasurable stroll. He made some casual remark and, handing me his   May

6, '64   field glass, asked if I would enjoy seeking the battery through it. He left me after I had had abundant time to look, but all of the fear had gone and did not return. When I next saw the glass it had been ruined, smashed by a shell which had nearly taken the life of the Lieutenant Colonel at Spottsylvania. All night I walked back and forth on the slope.

When we took our position upon the Brock Road, volunteer skirmishers were again called for and I responded as before. I was placed perhaps three hundred feet in front of the Regiment in a typical Wilderness forest tangle. Here were hardwood trees several inches in diameter, and in an almost impenetrable mass between them were quickly grown hardwood saplings of the diameter of one's finger and perhaps twenty feet in height. These were in the beautiful, tender green, full foliage of May and often woven all through between their interlacing branches were strong, green, horse-briar vines in so high and dense a hedge that had a line of battle been in your front not twenty feet away you probably could not have seen it. My part was to watch the thicket in front of my post and to give warning of the first appearance of the enemy. My fear of the day before did not return. I had excellent opportunity to hear the rapidly detonating musketry on my left and front, varied by the deep bass of occasional artillery. As the firing quickened I could no longer distinguish intervals between the sounds. I heard only one clear, loud, inspiring, uplifting, musical sound punctuated by artillery.

Suddenly, upon my left and behind me all was commotion. The Sixteenth Maine on our left fired volley after volley toward the front. My regiment, the

Thirty-ninth Massachusetts, followed their lead. I threw myself upon my face until the fusilade had ceased. Then I lost no time in reaching the Regiment. I saw no wounded in our immediate front, but a number in butternut clothing crawled toward the Sixteenth Maine or lay prostrate in their front. One in particular, I remember, he was crawling upon his hands and knees toward the Sixteenth, while a large, red stream flowed from his throat as I had seen blood flow from the throat of a slaughtered pig.

I now saw that a wonderful change had occurred in front of the Thirty-ninth. A wide belt of the forest had disappeared. Three parallel lines of breastworks, with an abatis in their front, were undergoing construction along the Brock Road. Men without axes had felled large trees with hatchets, and saplings with knives. Bayonets instead of pickaxes had loosened the sun-baked Virginia clay and tin plates instead of shovels had transferred the soil. The trees, the saplings and the clay, under the direction of skilled mechanics and by the herculean efforts of determined and rapid workmen, had taken and were taking effective defensive shape. The moment the firing ceased the constructive, defensive work again began. I saw upon the Brock Road a mounted officer, riding and swinging his sword. I heard him say, "General Grant says, 'If you hold this place until night, the enemy must evacuate Petersburg and Richmond, is ours.'" I began to use my bayonet and tin plate with the rest in constructing breastworks, but the call for skirmishers soon came again and I went back to watch through the night and the following day for the first signs of another frontal attack, which happily did not come. Before we left this place I listened to the account of my messmate, George V. Shedd, who, as one of a squad, had passed on duty through a part of the woods where men wounded, dying and dead had been blistered, blackened and burned by ruthless forest fires.

I have learned since that on the morning of May 6th a Confederate engineer officer reported to General Longstreet that the extreme left of the Infantry of the Army and of the Second Corps was in the woods in front of the Brock Road and exposed. A flank attack by four Brigades was immediately made, following first the unfinished railroad bed where their march was practically unimpeded and then advancing north through the woods. Our men, who were cooking coffee, were completely surprised and routed, and this explains the confusion which prevailed along the Brock Road when we arrived a little later. The Brock Road was now almost in the grasp of Longstreet, who hoped to seize it and to "put the enemy back across the Rapidan before night." "Longstreet, followed by fresh Brigades at double-quick," began to follow up the victory when he and his staff were mistaken for Federal troops and fired upon by the Sixty-first Virginia of Mahone's Confederate Brigade. Longstreet was severely wounded. General Longstreet says, "I immediately made arrangements to follow up the successes gained and ordered an advance of all my troops for that purpose."

(Here the hand of our comrade ceased, for fatal illness came upon him ere his task was ended.—A. S. R.)

One of the saddest features of the Wilderness struggle was the fire kindled by exploding shells and which raged unchecked over much of the fighting area, enveloping in its destroying embrace with equal fury the blue and the

May 7, '64 gray, whether living or dead, and we can never know how many among the missing were thus ushered into eternity. In Northern burial grounds, no unusual sight is that of a cenotaph or memorial to the memory of a departed soldier whose body was cremated or burned beyond recognition in the Wilderness. Save for the industry displayed in the building of rifle-pits, and the fruitless rebel assault on the Sixth Corps at our right, the night connecting the 6th and 7th of May was a quiet one; both sides were weary to the pitch of exhaustion, and both had learned that breastworks had wonderfully preserving qualities and, while Sheridan makes something of a stir at our left, as far away as Todd's Tavern, the day is relatively a peaceful one. Very likely the respective heads of the two great armies are taking inventories of their losses and gain, if any of the latter were observable. Both leaders had suffered sufficiently in the Wilderness, yet each one is perfectly willing that the other should attack, and when Grant's tentative skirmish line fails to draw the men in gray from their intrenchments, the Union commander knows that the time for him to continue his march towards Richmond has come. There appears to be a general agreement among those keeping diaries that the Thirty-ninth, with the other regiments of the brigade remained in or near the intrenchments till well along in the afternoon, when it was withdrawn, and in the rear had the privilege of preparing something to eat. Davis, in his story of the Thirteenth Massachusetts, says fresh meat rations were drawn and cooked and coffee was boiled, a most grateful relief, if only a brief one.

Of this day General Warren says that the army took up defensive positions and spent the time getting together the several commands which had been detached to defend parts of the field in the varying emergencies of the previous days' battles. Of himself he remarks that he had received, on the 6th, eighteen orders to send reinforcements to other parts of the line. It is nine o'clock in the evening of the 7th that the Fifth Corps takes up its line of march towards the left. Men of other corps are seen asleep as we pass by, and it is no craven thought for us to wish that we might slumber also, but "Forward" is the word. Lieutenant Schaff, more than forty years later to produce one of the most remarkable battle descriptions ever given, his story of the Wilderness, an officer on Warren's staff, says this of the scene:—

"Here comes the head of Warren's Corps with banners afloat. What calm serenity, what unquenchable spirit are in the battle-flags! On they go. Good-by, old fields, deep woods, and lonesome roads. And murmuring runs, Wilderness, and Caton, you too farewell. The head of Warren's column has reached the Brook Road and is turning South. At once the men catch what it means. Oh, the Old Army of the Potomac is not retreating, and, in the dusky light, as Grant and Meade pass by, they give them high, ringing cheers.

"Now we are passing Hancock's lines and never, never shall I forget the scene. Dimly visible, but almost within reach of our horses, the gallant men of the Second Corps are resting against the charred parapets, from which they hurled Field. Here and there is a weird little fire, groups of mounted officers stand undistinguishable in the darkness, and up in the towering tree tops of the thick woods beyond the intrenchments, tongues of yellow flame are pulsing from dead limbs, lapping the face of night. All, all is deathly still. We pass on, cross the unfinished railway, then Poplar Run and then up a shouldered hill. Our horses are walking slowly. We are in dismal pine woods, the habitation of thousands of whippoorwills uttering their desolate notes unceasingly. Now and then a sabre clanks and close behind us the men are toiling on.

"It is midnight. Tood's Tavern is two or three miles away. Deep, deep is the silence. Jehovah reigns; Spottsylvania and Cold Harbor are waiting for us and here The Wilderness ends."

SPOTTSYLVANIA

Of this same day and evening, our own Colonel Peirson has also given a vivid picture; after quoting Grant's words to Colonel Theodore Wyman, sitting under a pine tree, May 7, '64 on the 7th, "To-night Lee will be retreating south" he says, in his Loyal Legion paper:—

"Lee did retreat south, but only for the purpose of intercepting the onward movement of Grant, and he retreated so rapidly that we found him at Spottsylvania when we emerged from The Wilderness. Nightfall of the 7th saw our whole army on the march for Spottsylvania—Warren leading with Robinson's division by the most direct route, which was by the Brock Road, via Todd's Tavern,—leaving on the field all our dead and wounded Grant remarked that if Lee thought he was going to stop to bury his dead he was mistaken, but a few days later he sent a cavalry force back with ambulances, who succeeded in saving some of the wounded men.... The 7th was hot and dusty, and as it was necessary in order to clear the roads of trains by daylight, the movement was discovered by the enemy. The Fifth Corps in the advance, preceded by cavalry and followed by the Second Corps, took the Brock Road. The Sixth Corps moved by the Plank and Turnpike roads via Chancellorsville, preceded by the train, and followed by the Ninth Corps, who were the rear guard.... The Fifth Corps, led by Robinson's division, marched all night and about six on the morning of the 8th emerged from the wilderness near Todd's Tavern, and after marching a mile or two came up with our cavalry, who, as evidenced by several dead cavalrymen by the roadside, had recently been engaged with the enemy."

General F. A. Walker, in his history of the Second Corps, accounts for the presence of the Confederates at Spottsylvania on the arrival of the Union army in a very interesting manner. He says that Lee, convinced of the intention on Grant's part of moving towards Fredericksburg, ordered Anderson, who had succeeded to Longstreet's position, to move in the morning of the 8th to Spottsylvania. We remember that the whole battle section had been overrun with fire and that it was still burning when the orders came. Anxious to escape its unpleasant nearness, he determined to set out in the evening of the 7th and so make a night-march of the fifteen miles intervening. By what Southern pietists might call this Providential procedure on the part of the Confederate leader, he got there ahead of Warren.

Resuming Colonel Peirson's excellent paper bearing on this campaign, we find him recording as follows:—

"As soon as the cavalry got out of the way Robinson's division at once deployed, with Lyle's brigade on the left and leading, the Maryland brigade (Third) coming upon his right, and Baxter's brigade (Second) supporting still further on the right. In this way they advanced, driving the skirmishers before them by and beyond Alsop's house, and, reaching a wooded knoll, reformed the line, which had become somewhat disordered, casting off their knapsacks in order to move more quickly, and because the heat made them almost unsupportable. Pushing forward again, they came in sight of a part of a light battery of the enemy, which was firing down the Brock Road, and breaking into a run nearly captured the two guns, driving them well to the rear. The leading brigade had now advanced some two miles since its deployment, and had reached a heavily wooded rise of ground, where they halted for a moment to get breath and some alignment; and having run much of the distance, had left the rest of the division far behind. The men were very much blown, and many had fallen from the way from sunstroke and fatigue. General Warren here rode up and, saying to General Robinson that his orders were to go to Spottsylvania Court House, ordered him forward. Robinson asked for time to get up his other brigades, but after a few moments of waiting Warren became impatient, and General Robinson ordered an immediate charge upon the enemy's line, then in plain sight behind some rude breastworks, saying, 'We must drive them from there, or they will get some artillery in position.'

"The enemy's line was formed on a ridge across the Brock Road, near its junction with a road leading to the Block House, and was protected by an incomplete breastwork, with small pine-trees felled for abatis and a rail fence parallel with the line to the front. The enemy was hard at work finishing their breastworks. They were two brigades of Kershaw's division of Longstreet's corps.

"Lyle's brigade, in which my regiment was, charged over 500 yards of open, badly gullied ground under a rapid fire from the enemy's muskets and from the artillery we had so nearly captured. The troops went over the rail fence, into the abatis, and up to within 30 feet of the works, getting shelter then from the hill and the felled pine trees. Here they lay to recover their wind, easily keeping down the fire of the enemy in their front, who fired hurriedly and aimlessly, and while waiting saw the   May 8, '64   Third Brigade (Marylanders) advancing gallantly across the field to their support. The latter, however, after getting halfway to the rebel works, broke under the enemy's fire from the right and retreated in confusion, General Robinson being shot in the knee while trying to rally them. The remaining brigade was too far to the right and rear to assist in this assault. Lyle's brigade, having rested these few minutes, started to go over the works, and would have gone over, but at this moment, discovering a fresh brigade of the enemy advancing in line of battle upon our left, I (a lieutenant-colonel, upon whom the command had devolved, so few were the men to reach this spot) reluctantly gave the order to retire, and the command fell back in some confusion, but reformed when clear of the flanking fire, and taking advantage of the accidents of ground checked the advance of the enemy. The sun was so hot, and the men so exhausted from the long run as well as from the five days and nights of fighting and marching, that this retreat, though disorderly, was exceedingly slow, and we lost heavily in consequence from the enemy's fire. My own experience was that, while wishing very much to run, I could only limp along, using my sword as a cane. My color-bearer (Cottrell) was shot by my side, and unheeding his appeal to save him, I could only pass the colors to the nearest man, and leave the brave fellow to die in a rebel prison. The flanking brigade of the enemy, which so nearly succeeded in surrounding us, was part of Longstreet's corps (now under command of General R. H. Anderson) and it was his line we had so nearly broken.... That Longstreet's corps had but just arrived at the line of our assault is evident from the incomplete nature of the breast works, and from the fact that they had no artillery in position. Had there been any support for the brigade which got up to the rebel works, the enemy's line would have been broken, and our army would have been between Lee's army and Richmond; but as we have seen the only supporting brigade was far behind, and the rest of the Fifth Corps not yet up....

"The delay in Robinson's movement caused by the cavalry was unfortunate, and gave rise to a good deal of feeling at the time. General Meade, who was always for giving the infantry a free foot, had sent orders to General Sheridan, on the night of the 7th, to have his cavalry out of the Brock Road, but Sheridan, not receiving them, obstructed the road with a brigade, and as the cavalry and infantry became unavoidably mixed up, this delayed the advance.... It is known that in an interview at this time, General Meade was very indignant with General Sheridan, until he learned from him personally that he had never received the orders to clear the road, when Meade frankly apologized for what must have been harsh censure. In this interview which was described to me by Colonel Theodore Lyman, who was present, General Sheridan, being much chagrined by the censure of his superior officer, stated there was no force worth speaking of in front of the advance of the Fifth Corps; but he seems to have withdrawn this view, when in his cooler moments he came to write his report. Perhaps the feeling which caused Warren's unjustifiable removal from the command of the Fifth Corps at Five Forks began here.... The advanced troops fell back to the line which had been taken up by the Fifth Corps, intrenched, and waited for the Sixth Corps to come up, which they did in the afternoon, going into position on Warren's left. Crawford's division of the Fifth Corps made an attack in the afternoon, but with little result beyond capturing some seventy prisoners and losing considerably in killed and wounded."

In the preceding pages General Peirson refers to the fact of the command of the Regiment devolving on himself; it might have been stated that Colonel Davis, a very large and stout man, though doing his best to lead his men whose pace was more than double-quick, was completely overcome by the heat and mounted upon one of the Rebel Battery horses, cut out by Milton F. Roberts of "C," was carried to the rear. Modesty no doubt influenced General Peirson not to state that he was, himself, hit by a portion of a buckshot-cartridge, three of the missiles lodging in his right arm or shoulder, his sword-cane giving place to the stalwart shoulders of Isaac H. Mitchell of "A." Two of the bits of lead were picked out by the surgeon, the other is there yet. The wound did not keep the resolute officer long from his post.

Here is the story as told by I. H. Mitchell, Company A, and transcribed by Channing Whittaker, Company B.:—

"It must have been very near to where the Johnnies were that Lieutenant Colonel Peirson received three buck-shot in his right arm above the elbow, on May 8th, 1864. It was after we had been ordered to fall back that I first saw him after he was wounded. He was conscious, but perfectly helpless. He was trying to get back. I took him right upon my shoulder and carried him quite a distance into and part way through the woods, where we May 8, '64 had formed line just before the last charge in which he was wounded.

I had carried him 100 yards sure, and was still carrying him to the rear, when we met a man with a horse who was looking for some officer. I told him that I had got to have the horse to carry the Lieutenant Colonel. He did not object, because he could not find his man, and the bullets were whistling about pretty thick at that time. He then led the horse and I held the Lieutenant Colonel on his back, while I walked by his side. We followed the general direction of those who were going to the rear. I was not sure whether we were going in the right direction, and fearing that we might get into the hands of the Johnnies, I stopped, took him from the horse and carried him a little distance from the road into the woods. If I remember rightly, I made some coffee for him there waiting perhaps two hours, before we could get a stretcher for him. While we were there General Robinson was carried by. He had been wounded and he was saying things. In the meantime they had established a division hospital in the rear, and I then hailed some stretchers bearers, who took the Lieutenant Colonel there and I returned to my place in the Regiment. He came back to the Regiment very soon and was in our next fight."

As the day advanced the other corps came into their respective positions, the Second being massed at Todd's Tavern, protecting the rear of the army and the Ninth was at the extreme Union left, and there was more or less fighting along the whole line at some time in the day. A melancholy train was that made up of ambulances and baggage wagons which on the 8th set out for Fredericksburg, bearing 12,000 wounded men, thence via Belle Plain Landing and the Potomac to be distributed to the great hospitals of Washington and points further North. Sheridan and his troopers also received orders to set out upon their famous raid which would flank Lee's army, reach the outer defenses of Richmond, slay J. E. B. Stuart, the most remarkable cavalryman of the Confederacy, and leave a gruesome token of its venturesome trip by a trail of decaying horseflesh and freshly made graves for considerably more than a hundred and fifty miles. The magnitude of this adventure, which began Monday morning, May 9th, may be seen when we know that it comprised 10,000 horsemen, riding in fours and well closed up, yet constituting a column thirteen miles long requiring, according to a rebel authority, four hours at a brisk pace to pass a given point; what an eye opener such a force must have been to the Confederates at home, who had little notion of the resources of the North. Rejoining the Federal army at Chesterfield Station, on the 25th, its results were summed up in having deprived Lee's forces of their "Eyes and Ears" (cavalry) since all of the mounted rebels started in pursuit, as soon as the move was understood; it had damaged Lee's communications, liberated nearly four hundred Union prisoners, destroyed an immense quantity of supplies, killed the leader of his cavalry, saved the Union Government the subsistence of ten thousand horses and men for more than two weeks, perfected the morale of the cavalry corps and produced a moral effect of incalculable good to the Union cause.

Returning to the incident of the artillery referred to by Colonel Peirson in his paper, it is interesting to find the same affair recounted by one of the leading Confederates, General Fitzhugh Lee, in one of his war sketches. After alluding to the ubiquity of the cavalry and the work it had done in preparing the way for the arrival of R. H. Anderson's (Longstreet's) Corps, he says:—

"Major James Breathed, commanding my horse artillery, remained behind and by my order placed a single gun in position on a little knoll. We knew the enemy's infantry was marching in column through a piece of woods, and the object was to fire upon the head of the column, as it debouched, to give the idea that a further advance would again be contested, and to compel them to develop a line of battle with skirmishers thrown out, etc. The delay which it was hoped to occasion by such demonstration was desirable. Under Major Breathed's personal superintendence shells were thrown, and burst exactly in the head of the column as it debouched. The desired effect was obtained; the leading troops were scattered, and it was only with some difficulty a line of battle with skirmishers in its front was formed to continue the advance. I was sitting on my horse near Breathed, and directed him to withdraw his gun, but he was so much elated with his ┆ May 8, '64 ┆ success that he begged to be allowed to give the enemy some more rounds. He fired until their line got so close that you could hear them calling out: 'Surrender that gun, you rebel scoundrel.' Breathed's own horse had just been shot. The cannoneers jumped on their horses, expecting of course the gun to be captured, and retreated rapidly down the hill. Breathed was left alone. He limbered up the gun and jumped on the lead horse. It was shot from under him. Quick as lightning he drew his knife, cut the leaders out of the harness and sprang upon a swing or middle horse. It was also shot under him just as he was turning to get into the road. He then severed the harness of the swing horses, jumped upon one of the wheel horses, and again made a desperate attempt to save his gun. The ground was open between the piece and woods; the enemy had a full view of the exploit; and Breathed at last dashed off unharmed, miraculously escaping through a shower of bullets."

In confirmation of the foregoing, is the statement of Sergt. Wm. A. Mentzer, Company A, as follows: "After advancing about two and one-half miles we came to a piece of artillery on a knoll. While the Rebs fired at us, to our pleasure as well as surprise, they fired over our heads. We drove them from their position about half-a-mile, when they opened on us again. We in the front rank gave them a Yankee yell and charged for the gun. We shot one horse and drove away all the men but one, who dismounted, cut the traces of the dead horse, remounted in a hurry and got away with the gun just as we thought it was ours."

Battle scenes and incidents, we think, are indelibly impressed upon the memory. Sometimes they are; more often many of the prominent features disappear entirely, so that when the locality is revisited, difficulty is found in reconciling the past impressions with those of the present. Thus many of the Thirty-ninth who made that exhausting charge under fire, in the morning of the 8th of May, would find themselves at fault at many points, and would wonder at the changes in the face of nature, had they the opportunity to go over the route followed under such adverse circumstances. Channing Whittaker of "B," however, is sure he could recognize the spot where the Regiment reformed and momentarily rested; the place where Colonel Peirson and General Robinson were wounded; the road cut through the hill which Grant's army did not pass over on May 8th or 9th, the hillside on which he was wounded and where he spent the night after the fight; the point whence he saw three mounted Confederate Generals and where he saw Sergt. Major Conn, hacking away with his short Sergeant Major sword at a multitude of

Confederates who had set upon him and finally carried him away captive and, above all, just where Breathed's rebel battery was dislodged.

Of the exactions of this day, M. H. Mentzer, "A," says, "Many were exhausted but an officer begged us to cross over one field more. We had been advancing and under fire from early morning, but we started again, a very thin blue line, through a valley, up a rise, when a terrible hail of bullets met us; we lay down and hugged the dirt; a lull, and then distinctly from the enemy came the order, "Now rally —— North Carolina and give them H—ll!" Over they came, taking many prisoners from our little line. I started to run as others did but tripped and fell headlong down the hill lying still until they had pushed our boys well back, when I crawled a short distance to cover, several shells bursting in my path as I got away. Out of the way, covered with sweat, dirt and ashes, for the cinders of the Wilderness were yet on us, I fell asleep, and remained here till about four o'clock in the afternoon. I fell in with a Natick boy, Company I, who had a bullet hole in his wrist; I washed out the wound, tore a piece from my shirt and bandaged it as well as I could, washed his face and hands, made some coffee to cheer him up and then took him to a hospital on the field. Then I set out to find my Brigade and Regiment and found them at twilight; my brother, Sergt. Mentzer, had reported me as dead with a bullet-hole through my forehead; those who saw me trip and plunge forward must have mixed me up with someone that looked like me. It was in the work of this   May 8, '64   forenoon that General Robinson was wounded and Jeff. Cottrell, of "A," Color Sergeant, was wounded and was carried part way off the field by Charles Goodwin, only to die at last in a rebel prison. My brother, Sergt. W. A. Mentzer, then took the colors and carried them until Major Tremlett reorganized the color-guard."

J. H. Burnham also of "A," recalls, "The march down the Brock Road with the Fifth Corps from the Wilderness, the night of the 7th of May, and our running into Longstreet's corps, then under General Anderson. The rebels were behind, hastily erected breast works and were ready for us. We advanced across an open field and suffered much from the rifle fire. When near the works, I was hit in the abdomen. Throwing down my gun, I made my way back across the field, over the dead and dying, and lay down under a tree in front of a house. As this was early in the morning of the 8th, I don't think there were many other wounded men there then, but later others came. Sometime in the forenoon, a lady came out of the house and asked me if I was badly hurt. She also said that she was from New Jersey. It seems as though she said the place was the Laurel Hill farm, though I understand it is known in history as the Alsop farm. The next day came the ambulances, tents and other outfit of the Fifth Corps. I should like to go there some day and have a look at the place where I expected to give up my life. I carried the ball in my body for months and have it now. I never rejoined the Regiment."

We owe much to Colonel Peirson's recollections of the service of the Regiment, but in this affair at Alsop's he fails to recount a story remembered by McDonald of "B," who says that in the company was a tall Scotchman, Hunter by name, much inclined to stoop and, for this reason was frequently enjoined by the critical Lieut. Colonel to take "the position of a soldier." In the advance of this trying Sunday, Robert was stooping as usual when a bullet went through his cap. When the ball was over and the opportunity came, Hunter sought the officer and, holding up his headgear, remarked, "Now, look at that; if I had ta'en the position of a so'ger, be G-d, that ball wud a gone thru' my heed." R. W. Hall of "F" recites an interesting experience of this 8th of May, "I had penetrated the abatis in front of the Rebs and was unable to extricate myself in time, when our boys fell back, and with about one hundred and fifty others was taken prisoner, but I never saw the inside of a rebel prison, as Sheridan in his great raid overtook us toward evening of the following day at Beaver Dam Station on the Virginia Central Railroad, where we were waiting. How plainly I can see General Custer and another cavalryman in the lead, when they dashed down the road as we were about to take the train for Richmond. Of course we had to keep up with the cavalry during the raid and to dodge the Rebs who, in small squads, contested the way. Their General Stuart was killed or mortally wounded, May 11th, at the Yellow Tavern, in a very hot fight. After several days' rapid marching, we came out at Malvern Hill, on the James. The gunboats took us for Rebs and gave us several shots. City Point, on the other side of the river, was not so very far away and thence we ex-prisoners took a transport for Alexandria, where we were re-equipped and sent to the front as guard for a supply-train of the Ninth Corps. When Nelson and I reported for duty the surprise we gave our comrades may be imagined."

The 8th was a bloody day for the Thirty-ninth, the summary of losses revealing ninety-three killed, wounded and missing. Lieutenant Dusseault was wounded in the breast but an army button diverted the bullet. As he wrote in his diary, "I was within thirty feet of the enemy's works, and when I was hit, I was sure I was killed, as the force of the blow caused me to spin round and round like a top, and I fell to the ground. Finding I was not seriously hurt, I jumped up and joined in the retreat. When we May 8, '64 got back, we found Captain W. C. Kinsley of Company K in tears; 'Look at my company!' he cried, 'Only seven men left out of eighty-seven!' But he was assured that the woods were full of our men and that his would be in shortly. It proved to be so. We were not called on for the rest of the day, and that night we obtained some sleep."

During the closing hours of the 8th, there was digging for the Fifth Corps and the early hours of the 9th found the hard worked soldiers still using the shovel; the night and the following day showing no less than three distinct efforts in this direction for the Thirty-ninth, a record in which the stories of the Sixteenth Maine and Thirteenth Massachusetts accord. Of the day itself and the new positions of the several corps, Colonel Peirson remarks, "The 9th was another hot and dusty day, and the Fifth and Sixth Corps occupied it in pressing the enemy and developing his position, seeking points of assault. The enemy were still passing down during the morning the Parker's Store Road, in dangerous proximity to our right and rear, and Hancock's Second Corps was at 10 a. m. moved into position on Warren's right, making lines of battle along the crest commanding the valley of the Po, the artillery shelling the rebel trains which were in sight, causing them to take a more sheltered road." The new position of the opposing forces might be stated, briefly: from the northwest to the southeast, a distance of two miles, were Hancock and his Second Corps at the right, next to Warren and the Fifth; then Sedgwick with the Sixth; and at the extreme Union left, Burnside and the Ninth Corps. At the rebel right was Hill's Corps, now under Early; the extreme left was held by Longstreet's men, under Anderson; and the intermediate distance, including the famous Salient, was occupied by Ewell's Corps.

The event of the 9th which emphasized it in the annals of the campaign was the death of Sedgwick, Commander of the Sixth Corps. Since the fall of Reynolds at Gettysburg, no similar misfortune had befallen the army of equal importance; universally respected, all but idolized by his own men, his very presence at any time was worth whole brigades to the cause he loved. "While standing behind an outer line of works, personally superintending and directing, as was his custom, the posting of a battery of artillery at an angle which he regarded of great importance, he was shot through the head by a rebel sharpshooter, and died instantly. Never had such a gloom rested upon the whole army on account of the death of one man as came over it when the heavy tidings passed along the lines that General Sedgwick was killed." He was Connecticut born, West Point, 1837, having as classmates, Hooker, E. D. Townsend, and Wm. H. French, late Commander of the Third Corps, all of the Union Army; while his rebel fellows included Braxton Bragg, Pemberton of Vicksburg fame, and one might wonder whether Jubal Early, over at the rebel right, had a twinge of sadness over the summary taking off of the man who, in earlier times, had stood by his side on the West Point parade ground. Born in 1813, Sedgwick was not yet fifty-one years old when sought by the enemy's bullet.

Some of the besetments of army life and duty at this time are well set forth in the story that Lieutenant Dusseault, of Company H, tells of his efforts to replenish the supply of ammunition for the brigade: "That same night—and it was a dark one too—I was detailed to go back to the ordnance train for ammunition. I had sixty men from the five different regiments of our Brigade to help me. I was ordered to bring 25,000 rounds (twenty-five boxes). We had secured the requisite amount and were returning to the brigade in the thick darkness. As it took two men to carry a box, which was supported on a blanket between them, it was impossible to keep the men together, and as I did not know them, many of them dropped their burdens and ran away. When we got back to our camping place, we found that the brigade had moved on a mile and a half May 9, '64 further. When I came to my superior officer, I had but seven boxes to deliver to him. Rousing from his sleep, he ordered me to go back immediately and secure the rest, and then turned over and went to sleep again. It had to be done and at about two or three o'clock in the morning I reported the second time, not with the lost boxes, but with enough others that had been obtained in a way which I will not stop to explain."

May 10th adds another day to the long battle list of 1864; while a part of the Spottsylvania encounter, it bears to those who had a part, the sub-title of "Laurel Hill," the location being in the same vicinity as that of Sunday's fight at Alsop's Farm, possibly somewhat further towards the south. While there was fighting along the entire line, of that portion of the same in which we are directly interested, Swinton, in his history of the Army of the Potomac, says:—

"The point against which the attack was designed to be made was a hill held by the enemy in front of Warren's line. This was perhaps the most formidable point along the enemy's whole front. Its densely wooded crest was crowned by earthworks, while the approach, which was swept by artillery and musketry fire, was rendered more difficult and hazardous by a heavy growth of low cedars, mostly dead, the long bayonet-like branches of which, interlaced and pointing in all directions, presented an almost impassable barrier to the advance of a line of battle. The attack of this position had already been essayed during the day by troops of the Second and Fifth Corps, and with most unpromising results. When Hancock's divisions joined the Fifth, an assault was made by the troops of both corps at five o'clock; but it met a bloody repulse. The men struggled bravely against an impossible task, and even entered the enemy's breastworks at one or two points; but they soon wavered and fell back in confusion and great slaughter. Notwithstanding the disastrous upshot of this assault, the experience of which had taught the troops that the work assigned them was really hopeless, a second assault was ordered, an hour after the failure of the first. The repulse of this was even more complete than that of the former effort. The loss in the two attacks was between five and six thousand, while it is doubtful whether the enemy lost as many hundreds. Among the killed was Brigadier General Rice[M] of the Fifth Corps, distinguished for his intrepid bearing on many fields."

This was the day, when at the left of the Fifth Corps a portion of the Sixth was more successful, yet even its fruits were not held. General Emory Upton of the First Division, Second Brigade, in a vigorous charge carried the enemy's first line of intrenchments, capturing nine hundred prisoners and several guns. This attack, however, was unsupported and the advantage could not be maintained, so that at nightfall Upton withdrew and the captured guns were left behind. General Meade ascribed the failure of the movement to the lack of expected support from Mott's Division of the Second Corps on his left. The reports of Generals Meade and Warren add nothing to the foregoing while Lieutenant Colonel Peirson particularizes as follows:—

"The ground in front of the Laurel Hill position was swept by the enemy's artillery, and our men suffered severely from it. In our own Regiment, we lost several men, killed by the falling limbs of the huge pine trees cut off by the enemy's artillery fire. One of our men was pinned to the ground by one of these limbs, so near to the enemy's line, that, when we retreated, as we did upon receiving a terrific musketry fire at point blank range, he was the only one who saw that after the volley the enemy ran as fast as we did, but in the opposite direction. They soon returned, however, and captured the observer. At some points our troops even entered the breastworks, but the men though brave were easily discouraged, and the long continued strain and fatigue told upon their spirit; and while they would defend their position to the May 10, '64 last, or retire in the face of heavy odds with the utmost coolness, the fact remains that the men of the Second and Fifth Corps were not as ambitious on the 10th, as they had been on the 6th and 8th of May."

While the Ninth Corps, General Burnside, did no severe fighting on the 10th, the day nevertheless was significant in Bay State records through the death of General Thomas G. Stevenson, commanding the First Division of that Corps. Born in Boston, February 3, 1836, he early displayed a bent for military matters and at the outbreak of the Rebellion commanded a battalion of militia in Boston harbor. At the head of the Twenty-fourth Massachusetts Infantry, he accompanied the Burnside Expedition to North Carolina, winning laurels everywhere. On the return of Burnside from the Southwest, Stevenson who already had won his star, was made commander as above and like Rice and Sedgwick is supposed to have been the victim of a sharpshooter.

While Colonel Peirson has given us a deal of information concerning the beginning of the Battle Summer, he says nothing of the fact that he had, himself, a narrow escape from death. Colonel Theodore Lyman, in his diary, writes of a visit made by himself and General Peirson to these scenes, and has this to offer on his observations:—

"A few hundred yards to the right of where this attack was made, we visited the patch of pine woods, where, on the 10th, Peirson's brigade again advanced to the attack. The brigade advanced to within about one hundred yards of the works, and then began firing in the thick woods, being exposed to a tremendous artillery enfilade, whose marks still remained in the fallen timber. Peirson said he ordered his men to cease firing, finding few balls coming the other way, but got an order from the brigade commander to open again. Then Peirson was knocked senseless by a shell."

Concerning the injury to Colonel Peirson, Lieut. Dusseault of "H" has this version:—

"On the 10th of May at Laurel Hill, our men were lying flat upon the ground, under the enfilading fire of artillery from the left and the direct fire of musketry from the front. As an officer of Company H, I had been trying to get up into the line a private of that company who was lying forty or fifty yards behind it. I had tired of exposing myself in the endeavor and had left him and taken my place in the line. At about that time, Lieutenant Colonel Peirson, who was walking back and forth, erect, as was his custom, saw him and went back to get him up into his place. I went back to help him. We had succeeded in getting him up to within eight or ten feet of the line. The Lieutenant Colonel who was within two feet of me, had his sword in his hand, both arms extended, and was leaning forward a little, when a piece of a shell came between his arms and his body, ripped out the breast of his coat, smashed his field glasses in their case, and jammed the hilt of his sword. He doubled up, fell forward on his head, and then over sideways. Colonel Davis, who was standing eight or ten feet in our rear, asked, 'Lieutenant, is he dead?' and I answered, 'Yes.' I called two men of my company and told them to take him to the rear. They turned him over upon his back, one taking hold of him near the head, and the other by the feet. When they commenced to raise him, his eyes began to blink and he answered the question which had been asked three or four minutes earlier by Colonel Davis, saying, 'No. I guess it isn't much.' He was sent back to the hospital and was very sick there, but he rejoined the Regiment on the 9th of June. Lieutenant Colonel Peirson was strictly a temperance man, but he carried a flask of brandy for emergencies, and he had requested some of the officers to give some to him if he should be hurt. It happened that the shell cut off the lower half of the flask and it fell in front of Private Richardson of Company A. A few drops remained in the flask which Richardson immediately drained, saying, 'They are throwing good brandy at us.'"

Of this same event, one of the men of "A" writes, "One piece of shell wounded Colonel Peirson, ripping off a row of buttons from his coat. I picked them up and divided them with the boys. I have one left now. Salem Richardson got the bottom of the Colonel's brandy flask, which was shot away by the same bit of shell, and I wish you could have seen him empty it." The same incident is called up by S. H. Mitchell, also of Company A, whose members evidently were keeping their commander under observation. The flask was carried against an emergency, May 10, '64 when it might be of great utility. It offered no resistance whatever to the Confederate missile but Comrade Richardson always averred that the coming of the drink was most opportune. From the story of the Sixteenth Maine, it is learned that this day the brigade was temporarily assigned to the First Division, General Cutler commanding. The Second brigade was placed in the Third Division, under Crawford, and the Third was made independent to report directly to General Warren, these changes being induced, supposedly, on account of the heavy losses and the wounding of the commanding officer, General Robinson.

Possibly the doings of the 11th can be described no better than by copying the record as made at the time by John S. Beck, "Rested all day to-day, if you can call it rest, for we were in a mudhole, out of the range of Rebel shells. Our brigade looks small; drew rations; raining hard, everything wet through, no blankets or shelter tents. I should have been sick were it not for the excitement of battle. Our position here looks dubious, as we have to fight the enemy behind concealed breastworks and in dense woods. To-night we lay down on the wet ground with an old, wet, woolen blanket which I picked up." Considering that this rain was the first since crossing the Rapidan, it really was a comfort even if it did make some, for the time, unpleasantly wet. The 11th is noteworthy from another fact, viz., that it is on this day that Grant telegraphs to Washington the prominent features of the campaign thus far, that reinforcements would be encouraging, and that he purposes "to fight it out on this line, if it takes all summer."

Thursday, the 12th of May, is the day of the dread "Salient" or the "Bloody Angle" of Spottsylvania. Had our Regiment been with Barlow's men of the Second Corps, or with the Vermont Brigade of the Sixth, the mortality record of the Thirty-ninth might have been far different, though all participants in any portion of this bloody field have ever thought their losses severe enough. The vision of that First Division of the Second Corps, in the morning mists emerging from the woods at the Union left centre, and with determined rush, "a narrow front, but extending back as far as the eye could see," seeking the Confederate works, is one that memory needs no assistance in recalling.

Through wonderful good fortune for us, the artillery of the enemy had been withdrawn and the guns which might have cut wide swaths through that disordered mass of blue, were hastening back, arriving just in time to be captured, the assault resulting in the capture of General Edward Johnson's Division of Ewell's Corps, including the commander, with twenty pieces of artillery and thirty stands of colors. But this did not end the day. So furious was the foe over the loss of men, munitions and position, that the struggle for reinstatement became possibly the fiercest and most deadly of the entire war. Once at least, the bayonet became a weapon of real contact. Here it was that the large oak tree was actually cut down by bullets from both sides. The ground, at the margin of the works, was covered with piles of the dead, and for twenty hours the battle raged, until the wearied rebels withdrew, unable to retake the lines lost in the morning.

In this rapid survey, no mention is made of the Sixth and Ninth Corps, but each one accomplished the task assigned, nor was the Fifth by any means idle. Inferring from the forces pressing upon Hancock in his endeavor to hold advantage of the early morning, that the enemy must be withdrawing his right and left to assist his centre, both Burnside and Warren were ordered forward. Warren obeying, advanced at something after nine o'clock, but was repulsed, "for Longstreet's corps was holding its intrenchments in force." Of this in his report, Warren says:

"The enemy's direct and flank fire was too destructive. Lost very heavily. The enemy continuing to fire on the Second and Sixth Corps, I was compelled to withdraw Griffin's and Cutler's divisions (First and Fourth) and send them to the support where they again became engaged. My whole front was held by Crawford's Division (Third) and Kitching's and the Maryland Brigades, presenting a line of battle not as strong as a single line. The   May 12, '64   enemy made no serious attempt to force it. My divisions on the left were relieved during the night from their position, and returned to the right in the morning, having been kept awake nearly all the night, which was rainy."

A graphic picture of the work of the Brigade is painted by Adjutant Small of the Sixteenth Maine in his history of the Regiment, and a portion of it is reproduced here:

"The men, thoroughly exhausted, would lie at length on the cool, fresh earth, some of the timid ones hugging the bottom of the trench, painfully expressing the dread of something to come. And yet these timid ones, at the first rebel yell, would over and 'at them,' or draw bead on some venturesome Johnnie, and shout with derision if he was made to dodge. If they dropped him, a grim look of satisfaction, shaded with pity, passed over their dirty faces. The quiet was almost unbearable, the heat in the trenches intolerable, and rain, which commenced falling, was most welcome. Time dragged. We had not the slightest hint of what was developing. The rebels seemed very far off and trouble ominously near. From the right came an aide, and, quietly passing down the line of works, he dropped a word to this and that colonel; only a ripple, and all was again suspiciously still. 'What was it, Colonel?' asked the adjutant. The Colonel made no reply but simply pointed up the hill. Soon he took out his watch and looked anxiously to the right. Suddenly a commotion ran down the line, followed by the command, 'Attention! Forward, double quick!' On went the Brigade with a yell which was echoed by thousands of throats in front and was thrown back by the double columns in our rear. Down from the rebel right thundered shot and shell, making great gaps in our ranks, while on swept the Brigade, until suddenly loomed up in our front, three lines of works—literally a tier, one above another,— bristling with rifles ready aimed for our reception. There was lead enough to still every heart that was present, and yet, when sheets of flame shot out in our faces, scarcely a dozen of the Regiment were hit. Then men tore wildly at the abatis, and rushed on only to fall back or die. Again and again did the Brigade charge, and as often came those terrible sheets of flame in our faces, while solid shot and shell enfiladed our ranks. The crash which followed the fearful blaze swept away men, as the coming wind would sweep away the leaves from the laurel overhead.... Just as the last charge of ammunition was rammed home, relief came, when the Brigade retired to the works in the rear, to learn that it was not expected of the Brigade to carry the works, only to hold a strong force of the enemy, while Hancock carried the lines in his front, which were more favorably situated for a successful attack."

It was in the trying scenes of this exacting effort that Major Leavitt, of the Sixteenth, so endeared by his manly character, received the wound from which he died on the 30th instant in Washington. His was a nature too broad and brave to be confined to the limits of his own Regiment. "None knew him but to love him."

How the day seemed to a Company C man appears in his diary entry for the day: "Still damp, wet and rainy; the day opened with an advance of the Second Corps under Hancock, who carried the enemy's front line of breastworks and captured a division of the rebels and their General, Johnson. We were soon on the move to support our First Division in a general charge and were soon into it, hot and heavy. The enemy soon had another enfilading fire of grape and canister on us, and we could do nothing. Edward Ireland was killed by a solid shot and Henry Ireland was wounded in the arm. Soon after being withdrawn to the rear, we were sent to the left to support the Sixth Corps, and lay in a line of rifle-pits about two hours, when again we advanced through the woods and joined the Sixth Corps on the right, where we lay all the afternoon. We heard our folks pouring shells into the enemy from mortars. We turned in for the night, resting on our arms, wet through to the skin."

The night was uncomfortable enough and during its hours there was an alarm that the enemy was advancing, while the truth was that Johnny Reb was quite as tired as the Yankees. Even soldiers must rest sometime, and early in the morning of the 13th the division was withdrawn to the rear, and for a short time laid aside responsibility, but it was not a long rest, since those rifle-pits must be filled with someone, and all too soon "we were moved up to the right, into works along with the One Hundred and Forty-sixth New York. Nothing here but water and mud.

May 13, '64 Showery all day, though the men are in good spirits, notwithstanding. About 8 p. m. when we were beginning to arrange to stretch out for the night, orders came to move, and we fell in, following the rest of the corps to the left. The mud was dreadful, the night dark, we forded streams up to our knees, and the mud all the time was over shoes." Grant had not yet found the spot through which he could force his way, so the Fifth Corps once more essays the part of pioneers, and leads the move towards the inevitable left, seeking in vain for some point not bristling with rebel bayonets, or threatening with black throated cannon. Truly our Lieutenant General is finding out, not only how strenuous is the Eastern Union soldier, but his eyes are opening wide as to the resourcefulness of the Eastern Confederate and his eternal vigilance.

It is another flank movement, and the men of Warren's Corps are moving to Burnside's left with orders to assault with that Corps at four o'clock in the morning of the 14th. Very likely the difficulties of this night, with its more than Egyptian darkness, had not been reckoned upon by the Commander and the appointed hour found the would-be assailants a long way from the point of expected advance. The route was past the Landrum House to the Ny River, which had to be waded, and beyond the route did not follow any road, traversing the fields, and a track was cut through the woods. Then came a fog, so dense that not even the fires built to light the way could be seen. Men exhausted by the difficulties of the move and previous exactions fell asleep all along the way. The new locality was quite unknown and by daylight when the expected attack was to take place, only Griffin with his First Division, having only twelve hundred "fagged-out men" had arrived. It was seven o'clock before General Cutler got thirteen hundred of his men together. Naturally the four o'clock charge was not made.

Wright and the Sixth Corps moved still further to the left, but had to do some fighting to get just the position wanted. All observers, whether of Regiment or Brigade, agree that the day was wet and comparatively quiet, though the enemy's shells passed harmlessly over the heads of the tired men, many of whom slept the sleep of utter exhaustion, the waking ones thankful that the fuses in said shells were long enough to keep up their hissing until a considerable distance beyond us before bursting. In the mutations of fighting and moving about, all the regular contents of knapsacks had disappeared, the most of the men retaining, in addition to canteen and haversack, rubber blankets only; besides, rations were scarce, yet men were content to rest without food, so trying had been the ordeal of the preceding ten days. After all, the average Yankee is ever anxious to know just where he is, and several entries of the 14th are to the effect that the Regiment is near the Fredericksburg turnpike, about eight miles from the city itself and, from a mile and a half to two miles from Spottsylvania Court House. With only the canopy of the sky as a covering, a large part of the Thirty-ninth slept through the night of the 14th-15th.

The 15th is Sunday, and just a week away from the sad experience of Alsop's farm. These men of the First Brigade are fast becoming hardened veterans, and they have the privilege of greeting as such the comrades who had been home on re-enlistment furloughs and who, this day, got back again. There are many comparisons between the spic-and-span attire of the just-returned, and the "of-the-earth, earthy" apparel of men who, for ten long days and nights have fought and marched, at intervals hugging muddy mother-earth, till all semblance of cleanliness has disappeared, and dress parades have faded out of the recollections of all concerned. Then too the ravages of the hotly contested field have torn great gaps in the erstwhile well-filled ranks so that only squads of men constitute what have been long company lines. Some boys remark on the quiet of Sunday and think it properly kept; three days' rations are drawn, including fresh beef, and,　May 15, '64　with returning vitality and spirits, learning that the Eleventh Massachusetts Battery, in the Ninth Corps, is hard by, men of the Thirty-ninth make friendly visits to their acquaintances therein. Colonel Davis comes back to the Regiment to-day, looking much better than when he dropped out. Towards night, six o'clock, the troops are formed in line with expectation of an attack; four lines deep, our right rests on the top of a hill whence, as far as the eye can reach, armed men are seen awaiting the attack which is not made. It is a sight to remember!

Monday, the 16th, is also a quiet day for this campaign. Beginning foggy and damp, with the rising sun the mists clear away and it is very warm. On some sort of an alarm we are deployed, in line with the One Hundred and Seventh Pennsylvania, Colonel McCoy, that has just got back from its home trip on account of re-enlistment. On being recalled to our former station, we are set to work entrenching, introducing heavy timbers into our lines of works, three deep. About 9 p. m., we have to stop work, because the tools are needed elsewhere. Though there are showers in the evening, the moon finally shines through and, under her benign light, the Regiment sleeps. Nor does the record of the 17th differ essentially from that of yesterday. Foggy in the morning, then clearing and warm; picket or skirmish line duty for some and, about 4 p. m., our lines are moved to the right, nearer those of the Ninth Corps where there is more digging to render safe our position in case of attack. It is about this time that General Grant finds the army encumbered with an excess of artillery and, accordingly, sends back to Washington over a hundred guns; how the Johnnies would like to have some of these same weapons! All of them will come back again before the Petersburg siege is over.

Those who remember clearly the events of the 18th will agree that the most important one was the arrival, at 5 p. m., of the first mail since leaving camp at Mitchell's Station. What joy its contents gave those loyal hearts! Yet there were missives, in that coming of the postman, for faithful lovers whose eyes, many hours before, had closed in dreamless sleep, and in this life could never know how fondly they were remembered. The enemy, as if to make amends for continued quiet, began to shell the Ninth Corps just after our early breakfast, which we had soon after four o'clock. For some reason, General Warren wanted our Brigade nearer him, so at seven o'clock we were moved over towards the left and, under a shelling fire, lay till well along in the afternoon. Though there were six regiments in the Brigade it numbered, all told, less than a thousand men. About two o'clock, we returned to the right and, at eleven o'clock, reoccupied the works on which we had labored the night before. General Warren in his report for this day states that General Richard Coulter, commanding our Brigade, is severely wounded. This, too, is the day of the arrival at the Front of the First Massachusetts Heavy Artillery from its long service in the defenses of Washington. It is assigned to the Second Brigade, Third Division, Second Corps, though at present it is with the Second Brigade of General Robert O. Tyler's Artillery Division.

For the greater part of the Potomac Army, the 19th is a quiet day, though the men in their breastworks notice some sort of change on their left. Of the day, General Warren says, "All our forces took up position on my left. This brought out General Ewell's Corps, who attempted to turn our right. He was repulsed, etc.... Rained in afternoon." Regimental note-takers remark on the drawing of rations, including fresh beef, and the fierce attack on their right, well along in the afternoon and of the fact that their friends in the First Massachusetts Heavy Artillery had a severe experience.

The hot reception accorded the First Heavies is worthy of more than passing mention. Recruited to the maximum of such organizations, the Regiment was a wonder to the   May 18, '64   men who had been long in the field, for it numbered about 1800 men, as large as two brigades of those who had been in the thickest of the fray. The Confederates of Ewell's command, desirous of ascertaining whether the Union forces were moving and, incidentally, to capture if possible a tempting wagon train, in the afternoon of the 19th, undertook to steal around the Union right, bearing down thus about 5 p. m. along the Fredericksburg Pike on the line of Federal supplies. Whatever the expectations of the enemy, the point of attack was by no means unguarded, and in history, the engagement is known as that of the Heavies, since not only were our First men there, but the First Heavy of Maine was in line, and the Second, Seventh and Eighth of New York as well. Swinton says that the artillerists had not been in battle before, but under fire they displayed an audacity surpassing even that of the experienced troops. "In these murderous wood-fights, the veterans had learned to employ all of the Indian devices that afford shelter to the person; but these green battalions, unused to this kind of shelter-craft, pushed boldly on, firing furiously. Their loss was heavy, but the honor of the enemy's repulse belongs to them." Excellent evidence of the sturdiness and steadiness of the men, with crossed cannon on their caps, is found in the words of an old Confederate, spoken in 1901 at the dedication of the regimental monument on the scene of the fight, known in the annals of the First as Harris Farm:

"I saw your men march on this field, not deployed, but like soldiers on parade, take aim and fire a volley straight from the shoulder. You seemed to me the biggest men I had ever seen. You were so near that I noticed that all wore clean shirts. There was the most perfect discipline and indifference to danger I ever saw. It was the talk of our men."

In Fox's book of Regimental Losses, he puts the killed and mortally wounded of our friends, in this engagement, as one hundred and twenty men.

NORTH ANNA RIVER

All agree that the 20th was a quiet day, though signalized by the arrival of a mail with so many letters and papers that for a while the general appearance was one of an out-of-door reading expanse, rather than a vast army under fire from a vigilant foe, though the latter also appeared to be quite good natured, and the bands of both armies made the air resound with music. Even the evening following the torrid heat of the day is described as moonlit and beautiful. General Meade says of the 21st, 22nd and 23rd, that they were employed in moving the army from Spottsylvania Court House to the North Anna River, and General Warren states that his artillery began to move at 10 a. m. of the 21st, that the enemy did some artillery firing and that the men stood to arms. His headquarters set out at noon. Local observers chronicle some activity on the part of the foe with certain changes in regimental positions and the actual starting at about noon, leaving pickets on their stations to shift for themselves. They march through a part of the country hitherto untouched by Union soldiers, and the people are seemingly badly scared. The stop for the night is at Guinea Station, covering a distance, someone says, of eleven miles. Though the men turn out at three o'clock in the morning of Sunday, the 22nd, they do not advance until almost noon, and then under a hot sun they marched ten miles to a certain Bull's church (St. Margaret's) where are seen a number of Confederate prisoners, and it is said that Lee passed through in the morning. The worst feature of the march is the fact that it is made on empty stomachs, for the rations have not come up.

Of the country through which Grant and his soldiers are making another flank movement, many remarks are made because of its improved appearance over that of the region about Fredericksburg and northward, where war had been raging for three years, and it had become a veritable

May 22, '64 land of desolation. To the eyes of the soldiers it was a delightful

sight, and one writer in the Thirty-ninth pays it the highest compliment possible by saying, "It looks like New England," and the same chronicler says he can't bear to see the men foraging for pigs, hens and everything edible, somewhat forced thereto, on account of the wagons being so far behind, and the tender hearted fellow continues, much to the credit of his bringing up, "Many of the people are poor and they need all they have for their own keeping." In army annals, the 23rd is known as the day of the North Anna River. In his report, General Warren states:

"General Cutler's division leading got off promptly at 5. a. m. Reached forks, where one road goes to the ford and one to the bridge, at 9. a. m. Cavalry skirmishing a little in advance. A deserter says it is Rosser's cavalry; says there is artillery and infantry on the other side. Turned back to give that road to Hancock and got possession of a crossing at a mill at 1 p. m. By 3.10 p. m., General Griffin's division had nearly all forded, and at 3.10 p. m. bridge-train began to arrive. About 4.30, bridge (pontoon) was completed and last of General Cutler's division crossed. About 6 a. m. enemy assaulted us. My right gave way, and the artillery drove back the enemy. We repulsed them everywhere."

From internal sources, we learn that the Thirty-ninth was started out before 5 a. m., and marched rapidly towards the North Anna. Getting on the wrong road a halt was had for an hour, and certain portions of the Second Corps passed by, including the Tenth Massachusetts Battery, the old friends of Poolesville, and later we got the right road and reached Jericho Ford, though it was pretty deep for men of ordinary stature. However, the crossing had been effected by others and the pontoon bridge laid so that we went over dry shod. An attack was made upon us soon after reaching the south side, the fight continuing until after dark. The enemy had expected to drive us back to the steep banks of the river, and possibly into it, but they made the error of letting over too many of us, and our artillery was quite too effectual for them. The high banks of the North Anna, would have made matters very bad for us had not the rebel calculations miscarried. While there was some loss, one killed in Company H, and several wounded, the loss of the Confederates was considerable. We lay very quietly on our arms throughout the night, no lights being tolerated lest we might reveal our location to the foe.

While the Second Corps is doing considerable fighting on the Union left and though the Thirty-ninth shifts its position, relatively the 24th is a quiet day. The enemy has fallen back a mile or so and he is followed up, advantage being taken of the opportunity to tear up some long stretches of the railroad and to bend the rails around trees, thus rendering them quite useless for the future. The wagon train having crossed the river, rations for four days are distributed and, as one man states, "They are badly needed." Large numbers of the enemy keep coming in, and they appear, for the most part, very glad to reach a point where food is possible, even if the wagons are sometimes slow in reaching us. As a variant on the unusual quiet of the day, a heavy thunder storm imparts noise and moisture to the scene. It is on this day that the Ninth Corps is formally incorporated with the Army of the Potomac, General Burnside generously waiving any rights possessed by the priority of his commission over that of General Meade. General Warren speaks of spending all of the 25th in getting into position in front of the enemy's line and driving in his (the enemy's) light troops to his main force. "Found Hill's Corps intrenched between the North Anna and the Little River. Lost about one hundred and fifty men and officers during the day." During this day, some of the men had severe experience on the skirmish line, fully nine hours of tedious duty, with incessant firing along the line. A severe thunder shower marked this day also, and it was a wet earth upon which the men undertook at last to sleep.

May 25, '64

Again the flank movement had failed to discover an assailable point in the confederate lines. They had been thoroughly reconnoitered and "so great was the natural strength of the ground, so well were the intrenchments traversed, so tenacious was the Southern infantry, that it seemed impossible to produce any serious impression upon them. To have attacked the army of Northern Virginia across intrenchment of the kind found here, would have involved a useless slaughter." The Corps Commander reports for the 26th, "Hard rain in morning at seven o'clock. Remained in position all day. Rained in afternoon. At dark, began to recross the North Anna River at Quarles' Mills. Roads heavy and slippery with mud and approaches to stream bad. All not over till near daylight." The day proves to be more than usually wet and disagreeable, but in the forenoon many are surprised and pleased at the return of the men, captured on the 8th at Alsop's farm, and retaken by Custer the next day at Beaver Dam Station, who now rejoin the Regiment ready for duty.

Skirmishing continues all day and the pickets are active, yet there is no set engagement, the head officers having decided on still another movement towards the inevitable left. At nine o'clock in the evening, we move out of our works, under orders to not speak above a whisper, so that our departure may not be suspected and the end of the 26th of the month beholds us approaching the recrossing of the North Anna.

Early in the morning of the 27th, we recross the river and at 2.30 a. m., some distance beyond the stream must halt and draw three days' rations, which we are told must last us six. An hour later we are on the march and struggle on through characteristic Virginia mud, so thick and adhesive that many a footgear is left in its tenacious clutches. There is very little halting for us, since we are trying to interpose ourselves between Lee and Richmond, and we must move more rapidly than the latter since he, being on the arc of an inner circle, has a less distance to overcome than we. At eight o'clock comes a welcome halt for breakfast, the pause being protracted for rest until nearly noon, when we are up and off again, with very little cessation till seven in the evening, having marched almost continuously twenty-two hours and covering twenty-five miles. We had not had our clothes off in twenty-four days; not a man thought of washing his face, much less of taking a bath; nor is the strain over yet. In what condition men, gently reared, found themselves may be imagined. Camp is pitched near Mangohick Church. The 28th begins as early as four o'clock, and following breakfast the march is resumed at six, and the Pamunkey River is crossed at Newcastle. Halting some three miles beyond the river, breastworks are built, the men proclaiming the digging easy, and here we halt for the night, being about fifteen miles from Richmond, the nearest point to the confederate capital as yet reached by the Thirty-ninth.

The record for the 29th is one of marching, waiting and digging. Though ordered out at four o'clock in the morning with the further direction to be ready to start at five, we wait till nearly noon, in the meantime seeing the arrival of the Ninth Corps, after an all night's march. On starting we find great masses of troops assembled in every direction, our Regiment halting near the Fifth Corps' headquarters, where we remain till near seven o'clock, when we proceed to the left, some two and a half miles, where the Brigade throws up breastworks; the Thirty-ninth going on picket later, the night proving a quiet one. It would have been enjoyable if our haversacks had not been empty, the injunction to make our last rations hold out six days not having been found practicable. Though we find roses in full bloom considerably earlier than at home, this does not offset hungry stomachs. About 7 a. m., we retire from the picket line and join the other troops of our Corps, and after a short march of about one mile, we draw rations of fresh beef, which help out somewhat, and later still came the rations we so much needed. The wagons could not come up so   May 31, '64   one hundred men were detailed to go back to the train and bring the food with them, this being after a day given to efforts to repel attacks that did not seriously affect our Regiment. Beck of "E" Company records that this day the old Second Division got together again under the command of Brigadier General Henry H. Lockwood, though the fact is stated elsewhere as provisional.

COLD HARBOR

The sun of May 31st rose red and torrid and the day proved to be terribly hot. Fortunately the exegencies of the campaign did not require any considerable activity, and the men had the privilege of "sweltering" in the breastworks or of "lolling" under their shelter tents, just back of the trenches. General Warren records of the day that the skirmishers were pushed forward about one mile, without opposition, beyond Bethesda Church. While there is the sound of cannonading on both the right and left, the last day of May, so far as our Regiment is concerned, is the safest seen since crossing the Rapidan. The day is the prelude to the opening of the Cold Harbor fight, one which will cover June 1-12, and it closes with the Union forces extending nearly North and South. White House on the Pamunkey has become the new base of supplies and here the Eighteenth Corps, under General W. F. Smith, landed on the 30th, and by forced marches will be able to take position between the Fifth and Sixth Corps on the 1st of June. The section now harried by the opposing armies was the scene of active warfare two years ago, for Fair Oaks began on the 31st of May and to-morrow's Cold Harbor will begin to repeat the horrors of the Seven Days' Fight.

The efforts of Generals Grant and Meade to find an unguarded point through which the Union Army might interpose itself between Richmond and the Confederate Army have thus far proved unavailing. Whether active at the head of his forces or weak and ailing, borne along his line in a carriage, General Lee is still untiring in his watchfulness and, loyally supported by such lieutenants as Ewell, Hill, Early, Anderson and others, there is always a firm gray wall confronting the determined line in blue. Attempts to force it had been unsuccessful at the North Anna and Totopotomy and now, on McClellan's old battle fields, another fierce assault is to be made on the enemy's works, though the brunt of the charge will not come on the Fifth Corps this day; rather will the story be told by those who fought in the ranks of the Sixth and Eighteenth Corps, which had gained their places, some portions thereof, late in the afternoon, and after desperate fighting carried certain of the Confederate defences. Turning again to the words of General Warren, we learn that there was a movement against the rebel position which was intrenched with a large space of clear ground in front, swept by artillery. The Corps suffers a loss of two hundred killed and wounded and the line is extended four to five miles; the Corps is attacked in several places, quite severely on the right just before dark.

Lieutenant Dusseault of Company H has the following account of the night of the 31st of May and the 1st of June, showing very well what a portion of the Thirty-ninth was doing:—

"On the skirmish line, last night, I became completely exhausted. We were a mile and a half in advance of our main line; the sergeant with me was of the One Hundred and Fourth New York; I left him in charge and went to sleep. About midnight, when it was pitch dark, he roused me, with the words, 'They are coming! They are coming!' It seems that the enemy were marching in one, long, steady column towards our right. They were so near that we could hear their voices, and their tramping shook the earth where we lay. In the morning we found their earthworks empty, and we so reported at headquarters. June 1st was pleasant but hot, our skirmish line, a mile and a half from our main line, was in the woods and close up to the enemy. At daybreak when we found their works vacated, I reported to division officer of the picket, Major Pierce, of the Thirteenth Massachusetts, who ordered me to advance my line. But just as I was about to   May 31, '64   do so, we found the enemy were moving back to our left. They passed within three hundred feet of our picket line, thus putting us in a precarious position. Their flankers were within two hundred feet of us, and we did not dare to move in the hour or more that it took them to pass. There must have been five or six thousand of them. They finally halted and slipped into their old works. Just then, the New York Ninth Infantry, deployed as skirmishers advanced to relieve us, making so much noise that they drew the enemy's fire and several of the New York boys were killed. The rebels must have thought the whole Yankee line was advancing, for they shelled the entire woods severely. We lay as closely as possible, and when there was a lull in the firing, we would fall back and thus gradually regained the Regiment, and went to work at building breastworks. About 7 p. m., we moved to our left, into an open field, where we threw up a new line of works, making the eighteenth that we had started in this campaign. There was a terrible battle in progress at our left, lasting till 9 p. m., the Sixth and Eighteenth Corps losing heavily."

Though no part of the experience of the Fifth Corps, it is quite in place to state that the battle which was heard at the Union left was that of the Sixth and Eighteenth Corps in the beginning of the sanguinary contest which was to rage along the lines of blue and gray for almost two weeks and which, in these, the opening hours, marked the attempt of the above named bodies to dislodge the Confederate divisions of Hoke, Kershaw, Pickett and Field, reading from rebel right to left, resulting in partial success but at the cost of between two and three thousand men on our side. During the night of the 1st Hancock and his Second Corps were withdrawn from the Union right, and by dint of a very trying march were found at the extreme Union left in the morning of the 2d of June, yet not in time for the early charge which had been ordered for that day. The several corps are now in order from left to right, Second, Sixth, Eighteenth, Fifth and Ninth, with a considerable gap between the Eighteenth and Fifth, covered by a picket line only. Captain

Porter of the Thirty-ninth, in a paper read in 1881 before the Military Historical Society of Massachusetts, refers to this hiatus as an "interval over a most desolate piece of country, woody, rocky, and quite hilly." The great 3rd of June charge, that to which Grant in his Memoirs refers, saying, "I have always regretted that the last assault at Cold Harbor was ever made," this bloody scene, also, was at the Union left, the brunt being borne by the Second Corps, and in less degree only by the men of the Sixth and Eighteenth Corps. Of the Fifth Corps, Porter says, "Warren, who occupied a front of nearly four miles, was altogether too much extended to allow of his having any available force to assault with, and he was content with carrying the enemy's skirmish line on his front." The Ninth Corps attacked the foe with some success, pushing its lines well to the right of the enemy's left.

At noon of the 3rd, owing to the opinion of the several corps commanders that further assaults would prove futile, General Grant issued an order to the effect that there should be a suspension of assaults until further notice. Then followed many days of digging, applied to parallels and approaches and the making of reconnoisances, thus keeping the enemy in a state of apprehension, lest he should detach a portion of his forces to assist in the effort to head off General Hunter in the Shenandoah Valley. General Warren's account of the period gives very little of interest save that on the 4th, owing to the withdrawal of the enemy from the front of the Ninth Corps, the latter was moved around the Fifth to the space between the Fifth and the Eighteenth Corps. On the 5th Warren made a reconnoisance on Shady Grove road, and in the night withdrew to the rear, and was on the road all night. The 6th he devoted to "putting things in order"; the 7th, he sent Griffin's and Cutler's divisions to picket the Chickahominy, and held Ayers and Crawford to support Burnside; 8th, 9th and 10th, remained in camp; 11th, with all his corps, except Griffin and Cutler, to Moody's, south of railroad, preparatory to further movement; 12th, June 3, '64 Generals Grant and Meade reached his headquarters at 5.30 p. m. Corps started at 6 p. m. Reached vicinity of Long Bridge before midnight.

The notes made at the time by men of the Thirty-ninth consist largely of statements of moving to the right or left and of coming back to positions formerly occupied; of picketing and of sundry incidents, some of which are appended, though, in the fighting for which the period has such a bloody record, the Thirty-ninth bore a very small part, yet it played its assigned rôle well, at no time failing to do with alacrity whatever duty came in its way. While not actively engaged in the assault of the 3rd, as stated above, the men were all on the alert and anxiously expectant. On the 2nd General Lockwood, who had commanded the reorganized Second Division a few days, was relieved and ordered to Baltimore, there to await further orders. His methods were not to the liking of General Warren. The general trend of the army was towards the left, and in two installments the Corps marched on the 5th several miles, fetching up at midnight at Cold Harbor, near the fighting points of the 1st and 3rd days of the month, camping in the rear of the Second Corps. Here follow three days of relative peace and quiet, in which rations are drawn, cooked and consumed with relish and dispatch. "The quietest time since the 3rd of May" is the record of one observer, and another says, "It seems nice to be free from firing all the while, though the bugles keep us in touch with camp life." Baggage wagons get up on the 6th and officers, after picking out their valises are able to enjoy a change of linen and, on this day, is promulgated the order that our old brigade relations are changed and the whole organization is transferred to the Second Brigade of the Third Division, the latter being under the command of General S. W. Crawford while Colonel Lyle remains at the head of the Brigade. The day also marks a slicking up time, the camp being policed and the quartermaster deals out much needed wearing apparel. Our camp is not far from the headquarters of General Warren. Our change to the Third Division also changes the hue of our corps badge, the maltese cross, from white to blue.

On the 7th, B. H. Dow, the only man wounded at Mine Run, returns to his "C" Company. That an unusual degree of quiet prevailed in these days appears when, on the 9th, the wagons brought up a desk for the adjutant, the bands begin to play again, drilling is resumed and the Second Brigade has a dress parade, but the event of all which pleased the Thirty-ninth most was the return of Lieutenant Colonel Peirson, who had been absent after his wounding at Laurel Hill. One of the boys thus entered the incident in his diary: "We cheered him heartily; a brave man commands the respect of all; his patriotism cannot be questioned, when he has the privilege of a furlough of thirty days, but instead of taking it comes back to his Regiment."

In Charles E. Davis's history of the Thirteenth Massachusetts Infantry, we may read an excellent statement of the soldiers' feelings toward General Grant:—

"No matter what happened, we moved forward. No backward steps were taken—an experience to which the Army of the Potomac, hitherto, had been unused. The consequence was that the "Old Man," as General Grant was called, was always greeted with genuine enthusiasm, though he didn't seem to care very much for it. In his old blouse and hat he appeared like the rest of us,—ragged and dirty. Once when we passed him, he sat on a platform car, gnawing away on an old ham bone. As the boys cheered him, he gave the bone a flourish for a second, and then went on gnawing it as though we were miles away. It was wonderful how thoroughly this retiring, undemonstrative man had gained the confidence of the army. In spite of the hard work we had been having, the men were in good spirits, pleased that at last we were accomplishing something."

The 7th marks the departure from the corps of the Eighty-third New York, Ninth Militia of the Second Brigade, its terms of enlistment having expired, and it is to ⸢June 7, '64⸣ offset the going home of regiments, through reaching their end of service, that great numbers of recruits are coming in constantly. In the case of the Eighty-third, so severe has been its losses, it takes away only one hundred and fifty men. The ninth day gives the men a new exhibition, that of a correspondent of the Philadelphia Inquirer being escorted through the army by a Provost Marshal's guard, bearing on his back, a board labelled, "Libeller of the Press," on account of certain libellous letters he had written to his paper. However sad the man may have been, through his punishment, his plight affords the observers a deal of amusement. During these days mails arrive and depart and, after the complete rest of a few days, to the survivors of the May experience, life really seems to be worth living. With the 11th is associated the memory of reveillé at four o'clock, breakfast at six, and then a march which takes us across the York and Richmond Railroad at about 11 a. m. and a mile or so south of it we halt for dinner. The march ends near Bottom's Bridge on the Chickahominy River, camps being pitched on the very ground occupied by McClellan's troops two years before. The 12th is Sunday and so long has been the interval since religious services were held, some men are glad of the chance to hear a Christian Commission man preach; and the Thirty-ninth is inspected by Colonel Lyle, brigade commander. At 7 p. m. the line of march is once more taken up and we proceed some miles towards the east, halting at eleven o'clock for a rest and supper.

TOWARDS THE JAMES RIVER

The veteran soldiers who are participating in this southward movement, though they may not know the details that are in the minds of Grant and Meade, are well aware that the grand purpose announced in the Wilderness is still being developed and, that the "summer-long line" is that which they are following. The Lieutenant General, having found the way too effectually blocked via Cold Harbor as early as the 5th of June, when Warren's men were withdrawn and sent towards the left of the Union line, had determined to change his base of operations and, after crossing the James, to lay siege to Petersburg, and thus to capture the Capital of the Confederacy. The pause of the Fifth Corps for several days had given the men the necessary rest and recuperation for the lead they were to take in the new flank movement and now, just before midnight of the 12th of June, they are awaiting the completion of a pontoon bridge over which they may pass to the south side and so hold the way open for the other troops to follow. General Warren refers to the locality as Long Bridge, but the map which accompanies Humphreys' "Campaign of '64 and '65" has it as "Long's Bridge," but in either case, whether called for its length or some family resident near, the structure had disappeared through the ravages of war, and a temporary bridge becomes a necessity.

The Journal of the Fifth Corps Commander for this 13th of June has the following entry:—

"Our cavalry drove back the enemy's to New Market Cross Roads. Crawford's (Third) Division went to White Oak Swamp bridge to cover passage of trains and Second Corps. At 8 a. m. began to withdraw, bothered by McIntosh's (union) cavalry brigade, and only got as far as St. Mary's Church, though traveling nearly all night. Enemy did not follow."

Lieut. John H. Dusseault says:—

"On June 13, we resumed our march at 1 a. m., and crossed the Chickahominy near Long Bridge, on pontoons, just before daylight. There was some slight skirmishing. At 6 a. m., we marched for two hours, covering about two miles only, and formed in line of battle. We were now in White Oak Swamp, between the James River and the Chickahominy, and the skirmishing was lively. We were marching on a straight road and we could see a fort nearly a mile in front of us. They opened upon us from the fort, and the first shell struck the road before it reached our column. The men opened to the right and left, and June 13, '64 the shell ricocheted down between them. We then left the road and went into the fields and woods. If I remember correctly we went to the left of the road. Our Brigade advanced some ways in the direction of Richmond, which was perhaps seven or eight miles away, the balance of the division remaining in the rear as a support. We did some light skirmishing during the afternoon, and the enemy charged some dismounted cavalry, who were located upon our right, and drove them back some distance. Shortly after dark, somewhere between 8 and 9 p. m., all of the officers of the brigade were ordered up to Colonel Lyle's (the Brigade's) headquarters. The Colonel told us of the position which we were in, stating that we were nearly surrounded, and that an attempt would be made at about midnight to get out. He also told us to tell our men of our position, also that no orders above a whisper should be given, and, that if we heard so much as a tin dipper jingling upon a man's haversack, to cut it off. We were told to get what rest we could between then and midnight. At about midnight the line fell in, seemingly without orders, faced to the left, and marched through a field where some tall grain was growing, and the men, knowing our position and being anxious to get out, kept increasing their pace and rattling the grain, so that it was necessary to halt them and to start them again from time to time until we had cleared the grain field. The night was very dark and the darkness favored our escape. We started again at Charles City Court House, not far from the James. At this time the Second Corps was crossing the James. We then found that while we were making this demonstration toward the enemy and occupying their attention, Grant had been moving the chief part of the army across the peninsular, toward the James River, and Petersburg. In fact, when we arrived, the Ninth Corps had crossed and the Second Corps was crossing the James. We crossed the James on the 16th, on the transport General Howard and were landed upon the Petersburg side at 9 a. m. I was told by another officer that it was understood that it was necessary that some small portion of the army should make this demonstration and occupy the attention of the enemy while the chief part of it should be crossing to the Petersburg side of the James and it was thought to be our turn to take the risk which attended it. General Warren is said to have remarked that he never expected to see us again."

After dark, we were withdrawn and started on a march which involved the taking of a wrong road and the consequent loss of valuable time, passing St. Mary's Church and just before daybreak of the 14th halted on the road to Charles City Court House. Starting again at six, by ten o'clock we were near the place named for that unfortunate British King who lost both crown and head, the place showing plainly the effect of McClellan's presence two years before. Were it not for the Court House itself, a one-storied edifice with a porch, and a blacksmith shop the place would be scarcely more than a name, but some one remarks, "We must be getting somewhere for I can hear the steamers whistle on the James River." Had we been supplied with rations our pleasure at the prospect and the rest would have been greater, but our haversacks were quite empty. However, we could go to sleep, which we proceeded to do at the early hour of eight o'clock.

The 15th was not eventful save as it brought the long expected wagon train and rations galore. There was a complete filling of all receptacles with the necessities of army life, and after stuffing ourselves with hardtack and the other good things that those wagons carried we were in a mood to enjoy ourselves, though we couldn't help wishing that the mail would come, bringing news from the far-away homes in the North. With a sort of forewarning that exactions would be made upon our vigor and strength on the morrow, again we turned in early. Sure enough we were turned out at two o'clock in the morning of the 16th for a march of three miles to Wilcox's Wharf on the banks of the James and the sight of the glorious river and the banks, in many cases, crowned with the mansions of aristocratic Virginians. The entire country, robed in the brightest of green, was one to make an indelible impression on the memory. The Thirty-ninth crossed the river on the transports, "General Howard," "George Weems" and possibly others, and by 9 a. m. we were all on the southern side. Here we found the Seventh Massachusetts, an Old Colony regiment, just taking boat for home. A splendid fighting body of men, they had earned the long rest that was coming to them. The pause, when   June 16, '64   over the river, afforded an opportunity for a plunge into the waters of the classic James, a chance that thousands of the men embraced, the very first one since crossing the Rapidan, and many declared that in all their army experience they had found no place equal to it, certainly none that they enjoyed more.

Concerning this movement to the south of the James, a dispatch was sent from army headquarters to Washington as follows:—

"Our forces withdrew from within fifty yards of the enemy's entrenchments at Cold Harbor, made a flank movement of about fifty-five miles march, crossing the Chickahominy and James Rivers, the latter two thousand feet wide and eighty-four feet deep at the point of crossing, and surprised the enemy's rear at Petersburg."

PETERSBURG

The long-continued battle of Petersburg had already begun before we were in battle line. General Butler, on the other side of the Appomattox, on this Thursday morning through General Terry, had assaulted Port Walthall with the intention of interrupting the coming of rebel re-inforcements on the Richmond & Petersburg Railroad and, the night before, troops of the Eighteenth Corps, which had been with us at Cold Harbor, had attacked south of the river, and had there been a supporting force at hand, the second as well as the first line of works might have been carried. As troops of the Second Corps came up they were sent against the works and, during the night and the following day, the 16th, the contest continued along the line composed of the Eighteenth Corps on the right, the Second in the centre and the Ninth on the left. All this while we of the Fifth Corps were sporting in the waters of the James. Meanwhile other portions of the Fifth Corps had gone forward, and at four o'clock in the afternoon the Thirty-ninth with its neighbors started on the road to Petersburg. After covering some ten miles of the way, we halted at 10.30 p. m. for food and rest, the route having been over hills and through swamps, difficult at the best, all the more so at night.

It was early in the morning of the 17th when the march was resumed, and at 9 a. m. we halted in the rear of breastworks, our entire route having been enlivened by the sound of firing, more or less vigorous, indicating a resumption of the days at Spottsylvania and Cold Harbor. Moreover, Massachusetts men do not forget that it is the 17th of June, and noise they had grown to think a regular accompaniment of that illustrious date. We are at the Union left and massed in the rear of the Ninth Corps, under Burnside, and the duty of our Corps is to act as a support of the Ninth if needed. We are about two miles from Petersburg and from many points the city is plainly seen. The cupola of Dinwiddie County Court House will be a target for Union artillery during many coming months. Lying in the breastworks through the day and night, we were exposed to the missiles of the enemy; Lieut Wyman of "H" and Captain Willard Kinsley of "K" as well as others were wounded. Unless he could sleep in the direst confusion there was no closing of the eyelids during this first night in front of Petersburg. In this memorable siege, the 18th of June is a notable date, for then there was concerted action along the entire line, though not in such uniform time and order as General Meade desired. It was a bloody day in which a vigorous effort was made to force the rebel lines before the arrival of help from the Northward. This might have been done earlier in the day, but, before the advance could be made, re-inforcements had arrived to nearly, if not quite, equal the number of the Union soldiers, and General Meade's orders were to hold what had been gained and to fortify immediately. The casualties of the four days, 15th-18th, footed up nearly two thousand killed and more than eight thousand wounded, the charges of this 18th day ending assaults on intrenched positions. The work of the Fifth Corps is thus described by a war correspondent:

June 18, '64

"On the left of the Ninth was the Fifth Corps, in the following order of divisions: from right to left—Crawford (3), Griffin (1), Cutler (4), Ayers (2). At early morning the advance was made and the enemy's withdrawal discovered. The Corps then prepared for a new advance, meanwhile keeping up a fierce fire of infantry and artillery. At noon, simultaneously with the attack of the Second Corps, a determined and vigorous advance was made. The ground to be crossed was generally open and cultivated, slightly rolling, and here and there artificially prepared with abatis, as well as naturally defended by undergrowth. The advance was against the south side of the Norfolk Railroad, and was partially, but not fully successful. In the evening again, at the time of Mott's attack in the centre (when the First Maine Heavy Artillery was so badly cut up) Griffin's and Cutler's divisions once more assaulted with great vigor. But here as before the labor was lost. The enemy foiled all our desperate endeavors."

The advance of the First Brigade, Third Division, is made at daybreak and we find the enemy missing. We are passing over surface which was fighting ground yesterday and last night; encountering the dead in both blue and gray, a most gruesome sight, at the same time driving back the rebel skirmishers until we come in sight of the Confederate earthworks, when we halt and throw up works for our own protection. Even danger and death can not wipe out human or, at least, boyish nature. Near the brief halting place are mulberry trees, fairly black with luscious, well ripened fruit, and not even rebel riflemen can keep Yankee berry-pickers out of those tempting branches. We soon advance, however, across a field and towards a railroad-cut some distance ahead of us, and to reach it we have to run the risk of the foe's rifles and cannon, snugly entrenched beyond the cut. We make a rush for this cut and the tumbles that some of the men take in entering it are funny even in battle's din. Colonel Davis's well known avoirdupois gained such momentum in the rapid rush that halting on the brink was quite impossible, and he rolled rapidly down the declivity. There is skirmishing all day and an artillery duel in the afternoon. Just at dark, a rapid movement is made across a ravine and orders are quietly passed that when the Colonel's hat is raised on the point of his sword, we are to rush forward to the edge of a bank, so near and yet so far below the rebel works that they cannot depress their cannon sufficiently to hit us. Officers are summoned later to brigade headquarters where they are informed that there will be a night attack, but, for some reason, changes come in the programme and in a new position we again throw up breastworks. In an exposed condition, we lie in them through the night and are saluted in the morning of Sunday, the 19th, by the enemy's fire at closer range.

The 19th falls on Sunday, though the particular day of the week gives these soldiers very little concern, since each successive twenty-four-hours is only one day more of "smoke and roar and powder-stench" and of this particular interval, General Warren has only the words, "Remained in position. Loss about three hundred." If remaining in position brought such a record as this, what would it have been had there been another effort to advance? The night before had seen very vigorous work in the trenches and men tried to strengthen them against possible attack, and so close were the workman to each other and so emphatic their strokes, George A. Farrar of "E" was wounded in the knee by a pickaxe and was obliged to go to the hospital. Nothing in the world finds more ready and willing workers than the throwing up of breastworks that may be used for defense and, under the spur of hostile missiles, the laziest become most industrious. At such times there are no suggestions that the other fellow ought to do it, but everyone is doing something, if it is no more than loosening earth with a bayonet or case-knife and throwing up the results with a cup or tin-plate, hoping thus to stop a vagrant bullet. Continuous rattle of musketry recalls the noise of the Wilderness and, with the evident skill of the sharpshooters, it behooves everyone to lie low. Writes one poor fellow, somewhat discouraged,

June 19, '64 "When shall we get through this terrible campaign?" Another says, "The Thirty-ninth is about five hundred yards (others put the distance as low as eighty yards) from the Confederate works and our skirmishers are on a hillside, across a ravine. At nightfall, we begin on the works again." This, doubtless, is the point referred to by Captain Porter, years afterward, when at a reunion of the Regiment, he said, "our skirmishers were among the first to establish the line at what was afterward the Crater, blown up on the 30th of July, 1864, and that line was pushed nearest to the rebel line, not excepting that of Fort Stedman and Fort McGilvery, by twenty yards."

Of the 20th, an officer records, "We worked till two o'clock last night, and turned out at four this morning. The rebel sharpshooters are on the lookout for a man careless enough to show himself. I am twenty-four years old to-day." Another scribe in the same company enters these words, "Wish I were at home to-day for it is our boy's birthday," so closely does the absent soldier keep in heart and mind to the loved ones at the hearthstone. While there is a trend towards the west, General Griffin's Division (First) reaching the Jerusalem plank-road and the Second Corps crossing it, our portion of the Fifth Corps, except as a part of the Brigade moves off to the left to help fill the gap made by the withdrawal of Griffin, remains as before. The 21st varies little from yesterday, men keeping pretty closely to their places, the least exposure bringing attention from the enemy, and men are wounded in spite of all care to the contrary. One of Burnside's colored regiments is digging a traverse out to the picket line. Extreme vigilance continues into the night, through fear of an assault by the enemy, and at about 9 p. m., the most of the Regiment goes on picket. Picket duty on the 22nd requires vigilance, "Yank" and "Reb" exchange compliments whenever opportunity offers and Jonas P. Barden, Company A, is killed. Quite late in the evening, the Regiment is relieved and retires to its former location, the same being not remote from the spot which in a few weeks would be known as the "Crater," and somewhat further to the Union left, opposite prominencies will be called Forts Sedgwick and Mahone, or in army parlance, Forts "Hell and Damnation." It is on this day that the Second Corps suffers one of the severest set backs in its entire history, the enemy succeeding in getting at its left flank, in a manner unprecedented, and in carrying off four cannon and more than two thousand prisoners.

Everyone is learning caution, but there are mortalities still, as with S. B. Harris of "H" who is hit in the head and killed on the 23rd. It is fair to suppose that Union sharpshooters are just as vigilant as their opponents, and that Death visits, with no show of partiality, both blue and gray. As the stay in these advanced trenches has not savored at all of rest, any change seems desirable, hence orders to move early in the morning of the 24th are heard with pleasure and, before daylight, we are off to the left to take the places of Second Corps men who had gone still further to the left, while the Ninth Corps moves into our vacated places. One very careful observer states that we lost our way and had to back and fill, as it were, at one time coming near running into the enemy, who kept up an almost constant shelling during the change. There seems to be less activity among the sharpshooters, for which the soldiers are duly grateful. To-day the original members of the Twelfth Massachusetts, the Fletcher Webster Regiment, long in the Second Brigade of our Division, draw out of line and start for home. The recruits, re-enlisted and drafted men of the Twelfth are to become a part of the Thirty-ninth. The coming into our ranks of one hundred and twenty-five men from the returning Twelfth, is the crowning incident of the 25th. One hundred and six more men are nominally transferred, but they are absent on sick leave, in rebel prisons or elsewhere, and those received to-day, represent about all the real additions to come from our friends who, after three June 24, '64 years of arduous labor, are homeward bound. The new position of the Regiment is across the Petersburg & Norfolk Railroad and the depleted condition of the 39th, following the campaign, is evident from the fact that eighteen of the men from the Twelfth Regiment, added to those left in Company C of the Thirty-ninth, called for just forty three rations in the entire company.

It was not lack of excitement which prompted a certain Company A man to a prank which afforded him and his comrades a deal of pleasure, rather was it a desire for something out of the ordinary that, in the midst of this, the severest campaign in the progress of the war, suggested to him a variation. Taking pencil and paper, he wrote, "I should be happy to correspond with any young lady so disposed; address G. W. Cheney, Company A, 39th Regt., M. V. M., Second Brigade, Third Division, Fifth Army Corps, Army of the Potomac." Thinking the idea too good to be kept secret, he read it to the boys around the campfire who were delighted with the plan and he had to write another, couched thus, "I would be pleased to correspond with young ladies, 18 to 22, with view to matrimony." Both of the ads were sent to the Boston Herald and the writer thinks they were the first of the kind ever inserted there. Two weeks later, or after the ads had had time to circulate, the mail brought one hundred and six answers, representing every state then in the Union; long letters, short and pithy ones, some perfumed and embossed; no end of good advice, love, kisses, merry, sporting fun and blessings; it was understood that the Colonel's good wife was quite horrified at seeing the ad and there must have been some uxorious advice to Colonel Davis since, though the next mail had over two hundred letters for the advertisers, they were all destroyed on the pretext that there were no such persons in the Regiment as those addressed. This however did not prevent the enterprising young men doing extensive corresponding over their own names.

The 26th is a quiet day; the 27th has its alarms with prompt response but no attack. Long desired rain fell along towards night, but not enough to satisfy the overheated men and the thirsty earth; so near are pickets of the opposing armies, they could readily converse without raising their voices, but they have not, as yet, reached that degree of familiarity. The 28th, Tuesday, marks a change in the situation in that we move to the front and right and proceed to throw up a line of earthworks, stronger than those already in use with the expectation of thereby affording shelter for suddenly attacked pickets and to better resist any assault of the enemy. The month of June ends with the Corps stretched along the Petersburg line, with the Ninth and Eighteenth at the right and the Second and the Sixth at its left. By seeming common consent, pickets cease firing, though the heavy guns thunder away; evidently both Johnnie and Yankee would like a rest; after extremely hard work, the regimental rolls are got into shape for muster which is had on the 30th; another sign of semi-permanency is the coming up of some of the sutlers who are anxious to resume operations, especially in view of the possible coming of the paymaster. It is in these days that the 1st Massachusetts Heavy

Artillery, Second Corps, which received so severe a handling at Harris's Farm, May 19th, yet most manfully held its place, is once more encountered and the ravages of war were never more apparent than in the fact that only three hundred are reported present for duty out of eighteen hundred men who left the defenses in the month of May.

The first third of July, as far as the Thirty-ninth is concerned, is quite uneventful. The comparative quiet that the men are experiencing has become a necessity. The persistent bending of the bow, beginning at the Wilderness, is bringing expected results. The fire of conscious strength, so evident in the earlier encounters of the campaign, is nearly burned out and recent trials of courage and endurance have shown and, future struggles   July, '64   will exhibit, a lacking of that enthusiasm which characterized the early days of May. Human bodies cannot endure everything, their limitations are sooner or later determined and such is the case with these survivors of the terrible exactions so continuously made. General F. A. Walker says, "Men died of flesh wounds which, at another time, would merely have afforded a welcome excuse for a thirty days' sickness leave. The limit of human endurance had been reached." General Grant, in his Memoirs, writes of the situation after the assault on the 18th of June, "I now ordered the troops to be put under cover, and allowed some of the rest which they had so long needed." It is a protraction of this rest that our men are getting in earlier July. From the 1st to the 10th of the month, the diary of General Warren has no entry of greater importance than reference to the building of a redoubt or the development of some plan on paper and, though constant vigilance is evident, there are none of the exposure and tests characteristic of the Wilderness and Spottsylvania.

To supplement the somewhat stilted rations furnished by the commissary department, the sanitary commission is sending in a variety of vegetables, fresh and dried, as well as fruits that are most gratefully received by the men and they are working a great improvement in general health. In our Regiment, appearances begin to resemble those of winter quarters since roll calls, three times a day, are in order, falling-in with guns and equipments. Ground is cleared for inspection and those formal ordeals are had as of old, and guns have to be cleaned up accordingly; prayer-meetings also are resumed. The 4th, usually so noisy at home, is just the reverse in our particular locality, though away off to the right, Butler and Smith fire salutes. In the Fifth Corps, the impression apparently is that we have had noise enough of late. In the evening, the pickets on both sides celebrate a bit with cheers, perhaps in behalf of ancestors who, both North and South, fought for a common cause. The weather continues very hot and mutual forbearance permits the men to stretch their tents as awnings back of the earthworks into which they are ready to tumble instantly, should occasion arise. Heavy details are made of men for labor on a new fort in process of erection to the southwest of our position, to be called, at first, Fort Warren, but later to take the name of our Colonel who, all unconscious of the fact, is rapidly approaching the day of his departure. On the 7th of July the Third Division of the Sixth Corps is detached and, by way of the James and Chesapeake Bay, is sent to Baltimore to head off near Frederick, Maryland, the movement of General Early and his men on Washington. This Confederate officer had been ordered to leave the vicinity of Cold Harbor on the 13th of June, and to proceed towards the Shenandoah Valley for the purpose of making trouble for General David Hunter, who had been operating in that section, Lee evidently thinking that his lessened battle front could afford the withdrawal. A considerable battle followed on the 9th, at Monocacy Junction, where Lew Wallace with a force made up of local militia and certain Ohio one hundred days' men and the Third Division of the Sixth Corps, was able to hold the Confederates long enough to permit the arrival in Washington of the remaining two divisions of the Sixth, the same leaving City Point the night of the 9th, and to successfully repel the rebel assault upon Fort Stevens on the 12th. Considerable effort was necessary to persuade General Grant that any portion of the Confederate army was missing from his front, luckily he was convinced in time to send a sufficient force to Washington to destroy all of Early's expectations.

The comparative calm of the first third of July was rudely broken on the 11th. The day had begun much as usual and, from five o'clock in the morning till five-thirty in the afternoon, there was the regular round of camp and other duties when, for some unexplained reason, the July 11, '64 enemy began a fierce fire of artillery on our rations-train. As hitherto, nearly all of the shells exploded way back of our lines but one, and a man states distinctly in his diary, "the only one," struck close beside Colonel Davis and, exploding, wounded him so severely that he died very soon afterward, 7 p. m. Private Mentzer of "A," long years later, recalls the sad happening thus: "Streets, tents, stockades, properly aligned; camps, graded and drained; constant discipline, inspections, dress parades, deportment, all better than those of any other regiment I ever saw, tell me that Colonel Davis did his work thoroughly and well. He sat on a rustic seat or bench, talking with a friend (Asst. Surgeon of the Thirteenth), none other near, save a detail of pickets, of whom I was one, just reported at headquarters, when a shell burst and tore his body dreadfully, still he was the commander to the end."

Lieut. J. H. Dusseault, "H," describes the sad event thus:

"The first shot fired, which we were wont to call the five o'clock express, hit a tree about fifty feet in front of our lines, cutting it off some forty feet from the ground; the rebels were really shelling our baggage train, some distance in the rear. Hitting the tree deflected the shell so that it passed downward through the canopy of leaves, arranged for shade above the officers' quarters, and burst under the Colonel, who was sitting cross-legged on a rustic seat with Assistant Surgeon L. W. Hixon of the Thirteenth Massachusetts. Both men were thrown down and the lower part of Colonel Davis' body seemed completely torn to pieces. My own quarters being not more than ten feet away, I was able to see the missile as it passed downward, after striking the tree. I helped pull the Colonel into his pit. His mind was clear and I heard him converse with Lieut. Colonel Peirson to the purport that he would be colonel now. To this Colonel Peirson replied, 'Oh no! You are going to get out of this.' The wounded officer, however, insisted that it was all over with him and he gave certain directions to the Lieut. Colonel saying that he would like to have him recommend Capt. F. R. Kinsley to be Lieut. Colonel and, his passion for details being strong even in death, he named a member of the drum-corps, who had overstayed his leave of absence and wanted him attended to when he returned. He requested also that a letter he had just written to his wife should be mailed and that the circumstances of his death should be added. Dr. Hixon, proclaiming himself also wounded, said he was unable to attend to the dying officer and it is possible that the surgeon of the First Massachusetts Heavy Artillery was called in to help dress the wound. After this he was placed on a stretcher and William S. Sumner of "H" was one of the men who carried him to the rear. As the enemy was shelling the road, they felt obliged to carry him through the woods and the way being very rough, the officer suffering terribly said to the bearers, 'Men, I wish you would take the road, I hate to ask you to do so, but this is terrible.' He died about the time the hospital was reached. A veteran of the Thirteenth Regiment claims to have a piece of the shell which killed Colonel Davis."

At this very time Colonel Davis was president of a court martial at the headquarters of the Third Division and had been there earlier in the day but, as the business in hand was not in proper shape, the court did not convene and its president returned to his Regiment. Had it been in progress, the chances are that our colonel would not have passed out of life as he did. John S. Beck, "C," detailed as a clerk at the court martial, writes thus: "I did not think it was the last time I should ever see him.... I felt very badly about it, for he seemed like a father to me. The boys felt blue enough. I think it will be hard to fill his place. I turned in feeling very sad and downcast."[N]

As with Tennyson's Brook, "Men may come and men may go," but the war "goes on." The gallant officer, into whose care the dying colonel committed the Regiment, was fully equal to the task. A member of the famous Fourth Battalion, which served its period of volunteer duty in Fort Warren at the breaking out of the war entirely without compensation, he had been one of the first to volunteer in the Twentieth Massachusetts where he was first lieutenant and adjutant and, captured at Ball's Bluff, had experienced

July 11, '64 Richmond inhospitality. Then as a staff officer, he had seen the fierce Peninsula campaign along with Generals Dana and Sedgwick. An early selection of Governor Andrew, he was made second to Colonel Davis in the raising of the Thirty-ninth and we have grown pretty well acquainted with him during the preceding months. As close to the enemy at Laurel Hill as he well could be, he was severely wounded and he now takes his promotion with the good will and thorough loyalty of every officer and man under his command. Major Henry M. Tremlett who was still absent on detached service in Boston becomes lieutenant colonel, and Captain F. R. Kinsley of the Somerville Company, "E," succeeds Tremlett as major.

Were this history that of the entire war or even that of the Army of the Potomac, the story of the remaining days of July would occupy very little space, for the siege of Petersburg, actually beginning on the 15th of June, is to continue until the 2nd of April, '65, and may be characterized as an unbroken engagement of almost ten months' duration with occasional extra emphasis laid on this or that point along the battle line, many miles in extent. Away at the right is the Eighteenth Corps, holding the space from the Appomattox to the Ninth Corps which stretches out till its left joins the right of the Fifth, which in turn touches the right of the Second; this corps since the withdrawal of the Sixth for service in Maryland, in Washington and later in the valley of the Shenandoah, has become the extreme Union left, with its line refused towards the south, and west of the Jerusalem plank-road, only a fraction of the distance to be covered before the winter's stay is ended. Even now the enemy is making vigorous effort to defend the several railroads which connect Petersburg with the south, feeling certain that Grant and Meade will not long delay trying to cut off the city from its Weldon Railroad connections and, until that time arrives, there will be more digging than charging along the rival lines, though the exchange of sulphurous compliments will be so constant that cessation rather than continuance will arouse remark.

General Warren, who has his command well in hand, has no conspicuous statement for this period, and even some regimental historians pass over the interval with only a few and scattering remarks. It will be understood that the most diligent picket and camp duties are maintained all of the time, and very few if any idle days come to either commissioned officer or enlisted man from one week's end to another. Never was there a better illustration of eternal vigilance than that displayed by both sides in this long game of opposites; hence in our progress it will be unnecessary to mention more than the passing events, in the least out of the ordinary. Colonel Thomas F.

McCoy of the One hundred and Seventh Pennsylvania succeeds Colonel Davis as president of the court martial, while the body of the deceased officer, with his faithful steed and Chaplain French, starts July 12th on its long journey homeward. Many a member of the Regiment felt, if he did not so express himself, as did the writer who put these words in his diary, "I can't realize that he has really gone and will not be with us at the front again." Early in the morning of this day, the Regiment is aroused and at 2.30 a. m. moves into the large fort or redoubt, for some time in process of erection. Of this, General Warren makes mention, saying that he spent the day here, planning and cutting timber, etc. At daylight of the 13th, everyone goes to work with pick or shovel in making defensible the new fort. Here we are to remain till the middle of August. Named at first for the commander of the Fifth Corps, it will soon take the name of our late colonel. Covering about three acres of ground, it is capable of holding a brigade. Situated a mile or more below Petersburg, it is on the Jerusalem plank-road and the next fortification south of Sedgwick, the Fort "Hell" of rebel parlance. Lieutenant Dusseault says, "In building our fort, we dug a trench twenty feet wide and ten feet deep, and threw   July 13, '64   up the rampart on the inside. Thus there were eighteen or twenty feet of banking. The fort was made square with a diagonal through it. We had a magazine in it, and two wells were dug for a water supply. Besides our Brigade there was with us also the Ninth (Bigelow's) Battery, which had suffered so severely at Gettysburg."

The routine of duty, including at least three hours' work daily on the fortifications, continues to-day, and all day and all night, too, for that matter, since the stronghold must be one in fact as well as name, men being so detailed as to keep the dirt flying; a writer in the story of the Thirteenth Massachusetts Infantry says it took eight men to get one shovelful of dirt from the bottom of the ditch to the top of the work, the men standing in little nitches cut in the side of the bank and passing the earth from one to another. This day also marks the transferral of recruits and re-enlisted men of the Thirteenth Regiment, the time of this staunch companion on many a march and hard fought field having expired and the original members being about to withdraw for their joyful journey home, though the actual union of the one hundred remaining men of the Thirteenth and the Thirty-ninth does not take place till the 14th of July, the only noteworthy event of the day, unless mention is made of the withdrawal of the Second Corps from its western position and its encampment south of the Fifth Corps, thus leaving the Fifth at the extreme Union left. On the Fifteenth the camp ground is thoroughly policed and General Warren superintends the laying out of a camp for the men and pitching our tents, regular living seems probable for a time at least. It is related that, reviewing some of the work as already laid out, General Warren, who had been Meade's chief engineer, asked who had projected certain lines and, when a division commander was named, he sharply remarked, "General —— had better stick to his pills," and seizing a shovel worked off some of his indignation by making the dirt fly with his major general hands. The Masonic Lodge held its first meeting for many a day and voted to pay for the embalming of Colonel Davis' body, and the expenses incident to sending it home, also appointing a committee to look after the families of brother Masons killed in the campaign.

The passion or appetite for drink is well illustrated on the 17th in Lieut. Dusseault's effort to properly distribute eight canteens (twelve quarts) of whiskey among one hundred men, on police duty, the ration being one gill for each one but, for fear that the quantity might intoxicate them, he discreetly gave out one half a gill per man, thus retaining four canteens for a subsequent occasion. When he lay down at night he put the canteens under his head, but despite his care the canteens were stolen with no clue to the thieves, save the maudlin condition in which several men were found. There seemed to be no risk that men would not take to secure that which was worse than useless for them, an enemy to steal away their brains. Several days of continued routine of police, picket, drill and other features of camp life follow, but entirely agreeable after the exactions of May and June. Thursday, the 21st, the enemy varied the monotony by making an artillery demonstration against Fort Sedgwick, possibly lest its occupants should forget its nick name, "Hell." The cordial relations existing on picket are well illustrated by an incident related of the period where a Union soldier, crawling out carefully to reach his station, was more than surprised to hear in unmistakable Southern speech, the words, "Say, you Yank don't belong thar'; that's we uns place; you uns place's over thar," a bit of information that the Yank did not hesitate to avail himself of. Deserters are in constant evidence, all coming in ragged and hungry.

It was at Fort Davis that Corporal Dow of Company C got one of his first experiences on horseback. Captain Hutchins sent him to Colonel Peirson, one morning, in answer to the latter's request for a messenger to City Point.

On the Colonel's telling Dow that he was to ride July 21, '64 a horse to City Point, ten miles away, the poor Corporal stood aghast and avowed his utter ignorance of an equine, his vocation being that of a ship carpenter, saying, "I can tell you all about a boat, Colonel, but I know absolutely nothing about a horse." "Oh! That's nothing," replied the officer, "you can stick on and the horse you will ride is like a rocking chair." The animal that Colonel Peirson named was an exceedingly easy riding beast but, unfortunately, the same had been appropriated by an officer and ridden off on a somewhat questionable errand; to make a fuss about it would be to give the officer away, so Dow submitted to the caprice of the man in charge of the stable and went off mounted on the Adjutant's steed, notoriously the worst riding brute in the entire equine outfit. John Gilpin's condition after his ride to Ware and back was nothing compared to that of the Corporal when he returned; as he expressed it, if he had ridden a rail the entire twenty miles, with sledge hammers pounding the ends of the same, he could not have been more jolted and galled than he was at the end of his twenty miles. A whiskey ration was being distributed when he reached camp, and Dow remarked that he needed extensive application, both within and without. "I guess I've killed your horse or he has me," he remarked to the Adjutant as, walking very wide, he passed that officer. "I hope you have," said the officer, "for then I can get a better one." The steed really did die from the trip, and when the Colonel called for Dow again, luckily for him, the easy going beast was ready.

Lest we should forget that we are in a state of war with our Southern brethren, we are favored on the 24th and the 25th, late in the afternoon, with certain iron compliments, the rebels even shelling the picket line, a very unusual procedure, one shell entering the fort; as many of their missiles fail to explode, we conclude that they must be using a very poor grade of powder. The cannon opposite to us are manned by the Washington Artillery, that crack New Orleans organization whose batteries were found in all the great Confederate armies, east and west. Towards the end of the month, a greater degree of activity is apparent; the Second Corps moves out on the 26th and then returns the next day; on this same 27th, loads of ammunition are bought up and picket relations are less amicable than hitherto. We turn in July 29th, with orders to turn out at 2.30 the next morning; this we do on the 30th and the Fifth Corps moves a half mile or so to our right into trenches back of the Ninth, with the Second Corps similarly disposed at our right. As yet we do not know what a large part of the country is to learn soon, viz., that this 30th of July is to go down the annals of time as the day of the "Crater." For weeks, under the direction of Colonel Pleasants of the Forty-eighth Pennsylvania, his men have been digging an underground way, in front of Burnside's advanced lines, to a point beneath Elliott's or Pegrams' Salient, more than five hundred feet distant. It was finished on the 23rd and in it were soon placed 8,000 lbs. of powder. To divert the attention of the enemy, lest he might discover the undermining project, the Second Corps had been sent across the James, to assist the troops already there in a demonstration against Richmond, but when the mine was ready for exploding the corps was hastily called back. Pages have been written of the event, of the explosion, of the advance of troops, white and black, into the abyss caused by the eruption and of their sorry fate beneath the concentrated fire of the Confederates, under Mahone and his artillery, and the unkind words that for many a year were uttered concerning Burnside and his part in the well conceived though unfortunately consummated project. Many of our Bay State regiments are in the Ninth Corps and they perform with credit whatever duty falls to their lot.

We are not called upon for any part in the fight, though we have our share of earache at the terrific explosion and the artillery firing afterwards. July ends with the Fifth Corps back in July 29, '64 the same position as that held before the "Crater" episode, one of whose principal features was the practical demonstration that negro troops are much like those of other complexion and may be depended upon in an emergency.

Although August, 1864, is written deep in the hearts and memories of members of the Thirty-ninth, up to and beyond the middle of the month there is little to record except the regular round of camp life close to the enemy's lines, and the rumors that are ever afloat where many are assembled. The sending away of the Sixth Corps to the defense of Washington and the inauguration of the Shenandoah Valley campaign under Sheridan, whose only instructions, imparted to him by Grant at Monocacy, in that meeting of August 6th, are "Go in," making matters in the Petersburg Zone much more quiet than they would be otherwise. A southside view of the situation is not amiss and the words of T. N. Page, in his life of Lee, are appended:—

"Jefferson Davis has declared that the remainder of the Petersburg campaign is 'too sad to be patiently considered.' Locked in his fortifications, with Richmond hung like a millstone about his neck, while the South was cut off piecemeal from possibility of contributing to his support, Lee, faithful to his trust, and obedient to the laws, put aside whatever personal views he might have held and continued to handle the situation with supreme skill. Before that army had succumbed it had added to Grant's casualty list, from the time he crossed the James, another sixty-odd thousand men, thus doubling the ghastly record of his losses.... Grant seems to be the one firm, clear-headed, practical man in all of the muddle of conflicting ambitions and confused orders. 'This man Grant grows on me,' Mr. Lincoln had said a year or two before—'He fights.' It was the one solution of the problem—to fight and keep on, no matter at what cost, till the other side should be exhausted. Grant recognized it and acted on it. Happily for the Union cause, Grant was the commanding general of all of the armies of the Union. Unhappily for the Confederate cause, Lee had not been given similar power. As dependent as was the South on his genius, the military command was still reserved in the hands of the civil authorities. He could not even appoint his chief of staff."

Of the period between the Mine and the month of March, 1865, General Humphreys, in his story of the campaign, remarks on the movements of the Army of the Potomac and that of the James to the right and the left, resulting in the extension of our line of entrenchment in both directions, and causing a corresponding extension of the Confederate entrenchments on our left, and their occupation in stronger force of their entrenchments on the north bank of the James. Very likely these blazing, hot August days would have been blazing with gunpowder in the furthering of the investment of the Cockade City had not the departure of the Sixth Corps compelled the temporary suspension of the western project and a continuance of the strengthening of the works already built. So far, however, as anything akin to comfort beneath the midsummer sun, in the exposed earthworks was concerned, nothing of the sort was possible. Only when the king of day hid his shining face, during the hours of night, could the intensity of his heat be forgotten.

Still, time was passing, and every day marked the approach of the wind-up, so long and so devoutly prayed for. Regimental note takers were observing everything out of the ordinary, and Horton of "E" remarks, August 1st on a visit to the scene of the explosion, July 30, saying, "It is opposite the old brick house, where we were before coming here" and he also comments on the burial of the dead, while a flag of truce is up. Another, writing on the 2d, says, "Walked along the front of our Corps, everything is under ground, covered ways for teams and troops to pass out if the enemy is near, showing a vast amount of labor." Thursday, the 4th, was a Fast Day, appointed by the President, which was observed in Fort Davis by a suspension of fatigue duty and religious services at 6.30 conducted by the chaplains of the Sixteenth Maine, the One hundred and Fourth New York and the One Hundred and Seventh Pennsylvania. The day was not observed by all organizations, and along the line of the   Aug. 4, '64   Ninth Corps there was considerable firing.

The versatile accomplishments of Union soldiers are indicated in that on the 5th of August a member of Company H, suffering from toothache, sought out an ex-dentist in the One Hundred and Seventh Pennsylvania and had his aching molars filled; and the scarcity of proper material is also shown in that the substance, used for filling, was just ordinary lead, but it did the business. Who would suppose that, through all of the ups-and-downs of an exacting campaign the instruments, essential to such work would have been, carried and what a substitute for a dentist's chair, with its varied attachments, must have been the end of a log or an empty cracker box!

Almost every day brings one or more deserters from the rebel ranks, men who are convinced that the game is really lost and can see no pleasure or profit in the "last ditch" idea. They are invariably hungry, ragged and dirty. On the 9th, Fred. Glines of "E," a Somerville boy, visits the hospital of the Ninth Corps and there meets Professor John P. Marshall, a respected instructor in Tufts College, a most pleasant meeting for both parties. He also records the blowing up of an ordnance boat, lying at the wharf in City Point, receiving fixed ammunition. The incident is an item in the history of the war, whereby there were a great loss of life and destruction of property. All told, the value of property destroyed mounted into the millions and the number of lives lost was between sixty and seventy; one hundred and thirty were wounded; some battles had a smaller record. At the time the explosion was ascribed to the careless handling of the ammunition cases.[O]

In the night of the 10th-11th there was a little artillery play in the direction of Fort Davis, but it proved to be harmless. The 12th marks the second anniversary of the muster-in of Company E, the first one in the Regiment. This day also saw a new movement of the Second Corps across the James River, another blow to be struck at Deep Bottom, if practicable. Evidently Generals Grant and Meade thought the quiet period had lasted long enough, besides the Lieutenant General thought that the rebels had sent off three of their divisions to reinforce Early in the valley. The truth was that only Kershaw's had gone, and all the others were right on the spot, ready to receive callers or boarders, it was all the same thing, and the expedition was not as productive of results as the projectors had desired.

One scribe, on the 13th, writes, "Got paid off," and elsewhere mention is made of the proximity of sutlers who are ready to settle old scores and also to sell for cash. Rumors of coming activity are current on the 14th and the next day, Monday, the Brigade marched out of the fort giving place to the First Division of the Ninth Corps, negro troops, and going back about two miles, we pitch camp and are evidently in reserve for some project. The heavens also are active and the long delayed rain comes in torrents for two hours in the afternoon. The troops which relieved us were the colored division of the Ninth Corps, under General Edward Ferrero, and of their appearance as we marched out, Beck of Company C remarks, "Who of the Thirty-ninth will ever forget the appearance of the colored troops sent to relieve us, as they lay about outside, half buried in yellow mud and water, as we filed out of the fort on that rainy morning? They had been marching

Aug. 13, '64 | all night in the darkness, rain and mud, and were so completely

exhausted that sleep to them was the one great necessity, position and bed being secondary. We carefully stepped over their bodies and soon were beyond the sound of their snoring." A heavy detail is made on the 16th for work on Fort Sedgwick, but day work is impossible there on account of the nearness of Fort Mahone, or "Damnation," whose sharpshooters are regularly gunning for the "blues." The detail had hardly more than begun to work at 10 p. m. when the command came to cease from labors and to report to the Regiment at once. There the information is imparted that the corps will move at 3 p. m. of the coming day. On this next day, the 17th, when in line awaiting the expected "Forward" there comes the order to break ranks and encamp for the night. Concerning the movement against the Weldon

Railroad, whole volumes have been written. It was a part of Grant's effort to cripple the resources of the rebel army that was being hemmed in gradually by the Union forces. The necessity of the move had been recognized from the first and it had been delayed, as already stated, principally by the departure of Sheridan and the Sixth Corps to the Shenandoah Valley. We have noted the activity of Hancock and his Second Corps, north of the James, made in the hope that it might cause the return of some of the Confederates who had gone to Early's relief, thereby enabling Sheridan to strike a heavier blow in his present command.

Incidentally, it seemed that troops had been withdrawn from the rebel right to strengthen those fighting Hancock and others, at the Confederate left, and Grant saw his opportunity to strike again for the Weldon track, and this is what he says in his Memoirs:—

"From our left, near the old line, it was about three miles to the Weldon Railroad. A division was ordered from the right of the Petersburg line to reinforce Warren, while a division was brought back from the north side of the James River to take its place. The road was very important to the enemy. The limits from which his supplies had been drawn were already very much contracted, and I knew that he must fight desperately to protect it. Warren carried the road though with heavy loss on both sides. He fortified his new position, and our trenches were then extended from the left of our main line to connect with his new one. Lee made repeated attempts to dislodge Warren's Corps, but without success and with heavy loss. As soon as Warren was fortified and reinforcement reached him, troops were sent south to destroy the bridges on the Weldon Railroad, and with such success that the enemy had to draw in wagons for a distance of about thirty miles all the supplies they thereafter got from that source. It was on the 21st that Lee seemed to have given up the Weldon Railroad as having been lost to him; but along about the 24th or 25th he made renewed attempts to recapture it. Again he failed, and with very heavy losses to him as compared with ours. On the night of the 20th, our troops on the north side of the James were withdrawn, and Hancock and Gregg were sent south to destroy the Weldon Railroad. They were attacked on the 25th, at Reams Station, and after desperate fighting a part of our line gave way, losing five pieces of artillery. But the Weldon Railroad never went out of our possession from the 18th of August to the close of the war."

The foregoing extract from the memoirs of the Lieutenant General has been made as an indication of his opinion of the magnitude of the work of August 18th in the progress of the war. The Army and Navy Journal of August 27th, after noting the extraordinary storm of the 15th, "Which swept away many tents and sutler's booths and filled the trenches with water" and the fierce cannonading on the 16th, also that of 1 a. m. of the 18th, lasting for two hours, has this to offer concerning the event which figures so largely in the annals of our Regiment:—

"At four o'clock, on the morning of Thursday, the 18th, and shortly after the heavy cannonading ceased, the Fifth Corps started from its camp (which was rather in reserve) with four days' rations, towards the Weldon Railroad. It took some time to get across the ground formerly held by the Second and Sixth Corps. Then the column marched towards Ream's Station, driving in easily the enemy's skirmishers, of whom a part were captured. Between seven and eight o'clock, the advance arrived at Six Mile Station, and busily setting to work, a mile of the track was Aug. 18, '64 torn up and burned, and the rails destroyed in the usual manner. The skirmishing up to this time had been very light, the enemy having obviously withdrawn to his left, and the whole move being made with hardly a show of opposition. While the First Division was tearing up the track, the others passed on towards Petersburg and after advancing two or three miles, took position so as to repel an expected attack from the enemy. They did not have long to wait. About noon, Walker's Virginia and Davis' Mississippi brigades came hurrying down the railroad. Ayres' Second Division was stationed at this point; the Third and Fourth Divisions, at his right; and the First on his left. The battle opened very promptly on the arrival of the enemy with sharp artillery firing. The enemy, a part of Hill's Corps, then rushed in with great impetuosity, falling with most force upon Hayes', Lyle's and Cutler's brigades, and succeeding in flanking a portion of our force, including Lyle's First Brigade, Crawford's Third Division, the latter brigade being brought forward under a severe enfilading fire. For two hours the firing was very hot, and as it was an open fight the losses were heavy. The main battle lasted till about three o'clock; but the skirmishing and cannonading continued till night, when both forces went to entrenching, the possession of the railroad still being left to our troops. Our loss is still somewhat uncertain, but it is somewhere from five hundred to one thousand. The Second and Third Divisions suffered most and the Thirty-ninth Massachusetts and the Fifteenth New York Heavy Artillery lost heavily. The enemy claims to have captured eight officers and one hundred and fifty men from us in this fight. The enemy's loss in killed and wounded was probably nearly equal to ours, but he lost few prisoners.

Headquarters at night were at the Six Mile House, so called from its distance from Petersburg. That night and all the next day our forces were busily engaged in strengthening our lines, and in endeavoring to connect the right of the new position with the left of our old line. But towards the evening of Friday the enemy came out in force and pushed in between the new entrenchment and the old ones, flanking the Fifth Corps and sweeping off about fifteen hundred prisoners. The Ninth Corps arriving on the field of battle, checked the enemy. Our loss was about three thousand men. Saturday was comparatively quiet, but on Sunday the enemy again furiously attacked us, and was repulsed with heavy loss. On Monday and Tuesday, there was occasional firing along the centre, but our lines were otherwise undisturbed. Our forces still hold the Weldon railroad, the capture and retention of which have cost a week of the hardest fighting of the campaign."

General Humphreys, in his "Virginia, Campaign of '64 and '65," has the following version of the story that specially touches our Division and Brigade:—

"General A. P. Hill, with Davis' and Walker's brigades under General Heth, and Weisiger's, Colquitt's and Clingman's under General Mahone, with Lee's cavalry and Pegram's batteries, moved to the Vaughan Road intersection. Heth was to attack Ayers, while Mahone, familiar with the woods, was to move concealed by it some distance beyond Crawford's right, break through Bragg's skirmish line, and take Bragg and Crawford in rear. About half past four in the afternoon, General Mahone with his command formed in columns of fours, broke through Bragg's skirmish line, faced to the right, and swept rapidly down toward General Warren's right flank, taking all Crawford's skirmish line and part of his line of battle in rear. His skirmish line fell back in the greatest confusion, and in doing so, masked the fire of his line of battle, and forced it to fall back, together with a part of General Ayres' division. Heth at the same time opened on Ayres' centre and left. General Warren, reforming the parts of Ayers' and Crawford's divisions that were broken, brought them forward again and regained the ground temporarily lost, taking some prisoners and two flags. General Willcox was ordered up to attack; and White's division (Ninth Corps) was formed facing to the right, and engaging Colquitt's brigade drove it back, and captured some prisoners. Mahone's command fell back rapidly in great confusion to their intrenchments, carrying with them the parts of Warren's command disorganized by the attack on their rear in the woods, and a large portion of the pickets."

As an illustration of one man's appreciation of a great battle, of what he sees, the following extract is taken from the journal of Lieutenant Dusseault:—

"We turned out at 3 a. m. This was the day of the 'Battle of Weldon Railroad,' sometimes called that of the 'Six Mile House' or the 'Globe Tavern,' also 'Yellow House.' We began our march at five o'clock towards the railroad, southwest and towards our left, a distance of five or six miles to the 'Six Mile House,' it being just that distance from Petersburg. Here we found the rebel pickets and drove them before us. General   Aug. 18, '64   Crawford's Division (Third), to which our Regiment belonged, formed a line of battle on the right of the railroad, and General Ayers of our Second Division formed on the left of the road. General Griffin's First Division was in the rear, tearing up the tracks as we thus advanced towards Petersburg. We had proceeded about a mile and a half in dense woods, when Hill's Rebel Corps charged us. The 'Six Mile House' is now behind us, Ayers' Division gives way, letting the enemy in on our left flank. There is nothing for us to do but fall back or be captured. The rebel line in front of us is within forty feet. The order is given to fall back. All were lying down flat on the ground at the time, the enemy in the same position, but ready to shoot as fast as we stood up. Colonel C. L. Peirson was already badly wounded in the bowels by a minie ball. He was able to stand long enough to give the command and then he fell. Just as I rose, a bullet struck me in the right side, broke the eighth rib and entered the lower lobe of the lung. I was taken off the field, along with the Colonel, to the field hospital just back of us. Sergeant Bradshaw, afterwards second lieutenant, and Private Thomas, both of Company H, were leading me and while thus supporting me, the latter was shot in the wrist, in consequence of which, hesitating a moment, he was captured. For a time I occupied the next cot to the Colonel's. I heard the surgeon say that he could not live twenty-four hours. As I remember, he was placed outside in a tent by himself to die. Three or four hours later, when the surgeons looked in upon him they saw that he had revived somewhat, and he was taken to the division hospital. His life was long despaired of. Few men recovered from wounds of like character received during the Civil War. As Major Tremlett was still absent, the command devolved on Capt. F. R. Kingsley of Company E. Our side was beaten for a time but, after being driven about a quarter of a mile, the men reformed and held the foe."

Fred. Baker of Company H had joined the Regiment as a recruit in February, 1864; he was on the skirmish line on August 18th, and, the position being a pretty warm one, he had been digging a pit to get into for cover. About the time that the hole had become large enough for him to get into it, some rebel shot and killed him. He fell into the pit and some of the others covered him with the earth which he had removed. He had dug his own grave.

Dexter Gray of Company E, who had been a schoolmaster before the war, was shot in the head; he was so paralyzed that he could neither speak nor move. His comrades were preparing to bury him, thinking him dead. He knew everything that was being done but he could make no sign to them, neither could he help himself in the least. But just before they were ready to bury him, he recovered sufficiently to make them understand, and the burial was postponed for about twenty years.

Many years later, General Peirson, having been requested to give some personal reminiscences to the Salem Evening News, under what he calls his last battle, recites the story of his experience in the foregoing 18th of August. After some prefatory statements, the General proceeds:—

"General Grant's movements in that campaign were successively to the left, and the order soon came for us to move to the left until we crossed the Weldon Railroad, which was about the last remaining feeder for the secession troops around Petersburg and Richmond. Arriving there we began tearing up the rails for half a mile to pile up the dry sleepers and put the iron rails on top of the cobpile and then firing the sleepers, the rails by the heat and their own weight were rendered worthless."[P]

"Moving through small trees, we came upon the enemy, who immediately attacked. Our men were ordered to lie down, and to receive and return the fire from their position. The commander cannot avail himself of such protection, since the men are likely to be less homesick if they see him apparently indifferent. Notwithstanding these precautions, there were soon wounded men in plenty, the colonel being shot through the body, falling at once upon his knees from the shock. Just at that moment one of the lieutenants, Severand, from the left company of the Regiment came up and reported, 'Everything is swept away from the left.' He was ordered to go out to the left and investigate. He never returned. I went then to that company and sent out the captain to make the same investigation. He did not return. I then went out myself, and meeting a secession soldier, remarked with some

Aug. 18, '64   force, 'Drop that gun and come in here.' He obeyed, not understanding that I had no strength to compel him, and I learned from him that his troops had got behind our left flank. This view was soon confirmed by the direction from which the bullets came. I then gave orders, something like this, 'Fours, right about, forward on the left company, March' or words to that effect, and the situation was saved.

"By that time, I was so much exhausted by the loss of blood that I was carried to the rear, where there was a field hospital. When I met the regimental surgeon who was my dear friend, I saw tears come into his previously cheerful face, and I then knew that something serious had happened. They gave me a little tent and some of the wounded officers came to bid me good-bye. The major general, commanding the division, hearing that one of his colonels had come to grief, sent an aide to inquire what could be done for my comfort. From him I obtained an ambulance. Our chaplain went with me, also a wounded soldier, who died on the way, and we started for City Point, where were the main hospitals of the army. In a few miles we came to a field hospital, where I hoped to be allowed to remain, but the surgeon declined, I thought brutally, to receive me, though I afterwards learned that any other course would have been fatal to me. So we proceeded on our long journey. Arriving at the splendidly equipped hospitals at City Point, my wound was examined, the ball probed for, and found, and by an operation extracted. Inflammation had by this time set in, and I remained in a very dangerous state for many days.

"While I thus lay on my cot, the hospital was visited by some well meaning but clumsy Christians, whose mission it was to supply the patients with testaments and tracts. They, seeing me, stopped to urge me, since I was so soon to meet my Creator, to turn from my evil ways while there was yet time, and to read the instructive words with which they burdened my couch. One of my friends afterwards said, though I cannot vouch for the truth of the story, that I had only strength enough to reply, 'Go to blazes.' However, I grew better slowly, was sent North on a stretcher, and put to bed in Barton Square, where my dear mother nursed me back to life. Some months after, when the war had closed, I went into business on Kilby street, Boston. One day there came into my office a well remembered soldier who proved to be the captain of the left company. He gave the military salute, and remarked, 'Colonel, I have come to report what I found on the left.' It seems that coming upon a secession picket, they had captured him, taken his weapons with most of his clothes, and persuaded him to go through a course of southern prisons from which he had only just returned."

Of the 19th, Lieutenant Dusseault has this to say, "The fight was resumed. The rebels found a gap on our right and came through, thus flanking us again. Our artillery opened on them as they were between us and artillery, and the shells did us as much harm as they did the enemy. The men of both sides were now pretty well mixed up in the woods. Whichever squad was the larger would capture the other. This day our Regiment was in the worst part of the line and suffered more than any other, unless it was the Sixteenth Maine, which was captured almost to a man."

In a paper read before the Massachusetts Military Historical Society, December 13, 1880, Captain Charles H. Porter says of this day:—

"The morning opened dull and rainy, with the troops in good spirits. No changes were made. The troops of their own accord strengthened the field works, making them quite strong. Nothing happened until about 3 a. m., when the enemy showed considerable activity, the pickets firing and showing quite a bold front. General Lee, determining to drive us from the road sends two divisions under Heth and Mahone. The former has four brigades with eight pieces of artillery from Pegram's battalion. Six of the pieces are west of the railroad and two are east of the same. Mahone has Weisiger's, Colquitt's and a part of Clingman's brigades. Mahone has discovered that the right of the Fifth Corps does not connect with anything. The Ninth Corps, which has been ordered to fill the gap, has not yet reached its destination though it is two o'clock p. m. Doubtless the extremely wet day prevented the prompt arrival of the reinforcement. Our troops, finding everything quiet and not expecting an attack, disposed of themselves in every way, trying to keep as dry as possible, little thinking of the fate in store for them. Four o'clock was the hour agreed upon by Heth and Mahone, as the time when the flanking column should be in position and almost to the minute, Mahone's troops reached our skirmish line and drove it in. Then turning in the thick woods to the west, they moved in column directly upon the exposed right flank of the Federals. This exposed flank had been a subject of anxiety to General Warren, and he had issued orders accordingly.

Aug. 19, '64 "While the Third Division was passing a quiet afternoon, the officers at headquarters were informed that Heth was attacking vigorously in front, this being principally against the Second Division. Our Third Division is still undisturbed. The butchers of the division are slaughtering cattle when the pickets of the Ninth Corps come tumbling in, saying that the enemy is advancing upon them. The woods are so very dense that nothing can be seen through them. Not even General Warren, himself, can discern anything. When, however, a line of men is discovered approaching, Warren is so sure that they are the delayed Ninth Corps contingent, he will not allow artillery to open on them, a very serious error on his part, for they are soon discovered to be a portion of the flanking Confederates, and that a considerable part of them is between our artillery and the Third Division. Our artillerists spring to their guns at once and open a rapid fire upon them. How does this act bear upon our Third Division, where the Thirty-ninth Regiment is? The very first intimation that Crawford's men have that all is not well with them, is the bursting of spherical case from the rear, in their midst. They are aware that the artillery is massed behind them, and they realize that something must have happened to bring such firing from their own comrades. Now, the firing in front from Heth and his men begins again, and our pickets are again attacked. It becomes necessary to seek protection from our own thirty guns. The men spring over the breastworks and hold them in reverse, thinking the pickets able to check the attack in front, and that their chief danger is from the rear. The suspense is soon broken when a line of confederate infantry comes rushing in upon them. All is now confusion. Without leaders, the men are completely demoralized. In the dark and dismal woods, dismayed by the fire from our own guns, the men make but a short resistance and this flanking column under Mahone captures nearly two brigades of the Third Division. The attack of Heth in front continues, adding to the confusion, but the rapid firing of our artillery convinces the enemy that there is nothing more for them in that direction, so they content themselves with the 2700 prisoners, whom they have swept almost entirely from the Third Division, and move up the Halifax road with more captives than they themselves number. As they thus move away the captured men narrowly escape the fire of Mahone's two cannon stationed on the east side of the railroad; the gunners think so large an array of men in blue must be an attacking party, but the condition is disclosed soon enough to prevent the possible slaughter.

"Such men of the Third Division as have not been captured, seek safety in every direction, each man for himself. Dodging behind trees, now east, now west, some of the wrecked body of men get the true direction and come out at the edge of the clearing, looking towards our artillery. Here they behold a welcome sight. It is an advancing line of the Ninth Corps, responding to the evident need. It is the First Division of the Ninth Corps, composed largely of Massachusetts men, and they are friends indeed. We know that, having the situation well in hand, the position will be regained and the railroad held. The remnants of the Third Division are finally rallied near the Dunlock House. Picture, if you can, one little knot gathered together, about twenty-five in number, all that, at this time, can be assembled of a regiment that yesterday carried three hundred and fifty muskets into the first day's fight, whose commander was most grievously wounded on that day. They are soon marshaled to occupy, as far as they can, their old line of works. Very few sleep any during the night, as the weary hours roll on, and it seems as though daylight would never come to bring relief to the dread hanging over the command through the night. Mahone and his men retire to their defenses with feelings quite the reverse of those of their opponents and the 'Little Gamecock of the Confederacy' fully merits his appellation as he turns over his plunder to General Lee."

An excellent personal story of the second day is told by Sergt. George E. Fowle, Company K, whose experience quite likely was similar to that of nearly all the men of the Regiment who succeeded in getting out of the confusion, free:

"I was acting First Sergeant of Company K. Corporal S. A. McFeeley was my bunkmate, and was one of the color guard. We were stationed in the woods on the right of the railroad, where the rebels made vigorous demonstrations on our front while a large force turned our right flank. Our artillery was firing solid shot over our heads when the enemy broke through and came between us and our cannon. The guns were immediately depressed to reach the confederates and the shots coming through them and reaching us were the first intimation we had of anything wrong. McFeeley was sent back to stop the artillery and was captured. The line was doubled up as the enemy came down on our flank. I started back with the rest and came across a canteen with the string cut; picking it up, I took a drink and filled my own   Aug.

19. '64   canteen, but when this was done I found myself alone, but I

followed along in the direction which the others had gone. I came to a cart path, where I saw some of our men with a few Johnnies on the other side of the path. The bushes separating us were so thick and low that I had to spread them apart with my hands to get through, and when I did and straightened up, with my gun in my hand, I found myself looking into a rebel gun barrel, held by a Johnnie who was standing by the side of an officer, whom I took to be a colonel. I was told to throw down the gun, which I did and walked across the road where the officer took me by the shoulder and turned me around, saying, 'Get into the ranks, and we'll take good care of you.' There were so many prisoners that we were in all sorts of position, one, two and three deep. The man nearest me wanted to know where the Maryland Brigade was located.

"I unhitched my knapsack and turned around to see if anybody was looking, and gave it a throw into the bushes. As I did so, I saw Joe Adams, the National color bearer, come out into the road, look up and down the same, and then he raised the colors over his head and threw them into the wheel-ruts, there happened to be a break in the guards near him. I threw off my scabbard and cut the strap which held my cartridge box. We were nearing the railroad tracks, where the rebels turned and marched up towards Petersburg. When I saw a good chance I jumped into the bushes and soon heard someone behind me, and turning saw Joe, Adams and another man. All this time we were getting more or less missiles from our own guns; the solid shot had been changed to shells and we were troubled quite as much as the confederates. We soon encountered a rebel with a gun in his hand, just as a shell exploded near our heads. To Adams' query as to where was the direction of the rebel rear, he replied, 'I'll be d—d if I know.' At this, I left them to see what I could do for myself in finding our own breastworks. In a short time I came across a lieutenant of the Sixteenth Maine, who was behind a tree, whereupon I found a tree also, but I didn't stop long, since I was not gaining ground. We could see the prisoners and the guard and occasionally a rebel would come our way.

"I started back towards our works, but on arriving found no one there, so I sallied forth to where the right of the Regiment had been. Going some distance beyond where our right was, I saw some troops mount the breastworks. At first I couldn't make out who they were, blue or gray, but, stooping down, I found them to be our men, and I recognized Corporal Abijah Thompson, who beckoned me to come up his way. The ground was covered with muskets, which had been thrown down when the boys were captured. Colonel Wheelock of the Ninety-seventh New York, then commanding his brigade, was up on the right, and seeing the movement, he put his men in front of the works and charged out upon the enemy, capturing everything in sight, Yank and Reb, including the Colonel, who was going to take good care of me, a stand of confederate colors and, best of all, our own which Adams had thrown down.[Q] The state colors borne by Serg. William A. Mentzer of "A" were brought in safely by him, though by great effort.

"On getting out of the woods into the field, there stood the First Division of the Ninth Corps in line; I ran down and told General White that the rebels had got our Brigade, and that they were on the road in there, not ten rods from where he sat on his horse, and he could get them all if he went in. The General turned around and said to one of his staff, 'They have got the road we came down.' He was waiting for orders from General Warren. It had been raining and I didn't know whether the gun that I had picked up would go off or not, so I pointed the muzzle towards the ground and fired. Whereupon the General said, 'Don't you know any better than that?' I went back to the line, borrowed some cartridges and caps and loaded the gun, when Colonel Lyle and the remnant of the Brigade came out of the bushes. His command resembled a color guard. A staff officer soon ordered me back into the breastworks. I picked up a sergeant's knapsack and soon made a set of sergeant's chevrons. Our company made two stacks of guns that night, and I put my gun across the stacks, and was in command of the company. Lieutenant Tidd and twenty-seven men of Company K were taken prisoners. Our captain was sick and had been taken to the hospital."

Aug. 20, '64   Of Saturday, the 20th, Captain Porter remarks that it opened quite pleasantly and that the sunlight, struggling through the clouds, was cheering to the lonely feeling troops of the Third Division, those that remained in line. The Ninth Corps had made a complete connection with the right of our division and further danger in this direction was obviated. This day the engineers of the Fifth Corps marked out a new line of works to be occupied in the open, just in advance of the Dunlock House, about three hundred yards north from the Six Mile House. This line ran near the woods in which so great disaster had befallen our troops. Our Third division occupied ground to the right, east of the railroad, which still divided the forces of the Second Division. The breastworks were heavily made and were quite impracticable for an assault in front. The lines of the Fifth and Ninth Corps were continuations of each other. All lines in advance of this new one were abandoned in the afternoon and evening of the 20th. While there was hard work in the trenches there was no engagement with the enemy. The latter had by no means given up the recovery of the railroad and was making plans for the morrow. The juncture of the Fifth and Ninth Corps, leaving no aperture in that direction, his attention was necessarily drawn towards the left. It was said that General Roger A. Pryor of Virginia, conspicuous in ante-bellum days, by his altercation with John F. Potter, a fellow Congressman from Wisconsin, who named bowie knives as duelling weapons, having retired from active army service, in his capacity of independent scout, had climbed a tree and from this outlook discovered, as he thought, the vulnerableness of the Union left. Hastening to impart his discovery to General Mahone, the latter made plans for an attack on the 21st. With the details of this unsuccessful effort to repeat the tactics of the 19th, we have no especial concern, except to state that this time, Mahone carried back no prisoners and reported no victory. Ayers and his First Division were quite ready to receive callers.

Of this campaign of four days, General Warren says, "The heat of the first day (18th) was excessive, and on the march many fell out who are here reported among the missing, but who will soon rejoin us. About fifty were completely prostrated by sunstroke. The men were kept working night and day, and every day were wet through with the rains. The side roads and fields were almost impassable for artillery." However much the Confederates may have lamented the loss of the Weldon Railroad as a supply source, and to them it was a grievous one, the conditions brought about by these terrible battle days in August remained unchanged to the end. Grant was taking no backward steps and with the grip of a bulldog, whatever he grasped, he held.

The losses met by the Thirty-ninth were frightful. May 4th, when the Regiment crossed the Rapidan there were five hundred and thirty men in the ranks, fully twice the number in any other two regiments in the Brigade. Since then we had received from the Twelfth and Thirteenth Regiments two hundred and twenty-eight transfers, bringing the aggregate to nearly eight hundred men, yet so severe had been the tests of the Wilderness, Spottsylvania and the attacks on Petersburg, including this most recent calamity on the Weldon Railroad, on the morning of August 22d only one hundred and two enlisted men and nine officers reported for duty. Of course, some would eventually report from the missing, which included not alone prisoners and wounded, but stragglers as well, still the fact remained that the swoop that Malone made upon the First Brigade on that August afternoon came near finishing it. Colonel Peirson was seriously wounded and in hospital; Major Tremlett was away on detached service; Captain F. R. Kinsley was a prisoner in the hands of the enemy and the command devolved upon Captain George S. Nelson of Company A. We have already seen that Company K stacked nine muskets, under command of a sergeant, the night of the 19th; ten men were reported   Aug. 22, '64   left in Company C, and "E" Company had only seven or eight of the original number. Terrible are the ravages of war.

The several army corps along the southside of Petersburg are hereafter to gradually strengthen the lines already established, to build new forts and to place the Weldon Railroad in a condition that even its recovery would in no way profit the Confederacy, since the impoverished condition of the latter would be quite incapable of putting it into a running condition. Colonel T. F. McCoy of the Hundred and Seventh Pennsylvania, commanding the Brigade after the retirement of Colonel Lyle, accounts for the procedure of the First Brigade during these days. He says that the dead were buried on the 22d. On the 23rd the division under General Crawford engaged in destroying the railroad from the Yellow House in the direction of Petersburg, the First Brigade, however, acting as a reserve to protect the working parties. The 24th, what was left of the brigade rested quietly in camp. The 25th brought orders to change camps, in doing which, however, other orders were received to prepare for action, and the column immediately took up the line of march towards Reams' Station, where the Second Corps was heavily engaged with a large force of the enemy. It was at this point that Colonel Peter Lyle, Ninetieth Pennsylvania, who had commanded the Brigade so long, on account of severe illness, was obliged to relinquish his command. Colonel McCoy,[R] succeeding, marched the Brigade to the Yellow House, where he received orders from General Crawford to report with his command to General Bragg, which he did, and proceeded in the direction of Reams, but after marching about one mile he was ordered to countermarch and encamp for the night. Next day, 26th, camp was again changed and the men were ordered to throw up works, southeast of the Yellow House.

The digging that the Fifth Corps did in the vicinity of the Yellow House became a part of the system of fortifications that were gradually extended to Fort Fisher, the extreme western fort, where there was a turn or refusal of the line to the southward, lest the favorite maneuver of the rebels might be tried on the Union left. Day and night, the work progressed, every day strengthening the coils which Grant and Meade were casting about the doomed city, and every one knew that the fall of Petersburg meant the end of Richmond also. A deal of ammunition was wasted in the bombardment of Petersburg, yet it had to be kept up, or the enemy would have thought the Yankees quite inefficient. They grew almost indifferent to the missiles from the Union guns and fifty years later they will tell of the tons of ammunition that were wasted upon them and their city. The "Petersburg Express"[S]

located near the Friend House, and manned by the First   Sept. 2, '64

Connecticut Heavy Artillery, failed not in its two hundred pound compliments for weeks and months and in the Twentieth Century the mortar itself will form a principal part of the regimental monument in Hartford. Somehow there is more real fighting over on the other side of the James where the Tenth Corps is located and the enemy cannot dispossess themselves of the impression that the Yankees really mean to get into Richmond that way.

By the last of the month, matters have resolved themselves into a long steady round of fatigue and picket duty to the music of artillery along the entire line, the attitude of the opposing guardsmen on duty depending entirely on the agreements that they may have made with each other. September 2d, General D. McM. Gregg, supported by General Crawford's (Third) Division of the Fifth Corps started out on an errand of some sort up the Vaughn road, towards the Plank Road and Petersburg; in other words it was a case of marching up the hill and then marching down again, for finding the enemy strongly entrenched, the entire force returned to camp. This day also the foe forgot the tacit agreement of friendliness and opened up a fire of musketry along the entire line, killing a large number of men and effectually ending amicable relations for some time.

While the fact of the occupation of Atlanta by the Union forces had been understood as early as the 2d, no official notice of the success was taken until the 4th, Sunday, when one hundred shotted guns were fired from extreme right to the furthest left, the celebration lasting about an hour, the enemy thinking it so queer a way of observing the Lord's day that they, too, opened their batteries and added to the din, arising from their own misfortune. "Westward Ho!" is evidently still the watchword of our commander, for every effort is made to strengthen the extreme left, and both sides watch out with the utmost alertness. For the sake of rearranging a portion of our line of works it became necessary to gain possession of the rebel rifle pits at "The Chimneys," on the Jerusalem Plank Road, and General Mott, with a backing from the Second Corps, was directed to accomplish the task, this on the night of the 9th of September. The duty was done at the point of the bayonet and the works were immediately reversed, the same becoming of great advantage to the new possessors, General Walker of the Second Corps pronouncing the operation one of the most creditable in the entire siege. Of course, the foe did not let go without protest, and subsequent nights were rendered lurid by his efforts to regain the lost ground, but to no avail.

The thoroughness with which the campaign is advancing appears on Sunday, the 11th, when an engine is run over the newly laid railroad from City Point to the Weldon road at Yellow House. The Confederates are running trains to Stony Creek, twelve miles south of Reams; and the remainder of the distance, around the Union left into Petersburg, is effected by wagon, pretty slow and vexatious work! The firing along the picket line, annoying and useless, had become very obnoxious to General Birney of the Tenth Corps at the Union right, and to give the enemy something to think about opened a heavy fire on the works in his front and on Petersburg itself. The enemy also played during the afternoon on certain signal towers along the front of the Eighteenth Corps. A very tranquil evening followed this ebulition. Perhaps no event of the week gave the Confederates so much pleasure as their success in surprising a couple of cavalry regiments in charge of a large number of beef cattle, some 2500 in number, near Coggin's Point on the James River and running the vast herd into their lines and taking with them the careless guards. While the rebels were thus supplying their commissariat, others of their number made an attack on the entire skirmish line of the Fifth Corps and capture nearly a hundred of the men. On the 16th, the Second Brigade was assigned to forts on the left of the line, the Thirty-ninth being ordered to Fort Duchesne. Sept. 16, '64 Camp was pitched just outside the fort, along with the One Hundred and Fourth New York the Eleventh, Forty-eighth and Ninety-eighth Pennsylvania, all under the command of Colonel Richard Coulter of the last named regiment. The 19th was enlivened by telegraphic news of Sheridan's victory near Winchester where Early was sent "Whirling up the Valley," followed by salvos of artillery in honor thereof. On the 28th, the paymaster left six months' pay.

Ten days later, Thursday, the 29th, was a counterpart to a deal of activity on the Union right, when business was actually suspended in Richmond through fear that an assault was imminent; a column consisting of Gregg's cavalry, supported by two infantry brigades, set out towards the Poplar Springs Church road, beyond the Vaughan turnpike, advancing about two miles. On their return, they were attacked by Hampton's cavalry, the force that had stolen the cattle-herd, and a brisk encounter followed. Friday, the 30th, extending into Saturday, took place the battle of Peebles' farm between certain portions of the Fifth and Ninth Corps and the Confederates, General Grant having in mind a movement towards the Southside Railroad, expecting thus to still further cripple the cities of Petersburg and Richmond, the result being a considerable advance westward of the Union left. While all of this commotion was taking place, the Thirty-ninth Regiment moved into the fort, remaining there until the 16th of October, when it came out and took a position on the Weldon Railroad half a mile in front of Fort Duchesne, and a mile from the Globe Tavern or Yellow House.

So far as our Regiment is concerned, affairs are very quiet, though the extended Union line towards the west affords opportunity for constant work, day and night, for every man, and the number in the Thirty-ninth is not very great, so large a portion of the survivors of the Regiment being involuntary boarders in the Confederacy. The fact that less than eleven months remain of the service for which the men enlisted causes not a few remarks as to the gradual approach of the day of release, though all must know that the future holds many possibilities of battles and other exposure. Ignorance in this case is surely bliss. The first third of October covers considerable activity on the Union right, where Darbytown Road wins a place in battle lists, and the cooler nights indicate the approach of another winter with its peculiar exactions. The first frost comes on the night of the 9th-10th. From the 8th to the 11th all sorts of firing have been common in the vicinity of Sedgwick or "Fort Hell" in local parlance, on the last named night the pyrotechny being especially brilliant, a Richmond paper stating that it was the heaviest mortar shelling of the siege, "The heavens being ablaze with brilliant meteors, ascending, descending and shooting athwart the horizon in almost countless numbers and unsurpassed beauty."

During these early October days, General S. W. Crawford is in command of the Fifth Corps and with it, accompanying the Ninth Corps, a reconnoisance in force is made on the 8th towards the Union left, possibly with an idea of extending our works even beyond Fort McRae. After a day of hard marching and constant skirmishing the troops returned, wearied enough, to their starting point; but General Grant is not satisfied, even yet, that he cannot reach the Southside Railroad. A little past the middle of the month, or on the 19th, comes the most unqualified report of victory in the Shenandoah Valley that the country has yet heard. It is the story of Cedar Creek, fought on the 19th, when differing from the dispatches after Winchester, just a month before, where Early was sent "whirling up the valley"; so nearly annihilated is the rebel army, it would be a very stiff breeze which could find anything left to whirl. The activities for this month, as far as the Fifth Corps is concerned, terminated with the joint move, on the 26th, of the Second, Fifth and Ninth Corps along with Gregg's Cavalry against the Southside Railroad,

Oct. 26, '64 known as the Boydton Plank Road, some distance east of the railroad. Very full and explicit instructions had been issued to the designated troops, and the utmost care had been taken to insure the safety of the entrenchments during the movement. The Fifth Corps, or that part of it in the project, marched out on the Squirrel Level Road, in a southwesterly direction towards Hatcher's Run, a small stream rising near Sutherland Station on the Southside Road and flowing southeastwardly into Rowanty Creek, a tributary of the Nottoway River. The Lieutenant General was determined to leave no stone unturned to secure the longed-for source of Petersburg's supplies. The country itself revealed many of the Wilderness characteristics, there being no roads and no chances to move artillery. In this confusion, the right of the Second Corps, furthest west, was lost to the Fifth Corps, a fact which enabled the enemy to get in between the two corps and capture a considerable number of men, the Second Corps suffering more than the Fifth, one whole regiment being run in. The mix-up was not unlike that of the 18th of August, for rain set in and ammunition was scarce, our leaders were ignorant of the lay of the land which the enemy seemed to know perfectly; so the left flank movement ended with the return of the troops to their former positions. On this same 26th the Thirty-ninth moved to the left and garrisoned Fort Canahey.

A very good story of give and take is recorded of this week; at dusk in the evening of Thursday, the 27th, one hundred volunteers of the One Hundred and Forty-eighth Pennsylvania attacked the fort of the enemy which succeeded that blown up on the 30th of July, climbed the parapet, drove the occupants out and, for a brief period, were masters of the situation, this being a plan to hold the attention of the Confederates while the assault was progressing further to left, but the enemy rallying quickly drove the Federal force back with considerable loss on both sides. In return, Sunday night, the 30th, at about ten o'clock, the rebels "relieved the pickets" in front of Fort Davis where the Sixty-ninth and One Hundred and Eleventh New York were on picket duty, and managed to capture nearly four hundred men. So delighted were the Confederates with their success they proceeded to throw a strong column against the works which had been uncovered by the capture of the pickets, but the alarm had been given and the triumphant men in gray were met with a fire of musketry that sent them back in a hurry and, for a time, there was a merry firing bee along the entire line. For the nonce, honors between blue and gray were easy and regular, expected shooting was resumed.

Another and the last November for the Thirty-ninth begins and finds the remnant of the Regiment doing garrison duty under the command of Captain Nelson of Company A, and comparative quiet reigning along the extended battle line, now reaching from the north side of the James more than twenty miles to Hatcher's Run. Lieutenant Colonel Tremlett, so long absent from the Regiment, returns on Friday, the 4th, relieving Captain Nelson, who has led the organization since the capture of Major F. R. Kinsley at the Weldon Railroad. Barring considerable excitement on the 5th, near "Fort Hell," where lines were captured by the enemy and reversed only to be re-taken and restored, day and night fully sustaining the reputation of the locality, and efforts of like nature in front of Fort Steadman on the 9th, the game of life and death was played without special emphasis—just the steady, constant watchfulness of thousands of men unwilling to allow any act of their adversary to pass unnoticed. Tuesday, the 8th of November, brings the presidential election, and the triumphant re-election of Lincoln, all soldiers having the privilege of voting, a singular illustration of ways in a republic where, in becoming a soldier the man does not lose his citizenship.

The 24th was Thanksgiving Day in New England and many a prayer was offered for the men at the front and many expressions of love and recollection were speeded Nov. 24, '64 southward for the delectation of absent ones. Nearly thirty tons of turkeys were said to have been sent from the North to the armies, and this vast amount of food, accompanied by all sorts of other meats and luxuries, must have gone far towards furnishing forth at least one good old-fashioned dinner for many thousands of men. As a sort of godsend to the enemy, possibly that they, too, might be thankful, on the 19th, some forty or fifty head of cattle, escaping from our corrals, made for the Confederate works where they were received as enemies, yet later found a thoroughly warm reception. On the 26th, the Ninetieth Pennsylvania, having reached the end of its term of enlistment, started for Philadelphia. It had been in the same division with the Thirty-ninth from the time of our joining the First Corps and, for the larger part of the period, in the same brigade. Its good qualities we had learned to appreciate. An outgrowth of the Second Regiment, Pennsylvania militia, it had served, under Colonel Lyle,[1] in the Three Months' call and, again, for three years. Recruits and re-enlisted men were transferred to the Eleventh Pennsylvania and all that were left of the originals were off for home. Towards the end of the month summaries were prepared of the losses sustained by the Army of the Potomac in the campaign so relentlessly waged and, according to Surgeon Thos. A. McParlin, Medical Director of the Army of the Potomac, from May 3rd to October 31st, the number of wounded amounted to 57,496, exclusive of the Eighteenth Corps while serving in this army, and he does not include the Ninth Corps at the Wilderness and at Spottsylvania Court House. According to data prepared by General Warren the killed and wounded in the Fifth Corps, during this same period, amounted to more than eleven thousand. The precautions taken to preserve life, and at the same time offering readiness to receive as well as make attacks, taxed the highest talents and ingenuity of engineers and soldiers. To the right and left, as far as the eye could reach, were earthworks of the strongest character, though few cared to take the risk of prolonged observations. There were corduroy roads underground and covered ways of heavy trunks of trees under four or five feet of earth to prevent shells from reaching those beneath. Few men cared to be for any considerable time in these safety holes, the monotony and closeness being terrible.

Though the Army of the Potomac is nominally in winter quarters, this in no way prevents changes of location, the organization of raids and a degree of activity hitherto unknown among the veterans of one or more winter's experience, who are carefully watching rebels while, at   Dec. 1, '64   the same time, keeping a careful reckoning on the time intervening before their muster-out. December comes in with a salute to the effect that it is the last one the Regiment will see in the field. On Thursday, the 1st, General Gregg leads a cavalry raid down the Weldon Railroad, starting before daylight, riding as far as Stony Creek, twenty-two miles below Petersburg, for the sake of destroying whatever stores may be collected there and to destroy also whatever advance may have been made in a proposed railroad connection between Stony Creek, the present terminus of the Weldon Railroad, and the

Southside Road through a new track, laid down by way of the Dinwiddie and the Boydton Roads. With considerable adventure, this was successfully done and with a forty mile's ride, not to mention the fighting, to their credit, the expedition was back again at 11 p. m.

The early part of the month saw the return of the Sixth Army Corps from its experiences in the valley, and with the garlands of victory fresh upon it, the corps took its place along the Petersburg line. In July, when the Sixth started for Baltimore and Washington, the Union front extended only a little further than the Jerusalem Plank Road; now it is prolonged to Hatcher's Run, and every foot of the prolongation has cost effort and blood; eight miles of new frontage dearly won. Into this battle line Sheridan's "Foot Cavalry" settles as naturally as though it has been away only a day or two on a casual raid. What is left of Early's force has been back with Lee several weeks. Not satisfied with the cavalry demonstration of the 1st, General Warren is ordered to conduct a more formidable array on the 7th to the same region. The troops, Fifth Corps, Mott's Division of the Second Corps and a division of cavalry under Gregg, above 20,000 in number with twenty-two pieces of artillery, have been massed on both sides of the Jerusalem Road and after a cold night, in the face of a severe rain, are off. On the Nottoway River, they come to where Freeman's Bridge was formerly, twenty miles from Petersburg, and they cross the stream on a pontoon bridge. Next day (8th) the march southward is continued and at Jarratt's Station where the Weldon Railroad crosses the Nottoway, thirty miles from Petersburg, they burn the bridge, two hundred feet long, crossing the river. The railroad track is torn up in the effectual manner characteristic of the times and Thursday night is spent here. Friday (9th) the work of destruction continues down to Bellfield, twelve miles further along. Of course there is skirmishing with the enemy constantly, but he is not here in sufficient force to offer substantial resistance. The troops bivouac for the night at Three Creek, three miles this side of Bellfield. All the time the weather has been wretched, the constant rain rendering the roads almost impassable and, to crown all, this night (Friday) come snow and hail to add to the general discomfort. Saturday (10th) the expedition faces towards Petersburg, burning on the way back the buildings at Sussex Court House in retaliation, so said, for the shooting of some of our stragglers and here the army bivouacs; resuming the backward route the Nottoway was reached in the evening of the 11th and, on the 12th, the old quarters are struck by a very tired body of men; the net results being a march fifty miles long, three railroad bridges destroyed, fifteen miles of railroad track torn up and bent out of shape and a county court house burned.

No mention is made in the official report of the quantity of apple-jack which the curiously inclined Yankees sought and found and, to their own harm, imbibed. The section had not been overrun before, and consequently better stored farm houses were found than the men had been seeing of late and, notwithstanding the rigors of the campaign, possibly on account of them, they made merry with the seductive liquids made from innocent cider. The story was long current that one man, outside of fully three fingers of the booze, and growing correspondingly free with the dignitaries, slapped General Warren familiarly Dec. 10, '64 on the back, calling him "The little Corporal," a term which ever afterwards clung to the soldier himself. Canteens of the fiery stuff were carried back to camp for the benefit (?) of those who did not go. Had the weather been more propitious, it is possible that the expedition would have gone on twenty miles further to Weldon, on the Roanoke.

In the foregoing episode, the Thirty-ninth bore its part, having moved back to the rear line on the 5th and, at the start, taking the advance of the infantry. Just before reaching Halifax Road, the 8th, on indications of trouble ahead the Regiment was deployed and sent forward as skirmishers to hold the road. Having established a line of pickets, the Thirty-ninth stood by to guard the road while the main column passed on. Shortly after dark we followed the troops, overtaking them near Jarratt's Station, and there we took a hand in destroying the railroad. On the 9th we had a place at the extreme left of the corps, and picketed the front of the brigade, which was doing its best to make the road a hard one for the rebels to travel. At 6 p. m. we were withdrawn to Cross Roads, above Bellfield, one half going on picket, the other half into camp with the Brigade. In the movement backward, beginning on the 10th, we fetched up the rear and thus enjoyed frequent tilts with the close following cavalry of the enemy who, in spite of our best efforts, managed to capture any who straggled, in the number, our Regiment losing four men. On the 11th, starting before daylight, we crossed the Nottaway at four o'clock in the afternoon and at nine halted for the night. On the 12th, we were back again before Petersburg, having marched twelve miles. Encamping near the Jerusalem Plank Road, we were ordered to build huts for the winter and, following a week's work, we moved into our new quarters where, for about a month, we had almost easy times. At any rate we were not right under the fire of the enemy all of the time. We had to turn out at intervals on account of real or fancied dangers; drill and fatigue duties had their part and there were the regular details for guard and picket. Once we served as guard for a wagon train which went outside for bricks and boards, securing the same from a deserted house some five miles away.

It must be understood that absolute quiet in front of Petersburg was out of the question. The extended works were like a mammoth keyboard for an organ, whose dimensions transcended imagination and, seated thereat, all the gods and goddesses of War played music that rivaled the thunderbolts of

Jove, now the low mutterings of distant lightning, anon rising to the fierce reverberations of an equinoxial as when, on the 19th of December, doubly shotted guns told the joy of the Union that Thomas had annihilated Hood at Nashville or, on the 26th, when Mars himself seemed to press those keys in token of the termination of the March to The Sea and that Savannah had fallen. Always catching up the refrain, the unterrified rebels, aided by their own warlike deities, hurled it back upon us, sometimes like an echo, immeasurable augmented, till veritably it seemed that the opposing lines, stretching away beyond human sight, could not have evoked a greater riot of sound had they been exits of Aetna and Stromboli. A topmost gallery seat in this magnificent theatre of war afforded, in the very mildest passages of Freedom's Oratorio, all the sound, melodious or otherwise, that the average human ear could appreciate.

Christmas brought nothing more notable than a beautiful day, which in the midst of a cheerless winter was not unwelcomed, but there were none of the festivities which untold generations have developed as essential features of the coming of the Prince of Peace and, for that matter, what propriety could there be in observing the advent of the Christ Child in an army, yet the world is full of just such anomalies. As December nears its end and dies with the old year, careful observers scan the retrospect, and in the deeds of Grant, Sherman, Thomas and Sheridan, ⌈ Dec. 25, '64 ⌉ behold the utmost encouragement. Grierson, with his cavalry marching from Tennessee to Louisiana, has discovered the Confederacy to be a "shell with nothing in it." With Grant holding Lee in his relentless clutches at Petersburg, Thomas looking about for the scattered remnants of Hood's Army, Price driven out of Missouri, Sheridan, at the head of his troopers, ready to vault into the saddle, and Sherman turning his face towards Augusta and Charleston, seemingly the "last ditch" is very, very near. Yet, that the enemy is not disposed to yield till forced to do so, on the very last day of the year, when "Happy New Year" is already ready for utterance by millions of happy voices, the Union picket line, in the region of Forts Wadsworth and Howard is surprised by a party of the enemy who charging furiously, yelling and firing rapidly, drive our men back into their main works with hardly a chance to exchange a shot. We lose two killed, three wounded and thirty-five captured, and the Johnnies took back with them the blankets, knapsacks and whatever other belongings they could find. So alert and swift were the rebels, so well had they planned their attack that they were out of range before the men in the forts could return their compliments. So ends the year.

1865.

January, the month of good resolutions and merry greetings, finds the opposing armies in front of Petersburg still grimly plying their guns and wishing for the end of the war. In the campaign from the Rapidan southward to the end of the year, Grant has lost in killed, wounded and captured more men than Lee was reputed to have had under his command when the fight began, yet the line in blue in front of the beleaguered city is just as persistent, just as vigorous as when the siege was started. While the exhaustless resources of the North are indicated by Lincoln's call for a half million more soldiers and follows that with a proposition to draft 300,000 more, Lee is writing the Confederate Secretary of War, "There is nothing within reach of this army to be impressed. The country is swept clear. Our only reliance is upon the railroads. We have but two days' supplies." General B. F. Butler, after the failure of the Fort Fisher attack has been relieved and sent home to Lowell, and General Terry is organizing a new expedition against the great fortification and ere the month is over his success will be heralded the country over. In its snug cabins or huts, the Potomac Army is gaining strength for the signal which will draw the men from their repose and send them forward. The winter is unusually severe, but, well clad and covered, the men in blue wot little of the sufferings of their adversaries in gray who are passing through all of the anguish which their fathers knew at Valley Forge. Of the Fifth Corps it need be said only that it and its many regiments are writing letters home, reading the matter sent them from those same homes, watching the foe and looking toward the end. The end of the month was signalized by the arrival of the so-called Peace Commission, consisting of Vice-President Alexander H. Stephens of the Confederacy and others who, February 3rd, met President Lincoln and Secretary Seward at Fortress Monroe, but, as the President would not enter into any negotiations without assurance of unconditional acknowledgment of perpetual union and the abolition of slavery, which the Confederates were not prepared to grant, nothing came of the meeting.

It is in this same January that Major A. R. Small, in his history of the Sixteenth Maine[U] has the following very Jan. 31, '65 pleasant words about the Thirty-ninth, words that the members of the Bay State Regiment thoroughly appreciate and fully reciprocate:

Among the strongest and most lasting attachments formed by the Sixteenth for other troops during its term of service was that for the Thirty-ninth Massachusetts, Colonel Davis commanding. I have no record of the date when it joined the First Brigade, but it was a day which marked an era of progressive good feeling, which ripened into warm, personal attachments.

The Regiment was splendidly officered, and under its able commander was an ever present incentive for us to do our very best. We never reached its precision in the manual of arms. We doubt if in this particular qualification it had a superior in the army; certainly it had not an equal in the Corps. Colonel Davis had a quiet way of coming into our hearts and he came to stay.

Though the men in the ranks knew it not, nor for that matter did the majority of the officers, yet it is stated that on the last night in January orders went to the several Corps of the Potomac Army to be ready to march. From that moment activity was prevalent; increased firing along the front concealed to some extent the work of the railroad in bringing up the necessary supplies from City Point. As early as the 4th of February came orders to the Regiment to be ready to move at a moment's notice. The 5th brought the order to report at brigade headquarters where the other regiments of that body were found, and the Corps was joined at 7 a. m. As usual Gregg's cavalry had preceded us and as on several former occasions the Fifth Corps leads the infantry to be followed by the Second and a repetition of the Hatcher's Run incidents of last October and December. The Fifth Corps is to pass around the enemy's right flank while the other troops assail in front; Crawford's Division to which the Thirty-ninth belongs marches last. Our direction is toward Dinwiddie Court House within two miles of which we camp for the night. Monday, the 6th, we are detailed for picket duty; in the afternoon we cross Hatcher's Run and in the first battle-line we are at the right, the enemy being strongly entrenched at Dabney's Mills. The first attempt to dislodge the rebels is unsuccessful, but in a second charge we take the works which, however, we are compelled to vacate because of lack of support.

The events of this day so far as the Second Brigade is concerned are effectively told by Major Isaac Hall, historian of the Ninety-seventh New York, at this time a part of the Brigade:

Early in the afternoon of the following day (6th), Crawford's Division moved forward into the woods in search of the enemy. He was supported on the left by Ayers' (Second) Division; Gregg's cavalry being on the extreme flank. This movement covered the Vaughn and Dabney Mill roads, and Baxter's Brigade was on the right of the column. The enemy's skirmishers were soon reached and pressed back upon the main line of Pegram's Division of Gordon's Corps, which also retired to the ruins of an old mill, where it made a stand. As the brigade came to an opening, a formidable fort—as was supposed—presented itself to view, and a strife occurred between the color bearers of the Sixteenth Maine and the Ninety-seventh New York as to which should first plant its standard upon the fort. The contestant of the Ninety-seventh achieved the victory; but great was his disappointment when instead of a veritable fort he found only a huge heap of saw-dust. A lively musketry fire was kept up here for twenty or thirty minutes, when Mahone's heavy columns came to the support of the line in our front. This was a most inopportune moment for the Fifth Corps; many of the men were already out of ammunition and the line surged back in spite of the officers. General Warren was himself at the front and with his ready glass was coolly surveying the enemy. He was pointed to by the officers, and as if ashamed of themselves the men faced about, but this was of no account since only a few shots were fired; the best of men will not stand with empty muskets and be shot down, and to charge with empty cartridge boxes and unloaded pieces was out of the question; hence the retreat was continued, not precipitately, but the line surged slowly and sullenly to the rear. The enemy was not eager to follow, as if doubting the sincerity of our retreat. An ordnance wagon had been ordered up, and some four or five hundred yards in front of our works Captain Trembly was met with an ammunition wagon with which, in the narrow road, he could neither advance nor retreat and was about to destroy it. The wagon was caught by   Feb. 6, '65   the men and quickly changed ends, and when our trenches were reached the ammunition was quickly distributed. A part of the Sixth Corps had arrived, and as the Fifth emerged from the woods it was fired into by the former, which seemed inclined to dispute our passage to the rear, some raw troops mistaking our line for that of the enemy. The latter did not press heavily upon our fortified position but seemed satisfied to know that our forces were well up. Our men lay upon their arms through the long, cold night. The morning of the 7th was cold and rainy; the rain soon turned to sleet which covered the ground and rendered the movements of troops difficult and somewhat dangerous. Our hands became so benumbed that it was difficult to handle our pieces, still we held our positions and occasionally advanced upon the enemy, which seemed to consist of a thin, gray line covering itself in the woods.

The foregoing wagon incident is told in quite a different manner by a survivor of our Regiment who believes in giving credit to him to whom credit is due:

At the battle of Hatcher's Run, Feb. 6th, 1865, our forces made a charge on the rebels, driving them back quite a distance; four of our ammunition wagons followed in through a cart path, when all at once our line broke and began falling back. The Captain of the ordnance wagons became rattled and ordered Sergeant W. P. Brown of Company K, Thirty-ninth, who was ordnance sergeant under him, to have the drivers unhitch the mules and burn the wagons, he himself taking the first two wagons and destroying them. Sergeant Brown kept his head, turned his two wagons around and saved one of them, the other, breaking a pole, had to be abandoned; the Captain in the meantime lost his horse, which was caught by Sergeant Brown, who went back in search of the officer, whom he found wandering about like a crazy man. Brown managed to get him on his horse and piloted him to the rear. Now comes the injustice, the Captain was complimented very highly on his bravery, a picture came out in the New York papers showing him destroying the wagons to keep them out of the hands of the rebels, while Brown was never mentioned or noticed in any way. Brown said that if he had had full charge, he could have saved three of the wagons at least, for he would have been perfectly sober—"To him that hath shall be given."

The particular part borne by the Thirty-ninth was to form in line at 8 a. m. and then to be deployed as skirmishers in front of the Brigade. Thus advancing, the skirmishers of the enemy were driven from three lines of rifle pits back into their main works which were near. At 5 p. m. our line was ordered to advance upon them, but the assault proving unsuccessful the line fell back to its original position where it remained exposed to a galling fire till late at night, when it was relieved. Wednesday, the 8th, was spent in bivouac, a couple of miles back of the scene of Tuesday's activities. The next day (9th), the Regiment went on picket and, when relieved on Friday, the 10th, it moved back to its old camp, near the Jerusalem Plank Road to get the men's baggage that had been stored there. After this ebulition, which cost the Fifth Corps 1,165 killed and wounded and 154 missing, quiet again fell on the army, and on the 11th, moving out to the extreme Union left near Hatcher's Run, camp was again pitched and winter quarters were once more prepared. One writer says that the Brigade was camped near the Goshen House, the Fifth Corps being massed in rear of the Second. However disagreeable such variations in what many would have made a peaceful winter may have been to the soldiers, there is not a doubt that the lesson of constant watchfulness was thoroughly impressed upon everyone, officers as well as men. Here, subjected to the accustomed routine of camp and picket duty, February wore away.

The beginning of March brought little if any variation on the ending of the preceding month, yet there was a feeling in most minds that the month would bring on the commencement of active hostilities. Everybody knew that Sherman had reached North Carolina, and that General Joe Johnston, with such forces as he could secure, was trying to prevent the further advance of the triumphant army northward. The line whose beginning we heard announced amid the thunders of Spottsylvania had encompassed Petersburg and was slowly but surely extending towards that never ending left. Though the army   Mar., '65   did not know it, General Lee in these March days had sought an interview with Grant with reference to some solution of the problem so long under consideration. The latter had wisely referred the matter to Washington, whence Lincoln warned the Lieutenant General against having any conference with Lee unless to accept his surrender. Save for just a little vigor shown by Sheridan and his cavalry there was practically nothing doing in the Old Dominion till away past the middle of the month when, on the 25th, the Confederates made their charge upon Fort Steadman, in front of the Ninth Corps, the very last aggressive movement on the part of the Army of Northern Virginia, effectually demonstrating to the exacting Confederacy that its soldiery had fired its last charge of ammunition in attack and that hopeless resistance and flight were the only resources left.

As side lights to the story of a single regiment in the great struggle, it might be said that United States Senator E. B. Washburn of Minnesota came down from Washington, arriving at City Point March 10th, the bearer of the medal which Congress had voted to General Grant for his distinguished services; the presentation was made in the main cabin of the steamer which brought the Senator, the evening of the 11th, the day itself having been given to a ride through the army and a review of some of the troops. General Meade and staff were present at the presentation, which was made in eloquent words by Washburn, a personal friend of Grant, and the latter received his honor with all the modesty that ever characterized all of his acts. While all this was taking place and the infantry of the great army was gaining strength for the coming ordeal, Sheridan and his ever untiring cavalry were continuing the raid on which, with 10,000 riders, he had started from Winchester, February 27th and, like a cloudy pillar by day and one of fire by night, he had ridden southward, once more administering severe punishment to Early and his followers; between Staunton and Charlottesville, had destroyed mills and factories, a considerable portion of the James River Canal, railroad bridges and tracks; and now, with his wearied horsemen, is approaching White House on the Pamunkey River.

Nor was March altogether one of idleness for the Thirty-ninth, since the new quarters constructed in February had to be maintained, and ordinary policing of camp will insure an appetite for any healthy soldier, and picket duty added kept everybody busy even if they were not marching and fighting. A newspaper correspondent of the day, having been through the camp and finding it extremely well kept, commented on the same in exceedingly complimentary terms, concluding with, "and the soldiers are spoiling for a fight," which, coming to the observation of the men, one of them thus moralized in his diary, "To say that a soldier is anxious for a fight and is eagerly waiting for a combat with the enemy is talk that savors of nonsense; only a lunatic would use such words. A soldier can be brave and can most ardently wish for the overthrow of the enemy, and be willing to fight if he must, but he never desires battle when strategy will do just as well, unless drunk or crazy like some of the newspaper men." Thursday, the 9th of March, brought along a pleasure in that the Regiment passed in review before that most excellent former division commander, General John C. Robinson, who had been so severely wounded at Laurel Hill and was just getting about once more. On the 14th, General Warren conducted a review of the entire Corps, a fact that set men to remarking that a move-out would soon be in order. Two days later, the 16th, another exhibition of our soldierly attributes and attainments was made for the edification of Secretary of War Edward M. Stanton and others, the Thirty-ninth acquitting itself in a praiseworthy manner.

The expiring thrust of the Rebellion, the assault and temporary capture of Fort Steadman on Saturday, the 25th of March, called for immediate aid from different ⸏ March 25, '65 ⸏ parts of the line, the Thirty-ninth with others; coming at five o'clock in the morning it was a great surprise to all of us; though the attack was about ten miles to the right, the noise of heavy artillery was excessive, and the Fifth Corps in light marching order was ordered to the rescue at once. The response was immediate and eager, and the Corps had a commendable pride in itself as it moved out of its several camps with brave Warren at its head, marching briskly towards the conflict, but before the scene could be reached the firing ceased and we were halted till, all danger passed, we were ordered back to camp. Near the Gurley House the Corps was reviewed by President Lincoln, it being not a little interesting that the President and his family had arrived at City Point the night before and he was near enough to see the 1600 prisoners taken at the Fort as they marched by.

It was March 24th, or the day before the assault on Fort Steadman, that Generals Grant and Meade issued their orders for the general movement against the enemy, the same to begin on the 29th. The Fifth Corps was in reserve and occupying camps in the rear of and to the left of the Second Corps. Griffin's (First) Division was on the right, closely connecting with the Second Corps; Ayres' (Second) was next at Griffin's left and Crawford's (Third) was still further to the left and near the Halifax Road. The movable force of the Potomac Army consisted of the Second and Fifth Corps and Sheridan's Cavalry. By the orders of March 27th General Warren was to march at 3 a. m. on the 29th and, crossing Hatcher's Run at W. Perkin's house, thence to march to the junction of the Old Stage Road and the Vaughn Road and from that point to open communications with the Second Corps, having accomplished which he was to move to a position in the vicinity of Dinwiddie Court House. These orders were subsequently somewhat modified. How near these days were to the end no one realized, though Grant had been exceedingly apprehensive that Lee would endeavor to move out from his entrenchments and, if possible, effect a junction with Johnston to the southward, yet not even his far seeing mind realized that less than two weeks separated these late March days from the final wind-up.

History is to be made rapidly in the coming days; Sheridan is to "push things," and the latest enlisted man is to march and fight feeling that every step and blow are telling against the effort to disrupt the Union.

The right of Lee's army is the object that Sheridan and his forces are seeking. He has his cavalry well in hand and had asked for the Sixth Corps, having in the Valley learned some of its qualities, but that Corps was so placed in the entrenched lines that its withdrawal was impracticable, and the Fifth was sent instead. Proverbially rainy, March of 1865 outdid itself and so watered the scene of hostilities that movements of any kind seemed almost impossible. [V]Warren's advance began at 3 a. m. on the 29th according to schedule, General Joshua L. Chamberlain commanding the First Brigade of Griffin's (first) Division in the lead; the crossing was made by pontoons over Rowanty Creek, the name given to the stream made by the union of Hatcher's and Gravelly Runs. The Corps was halted at the Quaker Road whence, to insure against surprise, advance guards and supports were pushed to within two miles of Dinwiddie Court House. At 10.12 a. m. Warren was ordered by General Meade to move up the Quaker Road to Gravelly Run and thence to throw out parties to the right that he might find the left of Humphreys, commanding the second Corps. At noon he was ordered to cross the Run and advance to Boydton Plank Road which was done, though considerable delay was occasioned by reason of the stream not being fordable and the laying of a pontoon bridge was hindered by the exceptional steepness of the banks of the stream. About this time the enemy was developed and his

skirmishers   March 29, '65   were driven back till near the junction of the

Quaker and Boydton Roads. Here, supported by Gregory of Griffin's Second Brigade, Chamberlain attacked and drove the rebels beyond the junction. It was about 6 p. m. when the assault was made, the sun being about half an hour high. Pushing on rapidly to the Plank Road, we went into bivouac at nine o'clock, holding the Plank Road from Gravelly Run to near Rainey's house where Griffin halted for the night, his pickets on the right reaching those of the Second Corps.

Sergt. Wm. A. Mentzer, Company A, recalls that in falling back he and his tentmate, I. H. Mitchell, in their anxiety to get a few more shots at the foe stopped behind an old shed, but they waited a bit too long, for the Rebels were near enough to get a cross fire on them, on which they started back in a hurry, but within a very few rods Mitchell got a shot which went right through him; however, his height was just right to enable him to throw his arm over Mentzer's shoulder and thus they weathered the storm of bullets, which, he said, made the mud through which they were running fairly bubble, for the enemy was determined to get them, and glad enough they were to reach the reformed line of the Regiment. Mitchell's wound healed all right and in 1913 he survives with his Sergeant to tell the story.

From right to left, the Fifth Corps divisions are Griffin's, Ayres's and Crawford's, the latter in which was the thirty-ninth being nearest Gravelly Run. During the night began the severe rain already alluded to, coming in torrents till the afternoon of the 31st. Full of swamps and ravines, the sand and clay were easily transformed into quicksands; much of the way was quite impassable unless corduroyed; a part of the land was covered with dense forest and undergrowth, so that being very flat the water was quickly carried off. Rowanty Creek, over which the Corps had gone on the 29th, rose so rapidly that on the 30th the pontoon bridge was one hundred feet too short and the wagons of the Corps had to wait until mid-day of the 31st. Notwithstanding this condition, Griffin's Division was advanced up the Boydton Road until the enemy was driven into his main line of works along the White Oak Road. During the 30th, the Thirty-ninth Regiment was on the skirmish line all day while those behind were busy entrenching, though the work was slow since all the tools that could be obtained belonged to the pioneers, those in the wagons not being available, as stated before. It was observed, as an interesting fact, that the advance was then occupying substantially the same position held by Hancock in October of the preceding year. On this 30th of March, General Ayres, according to directions, sent out one of his brigades on a reconnoisance; his advance reached the Holliday house without opposition, crossing a stream which was to play an important part in the operations of the next day, going over the same with so much ease that he did not deem it worthy of mention as an obstacle in his report, though then the rain was falling furiously. Meanwhile Crawford and his Third Division had relieved the two remaining brigades of Ayres's Division and now occupied the line from Gravelly Run to Rainey's house.

During these movements the proceedings of the enemy were quite visible and from captures made by our troops it was learned that there was a considerable tendency of the Confederates towards Five Forks. In reporting this information to headquarters, Warren suggested that Griffin be relieved by Humphreys and that the entire Fifth Corps should support the advance of Ayres, intimating that, if allowed to do this, he could effectually block the White Oak Road and prevent its further use by the enemy. At 9 p. m. orders were received substantially in accord with General Warren's proposition, and Warren at once disposed of his forces so that Ayres should lead, supported by Crawford and Griffin whenever the arrival of Humphreys would permit.

At 8.15, in the morning of the 31st, March 31, '65 Ayres is informed by General Warren that Merritt's cavalry has been driven from the White Oak Road and that he must observe his left with the utmost care lest the enemy assail him from the west as well as from the north, a possibility at every step of the movement from the Rapidan southward. Still heavily falls the rain, diminutive brooks become swiftly flowing streams and ordinary creeks speedily grow to be roaring torrents.

LIEUT. COLONEL HENRY M. TREMLETT
Brevet Colonel

It was 10.30 when Ayres's advance was made, but it seemed that the enemy was like minded with the Union Army and he too was approaching with a far larger force than that of the Federals. The Union line slowly withdrew to its original position while other troops were hurried to its support but without avail and to add to the dangers of the situation a heavy column of the enemy was discovered approaching from the west. Unable to withstand the Confederate advance, our lines gave way in considerable confusion. Crawford's Third Division was thrown into the breach but was too unsteady to stay, and so fell into the general retreat before the enemy. The Thirty-ninth had been thrown forward as skirmishers, they were known as the skirmishers for the Brigade, being near the Holliday house and holding their place with steadiness, but, outflanked by the enemy, of necessity they fell back with the rest. General Baxter, commanding the Brigade, strengthened the line of the Thirty-ninth with the Eleventh Pennsylvania, both regiments being composed of hardened campaigners who did their best; but the odds were too great and they slowly gave way, expecting to rally on the division which, however, had fallen back to the branch of Gravelly Run. Lieut. Colonel Tremlett who, as a member of the Twentieth Regiment, had been inducted into battle at Ball's Bluff, here received his mortal wound and was borne from the field. Captain Willard C. Kinsley, Company K, was also mortally wounded and the command of the regiment devolved upon Captain Cooper of Company F.

When General Warren reached the scene of conflict and realized the situation he seized the flag of a Pennsylvania regiment and rode up and down the lines, trying to stem the retreat but without avail, it being evident that the men would not stop on the western side of the branch of Gravelly Run, mentioned in the advance of Ayres on the 30th. Still waving his flag and trying to halt the men on the eastern side of the stream, he succeeded in once more forming a well ordered line and the approach of the enemy was effectually withstood and Griffin's men recrossing the branch drove the enemy back. By this time Humphreys, still further to the east, sent reinforcements so that the rebels were effectually prevented from making any further serious attack. At 2.30 in the afternoon the Union Army again advanced and effectually drove the enemy back over all the ground won in the forenoon and never halted until it was on the White Oak Road, the Confederates themselves saying it was one of the most gallant charges that they had ever seen. "Crawford now reached the road and, following the line of the rebel entrenchment to the east, connected with Miles of the Second Corps, who had advanced and driven the enemy into their works to the east and to the Plank Road." Ayres also had not fired a musket in this advance, was halted just before reaching the road, and, still covering the left near the house of W. Dabney, looked down the road towards Five Forks. The enemy had failed in his effort to double up the Union left and what was worse for him had lost the White Oak Road and was effectually penned up within his works.

All this time Sheridan was having more trouble than usually fell to the lot of Little Phil. He was near Dinwiddie Court House and the cavalry of the enemy was making a more stubborn showing than was their wont, indeed the men in blue were yielding to those in gray and late in the afternoon, Warren sent a brigade (Bartlett's) of Griffin's Division to Sheridan's relief, this being the first of   April 1, '65   the Fifth Corps to move to the assistance of Sheridan in response to his call for infantry.

April 1st, so often mingled in Anglo Saxon minds with fooleries of all descriptions, was one of intense earnestness to the long time rivals along that line, reaching from the other or further side of James River to Five Forks, a distance of nearly or quite forty miles. Good Bishop Berkeley's aphorism as to the Star of Empire and its western way has another application as General Ord and his divisions from the Twenty-fourth and Twenty-fifth Corps leave the north side of the James to Weitzel and his colored troops, and moving westward occupy space to the left of the Sixth; from the right of the latter, Parke and the Ninth Corps extend to the James. Humphreys and the Second Corps are between Ord and the Fifth Corps, while Sheridan and his troopers are at the extreme left, making sure that the Confederates shall not escape to the southward. So generally have the rebel lines been reduced at Lee's left, it seems strange that the Union troops in that locality did not advance into the all but empty trenches. A wonderfully alert line of men is that which, looking northward, sees the earthworks which must be stormed, and that right early. The showing of Confederate cavalry at the Union left, with the constant coming of infantry, demands its destruction and this is the task that Sheridan has set for himself on this day.

The last day of March saw Sheridan at the close of a day not entirely to his liking, and a portion of the Fifth Corps was hurrying to his aid. General Horace Porter in his "Campaigning with Grant" says, "The Fifth Corps had borne the brunt of the fighting ever since the army had moved out on March 29th; and the gallant men who composed it, and who had performed a conspicuous part in nearly every battle in which the Army of the Potomac had been engaged, seemed eager once more to cross bayonets with their old antagonists. But the movement was slow, the required formation seemed to drag, and Sheridan, chafing with impatience and consumed with anxiety, became as restive as a racer struggling to make the start." For many reasons the advance of Warren's men towards Five Forks was slow; Ayres and the Second Division went first and reported to Sheridan or one of the latter's staff officers before daylight of the 1st; under orders, the commands of Griffin and Crawford began their march towards Five Forks before daylight of the 1st. The movement was made with considerable caution because of information as to the positions of the enemy, stated the night before by Sheridan, and with consequent slowness. At 7 and 8 a. m. respectively Griffin's and Crawford's Divisions halted and were permitted to cook their breakfasts and to rest, General Warren halting with them. In the formation of the Corps finally, Crawford was on the right, Ayres on the left with Griffin massed in rear of Crawford's right flank; Baxter's Brigade in which the Thirty-ninth was ranged held the extreme right of the Third Division.

The orders were to advance to the White Oak Road and to swing to the left, keeping the sun over the left shoulder. When the advance was made it was found that the line was half a mile too far to the right and a readjustment was necessary. In this effort, Crawford's Division was thrown directly into the air and it seemed as though he were marching away from the field. General Warren[W] hastened   Apr. 1, '65   to rearrange the confused line, an effort not unaccompanied with difficulty. In this particular movement, as a regiment in the Third Division, the Thirty-ninth bore its part and of this Captain Charles H. Porter says:—

After getting over the White Oak Road we never saw any clearing of any description until we came over the cleared field in which were the chimneys of some houses, which is marked "chimneys" on the map. We swung to the north of those chimneys and as the line came around we went into the woods again. Coulter, who had been in reserve, was now on the line of battle and connected with the Second Brigade, Baxter's.

It was a very wide sweep that the Third Division made and in its progress a battery was captured, the division being under fire all of the time, and this advance of Crawford's men caused an evacuation of the enemy's entrenchments. Again quoting Captain Porter, we have:—

As the Third Division neared Five Forks, under orders from General Warren, the troops were faced west and we pushed on with our left a little north of the White Oak Road, and when we reached the clearing known as Gilliams' we found the enemy had made a final stand and erected temporary earthworks at right angles to their original lines. The men being out of breath and the formation somewhat broken, the troops halted and opened a desultory fire upon the enemy. General Warren, hastening up, quickly discovered the cause of the delay and, after giving a little time to the reforming of the troops, a very good line was formed, and under the gallant leadership of him who had commanded us for more than a year the troops sprang forward and carried the works. General Warren's horse was shot under him, directly astride the works; and Lieut. Colonel Richardson received the bullet that would have struck our beloved corps commander. By this time, the night was well upon us, and, the enemy being thoroughly dispersed, the troops were halted and General Warren sent one of his staff to find General Sheridan and to ask for further orders. The aide reached Sheridan and received in reply the words that orders had been sent to Warren, and not long after Bankhead's return, Colonel Forsyth arrived with the order from Sheridan relieving Warren from the command of the corps.

Thus on the field of battle after the most successful day's work that he had ever taken part in, Warren was deprived of the command of the corps which he had commanded since March, 1864, and a position which he had earned by soldierly courage and brilliant conduct on many fields. Beginning at Great Bethel, his name is associated with every field upon which the Army of the Potomac was engaged. The insulting remark and the tone and gestures of Sheridan, when he alluded to Warren's services on this day, are a disgrace to this brilliant man. There is no excuse nor palliation for them. The most ardent friend that Sheridan has cannot explain away the insult conveyed to one of the bravest and most devoted of soldiers in the Army of the Potomac.

Crawford's Division suffered more than the other portions of the corps, its casualties being nearly equal to those of the other two divisions. We came under fire as soon as any of the corps and continued to be under fire until after the attack on Gilliam's field.

Long years after the war Sergt. Wm. A. Mentzer of "A" was wont to tell of seeing Sheridan at Five Forks with his Staff, riding along the rear of our lines, shouting, "See the Sons of B——s run! Give them H—L, boys!" "After going a little way into the woods we came to the rear of the Rebel works, where I saw a lad behind the same firing at our folks. Jamming on my bayonet I jumped to the works and ordered him to come out; he looked up and had the impudence, with a smile on his face, to say, 'I wish you would let me fire these five cartridges.' I think I swore some and told him I'd put the bayonet right through him unless he came out at once, and he came. When going to the rear with my prisoner I saw General Warren riding the same way, but not till the next morning did I know that our great and good leader had been relieved of his command."

April 2d, as usual when the most important military operations are to be undertaken, is Sunday and at 4.45 a. m. signal guns announced the general advance of the Union Apr. 2, '65 forces in front of Petersburg, from the Appomattox to Five Forks and beyond. Within half an hour, Wright of the Sixth Corps sends word to Grant that he has carried the enemy's lines in front of his position, and Parke of the Ninth reports that he has captured the outer works with artillery and 800 prisoners, and, before seven o'clock, the Lieut. General telegraphs President Lincoln at City Point the good news. This is the day in which Richmond, the Confederate Capital, lulled into fancied security, quite ignorant of the havoc along the Petersburg lines, is actually attending church and President Davis is summoned from his pew in St. Paul's church with the overwhelming news that the Yankees are coming. How pandemonium broke loose, how the iron clads and other ships in the James River were destroyed; how the three bridges which spanned the James were burned; and Richmond, itself, by a fire set by the Confederates and extinguished by the Union troops, suffered worse than Columbia from the alleged inhumanity of Sherman—all this is history. Every man who wore the blue seemed to have a mission to find someone in gray and the latter, be it said to his everlasting credit, was nothing loath to be found.

Until the afternoon of the 2d, the Fifth Corps was employed on the field of Five Forks in caring for the wounded, burying the dead and destroying the old arms of the captured Confederates. After these accomplishments the Corps, now under General Griffin, received orders to proceed towards Petersburg, Chamberlain's Brigade of Bartlett's Division (till yesterday, Griffin's) leading. Whatever opposition was encountered, it was speedily swept away and, at Church Road Crossing of the South Side Railroad, fifteen miles from Petersburg, a passing train of cars was captured. Crossing the railroad he was ordered to push out if possible to the Cox Road, crossing the line of march at right angles. The First Division continued towards Sutherland Station, still nearer Petersburg, while Crawford's coming up, at about 3 p. m., went over the road with cheers, thence passing down the same about seven miles it turned to the left, marching till 6.30 before halting for the night. In some places the stream at which the stop was made is called Namozine while General Humphreys' map has it Whipponock and here some annalist says the enemy got combative during the evening and the Thirty-ninth, as usual, went out on skirmish duty, when a few shots seemed to settle the matter for the rebels, of whom nothing more was heard during the night.

The great Confederate army that had withstood our onslaughts so many years is clearly trying to escape "on the run" is the thought in the minds of those who follow. The Union cavalry, led by the fiery Custer, is keeping the rear guard of the enemy in plain sight and the infantry is following as rapidly as it can. With the exception of Willcox's Division of the Ninth Corps, which is occupying Petersburg, the entire Potomac Army is in the chase; it is the day when Godfrey Weitzel marches into Richmond and extinguishes the conflagration started by the retiring foe; President Lincoln, leading his son, Tad, enters Petersburg and personally congratulates Grant on the great victory; of the meeting General Horace Porter says, "I doubt whether Mr. Lincoln ever experienced a happier moment in his life." The Fifth Corps follows hard after the cavalry, picking up many prisoners with five pieces of abandoned artillery and a number of wagons. At night, with Crook's Division of cavalry, the Corps encamps on the Nazomine Road, near Deep Creek. On the morning of the 4th, the Corps moves directly and rapidly towards Jetersville, a station on the Richmond and Danville R. R., Sheridan thinking that the rebels are collecting at Amelia Court House about eight miles northeast of Jetersville. On arriving we are ordered to entrench with a view of holding the point until the main army can come up. The position of the Corps is an exposed one, of which Sheridan in his report says, "The enemy lost its last chance of escape by failure to advance and attack the comparatively   Apr. 4, '65   small force and so march on its way to Burkeville." However, luckily for the troops at Jetersville, the Confederates are not reaching the Court House as rapidly as Sheridan thinks and by the afternoon of the 5th, the Second and the Sixth Corps are up and ranged in line with the Fifth. While not described in detail, the whole world knows that everybody was busy in those days with scant time for sleep at night, but through the bewildering maze of horse and foot, it is ours to follow only the men of a single corps and that the Fifth. Many a page might be given to reciting the incidents of Sailor's Creek, the last pitched battle in the East, but our regiment was not in it. At last Sheridan had obtained his wish and the Sixth Corps, having been sent to him, wins renown in this final struggle, while the Fifth moves off at the right of the Second through Paineville on Deatonville. It proved a long, rapid and tiresome march, a distance of thirty-two miles to Ligontown Ferry, experiencing no greater variety on the way than the destruction of abandoned army wagons, gun carriages and caissons of the enemy and the capture of some prisoners.

Says Powell in his History of the Fifth Army Corps, "No army in the world could stand such losses as Lee was meeting every day, and no troops could long endure the strain and fatigue of marching all night and fighting by day, as Lee's men were now enduring. They were by this time deprived of everything, even food, and those captured presented a pitiable condition." Though the slumbers of the Union Army are not as prolonged as they may have been at other times, nevertheless there are halts and rations are had, and with full stomachs and a boundless supply of ammunition the pursuit is maintained. Friday, the 7th, General Meade orders Griffin with the Fifth Corps to proceed to Prince Edward Court House while the Second and the Sixth keep up the direct pursuit. Our Corps crosses the South side R. R. at Rice's Station, just fifty miles west of Petersburg and forty from Appomattox. General Grant's first letter to General Lee, relative to surrender, bears the date of the 7th and the answer of the great Confederate, asking for terms, is dated the same day. Whatever his intentions, Lee does not await the statement of Grant, but pushes on through the night towards the west on his hopeless task. The morning of the 8th beholds the tireless Second Corps, closely followed by the Sixth, in eager pursuit. The Fifth Corps also has an early start and striking the Lynchburg R. R. at Prospect Station, twenty miles from Appomattox, at about noon, follows thence Ord's forces towards Appomattox Court House and at 2 a. m. of the 9th, Sunday, bivouacks about two miles from the site of the immortal scene so soon to be enacted having marched twenty-nine miles from Prince Edward's Court House.

Meantime, on the 8th, Grant and Lee had again exchanged courtesies, the former writing to Lee that his surrender could be accepted only on the understanding that his soldiers should not take up arms against the United States until properly exchanged, and the famous Virginia names the 9th as the day for their meeting, stipulating however that it need not necessarily lead to his surrender, and 10 a. m. as the hour. All this is not known to the rank and file, who for ought they know are still due for weeks of marching and fighting, though for the last few days there has been considerably more of the former than of the latter. Accordingly there was no surprise abroad when the familiar assembly call rang out on the morning air of the 9th and without rations the day before, or breakfast this morning, at four o'clock, the Corps moved from its bivouac and reached the headquarters of General Sheridan at 6 a. m. The cavalry evidently was hotly engaged and the Twenty-fourth Corps was moving out when Ayers of the Fifth (Second Div.), followed by Bartlett and the First Division, took position also. General Griffin reported that the failure of the Third Division to be in line with the others was entirely the fault of the commander, though Apr. 9, '65 he had been notified of the necessity of keeping well closed up; as a result the division did not reach its proper position till after hostilities for the day were over.

The 9th day of April will figure in history as one of the most important dates ever recorded; the correspondence, now passing between Grant and Lee, will rank with the other all but sacred documents in our national records. Hostilities had begun and our lines were pressing forward, driving the enemy, when a message was received from Sheridan that fighting should cease as the Confederates were about to surrender. On the scenes that follow—those beneath the famous apple tree and within the parlor of Wilmer McLean, where foemen "worthy of their steel" were assembled—it does not behoove us to linger, for they are as familiar as household tales throughout the land. The two pre-eminent figures, those of Grant and Lee, meet face to face, each one increasing the esteem in which he must be held as long as the Nation lives.

"These in the robings of glory,

Those in the gloom of defeat,

All with the battle-blood gory,

In the dusk of eternity meet."

While the great majority of the triumphant army, setting their faces homeward, start on the return march the next day after the surrender, to the troops of General Ord and the First Division of the Fifth Corps is entrusted the honor as well as task of receiving the formal "laying down of arms" by the beaten Confederates. This crowning event does not take place until the 12th, the Fourth anniversary of the firing upon Sumpter, when at nine o'clock in the morning General Joshua L. Chamberlain of Maine, having asked for the services of his old Brigade, the Third, had the same ranged in line to receive the oncoming Southrons. "It was not long before a column of gray was seen marching down the valley which sent a thrill of excitement through every individual present. The Union troops were brought to attention. Evans' Brigade of Gordon's Corps led the advance of the Confederates. As its head reached the extreme right of Chamberlain's line, it was wheeled into company line first and subsequently into general line confronting the Union troops. Then each regiment stacked arms, unslung cartridge boxes and hung them on the stacks, and finally laid down their colors. It was a trying scene. And then, disarmed and colorless, they again broke into column and marched off, disappearing forever as soldiers of the Southern Confederacy."[X]

While to the Fifth Corps came the honor of receiving the formal surrender of the Confederates the fact that the men had to linger here, at least some of them, until the 15th brought upon them certain hardships, disagreeable in spite of their pleasure over the successful ending of the campaign. For some reason, perhaps the destruction of bridges on the route, supplies did not reach the army, so that there was positive suffering on account of lack of food. Only a few days before, hungry rebel stomachs had been filled through the foresight and kindness of Grant, and now the victorious Yankees are experiencing want themselves; somehow there comes to mind the Scriptural expression, "He saved others, himself He cannot save." To crown all, a severe rain fell during the 14th, so without tents and minus rations, the soldiers passed a miserable day and night. It was about noon of the 15th, that the Corps began its retrograde movement, but the rain had rendered the roads well nigh impassable, hence the course backward had few of the features of a triumphal procession, everyone being on the lookout for expected rations, but none arrived, and after dark came the orders to halt, break ranks and make the best of the situation for the night; meanwhile the rain was falling incessantly. The 16th dawned cold and raw and under the circumstances the men were as comfortable when marching as when nominally resting. At noon the Appomattox was reached ⟨Apr. 14, '65⟩ and, on a temporary bridge it was crossed, and soon after Farmville was gained, a place more conspicuous in history than in fact.

Here, at 4 p. m., came the dispatch announcing the death of President Lincoln and the already discouraged men had a deeper pitch of woe to bear, naturally the rank and file of them ascribing the assassination to the Confederate leaders rather than to a half-crazed actor. It is said that to properly drape their colors, some of the bearers actually dipped their handkerchiefs in ink. The next day, Monday, the 17th, the homeward route was resumed by way of Burkeville, and on the 21st the Second Brigade encamped at Blacks & Whites Station on the Southside R. R. Evidently the Fifth Corps was distributed along the road, for Powell mentions Sutherland Station, near Petersburg, as the camping place, reaching the same on the 23d; and a diarist of the Thirty-ninth, who was at corps headquarters, places the same at Nottoway Court House. However placed, in due time the army learned of the surrender of Johnston in North Carolina on the 26th. Here too were welcomed back many of the men who were captured in the Weldon

R. R. incident, among them being Major F. R. Kinsley upon whom devolved the command of what was left of the Regiment.

We observed May Day by breaking camp and resuming the march towards the North, passing through Petersburg on the 3d, taking hurried glances at what had occasioned us so many months of toil and danger. The James River was reached at Manchester, just across from Richmond, so as to pass through the former Capital of the Confederacy on Saturday, the 6th, taking note in passing of Libby Prison, Castle Thunder and the State House. Near the latter to review the Army of the Potomac, excepting the Sixth Corps, were standing Generals Meade, Henry Wager Halleck and other officers. The Sixth Corps was still doing guard duty along the railroad, between Burkeville and Danville. On the 9th, we pass over the famous battlefield of Fredericksburg where Massachusetts regiments suffered so severely. We cross the Rappahannock on pontoons below the city, this being our tenth and last time, and Friday, the 12th of May, beheld us on Arlington Heights, near Fort Albany and almost on the very spot of our first camping ground when, in September, '62, we crossed the Potomac and entered the enemy's country, thus ending where we began. What days of wearisome marching, long and dreary vigils on picket line and vidette, what dangers of the embattled field the interval covers! The extended line marks our duties along the Potomac, in Washington, from Harper's Ferry to Antietam and thence southward to the Rapidan, with a backward turning to Bull Run and Thoroughfare Gap, through the Wilderness, Spottsylvania and Petersburg, the pursuit, surrender and return, till now the circle is complete. With so much behind us, what wonder that visions of home become more and more absorbing!

However, there yet remained the Grand Review for which in part Sherman's Army had made the trip from North Carolina, and it was an inspiring sight to see the many tents of the men who had made the world-famous "March to the Sea" as they were spread over the heights back of Alexandria. Very likely the Review was worth all it cost, but to the men who had to undergo the fatigue incident to it, there was no little bitter mingled with the sweet; some even claimed that the exhibition of Tuesday, the 23d, when the Potomac Army marched in review was the most exacting they had ever taken and they thought it was for the express and only purpose of gratifying a sightseeing proclivity of certain authorities well up the line; Sherman's men paraded on the 24th. The next night, that of the 25th, there was an illumination by the Army of the Potomac, candles being lighted on every tent and rockets were sent up. The brigades turned out, every man carrying a candle and thus marched to corps headquarters, May 23, '65 where hearty cheers were given for General Griffin. For the remainder of the month there is little more than a waiting for the final muster-out and occasional visits to Washington, Alexandria and other near-by points of interest.

The coming of June simply intensified the home-longing and the feeling that we must go very soon. The ceremony of muster-out began on the 2d, terminating on the 3d, on whose night comes the statement that we will depart at 8 a. m. of the 4th. According to schedule, we start, the day being Sunday, and march into Washington and there wait till 2 p. m., when the train is taken for Baltimore; the same proved to be a slow one for we do not reach the city until five o'clock. Then comes the march through Baltimore, the boarding of another train and an all night's ride to Philadelphia, arriving in time for a breakfast at the Cooper Shop, whose hospitality we had tested on our way southward in September, '62. Thence we ride through New Jersey to New York city, where a lunch is furnished by the New England Relief Association, before going on board a steamer bound for Providence, whence by rail we reach Boston early in the morning of the 6th. The wait in Boston is very short and another train transports us to Readville at 8 a. m. and we are assigned to quarters there. By a singular coincidence Lieut. Colonel Tremlett who had been severely wounded at Gravelly Run, March 31st, and was sent home to Boston, dies this very day in his Beacon Street home. While passes were readily given to the homes represented, all were glad to return and receive their discharges and pay on the 14th of June. Thus ends the story of devotion and sacrifice of a regiment that had gone forth to help save the Union and whose members now are returning to the paths of peace. They have made an honorable record, not alone pleasing to themselves but to the hundreds of those to follow and who, in the years to come, will call their memory blessed.

They are returning to their homes,

"Where the matron shall clasp her first-born

With tears of joy and pride;

And the scarred and war-worn lover

Shall claim his promised bride!"

—*Bryant.*

IN REBEL PRISONS.

While men of the Thirty-ninth suffered in nearly all of the prison-houses of the South, the greater number spent their periods of confinement in Salisbury, N. C. The two hundred and thirty-two swept off August 18-19, '64, at the Weldon R. R., after incarceration at Libby and Belle Isle, were taken to Salisbury and there spent the time till their liberation in February, '65. Among the unfortunates was John H. Eames who was First Sergt. Co. C, and whose diligent care secured the data concerning his fellow sufferers which perfected the State House rolls and gave the boon of certainty to many a stricken home in the old Bay State. His tabulated statement bears the following names:—

Company A:—Serg'ts, J. W. Cottrell, J. P. Dodge; Corp's, T. Bean, G. W. Cole, S. C. Packard; Privates, F. D. Adams, G. J. Boodry, G. W. Burnham, W. S. Evans, J. K. Gibbs, C. M. Goodwin, A. S. Haskell, R. E. Mears, W. Hunting, J. H. Mitchell, D. F. Morse, L. Marteau, W. Myers, L. E. Ordway, J. H. Perkins, J. M. Sawyer, E. Stevens, G. F. Whitcomb.

Company B:—Serg'ts, E. S. Davis, J. R. Robinson; Corp's, G. A. Andrews, E. H. Lewis; Privates, W. M. Bills, J. Cassidy, M. Cunningham, F. Edmonds, J. Gunning, J. Kilduff, Geo. McDonald, T. P. Mohan, P. Reaney, H. R. Smith, F. T. Start, D. O. Sullivan, Charles Swan, C. Wadsworth, J. Burns captured Dec. 11, 1864.

Company C:—Serg'ts, J. H. Eames, I. T. Morrison; Privates, J. M. Baldwin, S. C. Bowen, Wm. Cheeney, F. J. Curtis, E. C. Dean, B. J. Ellis, P. Gleason, E. Ireland, A. Joyce, J. Lange, J. McGee, M. F. Roberts, W. H. Rogers, W. S. Smith, Wm. Vaeight.

Company D:—Serg't, H. Curtis; Corp's, W. H. Burns, W. E. Colburn, A. Derby, C. C. Dickerman, H. Newcomb, E. Thomas; Privates, F. Becker, A. Bullard, C. Bushnell, E. Damon, S. DeForrest, T. Doyle, J. Durgin, J. E. Forbes, J. F. Green, W. Hayden, D. Kanily, W. G. Keep, T. H. Lunt, P. Moran, E. Pierce, G. W. Savill, H. Shavlin, J. Sheehan.

Company E:—Serg'ts, J. Kennedy, E. Ladd; Corp's, F. A. Glines, D. Gorham, J. E. Horton, W. L. Howard; Privates, J. M. Allen, W. H. Bartlett, J. Brown, J. B. Canfield, C. L. Carter, J. Creedan, Geo. H. Hatch, P. D. Horgan, C. G. Jones, D. Kendrick, J. F. Locke, A. W. Phillips, John Riley, T. P. Shaw, F. W. Thompson, L. Ulrich, J. Vancleff, H. K. Webster.

Company F:—Serg'ts, W. Doherty, H. B. Horton, D. Wood; Corp's, J. Bagth, B. J. Hall; Privates, P. Conway, J. Day, W. E. Dean, G. W. Gay, J. A. Hathaway, B. L. Howland, W. H. Jones, D. S. Kane, J. A. Lawler, S. Packer,

T. W. Paul, D. M. Phillips, F. C. Skinner, E. H. C. Smith, J. Smith, A. P. Terry, G. L. Titus, W. Walsh.

Company G:—Serg'ts, J. Adams, H. C. French, W. H. Jacobs; Corp's, J. D. Day, P. J. Shaw, T. G. Short; Privates, J. Bannon, W. Bright, C. Danbenmayer, W. G. Dodge, D. R. Ewell, M. Fitzgerald, C. E. French, M. Gorman, F. K. Hanson, Z. M. Hayden, H. F. Hersey, S. W. Hutchins, J. Kennedy, H. W. Leavitt, T. Murphy, J. S. Neal, S. V. Smith, C. A. Spaulding, E. A. Spear, N. W. Thayer.

Company H:—Serg'ts, C. W. Richardson; Corp's, E. J. Childs, B. F. Prescott, S. O. Savil; Privates, J. Brunel, P. Collins, M. Dailey, J. Davis, J. Doody, J. Farren, R. T. Gammon, R. T. Holmes, T. Kelley, J. Keniston, E. F. Kimball, E. McCarthy, G. C. Millett, J. H. Millett, R. Monk, T. Murray, P. Shean, D. Southworth, F. H. Sumner, G. N. B. Thomas, E. Tileston.

Company I:—Serg'ts, E. Brown, J. Currier; Corp's, W. H. Beal, W. H. Clough, W. Collins, S. Hardy; Privates, W. L. Allen, J. D. Bispham, C. B. Butterfield, D. O. Chamberlain, S. C. Chace, A. M. Cole, E. Curran, S. Gourley, T. Hoey, C. O'Brien, A. E. Smith, N. D. Stearns, F. E. Travis, C. H. Williams.

Company K:—Corp., S. Richardson; Privates, J. Bacon, M. Baldwin, J. Brannagan, F. M. Bryant, M. Butler, C. H. Colgate, R. Curry, G. W. Dean, E. Haskins, S. T. Hooper, W. H. Jones, C. H. Kingsbury, A. Lapurve, J. F. Leslie, R. Lombard, J. McGuire, T. Mahony, T. Marran, T. W. Morrill, E. O'Donnell, Peter Parks, J. F. Ramsdell, M. D. Reed, A. H. Richardson, M. Rowland, C. Scott, J. H. Sheehan, F. Spokesfield, G. A. Sprague, E. O. Hemmenway captured Dec. 11, 1864.

In Sergeant Eames' well preserved record, on its final page, is written,—"This book I arranged while in prison from information from the members of the reg't and, to the best of my knowledge and belief, is strictly true. The leaves I purloined from the rebel surgeon's hospital book; the cover I carried through prison, having received it with, of course, the original leaves through the mail, Aug. 18, 1864."

"Left Salisbury Prison at seven o'clock, Feb. 20, 1865; cars started for Greensboro at 8; we rode on top, very cold and slow riding; arrived at G. (fifty miles) at about 7 a. m. Changed cars and lay over until 7 p. m. Left for Danville, Va.; slept nearly all night, reaching D. at daylight; changed cars and started immediately for Richmond, enjoying the prospect of homeward bound. Washington's birthday, Feb. 22; arrived in Richmond about 2 a. m. Waited till 9 a. m. when we were put into Libby Prison, remaining there till nine o'clock of the following morning. Then we started by boat down the

River, passing safely through the obstructions; saw two rebel rams, Fort Darling and other places of interest, reaching the landing (Aiken's) after two hours' sail, and were received by Yankee cavalry and escorted to the Yankee truce-boat, some 3 or 4 miles down the river; passed through the Eighteenth Corps, mostly colored troops, who used us finely giving us bread, tobacco, etc. On seeing the good old Flag we felt that we were free again. We got to our boat all right, except wet feet and some weariness. We soon got the first drink of Yankee coffee for five months and more; it tasted splendidly and we got plenty to eat and felt like new men. We had a safe trip down the river, arriving at Annapolis Feb. 26, '65; started from Salisbury Prison, Monday; reach Annapolis Saturday. This journal was written on the way home, written under difficulties and excitement, and, as a consequence, is not very minute.

"P. S. Many of the poor fellows who lived to leave prison, died soon after reaching home so that, at the time Lee surrendered as far as I could ascertain, four-fifths of those sent to Salisbury were dead, the remainder being more or less broken in health."

CORPORAL F. A. GLINES' DIARY.

Of the foregoing list, Glines, Horton and Locke, all of "E," kept diaries or some form of record, as did Corp. E. H. Lewis of "B," the first two until a few days before their deaths; Private Locke, after the war, embodied his recollections in a very interesting lecture, delivered by him many times. From all of these sources items have been gleaned through the body of the history and especially in the following pages. From the carefully preserved diary of Corporal F. A. Glines extracts are made as follows:—

Fri., August 19, 1864—Lay in line all night; moved a little to the right; were attacked and flanked and I, with the greater part of my reg't, was taken prisoner; were taken to Petersburg under guard; very rainy and muddy.

Sat., 20—Lay in a field all night; very wet, cold and uncomfortable; were taken through the town and put on an island, at the north side of the Appomattox.

Sun., 21—Lay on the island all day; drew rations for one day; I had bread and a small piece of pork, full of worms.

Mon., 22—Were called up at 2 a. m.; left the island at 4; were put aboard the cars and sent to Richmond; are quartered in Libby Prison; drew rations for one day, half loaf corn-bread and a small piece fresh meat.

Tues., 23—Were sent across the street to another prison; were searched and all articles of any value were taken from us; were sent to Belle Isle this afternoon; met John Davis (H) here; am in the Forty-fifth Squad.

Wed., 24—Very hot; are having tents put up for us; we have two meals a day; quarter loaf of corn bread at 10 a. m. and corn bread and soup at 3 p. m.; have to sleep on the ground with no covering.

Thurs., 25—Very hot and uncomfortable; signs of rain to-night; had only one meal to-day.

Fri., 26—Very heavy thunder-shower; last evening several men tried to escape; do not know how many succeeded; several shots fired at them; one man killed and three wounded.

Sat., 27—Sergt. French, Co. G., shot by the guard, one other man wounded; got our tents to-day.

Sun., 28—Very hot; were counted this morning.

Mon., 29—2000 more prisoners sent here this afternoon; enlarging the space for prisoners.

Thurs., Sept. 8—My twenty-first birthday; pleasant weather.

Fri., 9—Were counted to-day; the squads, filled up, stayed outside nearly all day; took different tents when we came in.

Sat., 10—Great fire in Manchester last night; great deal of dispute about tents.

Thurs., Sept. 15—Those men whose terms of service have expired were sent for to-day and their names taken; there was quite a large number of them from nearly all the states.

Fri., 16—Slept cold last night; a warm day; the guard which has been guarding us has been relieved by a lot of old cocks who hardly know a gun from a broomstick; the old guard went off last night.

Thurs., 22—A Dutch reb lieutenant in here this afternoon, trying to enlist Germans in the reb. service; met with poor success, the boys were too loyal for him; the guard-tents on the hill removed.

Sun., 25—A lot of our men went out to-day to work for the reb government as coopers, carpenters and shoemakers; they are a small loss to us; the fewer such men the government has, the better for us.

Mon., 26—Some of our men building breastworks for the rebs opposite the camp; it is a pity that they cannot be made to charge on them with rebs behind the works; did not get anything to eat till about 2 p. m.

Tues., 27—John Davis sent to the hospital; a boat load of tents came over this morning.

Wed., 28—Counted this morning; two men buried themselves outside with the intention of escaping, but one of our men told the Lieutenant, who has kept them in their hole all day buried up to their necks.

Thurs., 29—Heavy cannonading in the direction of Fort Darling; some excitement in Richmond; a battery planted opposite us, across the river; counted to-day; had to stay out nearly all day; got nothing to eat till evening; was very hungry and faint; new tents put in place of the old ones.

Fri., 30—It is six weeks to-day since we were "gobbled" and about as miserable a six weeks as ever I passed, but "nil desperandum"; 670 prisoners sent here to-day, the greater part captured at Winchester.

Sat., October 1—Very heavy cannonading in the direction of Fort Darling; a great deal of excitement in Richmond; the guards have orders to shoot us if we make any cheering or noisy demonstration; rained all day, passed a cold, miserable and comfortless day.

Sun., 2—Rained nearly all last night; some cannonading this morning; a man shot by the guard last night; cloudy nearly all day; the quartermaster and quartermaster sergeant of the island sent to Castle Thunder for selling rations.

Mon., 3—Another man shot by the guard this morning; about 200 more prisoners were sent over here this evening from Libby.

Tues., 4—1100 men were sent away from here this morning; said to be going further south; they were furnished with two days' rations.

Wed., 5—600 more men sent off this morning.

Thurs., 6—900 of us were turned out at 2 a. m. and furnished with two days' rations; marched off the island and lay till four o'clock just off the island, got aboard the cars on the Richmond and Danville R. R. and started en route for Salisbury, N. C.

Fri., 7—Rode on the cars all night, reaching Danville at 10 a. m., a most painful ride; we were packed in like herrings; changed cars and reached Greensboro, N. C, at 10 p. m.; were marched out into a field for the night; very cold and windy.

Sat., 8—A very cold night, slept very little; left Greensboro this morning and reached Salisbury this evening, a very cold ride; 100 men were packed into each car; have drawn no rations since Thursday morning.

Sun., 9—We are in a field of about ten acres, we have no shelter and have to sleep on the ground with no covering, drew rations this morning. Saw Captain Kinsley and the rest of the officers; they are in the field with us in log houses, separated from us by a guard.

Mon., 10—Did not sleep any last night, it was so cold; drew rations of half loaf of bread and a pint of boiled rice; 2000 more men sent here from Belle Isle.

Tues., 11—Slept in the house last night, quite comfortable; drew only half loaf of bread to-day; two men died last night; strong talk of paroling; guess it's only "chin."

Wed., 12—Water very scarce, went outside to-day with some dippers after water.

Thurs., 13—Slept in the house last night, slept very cold; drew rations of hard bread and rice soup to-day; the best rations we have drawn since we came here.

Sun., 16—During the night Captain Davis of the 155th New York Regiment was shot by the guard through the head, he was killed almost instantly.

Wed., 19—All the officers sent away this afternoon; 500 more prisoners sent here this evening from Danville, Va. Have been a prisoner two months to-day.

Thurs., Nov. 10—One of our squad fell into the well to-day and escaped almost miraculously with a sprained shoulder.

Wed., 23—Cleared off this morning; pleasant but very cold; Charley Jones died this morning at eight o'clock; Allen died at 2 a. m.

Thurs., 24—Thanksgiving Day at home; we are on half rations to-day; a hard Thanksgiving day for us, but better times are coming, boys, "Wait a little longer!"

Fri., 25—Made a grand rush for freedom this noon, but we were driven back by the guard and about twenty-five or thirty were killed and wounded; we are on half rations again to-day.

Sat., 26—Phillips died this morning; received a letter from home this evening. It seems good to hear from the dear ones at home; it was written Sept. 27.

Mon., 28—146 colored prisoners came in yesterday from Richmond; they have been captured about two months.

Tues., 29—A large number of our men going out to enlist in the rebel service. I am pretty hard up, but I am bound to stick to Uncle Sam.

Fri., December 2—Rather cloudy but comfortable day; full rations again to-day, bread, meat and rice soup, so I satisfied my hunger for the first time in a long time.

Tues., 6—400 more prisoners arrived here yesterday, mostly cavalry captured in the Valley; 525 men enlisted in the reb service.

Tues., 13—350 men enlisted in the reb service to-day; Thompson of our company went with them; he is the first man to enlist from our company.

Wed., 14—Slept in the hospital last night.

Fri., 16—30 men from our Corps sent in here to-day; three are from our regiment and bring interesting news from the boys.

The entry for the 16th was the last made by the young man, whose Somerville home was as pleasant and comfortable as any which that most attractive place afforded; whose father was fretting at the absence of his son, yet the latter, putting duty to his country before all others, was faithful to the end and died on the 6th of January following, his body sleeping with nearly 13,000 others in a nameless grave.

CORPORAL JOHN E. HORTON'S DIARY.

Corporal John E. Horton was a very regular observer and chronicler of passing events, seldom if ever missing a day. The following extracts are given, not all that he wrote but rather where his records add to those already given from Corporal Glines' entries. A faithful husband and father, nearly every day has some reference to the wife and the baby boy in the far away home and on the 21st of August he laments his inability to get a letter through the lines to Laura, his wife:

Tues., August 23—(The prisoners are in Libby.) Slept first rate. Wash up and eat breakfast. They put part of us into another building opposite; take our names, number of regiment and where we were born, then search us, take our haversacks, etc. Give us rations about 1 p. m., take us to Belle Isle; there are a little over 3,000 of us here. We are divided into squads of 30; Ladd is our Sergeant.

Thurs., 25—Brown is at work, outside, helping the cook; get our rations from across the river; attend prayer meeting.

Mon., 29—About 2100 came from Libby, of the Second Corps; they were taken the 25th at Ream's Station; am sorry to see them.

Tues., 30—Provisions are very high; small loaves of bread are $5.00 in Confederate money and $1.00 in greenbacks; coffee, $15.00; sugar, $12.00; onions, $1.00; apples, $2.00 and $3.00. For $1.00 we get one-fourth of a loaf of bread, a small piece of bacon and a little bean soup, just enough to keep us alive.

Sat., Sept. 3—They have stopped the speculation in corn bread. The Lieutenant says all of it is ours and he will see that we get it. Write a short letter to Laura; fear she may not get my letters; there is a prayer meeting every night. I attend and hope they may do me good.

Sun., October 16—Sell my ring for $60.00 Confederate money and buy a blanket for $40.00. Am sorry to part with the ring, but the blanket will do me more good. A number die every day.

Thurs., 20—Our rations are bread, molasses and rice soup.

Thurs., 27—500 more prisoners arrive from Richmond; they were taken in the Valley and belong to the Sixth, Eighth and Nineteenth Corps.

Fri., 28—Twenty-seven died in the last twenty-four hours; it is sad to see men suffer and die off in this way; my health is still good; have nothing but rice to-day.

Sat., November 5—A number take the oath of allegiance to old Jeff. The Union boys hooted them and kicked one so that he died; Creedon took the oath.

Tues., 8—To-day is Election; wish I were at home to vote for Old Abe. Get no bread or meat, but about a quart of rice soup; feel hungry and weak.

Wed., 9—Get some bread; went sixty hours on a little over a quart of poor rice soup. Felt quite weak and faint, but feel better since getting some bread; from twenty-five to fifty die every day.

Fri., 11—Get bread, meat and soup, but no salt in soup or on meat, there is none in camp.

Sat., 12—The long roll was beat three times last night; someone stoned the guard; have only nine months more to serve.

Mon., 14—The coldest night of the season thus far; sell a pair of socks for $5.00 Confederate money and buy some salt at $1.50 a pint.

Wed., 16—Rained a little in the night. The papers say Abe is elected sure.

Fri., 18—Help take Allen of the Fourth New Hampshire to the hospital; think he cannot live long. It is a sad sight to see how the men are dying off.

Sun., 20—This does not seem like the Sabbath; little Orren is seventeen months old; wish I were at home to see him.

Mon., 21—Rheumatism troubles me some; Allen of the Fourth New Hampshire died last night.

Sat., 26—Get a letter from Laura dated Oct. 2d, and another this afternoon, dated August 27th; they are all well; am very glad to hear from them. Phillips (E) died last night.

Mon., 28—The Rebs count every division at the same time to stop flankers; have an attack of diarrhea.

Tues., 29—370 take oath of allegiance to Jeff and go into the rebel army; short rations and so many dying urge them to this step; diarrhea a little worse.

Wed., 30—Am some better; this is my thirty-fifth birthday; hope to be able to spend my next at home. It is a real Indian Summer day. P. Merrill of the First Massachusetts Cavalry died in our tent. The chimney in the hospital fell, killing one man and wounding several.

Thurs., December 1—A fine day for the first of winter; am much better; sold my rations and bought some bread flour; Locke gave me some pills.

Fri., 2—It is just fifteen weeks since I was taken prisoner, am in strong hopes of being exchanged soon; feel about well.

Sun., 4—Could hear the church bells and it made me feel homesick; how I wish I could be at home with my wife and boy.

Sat., 10—Stormed all night; about three inches of snow fell; a cold, bad night for us prisoners, but I managed to keep warm. Gorham (E) died this morning about two o'clock; he was sick but a short time.

Mon., 12—It froze hard, very cold for those who have no blankets. General Winder and some other rebel officers were here to inspect the condition of the prisoners. Am some better to-day, got wheat flour.

Fri., 16—A few more Yankee prisoners come in, three of the Thirty-ninth, one (Burns) from "B" and one (Hemmenway) from "K," captured last Sunday (11), near Weldon. Sorry to see them here, but glad to hear from the regiment.

Thurs., 22—Drew bread, syrup and soup, no meat for a long time.

Sun., 25—Cloudy, with raw, cool wind; a dull Christmas for me. We got one-half a loaf of bread and a little rice soup for our Christmas dinner, breakfast and supper; wish I were at home, but see little signs of an exchange.

Wed., 28—Tipton was elected our squad sergeant in place of White (deposed); our tent run for Haun, but he got beat; think we have a good sergeant. Rumor says there is to be a general exchange of prisoners the first of January; hope it is true.

Thurs., 29—Rained quite hard all night and our tent leaked some; do not feel very well but hope I shall not be sick.

Fri., 30—A cool, dull day. Have the diarrhea quite bad, but am in hopes to get rid of it soon. John Locke gave me some pills.

Sat., 31—Rained about all day; comes on cold and snows some. Had the diarrhea very bad all night; a cold, dull, disagreeable day for the very last of 1864. It looks like a dark prospect ahead for us prisoners, but I am in hopes to be exchanged soon; so the story runs.

Sun., January 1, 1865—A fine pleasant morning but cool. It does not look like a very happy New Year for me, but am in hopes to get out of this soon. God grant it may be a happy and pleasant one to my wife and boy. Am a little better this morning.

Five days later the hand that wrote the foregoing and that had given daily evidence of its fealty to God, home and country, in devotion to duty and in a daily record of deed and thought, was cold in death, for on the 6th of January Horton died and what was mortal of him was borne out to the trenches to rest with the more than two score of his comrades of the Thirty-ninth who had gone the sad way before him. And thus perished almost 40,000 loyal men, faithful to the end and, "When the Roll is Called up Yonder," it seems highly probable that the most of those, who thus endured cold, hunger and every form of privation in token of their appreciation of duty, will stand a fairly good chance of being able to answer "Here."

FROM DIARY OF CORPORAL EDWARD H. LEWIS, CO. B.

As the Corporal's record goes over the same time and place of other diarists, care is taken to avoid repetitions.

Salisbury, the last of October—The death rate is heavy, owing to bad weather and small rations; the latter also being poor in quality, consisting of what is supposed to be coarsely ground corn meal, including a great deal of the cob. It is mixed with hot water, no salt or seasoning of any kind, and baked in large loaves, about three inches thick and these loaves are cut into squares of about three and one-half inches, the same being a ration for twenty-four hours. In addition to this we have been having about three-quarters of a pint of something called "soup." It is made of North Carolina peas (usually called "cow-peas"), decayed bacon very active with maggots, and water, the process of brewing being as follows: A large kettle receives its bushels of peas, along with its due proportion of the said animated bacon and the necessary liquid, and the combination is boiled until the outer cuticle of the pea is loosened, scarcely longer, and then is dipped out for the sustenance of Yankee unfortunates. Were this all, it would not be so bad, but the foam which appears upon the surface of the soup is very far from being unsubstantial, since therein float hundreds of the vermicular denizens of peas and bacon. Not exactly as appetizing as the bouillon of home preparation nor as clear, yet with closed eyes and bated breath, we manage to enclose it, probably to our bodily good, if not to the satisfaction of our several senses.

Nov. 10—Charles Wadsworth, Company B, dies to-day.

Nov. 24—Many of the boys suffering from hunger, thirst and general exposure, took the oath of allegiance to the Confederacy to-day, thinking by so doing to find an opportunity to escape and reach our lines; fully three hundred have done this during the month of November.

Nov. 25—The attempt to break out of prison to-day was unsuccessful. The prisoners were divided into three divisions, the first being called the Wood Division, since it was expected to make the attack on the big gates where wagons bring in our wood; the second division was to break through the bakeries, while the third was to spike the pieces of artillery that were trained upon the enclosure; mine was the Bread Division and in the effort we lost six killed and ten wounded.

Nov. 27—James Kilduff, Co. B, dies to-day.

Dec. 5—Was asked to enlist in the Confederate army and thus escape this terrible suffering. I replied most positively that I would stand by the old Flag if I died here.

Dec. 27—My shoes, such as they were, were stolen last night and I am barefooted. Could only wrap my feet in rags which I picked up in small pieces. Three rebel Catholic priests came into the prison to-day and tried to influence our Catholic boys to serve in the Confederate army and succeeded in getting many of them.

Feb. 19—Leave Salisbury early in the evening, we know not where.

Feb. 21—Arrive in Raleigh, N. C., this morning, where we are detained during active military operations on and near the Cape Fear River, near Wilmington, N. C.

Mar. 5—Leave Wilmington on transports for Annapolis, Md., which we reach on the 8th at 10 p. m. Here we are detained and enrolled, also relieved of all clothing and reminders of prison life, Uncle Sam issuing to us new suits of clothing.

Mar. 15—Receive two months' pay and commutation for six months and eleven days as prisoner, $84.50 in all. (The commutation covered half rations for the prison period at 25 cents a day.)

Mar. 16—Leave Annapolis, Parole Camp, for home, having a furlough till April 13.

April 14—Reach Baltimore on my return and at 11 p. m. hear the news of President Lincoln's assassination; the returning prisoners, several hundred in number, offer their services to the Provost Marshal in case of need.

April 21—Detailed to take charge of Barracks, No. 43 (Annapolis), and am put to work on the pay roll for this barrack.

May 3—Proceed from Annapolis to Camp Distribution, north of Alexandria, Va.

May 23—Leave camp for Washington via Chain Bridge and, having rejoined my regiment, take part in the Grand Review.

June 14—Paid off at Readville and discharged from the state service.

June 20—With Co. K of the Thirty-fifth, my Company (B) of the Thirty-ninth is given a reception and review by the City Government of Roxbury who were in office 1862, and those on duty now.

JOHN F. LOCKE'S RECOLLECTIONS.

'Twas a gloomy march from the immediate rear of the Confederate Army to Petersburg and a weary night that was spent in the yard of the penitentiary of that town. In the morning we were relieved of all military equipments such as knapsacks, haversacks, canteens, etc., and also all blankets, shelter-tents, overcoats, or extra clothing.... The next day we were removed to an island in the Appomattox and the rain, setting in, rendered the night hideous enough. The boys gathered in squads and, sitting back to back, on the damp, spongy ground, tried to sleep but, with such a hapless present and such a hopeless future, few could enjoy that luxury.

The next day the whole 1800 were escorted out of town about two miles, that we might take the cars for Richmond. Three hard-tacks (the first food received from our captors' hands) were given us to make us hungry and that we might enjoy our excursion. The sound of the battle in progress (the 21st) on the same ground where we were captured was plainly heard, and we could but wish that the results might be more favorable than those of the 19th.... Towards the last of the afternoon we arrived in Richmond and as we alighted from the coal cars we were told that only one hotel in the place could accommodate us and that one was "The Libby" and, as we were strangers in town and might wish to look around a little, we were escorted through some of the principal streets.

Finally the procession brought up in front of Libby and we were stowed away in it; thus in nine of its rooms were packed 1800 men. We spent a portion of our time in examining our new quarters, the walls of which were covered with the names of former fellow sufferers. Here we received our first half loaf of corn bread which was not so bad in quality as it was in quantity. Then came orders from the Prison Inspector, Dick Turner, to hand over all moneys to him for safe keeping, and some unsophisticated ones obeyed, having their names duly registered, but I have not heard that Turner gave any receipt or that anything ever came back. After a very uncomfortable night, owing to our crowded condition, we were glad to see the morning and soon afterward we were taken across the street (Carey) to Pemberton prison and distributed in its rooms in squads of twenty-five. Turner soon came in and, in his insolent, arrogant style, ordered us to strip ourselves that our clothes might be searched, for he was not satisfied with the amount already given up. Stripped naked, and with our clothing a few paces in front of us, we saw our garments searched for valuables.

Our wallets, watches, jackknives, rings and everything of comfort or value that was not absolutely necessary was gathered into a heap and Turner, with greedy eye, not only inspected but appropriated. At the end of a long half hour we were permitted to dress and then were conducted back to Libby, and other squads followed, the procession continuing till well into the next day, everyone being pretty thoroughly plucked. After all, many of the cunning Yankees were able to circumvent the rebels, since bills of large denominations were hidden in such queer places as ears, mouth and hair, thus enabling the possessor to procure needed comforts in coming days.

Having been, in this manner, completely robbed, we were formed in line for Belle Isle; as the dismal name was sounded our spirits fell, for we had heard the stories of suffering there, but to Belle Isle we went and were conducted to one corner, containing about an acre and a half of ground, enclosed by a low breastwork and a deadline. This part of the island was so low that the spring freshets invariably covered it. The soil is composed largely of sand and is prolific of fleas, bugs and other kinds of insects too disagreeable to mention. The place was extremely hot by day and, through its lowness, cold by night; alternately roasted and all but frozen we passed seven miserable weeks upon Belle Isle, but why thus named beautiful we could never imagine.

For three weeks we were without shelter, then came six good A tents for every squad of one hundred men. When it rained or was colder than usual, we were wont to lower the tent upon us, using it as a blanket; here we would lie and all but smother till the call for rations was sounded the next morning at about nine o'clock. Our rations consisted of a piece of corn bread, 5 x 2-1/2 in. in size and a small piece of rancid bacon or boiled fresh beef. Towards three in the afternoon a half pint of soup, composed of wormy beans, was issued and, though the hogs of the keeper usually tasted it first, we relished it and were glad to get it. While we thought this pretty hard fare, the time was to come later when we looked back upon these days as those of comparative plenty.

By new arrivals our numbers were soon swollen to fully 6,000 men, among them being a portion of a regiment of Germans so new to the country that they were unacquainted with our language, hence a deal of trouble for them, as in their ignorance they would wander over the dead line after a chip for fuel, but they never returned. During the day we were permitted to go to the water, through a narrow passage, as often as we pleased, but at night only five were permitted to go at a time. A sergeant (H. C. French) of Co. G, our regiment, having taken his turn, was coming back and of course there was a rush to be the next one to go down, by the boys in the yard, and in their haste they pushed the sergeant, who was quite weak from illness, into the ditch of the dead line. Without a word of warning he was instantly shot dead by one of the sentries, the bullet passing through his head. This sentinel was a young fellow of sixteen years who, with his mother, while living near Mitchell's Station had been supplied with food during the whole of the previous winter by the commissary of our Brigade. We were told that he was paid for this act of ingratitude by a two weeks' furlough home.

An incident will illustrate the straits to which the lack of food will drive otherwise decent men. We were counted regularly once a week, usually on Saturdays, the object being to find out whether any were escaping. To effect this numbering we were filed out, one by one, into a vacant lot which bordered on the river. While here one day, several of the boys completely buried themselves in the sand, hoping to get away from the island in the following night. No loss was suspected on our return but, during the afternoon, a poor hungry wretch went to the gate and, calling for the sergeant of the guard, offered to reveal something of importance if he would give him a loaf of bread. The rebel agreed, whereupon he was shown where the Yankees were concealed in the sand. It is only fair for the sergeant to state that he knocked the informer down with the butt of his musket, saying that if he were as mean as that, he would go and kill himself.

The Confederate mode of punishing petty offenses among us was most cruel. The culprit was placed astride a tall, carpenter's horse, some six feet in height, and ropes were tied to his feet, fastened to the ground and then drawn as taut as possible; his hands were fastened behind him and tied to the horse. In this condition the unhappy sufferer was obliged to pass three or four hours; most always they were taken down insensible and some of them never recovered from this brutal usage. On the 5th of October came orders to be ready to march. Joyfully we obeyed, confident that our destination was the land of the Stars and Stripes, though rations of a loaf and a half of corn bread clearly pointed in another direction, our halting place being on the south side of the James where, by the side of the Richmond and Danville R. R., we lay all day eating our three days' rations. At 5 p. m. a train of baggage cars drew up and the painful fact dawned upon us that we were simply going to exchange one prison for another.

So closely were we packed, lying or sitting was out of the question and all had to stand. We reached Salisbury, N. C., three days after leaving Belle Isle, and in the evening of the 8th we were turned into the prison enclosure where we saw very little to invite us, though the place was comparatively clean then. The light of fires revealed the shivering forms of unhappy prisoners who had preceded us to this place of detention. It was one of the coldest of autumnal nights and we came so late no provision had been made for us, so, hungry as we were after fasting two days, tired and cold, we faced the uncomfortable night. Worn out with hunger and fatigue, we threw ourselves on the frozen ground with no covering save the heavens, which were very cold that night; dressed, the most of us, in summer blouses with no underclothing, it was one continuous shiver till the rising sun gladdened our eyes and warmed our bodies. We lay down close to each other but, as the night grew colder and the wind whistled more sharply, the end men with one side exposed, unable to endure the cold longer, would leave for some fire or exercise till at last the entire line would dwindle away.

A day's ration of half a loaf of wheat bread and a nice slice of meat put us in proper condition to examine our quarters. The field comprised about seven acres, somewhat triangular in shape with a twelve-foot-high board-fence surrounding it, on whose outside, about four feet from the top, was a continuous platform for the sentries. Facing the entrance were three little brick houses about 30 x 15 and at their right, at right angles, were three other similar buildings; in one corner stood a large brick edifice, formerly a cotton factory, now called the penitentiary, adjoining which was the prison cook-house; near by were two wooden buildings, one a hospital, the other occupied by citizen prisoners; of the large structure, three rooms were occupied by deserters from our army, and two others by rebel deserters, than whom a more graceless lot I never saw. On the north side of the prison-yard and back of the brick buildings were four wooden shanties, built of rough timbers and occupied by our officers who were captured when we were, separated from us only by the beat and bayonet of the sentinel.

Wood was brought in and distributed in a very peculiar manner, since everybody attacked the load at once and to the strong went the major part of the fuel, while the weaker men had to suffer. On our arrival, the whole enclosure was covered with grass, but it soon disappeared. Meanwhile the days were growing colder and our appetites keener; on our way hither I had sold the stockings off my feet for a boiled beet, now I exchanged a good pair of pantaloons for a miserable rebel pair and five dollars, Confederate scrip, and though my blouse was about worn out I felt as happy as a lark in so doing, for by the proceeds I was able to buy another pair of socks and had enough money left for little extras of food for a week or ten days. There were only three wells in the enclosure (four more were dug later) which yielded hardly water enough for drink, thus putting bathing entirely out of the question. There being no bucket for drawing the water, we supplied its place by our tin cups, which we lowered with strings made from suspenders and bootlegs. Through constant dipping the wells were transformed into mudholes, so that a nominal quart of water was really one-fourth red clay.

Made desperate by the prospects of the coming winter, a plan for an escape was formed to be led by General Joseph Hayes (formerly Colonel Eighteenth Massachusetts Volunteers commanding First Brigade, Second Division, Fifth Corps; captured at the Weldon R. R.) but discovery of the plot resulted in the removal of the officers to Danville, Va., and the collapse of the scheme. For the distribution of food the prisoners were divided into divisions of one thousand each and these into squads of one hundred, each one being looked after by a sergeant from its own numbers. About the 1st of November tents were issued, two to a squad, ours receiving for one the fly of an officer's tent, the other a small McClellan, the two affording protection for only a small part of the squad, and those who got any good from them were the immediate friends of the sergeant. All others had to seek cover under ground which they secured by digging holes, somewhat larger than those of woodchucks, but of the same general nature. Pitiable indeed was the condition of the men by this time, since the heavy rains had turned the whole enclosure into a veritable pig-sty whose soft red clay could be made into bricks without further mixing.

The death-rate increased at an alarming rate, so that from forty to fifty were carried out each day to the dead-house. Nearly all of the workshops had been changed into hospitals, also two floors of the old factory building. The dead-house was one of the lower floors of one of the work-shops where, when the weather was bad and the dead were not readily removed, as many as eighty corpses, stark and cold, could be seen piled one upon the other like corded wood. On the coming of the cart to remove them, they were thrown into the same with the least formality possible and so carried off. As we had no means of bathing, one of the worst features of the yard was the mass of animated insect life. Oh! the horrors of such creatures! Through them it might be said that we suffered a thousand deaths. Never at rest, always vigorous, they inhabited every nook and crevice of that dismal yard. They were worse than death. The terrors of a Spanish Inquisition could not bring to bear a mode of torture so vile as these filthy vermin.

Then the state of the yard! The principal diseases were dysentery and pneumonia, so that disease bred corruption and malaria. Those who were taken sick, if their squad sergeant were attentive, were carried to Hospital No. 3, and if, on examination, it were evident that the ailment was incurable, he was sent to a hospital to die. The good wheat bread of our earlier rations was changed to corn bread, made of the coarsest cob meal and given to us with rancid molasses. Meat was issued, after a time, about once in fifteen days and then at the rate of eight pounds of beef and bones to a hundred men. At such times all parts of the creatures were used; the heads with eyes and horns still attached were often issued and in some way made victuals of. All small bones capable of being chewed were swallowed as a dog gulps his osseous food and the larger and harder ones were crushed with stones and boiled for hours; the soup thus obtained was thought a great luxury. To obtain salt a day's ration would be exchanged for enough of this necessity to last a fortnight or so, of course the exchange meant a fast for the day whose ration was traded.

Occasionally flour or meal was given us in the raw and without salt; this was cooked into paste and gruel and very thankful all were to get it; oftentimes the prisoners were kept on one-half the regular rations, possibly one-quarter of the time, and sometimes we went as many as three days with no bread whatever. It was this starvation process that drove good men to enlist in the southern army. About the 12th of November a thick cup of rice soup was given out; the next and the following day, we got only rice water, then came flour without salt. Wood was now issued regularly, each squad getting four sticks of eight foot timber. This particular afternoon it was green pine. To add to our troubles a mist arose, so that the only way we could cook our food was by piling the logs on top of each other and placing a coal underneath which we took turns in keeping alive with our breath, till all had cooked their meal. It was a hapless sight that we afforded that afternoon, black with dirt and smoke, as we ate our food. We had gone so long without food that we had almost lost the sense of hunger and this little meal only served to wake our appetite. Before eating my ration, I could walk about the yard without resting; afterwards I was so weak that I fainted in going to my tent, for I was failing rapidly; my old pantaloons were worn out and slit from the knee downward; the sleeves of my shirt and blouse were almost gone, my shoes and socks worn through, my hair matted with dirt and filth, my complexion that of a negro, my body truly was more dead than alive.

My condition was that of my associates in misery, and it was then that the rebel authorities opened a recruiting station in our midst, offering a loaf of bread and fifty dollars in gold to each one who would enlist; six hundred went out. With the exception of a few desperate characters, all hearts were softened at the sight of so much misery, the faint hearted had mostly enlisted in the rebel ranks and those who remained were true blue and had determined, live or die, to stand fast to their principles. Without anything being said, oaths began to be dropped and testaments to be read; while cant was never so ridiculous and intolerable, true religion and a pure morality began to be the life of the mass.

About the last of November, a friend with whom I had become acquainted on Belle Isle was appointed wardmaster of Hospital No. 5; hearing of my condition, he sent for me. I went and was received like a brother, the dirt washed from me, there being plenty of water in the hospitals, clothes taken from men who had died were given me and I was nursed, cared for and fed out of his own rations till my life, which was slowly ebbing away, was coaxed back again. This friend, a total stranger before my capture, was a sergeant in a Pennsylvania cavalry regiment and our acquaintance began at a devotional meeting where were laid the foundations of the strongest Christian friendship. He was a veritable ministering angel to all those who came under his care, and from his conduct I learned that Christianity was not merely a sentiment but a life, not an idea but a reality.

As remarked before, few cases were admitted to the hospital that were not considered hopeless; from our ward of two rooms, having forty patients, five or six would be carried to the dead-house every night. Army surgeons are bad enough anywhere, but those provided at Salisbury were worse than the common run. Coming in at the time appointed, they never came at any other, they would go along the line of men lying on the floor, hitting the patient with their feet to attract attention, would contemptuously inquire, "Well, what's the matter with you to-day?" and, without waiting for a reply, would prescribe any one of the medicines that happened to cross their minds. There were, indeed, three honorable exceptions, but they could only express their sympathy by words of encouragement. Our ward doctor, the most of the time, was a medical student of the latter class.

November 25th came a decided effort to break out; unfortunately the plot had not been worked up so that a sufficient number understood the plan, so that the effort was made at two instead of four o'clock, when only three divisions had been prepared. On the appearance of the relief at that time, someone gave the watchword, "Who's for liberty?" and, as quick as a flash, every one of those sentinels was disarmed and the boys were using their guns against the sentinels on the fence. The noise of the struggle of course soon brought the troops to the scene and forming on the fence began firing. If theirs had been the only resistance, we might have succeeded; unfortunately for us, the Sixty-ninth North Carolina, a newly recruited regiment, was just outside, awaiting transportation, and they were brought to the support of the guards, and many of the Salisbury citizens, afraid of their property if we got away, trotted down with their fowling pieces and old flintlocks. The fence was soon covered with enemies who began a murderous fire on every tent in the yard, though not a third part of the prisoners knew what was up until it was too late and then, recognizing the hopelessness of the effort, everyone tried to hide himself from the terrible fire. The guards having recovered from their fright proceeded to exercise vengeance by discharging the two pieces of artillery loaded with boiler screws amongst us. No one knows how many were killed, but sixty or seventy were wounded, most of them lying in their tents. The wounded were all placed in the same hospital, were all treated with the same surgical tools and gangrene set in with all, and all, save two or three, died.

Of my company (E) twenty-four were captured, the most of them strong healthy men. As the winter advanced and the cold grew more intense, many of them lost hope and dropped away. From my position in the hospital, to which I had been elected after recovering sufficient strength, I was able to be of help to them. I passed out crust-coffee and opium pills whenever I could get them. The stoutest hearted man in the company was the first to die. A native of Maine, a blacksmith by trade, Jones seemed the one best fitted to endure hardship, yet, allowing himself to become disheartened, he quickly fell a prey to disease. On one of my visits to the boys I found one of them, a corporal (Glines), failing fast. I asked permission of the superintendent to admit him to the hospital as a patient and it was granted. Two days later, I heard that another corporal (Horton) of my company, a near neighbor and friend at home, wished to see me. I found him lying in the mud of his tent, and I knew by the look of his face that he could not live. He asked me if I could do anything for him or, at least, give him some opium. I got some of the pills for him and told him I would do what I could towards getting him into the hospital. Knowing that he could not live much longer he said, "Tell the folks at home I died trying to do my duty and thinking of them." Going back to the ward, I besought the privilege of bringing him to the hospital. The superintendent replied that there was no vacancy, but would be on the morrow, but I might go after supper and get him and give him a place under a bunk. I went upstairs and cooked our scanty meal and, while doing so, the night patients were brought in. While eating my supper, one of the nurses, a pompous fellow, came in and said that one of the patients was a young fellow who insisted on seeing me before going under his bunk. On being told that I was busy upstairs the nurse said he whined, "I wish you would call Johnnie, one moment," but he put a stop to his "nonsense," as the nurse said, by showing him his place for the night and said that he had fainted in taking it. Indignant that my friend had been denied so small a favor, I hurried down to the place where he had been put and cried, "Fred," and, as no answer came I supposed him asleep and thought I would not disturb him. After finishing my work at midnight, I went upstairs to retire; shortly afterward the nurse in attendance called that a corporal, under the bunks, was dead. Hurrying down, I found my friend stiff and cold in death in the middle of the floor. A friend and playmate from boyhood, the merriest boy of us all, smart in school, most joyous in sport, he was the life of our youthful circle. We had enlisted together; his parents, brothers and sisters were all well known to me and I must tell the sad story to them—how he had died in a hospital of which I was an attendant, yet had been unable to comfort him in his dying hours. The sight of my grief was a good lesson to the nurses who were more ready to grant favors thereafter. Horton, the other corporal, died the same night.

A great many died from the effects of the cold weather; numbers of them had their feet frost-bitten and, as they were not taken care of, mortification set in, to be followed by death. Many a poor fellow, weak with disease, left his tent at night, and, stumbling in the darkness would fall and being too weak to call for help would be found in the morning a frozen corpse. Finally, without any warning, on the to us ever memorable 20th of February, '65, orders came to have the sick ready for removal. It was with joyful hearts that we obeyed and, when the gate was opened that we might carry them out, we could hardly contain ourselves for joy. Only when the cars had fully started could we realize that Salisbury, with its filth and dirt, its misery and degradation, its dying and dead, was being left for good. With feeble voices we sang "Praise God from Whom all Blessings Flow" and many a prayer of thanksgiving was breathed that we had lived to see the glad hour.

SERGT. MAJOR C. K. CONN

Sergt. Major Chas. K. Conn, originally of Company K, was wounded May 8, '64, captured and carried to Richmond. After recovering from his wounds he was retained as a clerk, one of his duties being to make out the lists of those who were to be paroled. Having a happy thought one day while preparing a roll of names, he wrote his own among those of men about to start for God's country, and when the party in charge called for those thus enumerated, Conn stepped forth with the invalids to whom parole privileges were confined in 1864. One of the Confederate officers, noticing him among the sick men, asked him what he was doing there. To the query the quick witted Yankee replied, "I heard my name called and so responded." The facts in the case were not discovered till after Conn had gone too far to be called back, though he felt extremely shaky until he was safely aboard the Union vessel.

J. F. LESLIE'S RUSE

This Company K man thought his liberty worth risking something for; captured Aug. 19, '64, he too had been taken to Richmond, "Libby" and Belle Isle, where he informed his comrades he purposed trying the sick dodge by way of the hospital, for he had discerned that the sick and wounded would go first. His friends tried to dissuade him, saying that he would surely be found out and might be made to suffer all the more on account of his attempted cheat. He tried the rebel doctor every morning with his complaints, but was careful to take none of the latter's medicine, throwing all of it away. At last the surgeon, suspecting shamming on the Yankee's part, prepared a Spanish-fly plaster, 4 x 8 inches in size, which could not be disposed of as his medicine had been. Leslie put it on his body, keeping it on all night, and when he visited the doctor in the morning and was asked if it had had any effect he was able to show a blister the full size of the plaster. This convinced the officer that our man was not shamming, for as he said, "Any man who could stand that could not be 'playing it'," so he was sent to the hospital in Richmond, "Yankee, 21," as it was called. On getting there he hardly dared move for fear of being sent back. One morning the hospital doctor, saying that he would give him something to make him sleep, left a potion with the injunction to make sure that it was taken; there was no way open but to take it, but it was spat out the moment the steward passed to the next patient. The look of astonishment on the doctor's face the next morning convinced the patient that it was a dose for final sleep that the surgeon had prepared; at any rate he never came near Leslie's cot again. In a few days the "artful dodger" was paroled, while his comrades were sent to Salisbury and Andersonville where the most of them died.

CORPORAL CHARLES H. BARNES' STORY.

A picture of Andersonville, as it appeared in the summer and fall of 1864 and the following winter, is drawn by Corporal Charles H. Barnes of Co. I, who was wounded the 8th of May and, two weeks later, while going from Fredericksburg to Belle Plain Landing, on his way with others to Washington and Convalescent Camp, was captured, carried to Richmond and shut up in Libby Prison, where he passed through the usual experience of being searched, etc. Three weeks later in company with more than a thousand fellow prisoners, he was started for Andersonville, Georgia; having ninety of them in an ordinary box car was pretty close work, since they could neither sit nor lie down, so had to stand. At Goldsboro they were unloaded and like cattle turned into a pasture without supper or shelter, but unlike cattle they could not eat the grass about them; rain was falling hard and, wet to the skin, they had to stand closely together for the sake of warmth. Starting again in the morning they reached Andersonville, just a week after leaving Richmond, the cars running only about three miles an hour, any greater speed being provocative of accident:—

I was wearing a pair of boots that came to me from home the day I was taken prisoner and I hated to part with them, but I got so hungry when on the cars that I traded them with one of the guards for a dozen biscuits and a pair of old shoes full of holes. I ate the biscuits pretty quick, and still was as famished as before, and I wished I had the boots back to trade again. We were told that it was a lovely place inside of the stockade, but we found it quite the reverse. There were 39,000 men within the enclosure living in holes and tents made of pieces of old shirts, blankets and anything they could get that would hold together. When we marched in, we had to stand a while before assignment to some place in which to stay, when some of the men, already initiated, said that we had better be looking for places to camp in, we having thought that some sort of shelter would be given us. So we hunted around and found a soft bit of earth which some fifteen of us occupied; ere long some of the old timers came round to see if we had anything they might wish. On waking, the next morning, each man found his pocket cut, but the thieves got nothing, since every man was dead broke.

There were two stockades, one inside the other, about twenty feet apart and as many feet high in most places; along the top were shelters for the guard and about twelve feet from the inner wall was the dead line. It was made of scantling nailed on the top of posts, about four feet in height and if a prisoner touched it, which he was quite likely to do, the guards would shoot him if they could. A small brook ran through the middle of the yard; sluggish generally, it became a raging torrent after severe rains. One day some of the stockade fell over into the water and some of the prisoners swam out to the floating logs and so raced out to freedom, for they were going too rapidly to be recaptured. For our first twenty days it rained nearly all the time and the only cover our party had was a piece of an old blanket, which as many as possible would put over their heads while the rest ran around trying to keep warm until the time came to exchange, an all day and all night series.

After some searching I found four members of my own regiment, they having a tent made of old shirts and parts of old blankets which they had pinned together with broken sticks. Three of the boys could scarcely move on account of the scurvy, but one of them asked me to come in and stay with them, which I was glad to do, though I had to lie at their feet until one of them passed on, only a few days later. Shortly afterwards the other ones died and two of the Thirty-ninth had what was left which, while it did not keep out the rain, did keep off the direct sun, a no small comfort in that terribly hot place. We had two half pieces of blankets, nearly used up and almost covered with what Robert Burns called "crawlin' ferlies," the fearful pests of our lives. I undertook one day to wash my shirt, trying first one corner of it which went to pieces, so I dried the garment carefully and without further effort at washing wore it almost nine months.

First and last many tunnels were dug, in several of which I bore a hand; I don't know how many succeeded in getting out but there must have been several hundred; bloodhounds were put on their track and those who were brought back were put in the chain-gang. Among so many men there must be some bad ones, a few very bad; they even resorted to murder in their efforts to secure what some of the prisoners possessed. To rid themselves of this terrible set of evil men a vigilance committee of the well disposed was organized and by sheer force of numbers, overpowered and sentenced to death six of them. The rebels, to their credit, furnished material for the gibbet and the execution took place, much to the relief of those who had to continue there.

Our drinking water came from holes in the ground four or five feet deep; while it was pretty clear, there were many dead maggots in the bottom, though we did not mind them, thinking the water so much better than that in the brook. One day in August a stream of water broke out just inside of the inner stockade; it ran all of the time, but the dead line was between us and the water; we procured boards and made a trough and then got permission to put it up, so that we had fine water all the rest of the time we were there. To this day it is known as the Providence Spring. Aside from scurvy, severe enough to loosen my teeth, I was not sick a day while in the prison. Our rations for the most part were a pint of boiled rice without any salt for twenty-four hours and oftener it would be forty-eight, for every time Captain Wirz discovered a new tunnel he would punish all of us by skipping our rations. Occasionally we would get some small black beans, such as the planters raised for their hogs; these we would try to cook with green pitch-pine with results that can be imagined. I have blown myself black in the face many a time trying to cook them and then had to eat them raw.

There was a sick call every day and when a man answered the same, all he got for his pains was a dose of sumach berries. No matter what the complaint might be the remedy was always the same, for it was all they had to give. Sometimes a man could be seen buried up to his chin; he had the rheumatism and if he could endure the antidote two or three days, he would come out cured. One boy, to get some extra food, told the captain one day where a new tunnel was in progress, and after the officer had gone out, the men shaved one side of his head and on his breast and back put big placards, bearing in big black letters the word "Traitor." He was then marched all over the camp and tormented almost to death; the enemy finally took him outside, which was just what he wanted.

After Stoneman's raid, the rebels thinking Andersonville no longer safe began to distribute us elsewhere and I sampled the bull-pen of Savannah, Ga.; the stockade of Millen, also in Georgia; and then was sent back to Savannah where I was paroled and sent down the River, to go on board a Union steamer; the sight of the Stars and Stripes brought tears to every eye. On board, our heads were shaved, we were bathed, clad anew and were judiciously fed; our old clothes went overboard. After reaching Annapolis I tipped the scales at seventy-five pounds, less than half my weight when I enlisted. After a brief stay in Parole Camp, I was paid off and sent home on a thirty days' furlough, where I was sick all of the time, but I returned to the camp at the end of the time to be furloughed again, this time for sixty days. On getting back to camp the second time, and wearying of it, I put my name down among those to be returned to their regiments and I reached mine the day after Lee surrendered.

REGIMENTAL VETERAN ASSOCIATION

The beginnings of the Association seem to have been lost in the interval between 1867 and the present; it is agreed, however, that the first four meetings were held in Boston hotels and that they were not very largely attended. The time was too near the date of getting home and the pleasures of that supreme event far outweighed any rehearsal of common dangers in war-experiences. Of the 5th gathering, the first basket picnic of the veterans of the Thirty-ninth and their lady friends, there is in substance the following account:

Downer's Landing, Hingham, was the place and Thursday, August 17th, the date; the party, numbering 300, left Litchfield's Wharf at 9.15 a. m. on steamers "Wm. Harrison" and "Emeline," arriving about 11 o'clock; a half mile walk brought all parties to the "Melville Gardens" which had been hired for the day. Noon saw the tables spread with the many good things brought by the members. Before repairing to the hall for dancing, Colonel C. H. Porter, President of the Association, introduced as speakers, Lieut. Colonel Hutchins, Major Graham, Captain Brigham, Lieuts. Mulligan and Mills, Sergeants Eames and Gardner. At 3 p. m. came a dress parade with one hundred and fifty men in line, Colonels Porter and Hutchins dividing the honors of commanding. A letter was read from General G. K. Warren, regretting his inability to be present, a disappointment to the veterans, as they had expected to meet their former commander once more; everyone of the Regiment and, for that matter, every regiment in the Fifth Corps, holding the officer in the highest esteem. On the formation of the line and led by Edmunds Band, the company marched back to the landing, reaching Boston at 5.15 o'clock, all happy and conscious that the presence of the ladies had added no little to the enjoyment of the day.

The reunions of 1872, '73 and '74 were held in Boston Hotels; in 1875, Oct. 6th in Woburn was held the most notable of the Association's gatherings thus far, General Warren being the distinguished guest and Company K, along with citizens of Woburn, the hosts. There were present 166 men with General Peirson at their head; drum corps and brass bands furnished music and everyone joined heartily in the reception to the eminent soldier. At the rooms of the selectmen, the public had a chance to meet General Warren. At the armory the meeting was called to order by Captain Hutchins and the chief feature was the presentation to General Warren of a magnificent Maltese Cross in Gold, the badge of the Fifth Corps, the cost $100.00 having been met by the veterans. In the afternoon a banquet was served in Lyceum Hall to more than four hundred guests, the good people of the town having vied with each other in making the occasion memorable. At the post prandial exercises, remarks were made by Captains Hutchins and Tidd; there was an extended address by J. A. Harvey, Co. C, followed by the introduction of Sergt. Abijah Thompson, Co. K, as Toastmaster, who read an original poem after which, and the playing by the band of "Hail to the Chief," General Warren spoke briefly to the following effect, "I rise to acknowledge the kind attentions I have received to-day. Those who have spoken have referred in such kind terms to me, and your marks of approbation have been so many that I do not feel prepared to speak for the Fifth Army Corps, as I could wish. I hope you will excuse me. I shall carry from this place a sense of having been honored more than I deserve. (Cries of no, no.) The feelings which this day has inspired will always remain, and you have laid on me a debt of gratitude I never can repay." Col. C. H. Porter responded for General Peirson, letters were read from General J. C. Robinson, and Colonels Farnham and Tilden of the Sixteenth Maine; further responses to toasts were given by Maj. Ambrose Bancroft of the Thirty-second Regiment, Capt. J. P. Crane of the Twenty-second, Capt. C. S. Converse of the Fifth, Lieut. John L. Parker of the Eleventh and others, the exercises terminating in an evening's levee which lasted till midnight.

The Centennial year, 1876, found the veterans 150 strong in Natick, the guests of Co. I.; 1877, August 28th, Co. D of Quincy did the hospitable act with 220 comrades present. In 1878, Co. E of Somerville, on the 6th of Sept, helped celebrate the 16th anniversary of the departure of the Regiment with 225 veterans in attendance, the event gaining unwonted interest through the presence of General John C. Robinson who had been the Division Commander of the Regiment at the Wilderness and at Spottsylvania, losing there a leg; there was a spirited address by Mayor Bruce of Somerville, an extended historical paper by Col. C. H. Porter with speeches of greater or less length by Gov. A. H. Rice, Gen'l N. P. Banks, Collector Beard, Secretary Pierce, Speaker Long, General Peirson and others, the celebration continuing with music and dancing till after midnight. A pleasant feature of the afternoon was the presentation of an elegant punch bowl and ladle to General Robinson by Lieut. C. K. Conn to whose words the General responded so happily that all recognized him as a good talker as well as fighter.

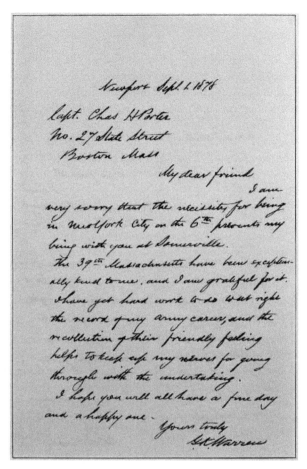

Newport Sept. 1. 1878

Capt. Chas H Porter
No. 27 State Street
Boston Mass

My dear friend

I am very sorry that the necessity for being in New York City on the 6th prevents my being with you at Somerville.

The 39th Massachusetts have been exceptionally kind to me, and I am grateful for it. I have got hard work to do to set right the record of my army career, and the recollection of this friendly feeling helps to keep up my nerves for going through with the undertaking.

I hope you will all have a fine day and a happy one.

August 27th, 1879, found the survivors of the Thirty-ninth in Taunton, guests of Co. F with Capt. J. J. Cooper president of the day and 125 veterans on hand; Adjutant O. A. Barker welcomed the old soldiers to the city and after a short business meeting, line was formed for the Agricultural Fair Grounds where Hiram Maxfield of Silver Springs fame served one of his imitable clambakes. In 1880, Sept. 15th, Medford was the entertaining place with Co. C at the front, Jas. A. Harvey being President. Oct. 5th, '81, the "old boys" came back to Woburn again, the reception being in the hands of the following named men of Company K., C. K. Conn., Geo. E. Fowle, Capt. L. R. Tidd, A. L. Richardson, J. F. Ramsdell, A. P. Barrett, J. Fred Leslie, A. Thompson and A. R. Linscott. Again Woburn has the honor of entertaining General G. K. Warren and he is accompanied by General J. C. Robinson, the valiant Division Commander, along with General Peirson, the ever popular regimental commander. At the dinner which was served in Lyceum Hall, remarks were made by those named above, Col. Porter and others. Before another reunion, General Warren will have passed away.

The regimental line formed again in Natick, Oct. 10, 1882; again Co. I plays the role of entertainers with fully 150 survivors to honor the occasion. Dinner was served in Concert Hall; Col. C. H. Porter spoke at length in praise of General Warren who had died the 8th day of the preceding August; resolutions of sympathy and respect were passed by the veterans and a contribution was made to a Fifth Corps fund to honor the General's memory. Remarks followed by Comrades Barrett, "K"; Beck, "C"; Locke, "E"; Eames, "C"; Oliver, "E," and others. 1883 brought the veterans to Quincy again with Co. D. Point Shirley in Winthrop was the place of meeting, August 26, 1884, with Co. H as entertainers. Roxbury, the home of Co. B, entertained next, Sept. 23, 1885. Company G came to the front Sept. 16, 1886, at Nantasket. The ladies of Somerville, in behalf of Co. E, furnish the dinner for the reunion of 1887, Sept. 6th. Through the selection of the Executive Committee, Bass Point was the place of meeting in 1888. Sept. 11, 1889, brought the clans to Medford, once more, with Co. C.

Sept. 24, 1890, the beginning of another decade, brings the veterans to Woburn, the home of Co. K, for the third time. As usual, great preparations were made for the reception, the principal guests, aside from the veterans themselves, being the widow and daughter of General Warren, and General Peirson and wife who with the wife of Mayor Johnson and the wife of the Hon. John Cummings formed the receiving line in the hall of the Y. M. C. A. The formalities of the occasion were conducted by Colonel C. H. Porter and Sergeant Abijah Thompson, "K," and 166 survivors pressed forward, glad of the opportunity of grasping the hands of their friends. Dinner was served in Lyceum Hall. The after-dinner exercises were presided over most happily by Sergt. Thompson who introduced Mayor Johnson, General Peirson, the Hon. John Cummings, Colonel Porter and others. Company A was the host Sept. 7, 1891, at the old Lynnfield camping-ground, and the occasion was rendered notable by the following paper, prepared for the day by Lieut. Elbridge Bradshaw of Co. H:

A VACATION IDYL

Some thirty years ago, leading a sedentary life and gradually sinking into a semi-bituminated condition, my medical adviser, alarmed at my symptoms, ordered travel and change of scenery. Having learned that Virginia contained more travel and scenery to the square mile than any other spot on the globe, I determined on visiting that State. Being of a timid nature and fond of Company, I joined myself to about a thousand other invalids, similarly afflicted, and seeking the same remedy, forming ourselves into a methodical organization. For convenience we divided ourselves up into groups of one hundred men each, using for purposes of distinction the first eleven letters of the alphabet, omitting the letter J. For menial service, i. e. to look after our physical wants, each group hired for such purpose, six servants, viz. a captain, two lieutenants, with a cook, a drummer and a bugler or fifer, the latter two being hired to wake the excursionists in the morning. To keep these captains and lieutenants in order, we placed over them a colonel, a lieut. colonel and a major, at the same time they being our head servants or butlers. These people added to themselves an adjutant to run errands, a chaplain, a doctor and a pill-driver. To insure a faithful discharge of duty, from each group were chosen a dozen fellows called sergeants and corporals who were set over the others.

Virginia at this time being in a tumultuous condition, and the U. S. Government having heard of our organization's plan of travel and objective points, invited us, through its Chief Magistrate, to walk over Virginia as peace officers, punching the heads of belligerants and arguing with the discontented, an invitation which we accepted. When President Lincoln secured our services he loaded us with benefits, first massing us at Lynnfield, giving us canvass houses to protect us from the dew and damp, sweet straw to nestle in, a pretty blue uniform, a belt to keep us from bursting, an iron toothpick, a tube of iron with a wooden handle, a little black bureau, in which to keep our collars, cuffs and bric-a-brac, a black cotton pantry for provisions and plates, with a round tin vessel for whiskey. Uncle Sam also gave our servants (the shoulder-strapped ones) toasting forks to stick pigs with and red sashes with which to gird their persons when running and chasing the pigs down. Rendered proud and arrogant by their good clothes and shoulder straps, our servants rose on us and captured our organization, styling themselves our superior officers, and our entire body the Thirty-ninth

Regiment of Massachusetts Volunteers. To give the usurpation a flavor of legality, they procured from Governor Andrew commissions indicating officially their rank and authority. On the whole they exercised their powers with great moderation and kindness.

Though to the last, we suffered them to think themselves our superiors, yet in reality, they still continued to be our servants, caring for our food, clothing and morals, furnishing us clean, airy lodgings having adequate fire-escapes, so that in fact we had nothing on our minds worth mentioning and all we had to do was to travel and fight; in a word, take our pleasure. They also taught us many pretty and amusing tricks; how to stand up straight in rows to be shot at; to abstain from whiskey (with quinine in it); to use the pickaxe and spade with the least expenditure of muscular energy and, in mud and night marches, to say our prayers without even stopping. As soon as we could march without scalping each other's heels, we left Lynnfield for active service and mighty active it proved on the start, our first engagement being a footrace against time through Boston. We left Lynnfield with cooked rations, meaning saltpork and hardtack.

How dear to this heart is the old army hardtack,

As Lynnfield's reunion presents them to view;

When eaten with raw pork or fried into doughnuts,

The rations that beat him, are scat'ring and few.

How oft in our marches, he's braced up our courage,

As with gnawing and growling we've hobbled along;

Oh! well may the hardtack, the old army hardtack

Prove a classical theme for an old veteran's song.

That dear army hardtack was a limber old codger,

In the hands of a Thirty-ninth's amateur cook;

In his grip, the old hardtack took metamorphosis

Not mentioned by Ovid, nor in Parloa's cook-book,

As a pudding or pie in a cob-house as a dumpling,

As a fry or a toast, or a raw on the shell;

That old army hardtack, that blessed old hardtack!

For every recipe turned out equally well.

I have eaten high banquets at Young's and at Parker's,

I have tasted their beef, roast turkey and lamb;

But all of these dishes are flat and insipid,

Beside the old hardtack of dear Uncle Sam;

For the old army hardtack is seasoned with memories

Of battles and sieges when wearing the blue;

Of marchings and flankings and digging of trenches,

And loving communion with old comrades too.

The old army hardtack speaks, too, of dear comrades,

Whose faces are missing to-day in our line;

Their battles all fought, their warfare all ended,

But whose virtues still live in mem'ry's pure shrine,

Then cheer the old hardtack, the square army hardtack,

Who was flinty and wormy at times, I must own,

But when at Mine Run, he took a vacation,

His absence was greeted with many a moan.

Chorus.

The old flinty hardtack, the iron bound hardtack;

The moss-covered hardtack, we all knew him well.

Travelling the next three years through Virginia and its environments, we were often obstructed by mud and other earthern impediments, and the scenery was much disfigured and frequently obliterated by sulphurous clouds of smoke, hence excursioning for health and pleasure was, on the whole, a failure. Speaking for myself, individually, the climate didn't agree with me a bit. This I attribute largely to the horizontal metallic showers with which that region was infested and against which no ordinary cotton umbrella was an adequate protection. Indeed the atmosphere was so impregnated with little pellets of lead and ragged chunks of cast iron, that my system must have absorbed about fifty-five pounds of old junk and brought it home with me for, on my return, I weighed 190 lbs. against 135 when I left Lynnfield.

Natick with its Company I entertained for the third time, October 5, 1892; Quincy and Co. D did the hospitable act, also for the third time, in 1893, August 30; Roxbury and Company B were the entertainers in 1894 and Co. H of Dorchester received at the U. S. Hotel, Boston, Sept. 25, 1895; for 1896, no record is found, but Sept. 6, 1897, Co. E and Somerville appear again; it is Medford and Co. C in 1898; Woburn and her K Company in 1899. The old century ends, as far as our Regiment is concerned, October 10, 1900, with I Company and Natick, while the new one begins Sept. 7, 1901, on the old campground at Lynnfield; Sept. 22, 1902, finds the veterans again in Quincy; Sept. 24, 1903, in Roxbury; August 19, 1904, with Co. H. at Nantasket. Then with no special company distinctions the reunions follow, directed by the Executive Committee, at Squantum Inn, Sept. 21, 1905; Bass Point, Sept. 6, 1906; in a Dorchester hotel, October 23, 1907; again at Bass Point, Sept. 29, 1908; at Revere Beach for three successive years, viz. August 30, 1909, August 18, 1910, and August 18, 1911. Fifty years after the departure of the Regiment from Massachusetts, nearly a hundred (92) veterans assembled again in Somerville with Company E and a large number of prominent citizens to celebrate the semi-centennial; the state armory was the gathering place and General Peirson was the marked figure on the occasion while wives, daughters and other lady friends added to the pleasures of the hour; Sergt. Abijah Thompson of Co. K was the oldest man present, he having seen fully 90 years. After the dinner, over which Comrade the Rev. John F. Locke said grace and at which Lieut. J. H. Dusseault, Co. E, presided, there was speaking by Ex-Mayors Edward Glines, C. A. Grimmons and John M. Woods, the latter a veteran of the war, and the first named a brother of Fred Glines of Co. E who died in Salisbury. Mayor Burns of Somerville extended the courtesies of the city to the veterans and welcomed them all most heartily. General Peirson was received with accustomed enthusiasm and was heard with rapt attention. The half century event was a great success. The 51st anniversary was observed in Medford, with the survivors of Co. C, Sept. 6, 1913; the day, the place, the guests, quite one hundred in numbers, made the event notable; the forenoon's meeting was in the hall of the S. C. Lawrence Post, G. A. R., while the dinner was served in the drill-room of the magnificent armory, presented to Medford and the State by General S. C. Lawrence.

REGIMENTAL ROSTER

Nothing in the story of a regiment is of greater importance than its Roster, for therein appears the record of the individual whether the same be good or bad. One man alone makes a small appearance, yet a thousand men make a regiment and every volunteer, whether commissioned or enlisted, is entitled to the best that can be said of him. If, in addition to his military service, his career in civil life may be given in outline so much the better, for in America every able bodied man is potentially a soldier. The foundation for the following Roster is found upon the muster rolls, carefully preserved in the State House, Boston, and additions have been made thereto through the information afforded by members of the Veteran Association.

The careful reader will observe in scanning the data afforded by the Roster that the ages of the soldiers almost entirely range between those of eighteen and forty-five years, these being the respective limits of legal enlistment; at the same time everyone is well aware that a large part of the army was made up of boys in their early teens; also we know full well that many a man went in long after reaching the maximum age for military service. As a fact, then, very many men lied their ages up or down; so far as the grand average, however, is concerned the "over" age compensated for or offset those who were "under." Since the muster-in rolls or enlistment papers are sources of all data concerning the age of volunteer and, it being well known that very many of them were and are incorrect, the wonder rises as to the source of statements that have gone the rounds of the public press in late years, wherein the ages represented by the soldiers are carefully tabulated. However, from whatever source obtained, as worthy of presentation here the following alleged facts are given:

Discussion has elicited an official statement that about 2,800,000 Union men enlisted; there were about 5,000,000 men called out on both sides. Of these nearly 4,500,000 were under twenty-one; there were about 332,000 who were under sixteen and there were 1,500 in the Union Army who were not fifteen years old. Less attention has been given to the men who were over age, but every regiment can give its cases of men fifty, sixty and even seventy years of age whose great excess would average up many a juvenile volunteer. When, however, the rolls afford no such statements, where is the statistician acquiring his alleged facts?

For the sake of brevity and economy of space the following abbreviations are used:

A. A. G. = Assistant Adjutant General; b. = born; bur. = buried; bvt. = brevet; batt. = battalion; Capt. = Captain; Co. = Company; Col. = Colonel; com. = commission or committee; Corp. = Corporal; cr. = credited; d. =

died or dead; des. = deserted; det. Serv. = detached Service; dis. = discharged; disa. = disability; en. = enlisted; ex. of s. = expiration of service; F. & S. = Field and Staff; G. O. = General Order; H. Arty. = Heavy Artillery; Infty. = Infantry; k. = killed; lat. add. = latest address; Lt. or Lieut. = Lieutenant; M. = married; M. I. = Mustered-in; M. O. = Mustered-out; mos. = months; mus. = musician; M. V. M. = Mass. Vol. Militia; N. F. R. = no further record; N. G. = National Guard; O. W. D. = Order, War Department; Pris. = Prisoner; prom. = promoted; re-en. = re-enlisted; rep. = reported; res. = resigned; S. = single; S. H. = Soldiers' Home; S. S. = sharpshooters; S. O. = Special Order; Sergt. = Sergeant; trans. = transferred; U. S. C. T. = U. S. Colored Troops; V. R. C. = Veteran Reserve Corps; w. = widower; wd. = wounded; W. D. = War Department.

In reciting facts pertaining to each name, the same order obtains throughout the Roster; first comes the family name of the soldier, next his Christian appellation; in some instances time and place of birth are given; as a rule, age, whether married or single, occupation and place of residence follow in order; next, date of enlistment or muster-in; incidents of army life are next in place, and then the time and manner of leaving the army; finally are given incidents of civil life and latest address if the same be known. The application of abbreviations and the order are seen in the following supposed case:

Jones, John, 20, S.; shoemaker, Natick; Aug. 22, '62; wd. May 5, '64, Wilderness; dis. disa., Aug. 20, '64; Selectman, Natick, 1880, '81; 1913, Natick.

Printed in full the foregoing would be as follows:

Jones, John, at the age of twenty years, single, a shoemaker living in Natick, enlisted August 22, 1862, or was mustered in on that date; he was wounded in the battle of the Wilderness and, on account of wounds or disability therefrom, was discharged August 20, 1864; he was a Selectman in Natick in 1880 and '81 and in 1913 is still residing there.

FIELD AND STAFF
COLONELS

P. Stearns Davis, 44, M.; stationer, Cambridge; August 29, 1862; Phineas Stearns Davis was born in Brookline, June 23, 1818, his Christian names coming to him from an ancestor who bore a part in the Boston Tea Party; his earlier education, received in the Brookline public schools, was supplemented by a journey around the world; in the publishing of schoolbooks he was long associated with his brother, Robert, on Washington Street, Boston; deeply interested in Free Masonry, Colonel Davis had been Master of Putnam Lodge, Cambridge, was a member of St. Paul Chapter, Royal Arch, and was a charter member of St. Bernard's Commandery, Knights Templar of Boston; entering the Militia at a very early age, the beginning of the War found him Division Inspector on the Staff of General Samuel Andrews of the First Division; later promoted to the rank of Brigadier General, he was serving in 1862 on a Board of Examination, thereby rendering signal aid to Governor Andrew; he passed thence to the Thirty-ninth Regiment. On leaving his home, he said to his mother who had expressed wonder, if not regret, at his going, "Mother, if I should live to see the end of this war without going and doing my whole duty to my country, I should never rest," and he went away with her blessing. Perhaps no man throughout the strife entered the service with higher motives than those which prompted Colonel Davis. Possessing as high an ideal of discipline and drill as he had of morality and patriotism, he proceeded to enforce them with the result that few if any organizations in the volunteer service excelled the Thirty-ninth in true soldierly qualities. Early called to the command of a brigade, it was truly said of him that he never was assigned to any position which he did not fill. The particulars of his death, July 11, 1864, have appeared in the body of this book; his funeral, held with Masonic honors in the Unitarian Church of Cambridge, was on July 18, the entire city being in mourning, with all places of business closed; flags were at half-mast and in the audience assembled to honor his memory were the City Council of Cambridge, Governor Andrew and Staff, Adjutant General Schouler, Mayor Lincoln of Boston and a wide range of other civil and military officers; Free Masonry in which he was so prominent was represented by Putnam Lodge to which he belonged, officers of the Grand Lodge, St. Bernard's Encampment of Boston, and the National Lancers also were present. Speakers at the services were the Rev. Chandler Robbins, who had officiated at his marriage, and Chaplain E. B. French who had accompanied the remains of his commander home. With the long escort, the body of Colonel Davis was borne to Mt. Auburn Cemetery, having as bearers General Samuel C. Lawrence, Colonels C. L. Holbrook and L. B. Marsh, Postmaster Leighton and Deputy Sheriff L. L. Parker, the burial being with Masonic rites.

Charles L. Peirson, from Lieut. Colonel July 13, 1864; owing to the stress of the "Battle Summer" campaign, his severe wound at the Weldon R. R. August 18, '64, and subsequent absence from the Regiment, not to mention the red tape that ever did hedge military matters about, it was not till the 23d of November, 1864, that Colonel Peirson was mustered in to his rank: the Records of the War Department, Washington, D. C., state:

Peirson is now held and considered by this Department, under the provisions of the Act of Congress, approved February 24, 1897, to have been mustered into the service of the United States in the grade of Colonel, Thirty-ninth Massachusetts Infantry, to take effect from July 13, 1864, and to have held that rank until the date of his discharge from service.

Upon the recommendation of Major General G. K. Warren, Peirson was commissioned Colonel of Volunteers by brevet, to date from March 13, 1865, for meritorious conduct in the battles of the Wilderness and Spottsylvania in May, 1864, and as Brigadier General of Volunteers, by brevet, to date from March 13, 1865, for gallant and meritorious conduct in the battle of the Weldon Railroad in August, 1864.

After months of prostration, incident to his wound, and on the clear evidence of his inability to return to the Regiment, Colonel Peirson resigned and was mustered out of the service January 11, 1865. Subsequent to the war, General Peirson was long in the iron business, Boston; on his retirement therefrom, he found occupation for his well earned leisure in historical studies, particularly with reference to the Civil War, being a member of the Loyal Legion, which he commanded, 1895, and the Massachusetts Military Historical Society. His city residence is at 191 Commonwealth Avenue; his summer abode is at Pride's Crossing, city of Beverly.

COLONEL CHARLES L. PIERSON
B'v't Brigadier-General

LIEUTENANT COLONELS

Charles L. Peirson, 28, S.; civil engineer, Salem; wd. May 8 and 10, '64, Spottsylvania; prom. Colonel; Charles Lawrence Peirson was born in Salem; was graduated from Lawrence Scientific School, Harvard, 1853; was a Corporal in the Fourth Battalion, under Major T. G. Stevenson, which in the spring of 1861 did gratuitous service in Fort Warren, Boston Harbor; later commissioned First Lieut. and Adjutant in the Twentieth Massachusetts, he was taken prisoner at the Battle of Ball's Bluff and suffered three months' confinement in Libby Prison, Richmond; on his return to his regiment he was detailed for special service on the staff of General N. J. T. Dana and also later upon that of General John Sedgwick, thus passing through the Peninsula campaign; it was while on sick leave from such service that he was notified of his appointment to his new position in the Thirty-ninth Regiment.

Henry M. Tremlett, from Major July 13, 1864; absent at the time on detached service in Boston Harbor he did not rejoin the Regiment until October following; wd. March 31, '65, at Gravelly Run, he died of wounds at his home in Boston, June 6th following, the very day of the return of the Thirty-ninth. The six weeks immediately following the battle were spent in the hospital at City Point; thence he returned to Boston, getting there May 9th, apparently on the road to recovery, but the setting in of intermittent fever proved to be too great a trial of his strength; his body was buried in Forest Hills Cemetery. Of him a writer in a Boston paper wrote at the time:—

His standard of manliness was one of noble action rather than of puling pretension, and his whole life showed him to be a loving son, a dear brother, a kind and generous companion, a devoted friend and a truly loyal man, willing to sacrifice his life for the noble cause for which he contended.

MAJORS

Henry M. Tremlett, b. Dorchester, July 15, 1833; 29, S.; merchant, Boston; Aug. 28, 1862; educated at Chauncy Hall School, Boston, he succeeded his father in mercantile life on Foster's Wharf; when Governor Andrew called for volunteers to serve in Fort Warren in the spring of 1862, he was one of those who filled the ranks of the Fourth Battalion, serving therein as First Sergeant. On the organization of the Twentieth Regiment, he was commissioned Captain and in that capacity bore his part in the fatal day at Ball's Bluff and was with the Army of the Potomac through the Seven Days' Fight. With the Thirty-ninth he participated in all of its experiences till, in the fall of '63, he was ordered to Boston where for quite a year, as Provost Marshal, he had charge of the draft rendezvous till after the death of Colonel Davis and the severe wounding of Colonel Peirson his return was necessary, serving thereafter as Lieut. Colonel.

Frederick R. Kinsley, July 13, '64, from Captain, Co. E; not mustered; captured, Aug. 19, '64, at the Weldon R. R., was held until the following March; came home in command of the Regiment; M. O. as Capt., June 2, 1865; soon after the war, with two brothers, he bought and worked a large farm in Dorchester, N. H.; represented the town in the Legislature; in 1911 he removed to Lowell where, in 1913, he makes his home.

ADJUTANTS

Henry W. Moulton, 21, M.; currier, So. Danvers; Aug. 18, '62; was first commissioned in the Thirty-fifth, Aug. 12, '62, and was trans. as above. Owing to the detailing of Adjutant Washburn, Lieutenant Moulton took his place; wd. May 10, 1864, Laurel Hill; absent, sick, until his discharge; dis. disa., Dec. 5, 1864.

Orville A. Barker, from Co. C, Dec. 5, '64; prom. Captain, April 3, '65; not mustered; M. O. June 2, 1864; a druggist for many years in Taunton, Captain Barker found time to serve as Treasurer of Morton Hospital and for thirty-five years was Clerk of the Baptist Church; he died Feb. 21, 1912.

QUARTERMASTER

Edward E. White, 34, —; —, Cambridge; August 25, 1862; prom. Captain, April 3, '65; not mustered; brevet Capt. and Major, U. S. Volunteers, March 13, 1865; M. O. as 1st Lieut., June 2, 1865.

SURGEONS

Calvin G. Page, 33, —; physician, Boston; August 22, 1862; dis. as Major, disa., Nov. 16, '63; an A. B., Harvard, 1852, he took his M. D. there in 1854; d. March 29, 1869.

William Thorndike, 29, M.; surgeon, Beverly; Nov. 17, 1863; an A. B. from Harvard, 1854, he also gained there his M. D., 1857; had seen service as Ass't Surgeon, Thirty-fourth Massachusetts Volunteers, whence he came to the Thirty-ninth; his efficiency in the Regiment was thoroughly appreciated by the men, and General Peirson affirms that recovery from the wound received at the Weldon R. R. was the result of the care and attention of his surgeon; the son of the latter, William, Jr., also Harvard, 1892, and M. D., 1896, is a Boston practitioner, whose wife is a daughter of the late General William Tecumseh Sherman; Surgeon Thorndike died in 1887.

ASSISTANT SURGEONS

James L. Chipman, 31, —; physician, Milford; August 25, 1862; dis. as 1st Lieut. disa., May 23, '64; later, June 26, '65, 1st Lieut. and Ass't Surg. Forty-third U. S. C. T.; M. O. Oct. 20, '65.

Henry H. Mitchell, 23, —; physician, East Bridgewater; August 25, 1862; res. Nov. 3, '64, as 1st Lieut. for prom. as Major and Surgeon, Thirty-sixth U. S. C. T.; res. June 15, 1864.

John F. Butler, —, —; physician, Chesterfield, N. H.; 1st Lieut. May 27, 1863; an M. D. from Harvard, 1854, a classmate of Surgeon Thorndike, he was M. O. June 2, 1865.

CHAPLAIN

Edward Beecher French, 29, M.; clergyman, Chatham; August 18, 1862; a graduate of Harvard's Divinity School, 1859, Chaplain French enlisted as a private from his pastorate, and was commissioned from the ranks; of him Thomas E. Small remarks, "At the battle of the Wilderness the Chaplain was right up at the front with the boys and when Daniel Burnham of our Company was shot and about to die, the Chaplain took his last message and whatever he had to send to his wife and family and comforted him in his last few moments of life; he accompanied the remains of Colonel Davis from Petersburg to Cambridge and spoke at the funeral; M. O. June 2, 1865; he was born in Lowell, Nov. 20, 1832; his earlier years were spent in Holliston; his first pastorate was in Chatham, whence he was the first man to enlist in the Thirty-ninth; after the war he served pastorates in Babylon, L. I., and Perth Amboy, N. J., but his health, enfeebled by exposures at the front, broke and recovery was sought in Texas and Wisconsin, but without avail. He died July 14, 1907, in Harwich with relatives of his wife, who had preceded him to the other world, and his body was laid by the side of hers in the Harwich burial ground."

NON-COMMISSIONED STAFF

Charles Henry Chapman, 21, S.; student, Cambridge; prom. 2d Lieut. Co. G, Nov. 11, 1862; Brown University, Class of 1861.

T. Cordis Clarke from Co. B; Dec. 8, '62; prom. 2d Lieut. Nov. 13, '62; vide Co. E.

Charles W. Hanson, from Co. A; Dec. 6, '62; prom. 2d Lieut. Jan. 25, '63; vide Co. H.

Joseph A. Merrifield, from Co. A, Feb. 20, '63; prom. 2d Lieut. Sept. 20, '63; vide Co. F.

Edwin Mills, from Co. E; Sept., '63; prom. 2d Lieut. Jan. 8, '64; vide Co. A.

Charles K. Conn, from Co. K, April 28, '64; wd. and pris. May 8, '64; prom. 2d Lieut. Feb. 1, '65; vide Co. H.

George H. Dennett, from Co. K, Feb. 1, '65; prom. 2d Lieut.; not mustered; M. O. June 2, 1865, as Sergt. Major; d. Malden.

Quartermaster Sergeant

Henry B. Leighton, 25, —; —, Cambridge; Sept. 4, 1862; prom. 2d Lieut. April 3, '65; not mustered; M. O. as Q. M. Sergt. June 2, 1865.

Commissary Sergeant

Lucius W. Hilton, 21, —; —, —; Sept. 4, 1862; M. O. June 2, 1865.

Hospital Steward

Frederick Harvey, 27, M.; apothecary, Dorchester; dis. Sept. 7, 1863, S. O. W. D.

Orville A. Barker, from Co. F, Oct. 13, '62; prom. 2d Lieut. Nov. 8, '63; vide Co. C.

George A. Stuart, 22, S.; chemist, Boston; March 9, 1864; trans. June 2, 1865, to Thirty-second Infantry.

Principal Musician

Matthew Woodward, from Co. F, Nov. 1, '63; M. O. June 2, 1865.

(To avoid needless repetition of dates in regard to transfers to and from the Regiment the following facts are stated here:—June 25, '64, on the M. O. of the Twelfth Massachusetts Infantry, the men whose enlistments had not expired were trans. to the Thirty-ninth, and on the 13th, of July, '64, under similar circumstances, men were received from the Thirteenth Massachusetts. When, June 2, '65, the Thirty-ninth was preparing to go home all members whose terms were not expiring were trans. to the Thirty-second Massachusetts and were M. O. with that organization June 29, 1865).

In battle-names, Spottsylvania may include both Alsop's Farm and Laurel Hill.

COMPANY A

From South Danvers, after the War to become the town of Peabody.

George S. Nelson, 27, M.; tanner, South Danvers; August 18, '62; res. March 2, 1865; had been commissioned Captain in the Thirty-fifth, August 12, '62, and was trans. as above; at last account, Capt. Nelson's address was 880 Seminary Avenue, Chicago.

As Acting Captain, 1st Lieut. Henry F. Felch of Company E commanded the Company on its return to Boston.

FIRST LIEUTENANTS

Emory Washburn, Jr., 24, —; lawyer, Cambridge; Aug. 25, '62; the son of Ex-Governor Emory Washburn, he was born in Worcester, Oct. 1, 1837; graduating from Harvard College in 1860, he had just taken his degree of LL. B. in 1862 when he was commissioned in the new regiment then forming; evidently his direct service, if any, in the Thirty-ninth was brief, for on the first Monthly Report he appears as detached and a member of the staff of General Charles Devens, also a Worcester man; in this capacity he did excellent work, as appears in the report of General Devens, after the battle of Fredericksburg, written Dec. 17, '62, wherein he says, "I am under especial obligations, for their zeal and fidelity, to my staff," including with two others, "my aide, Lieut. E. Washburn, Jr." It would appear that Adjutant Washburn returned to the Regiment for one week at Poolesville, Md., resigning, January 24, 1864; he died in 1885.

Charles H. Porter, from 2d Lieut. Co. D, Jan. 25, '63; prom. Captain, Sept. 8, '64; not mustered; M. O. as 1st Lieut. June 2, 1865; as a member of the Loyal Legion, Captain Porter was conspicuous in promoting its interests; was Junior Vice-Commander, 1897; Registrar, 1903-5; Recorder, 1906-11; no veteran of the Regiment took more interest in its annual reunions than did Captain Porter, and for years he was practically its motive power. His papers on the campaigns in which he bore a part were valuable contributions to the Massachusetts Military Historical Society. Born in Weymouth, 1843, he was only six weeks old when the family removed to Quincy; his early education was had in the Quincy High School; his business life was that of insurance; he was almost constantly in public life, twelve years on the School Board, three years Selectman, the First Mayor of Quincy, 1888, he was re-elected; several years on the State Board of Health; first Commander, Paul Revere Post, G. A. R.; commissioned as Lieut. Colonel in Seventh M. V. M. by Governor Andrew, he was widely known as Colonel Porter; he was seven years Trustee of the Chelsea Soldiers' Home and was ever prominent in local business organizations and in Masonic Circles; d. Aug. 10, 1911.

SECOND LIEUTENANTS

George H. Wiley, 23, M.; shoemaker, So. Danvers; Aug. 18, '62; res. Jan. 7, '64; had been commissioned in the Thirty-fifth Aug. 12, '62, and was trans. as above; was 3d Lieut. Co. H, Fifth M. V. M., three mos. service; d. May 19, 1910, Boston.

L. F. Wyman, Feb. 23, '64, from Co. K; returned to "K," Mar. 2, '64.

Edwin Mills from Sergeant Major, Jan. 8, '64; dis. on account of wds. rec'd May 10, '64, Oct. 19, '64.

ENLISTED MEN

Adams, Francis D. (Corp.), 27, M.; upholsterer, Boston; July 9, '63; recruit to Twelfth Infty.; trans. thence to the Thirty-ninth and later trans. to the Thirty-second and afterwards M. O.; Pris. Aug. 19, '64, Weldon R. R.

Adams, Joseph, 44, M.; mechanic, Stowe; Aug. 18, '62; wd. May 8, '64; dis. disa., Jan. 18, '64.

Aitken, Samuel, 19, S.; mason, Boston; June 26, '61, in Co. A, Twelfth Regiment; to compensate for protracted absence without leave to Oct. 1, '63, he was trans. to the Thirty-second and thence M. O.

Ames, John, 21, S.; laborer, Boston; July 9, '63; recruit to the Twelfth Infty., trans. thence to the Thirty-ninth; trans. to One Hundred Sixty-eighth Co., Second Batt. V. R. C.; dis. June 7, '65.

Andrews, Timothy, Jr., 33, M.; spar maker, Essex; Aug. 18, '62; M. O. June 2, 1865; d. 1896.

Badger, George H., 30, M.; shoemaker, Stoughton; Aug. 18, '62; dis. disa., Oct. 22, '63.

Bancroft, George W., Jr., 20, M.; teamster, So. Danvers; Aug. 18, '62; dis. May 20, '65—report of Adjutant General says, "ex. of s."

Barden, Jonas P., 18, S.; farmer, Lynnfield; Aug. 18, '62; k. June 22, '64, Petersburg, Va.

Barnard, Henry, 21, S.; stonecutter, Hanover; Aug. 15, '61; in Co. C, Twelfth Regiment by way of compensation for unexcused absence was, at last, trans. to Thirty-second Massachusetts Volunteers for final M. O.

Batchelder, Benjamin A. (Wagoner); 40, M.; teamster, Chatham; trans. Sept. 7, '62, V. R. C.; d. —.

Bean, Thomas, b. Mar. 19, 1833; 29, M.; shoemaker, Easton; Aug. 18, '62; Corp. April 27, '63; Pris. Aug. 19, '64; M. O. June 2, '65; shoemaker and farmer; in Legislature, 1870; has held all offices in G. A. R. Post; 1913, Easton.

Belcher, John, 28, S.; shoemaker, Framingham; July 13, '63; dis. disa., May 4, '65.

Bemis, Winfield S., b. Nov. 16, 1844; 18, S.; farmer, Stowe; Aug. 18, '62; trans. V. R. C. Jan. 18, '65; M. O. from Co. I, Eighteenth V. R. C. June 29, '65; lastmaker and shoemaker; 1913, West Medway.

Bessom, Edward A., 25, M.; barber, So. Danvers; Aug. 18, '62; prom. Corp., trans. Feb. 11, '64, Co. A, Twenty-fourth V. R. C.; M. O. June 28, '65.

Blaisdell, John O. (Corp.), 30, M.; shoecutter, So. Danvers; Aug. 18, '62; Sergt. June 1, '63; wd. Feb. 6, '65, Hatcher's Run, Va.; prom. 2d Lieut. June 7, '65; M. O. as Sergt. June 2, '65.

Blauvelt, James, 42, M.; carpenter, Chatham; Aug. 18, '62; trans. July 9, '63, V. R. C.

Bloomer, Joseph, N., 23, M.; mariner, Chatham; Aug. 18, '61; dis. disa., March 3, '63.

Boodry, George J., 35, M.; bootmaker, Easton; Aug. 18, '62; prisoner from Aug. 19, '64, to Jan. 2, '65; M. O. June 2, '65.

Bowker, Edward H., 21, S.; artist, Boston; Aug. 18, '62; trans., Jan. 5, '64, V. R. C.; dis. disa., Aug. 20, '66, Fort Wayne, Mich., from Third Independent Co., V. R. C.

Brennan, James, 21, S.; paper hanger, Boston; June 26, '61; in Twelfth Infty., re-en. Jan. 5, '64; trans. to Thirty-ninth, thence to the Thirty-second and M. O.

Brett, Charles G., 19, S.; blacksmith, Stowe; Aug. 18, '62; Corp. May 1, '65,; M. O. June 2, '65; d.

Brown, Frank P., 23, M.; telegrapher, Boston; June 28, '63; trans. to Thirty-second and M. O.

Burnham, Daniel, 32, M.; farmer, Essex; Aug. 18, '62; k. May 11, '64, Spottsylvania.

Burnham, Eli H., b. July 19, 1833; 29, M.; shoemaker, So. Danvers; Aug. 18, '62; M. O. June 2, '65; 1913, Lynn.

Burnham, George S.; 26, S.; shoemaker, Essex; Aug. 18, '62; wd. May 8, '64, Alsop's Farm; M.O. June 2, '65; 1913, Essex.

Burnham, George W., 32, M.; shoemaker, Essex; Aug. 18, '62; pris. Aug. 13, '64 to March 2, '65; M. O. June 13, '65; d. 1902.

Burnham, James H., 19, S.; farmer, Essex; Aug. 18, '62; wd. May 8,'64, Spottsylvania; M. O. May 11, '65; 1913, Essex.

Burnham, Wilbur (Corp.), 20, S.; carpenter, Essex; Aug. 18, '62; Sergt. Dec. 4, '62; d. May 21, '63.

Butler, Benjamin F., 29, M.; currier, Salem; Aug. 18, '62; trans. Navy, April 21, '64.

Channel, John F., 19, S.; shoemaker, Essex; Aug. 18, '62; dis. disa., Jan. 29, '63.

Clifford, James A., 23, S.; bookbinder, Boston; Aug. 18, '62; dis. disa., April 2, '63.

Cole, George W., 20, S.; shoemaker, No. Bridgewater; Aug. 18, '62; Corp. March 17, '63; pris. Aug. 19, '64; M. O. June 2, '65; 1 French Ave., Brockton.

Conant, Edward, 19, S.; pail maker, Stowe; Aug. 18, '62; Corp. April 29, '63; wd. May 8, '64; trans. Co. D, Twenty-fourth V. R. C.; dis. June 27, '65.

Cottrell, Jefferson T. (Sergt.), 21, —; mariner, Bangor, Me.; Aug. 18, '62; wd. May 8, '64, Spottsylvania; supposed to have d. in Rebel Prison.

Cottrell, Justin W., 19, S.; mariner, Bangor, Me.; Aug. 18, '62; Corp. Sept. 20, '62; Sergt. Feb. 11, '64; Pris. Aug. 19, '64; d. Parole Camp, Annapolis, Md., Sept. 10, '64.

Cunningham, Eugene B., 22, S.; mechanic, Saxton's River, Vt.; Aug. 18, '62; dis. disa., Dec. 13, '63.

Curran, John, 21, —; —, Boston, cr. Canton; July 1, '63; trans. to Thirty-second and M. O.

Darling, Ezekial B., 29, M.; shoemaker, So. Danvers; Aug. 18, '62; wd. Feb. 6, '65, Hatcher's Run; M. O. June 2, '65.

Dean, Samuel D., 19, S.; shoe dresser, No. Bridgewater; Aug. 18, '62; Corp. Feb. 11, '64; k. March 31, '65, White Oak Roads, Va.

Dodge, Harrison A. (Sergt.), 22, S.; tanner, So. Danvers; Aug. 18, '62; trans. V. R. C. March 18, '64.

Dodge, John P. (Corp.), 29, M.; tanner, So. Danvers; Aug. 18, '62; Sergt. Sept. 30, '63; 1st Sergt. Feb. 11, '64; Pris. Aug. 19, '64, Weldon R. R.; d. Jan. 15, '65; Salisbury, N. C.

Doyle, William A., 21, —; —, Charlestown; July 9, '63; from the Twelfth Infty., Co. C; trans. to the Thirty-second and thence M. O.

Dyer, Lewis R., 17, S.; printer, Lowell; June 26, '61, in Twelfth Infty.; re-en. Jan. 5, '64; trans. and prom. Sergt. June 25, '64; trans. to Thirty-second and M. O.

Eischman, John, 26, —; shoemaker, Marblehead; a recruit to the Thirteenth Infty., where he is entered as Ehrman, Co. A, and trans. to V. R. C., July 14, '64; however, his name is among those coming from the Thirteenth and is duly trans. to the Thirty-second, where he is recorded as "absent, sick"; the chances are that he never saw either the Thirty-ninth or the Thirty-second.

Eldridge, Prince, Jr., 31, M.; mariner, Chatham; Aug. 18, '62; trans. Navy, April 21, '64; dis. disa., Naval Hosp'l, Norfolk, Va., April 19, '65; d.

Ellis, Daniel W., 18, S.; mariner, Chatham; Aug. 18, '62; M. O. June 2, '65; Carver.

Evans, William S., 21, S.; brickmaker, Danvers; Aug. 18, '62; Pris. Aug. 19, '64, Weldon R. R.; d. Feb. 3, '65, Salisbury, N. C.

Fannon, John 38, S.; operator, Lawrence; July 16, '63; recruit to the Twelfth Infty.; trans. to Thirty-ninth, thence to Thirty-second and M. O.

Field, William, 48, M.; mechanic, Harwich; Aug. 18, '62; M. O. June 2, '65; b. 1800; was a soldier in the Mexican War, the oldest man in the Regiment; dead.

Fish, Henry F., 22, M.; laborer, Milton; July 17, '63; recruit to the Twelfth Infty.; trans. to the Thirty-ninth, thence to the Thirty-second and M. O.

Flint, James F., 30, M.; shoemaker, So. Danvers; Aug. 18, '62; dis. disa., June 11, '63; d.

Flynn, Daniel B., 18, S.; shoemaker, Stowe; Aug. 18, '62; Pris. Aug. 19, '64, Weldon R. R.; M. O. June 29, '65.

Fogg, Joseph 24, S.; tanner, So. Danvers; Aug. 18, '62; dis. disa., Feb. 19, '63.

Foster, Henry, 21, S.; boatman, Lowell, cr. Brighton; July 24, '63; recruit to the Thirteenth Infty.; trans. to the Thirty-ninth, and thence to the Thirty-second and M. O.

Freeman, Warren H., 18, S.; clerk, Boston; Dec. 1, '61; recruit to the Thirteenth Infty.; trans. to the Thirty-ninth and dis. Sept. 13, '64, S. O. W. D., No. 86.

Gibbs, John K., 44, M.; laborer, So. Danvers; Aug. 18, '62; d., a prisoner, Dec. 2, '64, Salisbury, N. C.

Goodwin, Charles M., 26, M.; brickmaker, Boxford, Aug. 18, '62; wd. May 10, '64, Laurel Hill; Pris. Aug. 19, '64; dis. May 15, '65, ex. of s.; Beverly.

Gould, Charles (Mus.), 23, M.; powder maker, So. Danvers; en. July 26, '62; des. Aug. 7, '62.

Gould, William A. 18, S.; Mariner, Chatham; Aug. 18, '62; wd. Aug. 18, '64, Weldon R. R.; M. O. June 2, '65.

Guilford, Jacob O., 21, S.; shoemaker, Middleton; Aug. 18, '62; dis. disa., Dec. 29, '63.

Guppy, George F., 25, M.; shoemaker, Essex; Aug. 18, '62; dis. disa., Sept. 9, '62.

Hampton, Samuel, 45, M.; physician, Stowe; Aug. 18, '62; Pris. June 5, '64; d. on or about Sept. 20, '64, Andersonville, Ga.

Hanson, Charles W. (1st Sergt.), 26, M.; clerk, So. Danvers; Aug. 18, '62; Sergt. Major, Dec. 6, '62; prom. 2d Lieut. Jan. 25, '63; vid. Co. H.

Haskell, Albert S., 19, S.; blacksmith, Essex; Aug. 18, '62; Pris. Aug. 19, '64, Weldon R. R.; d. Feb. 2, '65, Salisbury, N. C.

Hebard, Henry J. A., 18, S.; engineer, Milton; July 21, '61; en. in Thirteenth Infty.; re-en. Jan. 4, '64; trans. to Thirty-ninth and dis. Sept. 21, '64, O. W. D.

Hegner, Anthony P. (Corp.), 18, S.; locksmith, Lynnfield; Aug. 18, '62; wd. May 8, '64, Spottsylvania; dis. disa., Oct. 3, '64.

Henry Abial R., 29, S.; carpenter, Boston; July 14, '63; recruit to Twelfth Infty.; trans. to Thirty-ninth, thence trans. to Thirty-second and M. O.

Hilton, William L., 23, S.; painter, Medfield; Feb. 13, '62; recruit to Thirteenth Infty.; trans. to Thirty-ninth and dis. Feb. 12, '65, ex. of s.

Hunting, Willard, 24, M.; Aug. 18, '62; Pris. Aug. 19, '64; Weldon R. R.; d. Dec. 5, '64, Salisbury, N. C.

Jones, Asa L., b. June 20, 1840; 22, S; Aug. 18, '62; mariner, Harwich; Corp. Dec. 1, '62; Sergt. March 17, '63; prom. Lieut. Sixth U. S. C. T., Sept. 15, '63; wd. before Petersburg, June 15, '64; dis. disa., Sept. 22, '64; merchant, pilot, fishermaster, seven years; capt. of a lightship eleven years; keeper of lighthouse and undertaker since 1889; from 1892 to 1897, inclusive, Selectman; 1913, Harwich.

Johnson, George, 21, S.; shoemaker, Brunswick, Me.; Aug. 18, '62; des. Feb. 11, '63.

Knapp, Charles P., b. Sept. 13, 1843; 18, S.; farmer, Needham; Aug. 18, '62; trans. V. R. C., Feb. 5, '64; dis. from Co. I, V. R. C., July 3, '65; as patient, guard and nurse in smallpox hospital, Washington, May 17, '63—Aug. '64; guard duty, Elmira and Syracuse, N. Y., till April, '65; same duty in Indianapolis, Ind., till M. O.; farmer and machinist; 1913, Caryville.

Kraetzer, Julius F., 20, S. clerk, Boston; July 16, '61; en. in Thirteenth Infty. and re-en. Jan. 4, '64; trans. to Thirty-ninth and thence trans. to Thirty-second and M. O.

Lee, Edward, 35, M.; blacksmith, Boston; en. July 14, '63; recruit in Co. I, Thirteenth Infty.; trans. to the Thirty-ninth, and des. Nov. 14, '64.

Livermore, Lorenzo D., 26, S.; yeoman, Spencer; July 14, '63; in Twelfth Infty., Co. I; trans. to Thirty-ninth, thence to the Thirty-second and M. O.; was wd., shoulder, Wilderness, while in the Twelfth; b. So. Royalton, Vt.; Livermore had served in Co. H, Tenth Mass., Infty.; wd. at Fair Oaks, he was dis. Oct. 27, '62, for disa. and later was drafted; d. Leicester, Sept. 22, '85; bur. in Old Cemetery.

McArthur, Peter, 30, M.; farmer, So. Danvers; Aug. 18, '62; M. O. June 2, '65; d. June, 1896.

Mansfield, William O., 21, S.; farmer, Lynnfield; Aug. 18, '62; dis. disa., June 10, '63; Wakefield.

Marteau, Ludovic, 28, S.; baker, Worcester; July 24, '63; recruit to Twelfth Infty.; trans. to Thirty-ninth; Pris. Aug. 19, '64; trans. to Thirty-second and M. O.

Maxwell, John, 31, M.; July 13, '63; laborer, Spencer; recruit to Twelfth Infty.; trans. to Thirty-ninth, thence to Thirty-second and M. O.; d. May, '96, Spencer, bur. St. Mary's Cemetery.

Mears, Rufus E., 21, M.; shoemaker, Essex; Aug. 18, '62; d., a prisoner, Salisbury, N. C., Oct. 27, '64.

Mears, Samuel, Jr., 37, M.; laborer, Essex; Aug. 18, '62; dis. disa., Dec. 23, '63; en. V. R. C. July 30, '64; dis. Nov. 21, '65, O. W. D.; d.

Mentzell, Herman, 21, M.; merchant, Amesbury; June 28, '63; recruit to Thirteenth Infty.; trans. to Thirty-ninth, thence to the Thirty-second and M. O.

Mentzer, Moses H., b. Oct. 19, 1843; 18, S.; painter, Stowe; Aug. 18, '62; M. O. June 2, '65; painter and farmer; Com'der, G. A. R. Post; 1913, Bolton.

Mentzer, William A., Jr., b. Nov. 7, 1841, Worcester; 21, M.; grocer, Malden; Aug. 18, '62; Corp. Sept. 20, '62; Sergt. Sept. 22, '64; M. O. June 2, '65; provisions, farming and teaming; 1913, Hudson.

Merrifield, Jos. A. (Sergt.), 26, M.; —, Boston; Aug. 18, '62; Sergt. Major Feb. 20, '63; 2d Lieut. Sept. 20, '63; 1st Lieut. May 4, '64; wd. May 8, '64, Spottsylvania; res. Jan. 14, '65.

Miles, Edward P., 19, M.; farmer, Marlborough; Aug. 18, '62; Pris. Aug. 19, '64, Weldon R. R., to May 18, '65; M. O. June 2, '65; d. 1904.

Milliken, James (Corp.), 22, M.; shoecutter, So. Danvers; Aug. 18, '62; M. O. June 2, '65.

Mitchell, Isaac H., b. July 10, 1836; 25, M.; shoemaker, Lynnfield; Aug. 18, '62; Corp. Sept. 22, '64; wd. March 31, '65; White Oak Roads; no M. O.; carpenter, policeman, constable; 1913, Lynnfield.

Mitchell, Jonathan H., 33, M.; shoemaker, Lynnfield; Aug. 18, '62; Pris. Aug. 19, '64; M. O. June 2, '65; d. Sept. 3, 1891.

Mitchell, Samuel H., b. Nov. 2, 1844; 18, S.; shoemaker, Lynnfield; Aug. 18, '62; Corp. Nov. 13, '62; at Five Forks captured two rebels and turned them over to the Provost Marshal; shoe business; two years in Boston City Council; 1895-6 in Massachusetts Legislature; M. O. June 2, '65; 1913, Brighton.

Morse, Benjamin G., 25, —; shoemaker, Boston; Feb. 13, '62; in the Twelfth Infty., Co. D; trans. to the Thirty-ninth and dis. March 23, '65, ex. of s.

Morse, Daniel F., 18, S.; shoemaker, Needham; Aug. 18, '62; Pris. Aug. 19, '64; M. O. June 2, '65; d.

Moulton, William J., 20, S.; farmer, Lynnfield; Aug. 18, '62; M. O. June 2, '65, in Co. E; d. 1905, Wakefield.

Mullen, Patrick, 23, M.; laborer, Boston; July 14, '63; recruit to Twelfth Infty.; trans. to Thirty-ninth, thence to Thirty-second and M. O.

Murphy, James, 33, M.; shoemaker, Stoneham; Oct. 12, '63; recruit to Twelfth Infty.; trans. to Thirty-ninth, thence to Thirty-second and M. O.

Myers, William, 38, M.; shoemaker, So. Danvers; Aug. 18, '62; Pris. Aug. 19, '64; M. O. June 2, '65.

Nichols, Wendell G., 24, S.; farmer, Lynnfield; Aug. 18, '62; k. Aug. 18, '64, Weldon R. R.

Nutting, Albion, 34, M.; machinist, Stowe; Aug. 18, '62; d. Oct. 14, '64, Washington, D. C.

Ordway, Lewis E., 18, S.; farmer, Roxbury; Feb. 9, '64; Pris. Aug. 19, '64; M. O. May 20, '65, ex. of s.

Osborne, Paul, 22, S.; shoemaker, So. Danvers; Aug. 18, '62; d. of wounds, Oct. 26, '64.

Packard, Sylvanus C., 18, S.; shoemaker, No. Bridgewater; Aug. 18, '62; Corp. Sept. 27, '63; Pris. Weldon R. R., Aug. 19, '64, to March 2, '65; M. O. July 14, '65; d.

Patterson, Joseph R., 22, M.; butcher, So. Danvers; Aug. 18, '62; dis. disa., Feb. 19, '63.

Perkins, John H., 23, M.; teamster, Danvers; Aug. 18, '62; had been prisoner of war; M. O. June 2, '65.

Pierce, John, Jr., 22, S.; Aug. 18, '62; dis. disa., Jan. 2, '63.

Plummer, Nathan F., Jr., 26, M.; clerk, Boston; July 9, '62; recruit to the Twelfth Infty.; trans. to Thirty-ninth, thence to the Thirty-second and M. O.

Powell, David, 18, S.; farmer, So. Danvers; Aug. 18, '62; wd. May 5, '64; M. O. July 1, '65; Saugus.

Purcell, George J., 18, S.; laborer, So. Danvers; en. Aug. 6, '62; trans. Sept. 18, '64, from Co. H to V. R. C.

Purington, William E., 18, S.; farmer, So. Danvers; Aug. 18, '62; trans. Feb. 15, '63, to V. R. C.

Reynolds, Marcus (Mus.), 19, S.; clerk, No. Bridgewater; Aug. 27, '63; recruit to Twelfth Infty.; trans. to Thirty-ninth, thence to Thirty-second and M. O.

Richardson, Francis S., 24, S.; farmer, Lynnfield; Aug. 18, '62; M. O. June 2, '65; d.

Richardson, William L., 20, S.; hostler, Salem; Aug. 18, '62; M. O. June 2, '65; Cambridgeport.

Roy, John, 25, M.; seaman, Boston; Sept. 18, '63; recruit to Twelfth Infty.; trans. to Thirty-ninth, thence to Thirty-second and M. O.

Ryder, Alvah (Corp.), 48, M.; mariner; Aug. 18, '62; dis. disa., Nov. 26, '62.

Saunders, Charles R. P., 31, M.; carpenter, Newburyport; Aug. 18, '62; M. O. June 2, '65; d. 1906.

Sawyer, James M., 19, S.; farmer, Sudbury; Aug. 18, '62; Pris. Aug. 19, '64, Weldon R. R.; M. O. July 18, '65; Clinton.

Schoen, Frederick, 30, M.; clerk, Worcester; July 25, '63; recruit to the Thirteenth Infty.; trans. to Thirty-ninth, thence to the Thirty-second and M. O.

Schwartz, Jacob, 28, S.; clerk, Taunton; July 28, '63; recruit to Thirteenth Infty.; trans. to Thirty-ninth, thence to Thirty-second and M. O.

Shaw, Zenas, 38, M.; shoemaker, Halifax; Aug. 18, '62; M. O. June 2, '65.

Simonds, George N. (Mus.), 32, M.; clerk, So. Danvers; Aug. 18, '62; wd. May 5, '64, Wilderness; M. O. July 12, '65.

Small, Thomas E., b. Feb. 17, 1844; 18, S.; mariner, Harwich; Aug. 18, '62; M. O. June 2, '65; for past seventeen years, carrier of U. S. mail, passengers and express; many years secretary and treasurer Board of Trustees, M. E. Church; 1913, So. Harwich.

Smalley, Henry, b. Feb. 12, 1842; 20, S.; mariner, Harwich; Aug. 18, '62; Corp. Sept. 30, '63; M. O. June 2, '65; cashier, B. & M. R. R., since Oct., 1867; 1913, Winchester.

Smith, Cyrus D., 21, —; —, So. Danvers; N. F. R.

Smith, George, 21, S.; laborer, Bangor, Me.; Aug. 18, '62; M. O. June 2, '65.

Smith, Nathaniel, 21, S.; farmer, Chatham; Aug. 18, '62; dis. disa., June 12, '63.

Snow, Eric M., 42, M.; harness maker, Chatham; Aug. 18, '62; dis. disa., March 26, '63.

Spencer, Roland J., 18, S.; hostler, Nantucket; Aug. 18, '62; M. O. June 2, '65.

Stevens, Elbridge, 18, S.; Aug. 18, '62; Pris. Aug. 19, '64, Weldon R. R.; d. rebel Prison, Richmond, Va., date unknown.

Story, Asa, 33, M.; shoemaker, Essex; Aug. 18, '62; d. Nov. 11, '62, Washington, D. C.

Summers, George M., 34, M.; shoemaker, Lynnfield; Aug. 18, '62; M. O. July 12, '65.

Tyler, John O., 24, S.; morocco dresser, Salem; Aug. 18, '62; trans. Navy, April 21, '64; Lynn.

Varnum, John, 24, M.; shoemaker, Essex; Aug. 18, '62; wd. May 12, '64, Spottsylvania; M. O. June 2, '65.

Whitcomb, George F., 18, S.; farmer, Stowe; Aug. 18, '62; Pris. Aug. 19, '64, Weldon R. R.; d. Jan. 2, '65, Salisbury, N. C.

Whiting, Walter B., 21, S.; bookbinder, Boston; Aug. 18, '62; dis. disa., Oct. 23, '62.

Wiley, Samuel (Sergt.), 21, S.; shoemaker, So. Danvers; Aug. 18, '62; missing after July 16, '64; supposed to have been murdered by guerrillas.

COMPANY B

Roxbury

CAPTAIN

William W. Graham, 33, S.; machinist, Roxbury; Aug. 20, '62; wd. May 10, '64; prom. Major, June 7, '65; not mustered; M. O. as Captain June 2, '65.

FIRST LIEUTENANTS

William T. G. Spear, 27, M.; tradesman, Roxbury; Aug. 20, '62; k. Aug. 18, '64, Weldon R. R.; the Lieutenant, on account of ill health, had resigned before leaving Mitchell's Station, the resignation had been accepted, but the notification was lost in a mass of papers at headquarters, and was not found till after his death; very far from being religiously inclined, Lieut. Spear's whole nature was changed by certain revival meetings at Mitchell's during the winter, and when his death-stroke came his constant and only words, till death sealed his lips, were, "What a blessed thing is religion."

Joseph A. Merrifield, from Co. D, May 4, '64; wd. May 8, '64; res. Jan. 14, 1865.

Melville C. Parkhurst (B), prom. Captain, June 7, '65; not mustered; M. O. June 2, '65, as 1st Lieut.; long Chief of Police, Somerville; 1913, Somerville.

SECOND LIEUTENANTS

Julius M. Swain, 26, S.; cashier, Roxbury; Aug. 20, '62; trans. to U. S. Signal Corps, March 3, '63; bvt. 1st Lieut. and Captain U. S. Vols. March 13, '65; res. June 14, '65; dead.

T. Cordis Clarke, from Co. E; dis. disa., July 19, '64; on detached service Aug. 10, '63; Ordnance Dept., 2d Div. 1st Army Corps.

Melville C. Parkhurst, from Co. E; prom. 1st Lieut. (B), Jan. 15, '65.

Charles H. Perkins, from Co. D, March 1, '65; Com. Sept. 8, '64; M. O. June 2, '65; dead.

ENLISTED MEN

Adams, George E., 25, S.; sawyer, Boston; July 22, '63; recruit to Twelfth Infty.; trans. to Thirty-ninth; wd. Aug. 18, '64, Weldon R. R.; trans. to Thirty-second and M. O.

Allison, Joseph, Jr. (Sergt.), 38, M.; boiler-maker, Roxbury; Aug. 20, '62; prom. 1st Sergt.; wd. June 19, '64, Petersburg, Va.; d. July 10, '64.

Andrews, George A., 22, M.; teamster, Roxbury; Aug. 20, '62; prom. Corp.; Pris. Aug. 19, '64; M. O. June 2, '65.

Arnold, Edwin L. (Corp.), 20, S.; machinist, Adams; Aug. 20, '62; dis. disa., June 30, '63.

Arnold, William, Jr., 28, M.; moulder, Roxbury; Aug. 20, '62; M. O. June 2, '65; 1913, Stoneham.

Backup, James B., 18, S.; clerk, Roxbury; Aug. 20, '62; dis. July 17, '63, for commission, Thirty-sixth U. S. C. T.; 2d Lieut. Aug. 13, '63; 1st Lieut. May 1, '64; Capt. Oct. 21, '64; dis. Jan. 23, '65.

Bartlett, Abner D. (Corp.), 34, M.; pattern-maker; Blackstone; Aug. 20, '62; dis. Feb. 4, '63.

Bartlett, John L., 45, M.; rope maker, Roxbury; Aug. 31, '62; dis. disa., June 3, '63.

Batcheller, Holland M., 43, M.; provisions, Needham; Aug. 20, '62; dis. May 5, '63, for Commission, U. S. C. T.

Bell, James H., 26, M.; shoemaker, Ashland; July 21, '63; recruit to the Twelfth Infty., Co. H; trans. to Thirty-ninth; prom. Corp. March 1, '65; trans. to Thirty-second and M. O.

Bennett, Alden B. (Mus.), 44, —; —, Boston; June 10, '63; evidently a recruit; trans. to the Thirty-second and M. O.

Bennett, Harrison M., b. March 22, 1843; 19, S.; farmer, Springfield; Aug. 30, '62; prom. Corp.; wd. May 10, '64, Laurel Hill; dis. disa., Dec. 24, '64; graduated in Law, National University, 1870, Washington, D. C., also in Medicine, Howard University; practiced medicine 10 years, since then, clerk Treasury Dep't, Washington, 1913, Takoma Park, Washington, D. C.

Betts, Charles R., 25, S.; July 24, '63; recruit to Twelfth Infty., Co. A; trans. to Thirty-ninth, thence to Thirty-second and M. O.

Bills, Walter M., 26, S.; fireman, Roxbury; Aug. 20, '62; Pris. Aug. 19, '64, Weldon R. R.; d. Jan. 24, '65, Salisbury, N. C.

Blake, Daniel P., 27, M.; shoemaker, Halifax; Aug. 23, '62; wd. June 23, '64, Petersburg; trans. V. R. C., Jan. 10, '65; also recorded as dis. Dec. 2, '64, Rendezvous, Va.; vide letter, W. D., Jan. 6, 1888; 1913, Halifax.

Briggs, Arthur M., 33, M.; teamster, Roxbury; Aug. 20, '62; dis. disa., Dec. 16, '62.

Brown, George, 23, S.; farmer, Southborough; July 16, '61; in Thirteenth Infty.; re-en. Jan. 5, '64; trans. to Thirty-ninth thence to the Thirty-second and M. O.

Bryant, Roscoe L., b. July 12, 1849, Woburn; (Mus.), 13, S.; carpenter, Woburn; Aug. 20, '62; M. O. June 2, '65.

Burns, James, 41, M.; laborer, Roxbury; Aug. 20, '62; Pris. Dec. 11, '64; M. O. June 2, '65.

Butske, Carl, 30, S.; baker, Roxbury; Aug. 20, '62; died, no date or place.

Carleton, William, 31, S.; mason, Boston; Aug. 20, '62; k. May 8, '64, Spottsylvania.

Cassidy, John, 27, S.; laborer, Boston; July 20, '63; recruit to Twelfth Infty. Co. B; trans. to Thirty-ninth; Pris. Aug. 19, '64; trans. to Thirty-second and M. O.

Chapin, Charles H., 24, M.; artist, Boston; July 9, '63; recruit to Twelfth Infty.; trans. to Thirty-ninth, thence des. March 4, '65.

Childs, John F., 21, M.; shoemaker, Natick; March 11, '62; recruit to Thirteenth Infty.; trans. to Thirty-ninth, thence dis. March 11, '65, ex. of s.

Clarke, T. Cordis (1st Sergt.), 19, S.; clerk, Roxbury; prom. Sergt. Major, Dec. 8, '62.

Crafts, William G., 18, S.; painter, Roxbury; Aug. 20, '62; dis. disa., Nov. 12, '62.

Cronan, Daniel, 19, S.; plumber, Boston; June 26, '61; according to rolls, but '62 would accord better with the record; trans. from Co. B, Twelfth Infty. to the Thirty-ninth and thence dis. June 2, '65, ex. of s.

Cunningham, Martin, 22, S.; laborer, Acton; Sept. 26, '63; recruit to Twelfth Infty.; trans. to Thirty-ninth; Pris. Aug. 19, '64, Weldon R. R.; escaped from train on southern way; trans. to Thirty-second and M. O.

Curtis, John M., 45, M.; laborer, Roxbury; Aug. 20, '62; dis. disa., June 9, '63.

Dailey, John, 23, S.; lather, Roxbury; Aug. 20, '62; dis. disa., July 17, '63.

Daly, James, 24, S.; silversmith, Boston; June 26, '61; en. Co. B, Twelfth Infty.; trans. to Thirty-ninth, thence des. 1865; he had already des. in first enlistment and had come back.

Davis, Edward S., 18, S.; plumber, Roxbury; prom. Sergt.; Pris. Aug. 19, '64; d. March 20, '65.

Davis, Gardner C., 28, S.; fireman, Roxbury; Aug. 20, '62; prom. Sergt.; missing May 8, '64, Spottsylvania.

Devines, David S. (Corp.), 33, M.; tinsmith, Roxbury; Aug. 20, '62; des. May 6, '63.

Diguer, Richard, 34, M.; blacksmith, Roxbury; Aug. 20, '62; dis. disa., Feb. 18, '65.

Doyle, Patrick, 19, S.; paper stamper, Roxbury; Aug. 20, '62; Corp. March 1, '65; M. O. June 2, '65.

Draper, Curtis W., 18, S.; shoemaker, Wayland; Aug. 20, '62; Corp. March 1, '65; M. O. June 2, '65; b. Wayland, Sept. 27th, '46, he was not quite 16 years old at enlistment; was in every battle and skirmish in which the Thirty-ninth took part, never lost a day's duty and never was struck by an enemy's missile, save once, and then it was a spent bullet; youngest soldier from the town.

Dudley, Charles, 20, S.; farmer, Wayland; June 26, '61; in Co. B, Twelfth Infty.; des. and came back; trans. to Thirty-ninth, thence trans. to Thirty-second, to make up time, and was M. O. June 29, '65.

Dyer, Simon D., 43, S.; bookkeeper, Roxbury; en. Aug. 3, '62; N. F. R.

Edmands, Thomas, 18, S.; paper hanger, Roxbury; Aug. 20, '62; Pris. Aug. 19, '64, Weldon R. R.; en. in Rebel Army.

Ernest, Anet, 20, S.; farmer, Baltimore, cr. Springfield; Sept. 20, '64; July 13, '64, he had en. as 21 years old, a Boston shoemaker, in Co. A of the Fifth M. V. M., 100 days; M. O. June 2, '65.

Fisher, Andrew J., 22, M.; bootmaker, en. Concord, N. H., cr. Boston; July 27, '63; recruit to Thirteenth Infty.; trans. to Thirty-ninth, thence to Thirty-second and M. O.

Fizzell, James, 18, —; plumber, Springfield; Sept. 20, '64; from Co. A, Fifth M. V. M., 100 days, where he was carried as Frizzell; M. O. June 2, '65.

Flanagan, Anthony, 23, S.; lather, Roxbury; Aug. 20, '62; M. O. June 2, '65.

Foley, John E., 38, M.; tailor, Boston; Aug. 20, '62; dis., May 3, '65, O. W. D.

Frahm, Louis, 40, M.; shoemaker, Roxbury; Aug. 20, '62; k. Aug. 18, '64, Weldon R. R.

Frederick, Benjamin B., 34, M.; carriage painter, Roxbury; Aug. 20, '62; dis. disa., Dec. 4, '63.

Gallagher, Edward, 30, M.; laborer, Boston; Aug. 1, '63; recruit to Twelfth Infty.; trans. to Thirty-ninth, thence to Thirty-second and M. O.

Gordon, Horace, F., 36, M.; shoemaker, Roxbury, Aug. 20, '62; M. O. June 2, '65.

Green, John W., 25, M.; teamster, Roxbury; Aug. 20, '62; missing, May 8, '64, Spottsylvania.

Gunning, John, 25, M.; laborer, Roxbury; Aug. 20, '62; Pris. Aug. 19, '64; d. prison hospital, Dec. 10, '64, Salisbury, N. C.

Ham, Henry A., 28, S.; clerk, Boston; July 27, '63; recruit to Thirteenth Infty.; trans. to Thirty-ninth, thence to Thirty-second and M. O.

Henry, Daniel, 33, M.; piano maker; Roxbury; Aug. 20, '62; k. May 10, '64, Spottsylvania.

Hicks, William L., 18, S.; clerk, Roxbury; Aug. 20, '62; dis. disa., Nov. 11, '63.

Hiedenway, David, 37, M.; shoemaker, Roxbury; Aug. 20, '62; dis. June 9, '65; roll also says "d. Dec. 14, '66"; vid. p. 52 of the narrative.

Holbrook, Silas P., 28, S.; clerk, Dorchester; July 16, '61; in Thirteenth Infty., re-en. Jan. 4, '64; trans. to Thirty-ninth, thence dis., S. O. W. D., July 19, '64, for Commission, 2d Lieutenant, Forty-fifth U. S. C. T.; res. April 25, '65.

Howard, Ephraim F., 18, S.; blacksmith, No. Bridgewater; Aug. 20, '62; trans. V. R. C., Sept. 30, '63; dis. Aug. 25, '64, from 102d Co., Second Batt. V. R. C.

Huggins, Arthur H., 22, S.; plumber, Boston; Aug. 20, '62; dis. disa., Sept. 19, '63.

Hunter, James, 22, S.; carpenter, Roxbury; Aug. 20, '62; dis. disa., Feb. 6, '64.

Hunter, Robert L., 44, M.; carpenter, Roxbury; Aug. 20, '62; absent at M. O. in Philadelphia; vide letter, W. D., Jan. 22, '94.

Jones, William, 21, S.; bootmaker, Taunton; Aug. 4, '63; recruit to Twelfth Infty.; trans. to Thirty-ninth, thence to Thirty-second and M. O.

Kelly, Edward, 43, M.; carder, Roxbury; Aug. 20, '62; trans. V. R. C., Sept. 16, '63; dis. disa., Oct. 24, '65, from Sixteenth Co., Second Batt. V. R. C.

Kelly, John, 20, S.; ropemaker, Roxbury; Aug. 20, '62; d. Nov. 26, '64, Washington, D. C.

Kelly, William, 39, M.; laborer, Roxbury; Aug. 20, '62; trans. Jan. 5, '64, V. R. C.; dis. from Third Independent Co., V. R. C., Aug. 29, '66.

Killduff, James, 37, M.; ropemaker, Roxbury; Aug. 20, '62; d. a prisoner, Nov. 27, '64, Salisbury, N. C.

Landgreve, George, 39, M.; carpenter, Roxbury; Aug. 20, '62; missing, May 8, '64, Spottsylvania.

Leach, Rodney M., 28, M.; bootmaker, No. Bridgewater; July 16, '63; recruit to Twelfth Infty.; trans. to Thirty-ninth, thence to the Thirty-second and M. O.

Ledwith, John, 21, S.; laborer, Roxbury; Aug. 20, '62; prom. Corp.; M. O. June 2, '65; 1913, Peabody.

Lewis, Edward H., 18, S.; clerk, Stoneham; Aug. 20, '62; prom. Corp.; Pris. Aug. 19, '64; M. O. June 2, '65; 1913, 22 Quincy Street, Chicago; though b. in Roxbury, Jan. 5, 1845, his life has been spent largely in the West; his well kept diary was drawn upon in the making of this history; he is a member of U. S. Grant Post 28, Dept. of Ill.

Loker, James D. (Sergt.), 34, M.; policeman, Roxbury; Aug. 20, '62; d. Dec. 30, '62, Poolesville, Md.

Lull, Stephen, 29, M.; shoemaker, Halifax; Aug. 20, '62; June 2, '65.

Macarty, Edward H., 22, S.; provisions, Roxbury; Aug. 20, '62; d. April 29, '65.

McDonald, George, b. 1844; 18, S.; laborer, Middleborough; en. Sept. 2, '62; Pris. Aug. 19, '64; escaped; M. O. June 2, '65; machinist; ass't. chief, Fire Dep't; 1913, Pawtucket, R. I.

McDonald, John, 35, M.; en. Aug. 31, '62; wd. May 10, '64, Spottsylvania; M. O. June 2, '65.

Mackenzie, Daniel, 29, M.; baker, Roxbury; Aug. 31, '62; dis. disa., July 19, '63.

McNeil, William C., 32, M.; painter, Boston; July 13, '63; recruit to Twelfth Infty.; trans. to Thirty-ninth, thence to Thirty-second and M. O.

McNulty, Thomas, 33, M.; porter, Roxbury; Aug. 20, '62; wd. May 10, '64, Spottsylvania; M. O. June 2, '65.

McPherson, John J., 25, S.; baker, Boston; Oct. 8, '63; recruit to Twelfth Infty.; trans. to Thirty-ninth and M. O. May 19, '65.

Melton, Joseph L., 30, M.; shoemaker, Halifax; Aug. 20, '62; d. Nov. 9, '63, Alexandria, Va.

Milner, Thomas K., 34, M.; Carpenter, Roxbury; Aug. 20, '62; d. April 29, '65.

Mitchell, Franklin A., 41, S.; carpenter, Roxbury; Aug. 20, '62; d. from wds. June 2, '64, according to the rolls, but G. V. Shedd's diary has it June 20.

Mohan, Terrance P., 18, S.; painter, Boston; Aug. 20, '62; Pris. Aug. 19, '64, Weldon R. R.; paroled, Oct. 7, '64; M. O. May 18, '65.

Moore, Sidney, 19, S.; farmer, Westport; Oct. 12, '63; recruit to Twelfth Infty.; trans. as "returned deserter"; N. F. R.; not carried to roll of the Thirty-second.

Morgan, John, 33, M.; butcher, Roxbury; Aug. 20, '62; dis. disa., April 22, '63.

Moses, George F., b. Aug. 24, 1843; 19, S.; farmer, Milton; Aug. 20, '62; lost left arm, May 10, '64, Laurel Hill; dis. disa., March 17, '65; for many years, watchman at State House, Boston; resides in Roxbury, 1913.

Monroe, James, 18, S.; farmer, Provincetown; Oct. 19, '63; recruit to Twelfth Infty.; trans. to Thirty-ninth, thence to Thirty-second and M. O.

Murphy, Thomas, 24, S.; farmer, Charlton; July 25, '63; recruit to Twelfth Infty.; trans. to Thirty-ninth, thence to Thirty-second and M. O.

Murray, Patrick, 21, S.; painter, Roxbury; Aug. 20, '62; wd. May 10, '64, Spottsylvania; M. O. June 2, '65.

Noble, Joseph A., 33, M.; painter, Roxbury; Aug. 20, '62; dis. Dec. 22, '63; later in Co. H Fifty-sixth Massachusetts Infantry.

Nolan, Patrick, 39, M.; brass finisher, Roxbury; Aug. 20, '62; wd. no time or place given; M. O. June 2, '65.

Nute, Joseph, 40, M.; carpenter, Roxbury; Aug. 20, '62; dis. June 29, '65.

Palmer, Rensilleir L. (Corp.), 34, M.; piano key maker, Roxbury; Aug. 20, '64; Sergt. March 1, '65; M. O. June 2, '65.

Perkins, Henry S., 21, M.; provisions, Roxbury; Aug. 20, '62; dis. as Corp. June 16, '64, O. W. D.

Perkins, Jonathan, 36, M.; laborer, Roxbury; Aug. 20, '62; M. O. July 10, '65.

Plympton, William P., 23, S.; mechanic, Springfield; Sept. 20, '64; M. O. June 14, '65; had been dis. Sept. 19, from Co. A, Fifth Massachusetts Volunteer Militia (100 days), to re-en. here; 1910, Insurance, Southbridge.

Pyne, Frederick (Sergt.), 29, M.; carpenter, Roxbury; Aug. 20, '62; prom. 1st Sergt.; dis. O. W. D., July 29, '63.

Reaney, Patrick, 26, W.; laborer, Roxbury; Aug. 20, '62; Pris. Aug. 19, '64, Weldon R. R.; d. Feb. 26, '65, Salisbury, N. C.

Rich, Giles H. (Sergt.), 21, S.; lawyer, Roxbury; Aug. 20, '62; dis. June 20, '63, Washington, D. C., for Captain's Commission, First U. S. C. T.; prom. Lieut. Colonel, Oct. 13, '64; M. O. Sept. 29, '65, Roanoke Island, N. C.

Richardson, William R., 32, M.; teamster, Roxbury; Aug. 20, '62; prom. Sergt.; 1st Sergt., March 1, '65; M. O. June 2, '65.

Ricker, Oliver P., b. 1837; 26, M.; expressman, Roxbury; Aug. 20, '62; prom. Sergt.; prom. 2d Lieut. Sept. 8, '64; dis., June 6, '65; clerk; 1913, Dorchester.

Robinson, Andrew J. (Corp.), 28, M.; mason, Roxbury; Aug. 20, '62; M. O. June 18, '65.

Robinson, John R., 24, S.; mason, Roxbury; Aug. 20, '62; Pris., Aug. 19, '64; d. Dec. 6, '64, Salisbury, N. C.

Roland, Richard, 20, S.; waiter, Roxbury; Aug. 20, '62; dis. disa., June 9, '63.

Rosemere, Conrad (Corp.), 22, S.; pattern maker, Roxbury; Aug. 20, '62; M. O. June 2, '65; as Rosemeyer, he had served from May 24 to Aug. 31, '61, in the First Massachusetts Infantry.

Russell, Edmund, 27, M.; farmer, Wayland; Aug. 20, '62; by the fall of a tree, his leg was broken March 7, '63; on recovery he was sent to Readville, Mass. and detailed as cook; dis. May 16, '65; went West.

Saunders, Abraham, 25, M.; carpenter, Roxbury; Aug. 20, '62; dis. disa., June 9, '63.

Schaffer, Henry, 27, —; clerk, Concord; July 22, '63; recruit to Twelfth Infty.; trans. to Thirty-ninth; wd. March 31, '65, Hatcher's Run; trans. to Thirty-second and M. O.

Schroeffel, Phillip (Mus.), 35, M.; —, Roxbury; M. O. June 2, '65; 1913, Roxbury.

Scott, Peter F., 42, M.; laborer, Taunton; July 25, '63; recruit to Twelfth Infty.; trans. to Thirty-ninth, thence to Thirty-second and M. O.

Shea, Peter E., 32, M.; rope maker, Roxbury; Aug. 20, '62; dis. disa., Nov. 16, '62.

Shedd, Albert A., 23, S.; tradesman, Roxbury; Aug. 20, '62; dis. April 12, '64 for Commission in Forty-third, U. S. C. T.

Shedd, George V., 21, S.; clerk, Roxbury; Aug. 20, '62; M. O. June 2, '65; his diary enters largely in the history; 1913, Preston, Conn.

Skinner, George F., 19, S.; carpenter, So. Reading; Aug. 20, '62; wd. Aug. 18, '64, Weldon R. R.; M. O. June 2, '65.

Smith, Charles H., 26, M.; seaman, Boston; July 29, '63; recruit to Thirteenth Infty.; trans. to Thirty-ninth; wd. March 31, '65, Hatcher's Run; trans. to Thirty-second and M. O.

Smith, Henry R., 23, S.; farmer, Ashland; July 21, '63; recruit to Twelfth Infty.; trans. to the Thirty-ninth; Pris.; d. Nov. 6, '64, Salisbury, N. C.

Smith, Peter, 30, M.; laborer, Adams; July 14, '63; recruit to Twelfth Infty.; trans. to the Thirty-ninth, thence to the Thirty-second and M. O.

Smith, Sidney, Jr., 21, S.; machinist, Roxbury; Aug. 20, '62; M. O. June 2, '65.

Somerby, Frank (Corp.), 20, S.; clerk, Roxbury; Aug. 20, '62; M. O. June 2, '65; 1913, Roxbury.

Spellan, Dennis, 41, M.; farmer, Southborough; Dec. 22, '63; recruit to Thirteenth Infty.; trans. to Thirty-ninth, thence to the Thirty-second and M. O.

Stepper, Joseph, Jr., 19, S.; moulder, Roxbury; Aug. 20, '62; wd. May 8, '64, Spottsylvania; M. O. June 2, '65.

Stevens, Charles E., 18, —; student, Springfield; Sept. 20, '64; M. O. June 2, '65; had been dis. Sept. 18, '64, from Co. A Fifth Massachusetts Volunteer Militia to re-en. here.

Strickland, William, 23, —; butcher, Canton; Aug. 4, '63; recruit to Twelfth Infty.; trans. to Thirty-ninth; wd. May 8, '64, Spottsylvania; trans. to Thirty-second and M. O.

Strong, Edward A., 31, S.; farmer, Gt. Barrington; July 15, '63; recruit to Twelfth Infty.; trans. to Thirty-ninth, thence to Thirty-second and M. O.

Stuart, Thomas, 24, —; laborer, Taunton; Aug. 4, '63; recruit to Twelfth Infty.; trans. to Thirty-ninth; Pris. Aug. 19, '64; d. Dec. 4, '64.

Sturtevant, Henry B., 20, S.; cordwainer, Stoneham; June 26, '61; had deserted from Co. D, Twelfth Infty., Sept., 8, '61; was arrested Sept. 2, '64, and sent to the Thirty-ninth to serve out term; trans. to the Thirty-second and M. O.

Sullivan, Dennis O., 23, M.; lather, Roxbury; Aug. 20, '62; Pris. Aug. 19, '64; M. O. June 2, '65.

Sullivan, Thomas, 21, S.; laborer, Roxbury; Dec. 21, '63; wd. May 10, '64, Spottsylvania; dis. disa., no date; 1913, Roxbury.

Swain, Edwin A. (Corp.), 29, S.; tradesman, Roxbury; Aug. 20, '62; prom. Sergt.; dis. Dec. 3, '63, for Commission in Third U. S. C. T.

Swan, Charles, 21, S.; teamster, Springfield; July 15, '63; recruit to Twelfth Infty.; trans. to Thirty-ninth; Pris. Aug. 19, '64, Weldon R. R.; d. Feb. 2, '65, Salisbury, N. C.

Sweat, Charles W., 29, S.; machinist, Roxbury; Aug. 20, '62; M. O. June 2, '65.

Symmes, Alfred, 42, M.; organ builder, Roxbury; Aug. 30, '62; dis. disa., July 6, '63.

Taft, Isaac D., 31, S.; farmer, Uxbridge; July 18, '63; recruit to Twelfth Infty.; trans. to Thirty-ninth, thence to Thirty-second and M. O.

Turner, Charles, 21, S.; groom, Boston; July 29, '63; recruit to Twelfth Infty.; trans. to Thirty-ninth; des. from hospital, no date given.

Tyree, John C., 18, S.; laborer, Springfield; Sept. 20, '64; M. O. June 2, '65; had been dis., Sept. 19, '64, from Co. A, Fifth Massachusetts Volunteer Militia (100 days), to re-en. here.

Wadsworth, Charles, 30, S.; moulder, Plymouth; July 17, '63; recruit to the Twelfth Infty.; trans. to Thirty-ninth; Pris.; d. Nov. 11, '64, Salisbury, N. C.

Warren, George, 22, S.; agent, Boston; July 9, '63; recruit to Twelfth Infty.; trans. to Thirty-ninth, thence to Thirty-second and M. O.

Wheeler, George, 40, S.; teamster, Roxbury; Aug. 20, '62; M. O. June 2, '65.

White, William H., 38, M.; carpenter, Brookline; Aug. 20, '62; dis. disa., Jan. 21, '63.

Whitman, Henry B., 25, M.; shoe cutter, Middleborough; July 14, '63; recruit to Twelfth Infty.; trans. to Thirty-ninth; dis. May 15, '65, O. W. D.

Whitaker, Channing, 18, S.; farmer, Needham; en. Sept. 2, '62; wd. May 10, '64; M. O. June 19, '65; graduated at the Massachusetts Institute of Technology, 1869, as Civil Engineer, in which Department, for a number of following years, he was a professor; during his later years he was Consulting Mechanic and Patent Engineer with the Lowell Machine Shops, with residence in Tyngsboro; d. July 23, 1913; his contributions to this history are prominent features.

Wilborg, William, 32, M.; coppersmith, Roxbury; Aug. 20, '62; wd. May 12, '64, Spottsylvania; M. O. June 2, '65.

Williams, Henry, 20, —; merchant, Springfield; Sept. 20, '64; M. O. June 2, '65; had been dis. Sept. 19th from Co. A, Fifth M. V. M., to re-en. here.

Wilson, Thomas A., 25, M.; moulder, Roxbury; Aug. 20, '62; wd. June 18, '64, Petersburg; M. O. June 2, '65.

Winters, Thomas B., —, —; —, Sandy Hook, Md.; en. Oct. 1, '61; recruit to Thirteenth Infty.; trans. to Thirty-ninth; wd. Aug. 18, '64, Spottsylvania; dis. Oct. 1, '64, ex. of s.

Wood, James, 23, S.; clerk, Boston; en. Aug. 30, '62; M. O. June 2, '65.

COMPANY C

Medford

CAPTAIN

John Hutchins, 42, M.; ship-carpenter; Medford; Aug. 14, '62; Pris. Aug. 18, '64, Weldon R. R.; M. O. June 2, '65; Lieut. Colonel June 7, '65, not mustered; had served as Captain in the 3 mos. term of the Fifth M. V. M., Co. E, 1861; U. S. Navy Yard, Charlestown; d. Medford, Oct. 12, 1905; b. York, Me., Oct. 17, 1820; came to Medford when 16 years old; early in the Militia he also was foreman of the local fire company, and was a member of the Masonic order. Dying at the Medford Inn, his home for several years, Oct. 12, 1905, his funeral on the 15th was conducted in the Lawrence Armory with the highest military honors, many of his old comrades in arms being present; burial was in Oak Grove Cemetery; "He never shirked a duty."

FIRST LIEUTENANTS

Perry Coleman, 28, M.; clerk, Medford; Aug. 14, '62; res. Nov. 7, '63; was 2d Lieut. in Co. E, Fifth M. V. M. 3 mos. term, 1861; d. Washington, D. C.

Charles W. Hanson, from Co. E, Nov. 8, '63; Pris. Aug. 18, '64; prom. Captain Sept. 8, '64; vide Co. E.

Orville A. Barker, Sept. 15, '64; Adjutant Dec. 5, '64.

William McDevitt, April 3, '65; not mustered; M. O. June 2, '65, as 2d Lieut.; long in Paving Department, Boston, 1913, Allston.

SECOND LIEUTENANTS

Isaac F. R. Hosea, 30, M.; clerk, Medford; Aug. 14, '62; the most of Lieut. Hosea's service was with the Brigade Pioneer Corps and he was commanding it when captured, Aug. 19, '64; prom. 1st Lieut. Jan. 15, '65; M. O. June 2, '65, as 2d Lieut.; had served as 1st Sergt. in Co. E, Fifth M. V. M., 3 mos. term; long clerk B. & M. R. R.; d. April 16, 1893, Medford.

Orville A. Barker from Hosp. Steward, Nov. 8, '63, mustered Dec. 7, '63, vice Hosea on detached service; prom. 1st Lieut. Sept. 15, '64.

William McDevitt from Co. K, Sept. 15, '64; prom. 1st Lieut. April 3, '65.

ENLISTED MEN

Alden, William F., July 20, 1833; (Corp.), 29, M.; clerk, Medford; Aug. 14, '62; dis. disa., Jan. 21, '63; had been in Co. E, Fifth M. V. M., 3 mos. term, 1861; engraver, policeman and janitor, Medford; 1913, Cambridge.

Alley, Charles Q., b. Sept. 18, 1842; 20, S.; baker, Medford; Aug. 6, '62; trans., no date, Forty-eighth Co., 2d Batt., V. R. C.; dis. June 26, '65; wholesale notions and toys; for forty-six years a member of Methodist S. S., Rockford, Ill., for twenty-eight years Assistant Superintendent, for forty-four years church usher, for twenty-eight, Secretary and Treasurer of the Eastern Veterans' Association of the Civil War; he retains the knapsack received at Boxford, as well as cap, canteen and haversack, his old army overcoat dates from Thoroughfare Gap, Oct., '63; 1913, Rockford, Ill.

Baldwin, John M., 28, M.; carpenter, Ashburnham; July 15, '63; recruit; Pris. Aug. 19, '64; trans. to Thirty-second and M. O.

Ballou, Charles H., 34, S.; carpenter, Medford; Aug. 14, '62; M. O. May 18, '65.

Barker, William S., 29, M.; watchmaker, Medford; Aug. 14, '62; M. O. June 2, '65.

Barnard, David A., 19, S.; baker, Medford; Aug. 14, '62; trans. Co. A, Sixth V. R. C.; dis. July 6, '65.

Bates, Hiram W., 32, M.; carpenter, Brighton; July 10, '63; recruit, trans. to Thirty-second and M. O.

Baxter, George M., 35, M.; cabinet-maker, Medford; Aug. 14, '62; dis. disa., Oct. 31, '62.

Beck, John S., 18, S.; —, Medford; Aug. 14, '62; M. O. June 2, '65; his diary indispensable to the history; b. Portsmouth, N. H., 1838; engine and carriage painter till he entered U. S. Railway Mail Service; leader Medford Band, Commander Post 66, G. A. R., etc.; d. Jan., 1910, Gloucester.

Beirne, James, 18, S.; currier, Medford; July 29, '62; k. May 10, '64, Spottsylvania.

Blanchard, William H., 27, S.; pork packer, Medford; Aug. 9, '62; M. O. June 2, '65.

Bond, Dudley, 43, M.; Aug. 8, '62; dis. disa., Jan. 21, '63; confectioner, Medford.

Booker, George D. (Corp.), 23, S.; farmer, Medford; Aug. 14, '62; trans. Nov. 26, '64, to V. R. C.; M. O. June 28, '65, from Co. B Twelfth Reg't. V. R. C.; had been in Co. E, Fifth M. V. M., 3 mos. term, 1861; died in Medford.

Bowen, Samuel C., 22, S.; seaman, Barnstable; May 7, '64; Pris., d. Nov. 27, '64, Salisbury, N. C.

Briggs, Benjamin M.; 29, M.; ship carpenter, Walpole; Aug. 14, '62; M. O. May 19, '65.

Bunker, Benjamin, Jr., 44, M.; shoemaker, Medford; Aug. 14, '62; dis. disa., Oct. 26, '62.

Busha, Stephen, 25, S.; moulder, Medford; July 22, '62; missing, May 8, '64, Spottsylvania.

Caldwell, George F., 29, S.; merchant, Fitchburg; July 16, '63; M. O. May 18, '65.

Carr, Royal S., 23, S.; clerk, Medford; Aug. 14, '62; Corp. Nov. 1, '63; Sergt. May 10, '64; wd. May 23, '64, No. Anna River, Va.; M. O. June 2, '65; had been in Co. E, Fifth Massachusetts Volunteer Militia in 3 mos., term, 1861; 1913, Winchester.

Chaffin, James W., —, —; teamster, Boston; recruit to Thirteenth Infty., Co. I; trans. to Thirty-ninth; M. O. Feb. 27, '65, ex. of s.; real name Marion E. Fisk, vide letter, W. D. Jan. 30, 1904.

Champlin, George H., 19, S.; laborer, Medford; Aug. 14, '62; prom. Corp.; d. Jan. 4, '64, Culpepper, Va.

Cheeney, William, 45, M.; ship carpenter, Medford; July 16, '62; dis. disa., June 18, '63.

Chenery, George W., 24, S.; clerk, Sudbury; July 8, '63; recruit to Twelfth Infty.; trans. to Thirty-ninth, thence to Thirty-second and M. O.

Churchill, George A., 21, S.; laborer, Medford; Aug. 14, '62; June 2, '65.

Clapp, George L., 19, S.; clerk, Medford; Aug. 14, '62; M. O. June 2, '65.

Clapp, Meletiah O. (Corp.), 24, M.; ship carpenter, Medford; Aug. 14, '62; trans. Navy, April 19, '64; dis. from the "Mendota," June 11, '65; had been in Co. E, Fifth Massachusetts Volunteer Militia 3 mos. term, 1861.

Collins, John J., 22, S.; brick maker, Romney, N. H., cr. Boston; Dec. 1, '64; dis. Feb. 23, '65, Annapolis, Md.

Cooledge, Charles H., 22, S.; clerk, Medford; Aug. 14, '62; Pris., d. Nov. 27, '64, Salisbury, N. C.

Coughlin, Owen, 18, S.; laborer, Medford; Aug. 9, '62; M. O. June 2, '65.

Crockett, Edward F., 18, S.; clerk, Medford; July 29, '62; dis. Aug. 15, '64.

Currell, Henry G., 18, S.; clerk, Medford; Aug. 14, '62; Pris.; d. Sept. 14, '64, Andersonville, Ga.

Curtis, Frank J., 21, M.; bolter, Medford; July 18, '62; Pris.; d. Feb. 26, Richmond, Va.; had been in Co. E, Fifth Massachusetts Volunteer Militia, 3 mos. term, 1861.

Cushing, Henry H. D. (Sergt.), 21, M.; clerk, Medford; Aug. 14, '62; dis. disa., Jan. 27, '64; had been in Co. E, Fifth Massachusetts Volunteer Militia, 3 mos. term, 1910, Medford.

Cushing, Joseph M., 22, S.; baker, Medford; Aug. 11, '62; M. O. June 2, '65.

Cutter, Benjamin P., 20, S.; clerk, Medford; July 28, '62; absent at M. O. June 2, '65.

Dean, Elijah C., 31, S.; yeoman, Oakham; July 13, '63; recruit to Twelfth Infty.; trans. to Thirty-ninth; Pris. Aug. 19, '64; dis. May 25, '65.

Dow, Albert F. (Sergt.), 29, M.; ship carpenter, Medford; Aug. 14, '62; M. O. June 2, '65; had been in Co. E, Fifth M. V. M., 3 mos. term, 1861.

Dow, Benjamin H., 30, M.; moulder, Aug. 14, '62; prom. Corp.; wd. Nov. 28, '63, Mine Run, Va.; trans. Ninth Reg't, V. R. C.; dis. June 26, '64.

Dushuttle, Henry L., 18, S.; shoemaker, Medford; July 12, '62; dis. disa., Dec. 23, '62; later Co. I, Second H. Arty.

Dyer, Charles E. (Mus.), 17, S.; gold beater, Medford; Aug. 14, '62; M. O. June 2, '65.

Eames, John H., b. Dec. 16, '64; (Sergt.), 27, S.; carpenter, Medford; Aug. 19, '62; 1st Sergt. June 7, '64; Pris. Aug. 19, '64, Weldon R. R.; 2d Lieut. Sept. 6, '64; 1st Lieut. April 3, '65; M. O. June 2, '65; M. O. as 1st Sergt.; came home from the war broken in health and for several months totally blind; recovering his health, from 1870 to 1876, postmaster at Medford; later, removed to Marshfield Hills, where he now resides; the data, concerning war prisoners from the Thirty-ninth, are largely due to him; had been in Co. E, Fifth M. V. M., 3 mos. term, 1861; for 12 years, Selectman, assessor or overseer of the poor in Marshfield; 1913, Marshfield Hills.

Ellis, Benjamin J., 27, M.; cabinet maker, Medford; Aug. 14, '62; Pris. Aug. 19, '64; d. May 21, '65.

Ellis, Hezekiah C., 43, M.; laborer, Medford; Aug. 14, '62; M. O. June 2, '65.

Fisk, Marion E., vide Chaffin, James W.

Fletcher, Joel M. (Corp.), 26, S.; carpenter, Medford; Aug. 14, '62; wd. June 18, '64, Petersburg; d. Aug. 25, '64; had been in Co. E, Fifth M. V. M., 3 mos. term, 1861.

Fletcher, Thomas M., 21, M.; clerk, Medford; July 28, '62; wd. May 6, '64, Wilderness; M. O. Aug. 14, '65; had been in Co. E, Fifth M. V. M., 3 mos. term, 1861.

Fox, Terrance L., 24, M.; weaver, So. Hadley, cr. Easthampton; July 16, '63; recruit to Twelfth Infty.; trans. to Thirty-ninth; wd. Aug. 18, '64, Weldon R. R.; M. O. May 25, '65.

Gage, George W. (Wagoner), 45, M.; wood turner, Charleston; Aug. 14, '62; dis. disa., Dec. 9, '63.

Gilbert, Henry E., 26, M.; farmer, Southbridge; July 14, '63; recruit to Twelfth Infty.; trans. to Thirty-ninth; dis. disa., Sept. 20, '64.

Gill, Anderson L. B., 28, M.; gold beater, Medford; Aug. 14, '62; wd. May 10, '64, Spottsylvania; trans. Jan. 7, '65; V. R. C.; dis. disa., Aug. 7, '65.

Gillard, Thomas H., 31, S.; calker, Medford; Aug. 14, '62; M. O. June 2, '65.

Gleason, Patrick, 18, S.; currier, Medford; Aug. 6, '62; Pris. Aug. 19, '64; d. Nov. 14, '64, Salisbury, N. C.

Goodale, Edward, 36, M.; painter, Medford; Aug. 14, '62; trans. Feb. 15, '64, V. R. C.; dis. from Co. I, Second V. R. C., June 26, '65.

Gordon, Orange S., 22, S.; weaver, Worcester; July 14, '63; recruit to Twelfth Infty.; trans. to Thirty-ninth; dis. May 24, '65.

Graff, Frederick, 33, S.; baker, Westford; July 21, '63; recruit to Twelfth Infty.; trans. to Thirty-ninth, thence to Thirty-second and M. O.

Graves, Austin, 25, S.; bootmaker, Hopkinton; July 14, '63; recruit to Twelfth Infty.; wd. Aug. 18, '64, Weldon R. R.; trans. to Thirty-second and M. O.

Haley, James T., 21, S.; cooper, Waltham; Oct. 26, '63; recruit to Twelfth Infty.; trans. to Thirty-ninth, thence to Thirty-second and M. O.

Harding, William, 18, S.; mason, Medford; Aug. 11, '62; k. May 10, '64, Spottsylvania.

Hart, Michael, 30, S.; laborer, Boston; July 24, '63; recruit to Twelfth Infty.; trans. to Thirty-ninth; wd. Aug. 18, '64, Weldon R. R.; trans. to Thirty-second and M. O.

Hartshorn, Elbridge B., 35, M.; upholsterer, Medford; Aug. 4, '65; dis. May 18, '65, O. W. D.

Haskell, Charles F., 18, S.; laborer, Medford; Aug. 8, '62; dis. disa., Jan. 23, '63.

Hatch, Edwin B., 36, M.; Aug. 14, '62; prom. Corp.; k. March 31, '65, Hatcher's Run.

Hathaway, Henry R., 19, M.; laborer, Medford; July 29, '62; wd. May 8, '64.

Hathaway, Nelson F., 23, S.; carpenter, Medford; Aug. 14, '62; M. O. June 2, '65.

Hathaway, Rodney C., 22, S.; mason, Medford; July 31, '62; prom. Corp.; k. Aug. 18, '64, Weldon R. R.

Heath, Andrew J., 27, M.; farmer, Medford; July 18, '62; dis. disa., Oct. 26, '62.

Hervey, James A., 34, M.; lawyer, Medford; July 29, '62; M. O. June 2, '65.

Holbrook, Frederick W. D., b. Jan. 26, 1840; 22, M.; civil engineer, Medford; Aug. 14, '62; dis. Feb. 9, '64, O. W. D. to accept position in the Engineering Department Defenses of Washington, under General J. G. Barnard, remaining there till after close of the War. From discharge to date, every year is accounted for with service from Hoosac Tunnel to Puget Sound, largely in R. R. development. For twenty-five years he has been in or near Seattle, Washington, in whose professional and social life he has been and is a prominent factor; 1913, Bremerton, Wash.

Hoyt, Moses C., 42, M.; farmer, Medford; Aug. 14, '62; dis. May 15, '65, O. W. D.

Hubbell, Joseph P., 29, S.; clerk, Medford; Aug. 14, '62; d. July 7, '63, Washington, D. C.

Ireland, Edward, 19, S.; farmer, Medford; Aug. 14, '62; k. March 12, '64, Lawville, Va.

Ireland, Edwin, 19, S.; painter, Medford; Aug. 14, '62; Pris. Aug. 19, '64; M. O. June 29, '65.

Ireland, Henry A., Jr. (Corp.), 22, S.; wheelwright, Medford; Aug. 14, '62; wd. May 12, '64, Spottsylvania; Sergt. March 9, '65; M. O. June 2, '65, as Sergt.; had served in Co. E, Fifth M. V. M., 3 mos. term, 1861; 1910, Medford.

Jepson, Samuel G. (Corp.), 30, M.; machinist, Medford; Aug. 14, '62; M. O. June 2, '65.

Johnson, John, 25, S.; sailor, Gloucester; Jan. 9, '64; Pris. Aug. 19, '64, Weldon R. R.; trans. to Thirty-second and M. O.

Jones, Obadiah, 18, S.; farmer, Randolph; Feb. 25, '64; trans. to Thirty-second Infty. and M. O.

Joyce, Alfred, 32, M.; carpenter, Medford; Aug. 2, '62; Pris. Aug. 19, '64; d. Nov. 7, '64, Salisbury, N. C.

Joyce, Henry S., 33, M.; joiner, Medford; Aug. 14, '62; M. O. June 2, '65.

Joyce, Samuel W., 21, S.; clerk, Medford; Aug. 14, '62; d. July 20, '63; Middleburg, Va.

Joyce, Winslow, b. Feb. 6, 1844; 18, S.; clerk, Medford; July 31, '62; M. O. June 7, '65; sealer, weights and measures, and inspector of milk; 1913, Medford.

Kendrick, Coleman C., 44, M.; joiner, Medford; Aug. 14, '62; trans. Dec. 1, '63, Forty-eighth Co., 2d Batt., V. R. C.; dis. March 16, '65; also, Kenrick.

Kendrick, Edwin T. (Mus.), 17, S.; farmer, Medford; M. O. June 2, '65.

Lange, Joseph, 21, S.; clerk, Worcester; July 24, '62; recruit to Twelfth Infty.; trans. to Thirty-ninth; Pris. Aug. 19, '64; trans. to Thirty-second and M. O.

Lewis, Joseph, 24, M.; painter, Boston; July 13, '63; recruit to Twelfth Infty.; trans. to Thirty-ninth, thence to Thirty-second and M. O.

Litchfield, Otis V., 26, M.; carpenter, Medford; Aug. 14, '62; M. O. June 2, '65.

Livingston, Robert, 36, M.; bolter, Medford; Aug. 6, '62; Pris.; d. Sept. 14, '64, Andersonville, Ga.

McDermott, Bernard E., 29, S.; clerk, Boston; June 8, '63; recruit to Twelfth Infty.; trans. to Thirty-ninth; wd. May 6, '64, Wilderness; trans. to Thirty-second and M. O.

McGee, James, 23, S.; clerk, Stoughton; Oct. 28, '63; recruit to Twelfth Infty.; trans. to Thirty-ninth; Pris. Aug. 19, '64; d. March 21, '65, Annapolis.

McLaughlin, Michael, 19, S.; laborer, Calaise, Me.; July 21, '61; en. Twelfth Infty.; trans. to Thirty-ninth; dis. Aug. 12, '64, ex. of s.

McNamara, Bernard, 24, S.; painter, Medford; Aug. 14, '62; des. Feb. 6, '63.

Mahall, John, 21, S.; laborer, Fall River; July 24, '63; recruit to Twelfth Infty.; trans. to Thirty-ninth, thence to Thirty-second and M. O.

Manning, John A., 25, S.; teamster, Medford; Aug. 14, '62; M. O. June 2, '65.

Merritt, Benjamin F., 40, M.; sailor, Scituate; Aug. 14, '62; dis. disa., Aug. 21, '63.

Meston, Peter D., 36, M.; bookbinder, Medford; Aug. 14, '62; M. O. June 2, '65.

Mitchell, Thomas O. H., b. June 13, 1826, Bath, Me.; 37, M.; joiner, Medford; Aug. 11, '62; wd. May 12, '64, Spottsylvania; M. O. June 2, '65; ship-joiner and house carpenter; 1913, Medford.

Morrison, Isaac T. (Corp.), 41, M.; ship-carpenter, Medford; Aug. 14, '62; prom. Sergt.; Pris.; d. Feb. 23, '65, Salisbury, N. C.; had been in Co. E, Fifth M. V. M., 3 mos. term, 1861.

Northey, William H., 39, M.; mason, Medford; Aug. 14, '62; M. O. June 2, '65.

Osborn, Alvin W., 20, S.; gardener, Medford; Aug. 12, '62; Corp. March 1, '65; M. O. June 2, '65.

Pratt, James H., 33, S.; farmer, Belchertown; July 14, '63; trans. from Twelfth Infty., to Thirty-ninth, thence to Thirty-second and M. O.

Prouty, John L., 43, M.; mason, Medford; July 31, '62; dis. disa., June 17, '63.

Putnam, Charles, 29, M.; shoemaker, Grafton; July 14, '63; recruit to Twelfth Infty.; trans. to Thirty-ninth; wd. Aug. 18, '64, Weldon R. R.; trans. to Thirty-second and M. O.

Ramsdell, Emory W. (Corp.), 32, W.; shoemaker, Medford; July 22, '62; wd. Aug. 19, '64, Weldon R. R.; M. O. June 2, '65; had been in Co. E, Fifth M. V. M., in 3 mos. term, 1861; 1910, Medford.

Redman, Wallace St. C., 27, M.; civil engineer, Medford; Aug. 8, '62;, dis. disa., June 19, '63; later served in Navy as Assistant Engineer.

Richardson, Charles A., 18, S.; blacksmith, Medford; Aug. 8, '62; wd. May 8, '64, Alsop's Farm; M. O. June 2, '65; with Fairbanks Scales Co. forty-seven years; joining the East Boston Methodist Church in 1879, he has been S. S. teacher, Assistant Superintendent and Superintendent; of his S. S. class, four members became clergymen, one, John L. Bates, governor—there were no black sheep; successively Church Treasurer and Secretary of the Board of Trustees, he has been Class Leader for almost thirty years; an officer in the United Order of the Golden Cross in 1883, he has been Treasurer of the United Order of the Pilgrim Fathers since 1896; 1913, East Boston.

Richardson, Franklin, 36, M.; carpenter, Medford; Aug. 7, '62; prom. Corp.; M. O. June 2, '65.

Roberts, Joseph W., 24, S.; brakeman, Boston; July 22, '61; trans. from Co. C, Thirteenth Infty. to Thirty-ninth; dis. Aug. 22, '64, ex. of s.

Roberts, Milton F., 20, S.; carpenter, Medford; Aug 11, '62; Pris. Aug. 18, '64, Weldon R. R.; M. O. June 2, '65; appointed carpenter in the U. S. Navy Dec. 12, 1879, he served in this capacity till his retirement, Feb 21, 1903, as Chief Carpenter with rank of Lieutenant; his last sea service was on the Oregon, being one of those who saw the part taken by the vessel, under Captain Clark, in the destruction of the Cristobal Colon, near Santiago and the consequent end of Spanish rule in America. Lieut. Roberts was ordered to the Oregon while she was building in San Francisco, and was on board through all of the famous trip down the Pacific Coast, around Cape Horn and up the Atlantic, one of the most remarkable cruises in modern naval history; his experiences on this voyage would make a most entertaining volume; the results of the trip are matters of history, but every member of the Thirty-ninth feels a measure of reflected glory in that one of his comrades had a part in the building, cruising and fighting of the Oregon; since his retirement, Lieut. Roberts has resided in Medford; b. Medford, April 17, 1842, he attended the public and private schools of the town and Spaulding's Academy for Bookkeeping in Charlestown; for many years was a member of the Medford Fire Dept. and is in the Masonic Order Lodge, Chapter, and Commandery; for 27 years has belonged to the Royal Arcanum and for more than ten years has been a member of the Veteran Association, Lawrence Life Guard; from boyhood has attended the Universalist Church.

Rogers, William H., 18, S.; laborer, Medford; Aug. 14, '62; Pris.; d. Feb. 14, '65, Salisbury, N. C.

Rugg, George J., 43, M.; carpenter, Medford; Aug. 14, '62; M. O. May 31, '65.

Samson, Albert A., 21, M.; clerk, Medford; Aug. 14, '62; prom. Corp.; dis. Oct. 26, '63, for promotion; N. F. R.

Sargent, Walter H., 18, —; shoemaker, Bridgewater; Feb. 10, '62; trans. from Twelfth Infty.; dis. Feb. 28, '65, ex. of s.

Senter, John H., 38, M.; gardener, Medford; Aug. 11, '62; trans. Aug. 19, '63, to Co. E, Fourteenth Regt., V. R. C.; trans. back to Co. C Jan. 9, '64; M. O. May 24, '65.

Sheridan, James A., 20, M.; clerk, Dedham; Aug. 27, '63; recruit to Thirteenth Infty.; trans. to Thirty-ninth, thence to Thirty-second and M. O.

Simpson, John H., 21, S.; clerk, Medford; July 17, '62; wd. May 8, '64, Spottsylvania; dis. Dec. 20, '64.

Smith, William S., 35, M.; chemist, Boston; July 17, '63; recruit Co. I, Twelfth Infty.; trans. to Thirty-ninth; Pris. Aug. 14, '64; d. Nov. 17, '64, Salisbury, N. C.

Southworth, William B., 23, S.; clerk, Medford; Aug. 14, '62; dis. disa., Dec. 20, '64.

Stevens, Samuel M. (Sergt.), 27, M.; ship carpenter, Medford; prom. 1st Sergt.; k. May 10, '64, Spottsylvania.

Thompson, Edward, 20, S.; seaman, Methuen; July 13, '63; recruit to Twelfth Infty.; trans. to Thirty-ninth, thence to Thirty-second and M. O.

Thompson, James, 18, S.; laborer, Medford; July 23, '62; wd. Aug. 19, '64, Weldon R. R.; dis. disa., May 17, '65.

Trask, Charles H., 26, S.; shipwright, Boston; July 9, '63; recruit to Twelfth Infty.; trans. to Thirty-ninth, thence to Thirty-second and M. O.

Tucker, Aaron, 32, M.; teamster, Medford; Aug. 14, '62; prom. Corp.; M. O. June 2, '65.

Tufts, Augustus, 45, S.; farmer, Medford; Aug. 14, '62; dis. disa., Jan. 27, '64.

Tully, Isaac J., 21, —; framemaker, Boston; July 9, '63; recruit to Twelfth Infty.; trans. to Thirty-ninth, thence trans. to Thirty-second and M. O.

Turner, Samuel H., Jr. (Sergt.), 24, M.; calker, Medford; Aug. 14, '62; wd. May 8, '64, Spottsylvania; M. O. June 14, '65; had been in Co. E, Fifth M. V. M., in 3 mos. term, 1861.

Tyler, Henry H., 21, S.; clerk, Medford; Aug. 14, '62; M. O. June 2, '65.

Vaeight, William, 22, S.; blacksmith, Swanzey; Aug. 5, '63; recruit to Thirteenth Infty.; trans. to Thirty-ninth; Pris. Aug. 19, '64; M. O. June 14, '65; Schouler has "Voight."

Vickery, John F., 29, M.; June 10, '63; recruit to Twelfth Infty.; trans. to Thirty-ninth; d. Aug. 12, '64, Alexandria, Va.

Voight, Wm., vide Vaeight.

Walker, Benjamin, 45, M.; bolter, Medford; Aug. 1, '62; dis. disa., Nov. 20, '63.

Walker, William A., 18, S.; laborer, Medford; Aug. 11, '62; M. O. June 2, '65.

Wayland, Henry P., 22, S.; gardener, Swampscot, Aug. 14, '62; des. Feb. 6, '63.

Webb, Lemuel, 32, M.; sailor, Scituate; Aug. 14, '62; M. O. June 2, '65.

Welch, Charles, 22, S.; slater, Salem; July 26, '63; recruit to Twelfth Infty.; trans. to Thirty-ninth, thence to Thirty-second and M. O.

Whitney, Jophanus, 18, S.; painter, Medford; Aug. 10, '62; Corp., May 29, '64; Sergt. (Color bearer), March 2, '65; wd. April 1, '65; M. O. June 22, '65, Philadelphia, Penn.; b. Avon, Me.; en. Co. E, Fifth M. V. M., Nov. 12, 1859; through successive promotions became Colonel, Aug. 6, '97; commanded Regt. in Spanish War; Brig. Gen'l, 2d Brigade, Feb. 23, 1901; retired as Major Gen'l, Feb. 23, 1908; in early life, learned painter's trade; later was a cigar-maker; twelve years on Medford Police Force; for many years on State Police Force; since 1908, its Chief; 1913, Medford.

Whittaker, James L., 36, M.; machinist, Medford; July 28, '62; dis. disa., Dec. 15, '63.

Williams, John, 28, M.; Aug. 5, '63; sailor, Boston; recruit to Twelfth Infty.; trans. to Thirty-ninth, thence to Thirty-second and M. O.

Wilson John (1st), 21, S.; calker, Lawrence; July 28, '63; on M. O. of Reg't trans. to Thirty-second and M. O.

COMPANY D.

Quincy

CAPTAINS

Edward A. Spear, 45, M.; bootmaker, Quincy; Aug. 14, '62; wd. Aug. 18, '64; Petersburg; dis. disa., Sept. 9, '64; had been 1st Lieut., Co. H, Fourth M. V. M., 3 mos. term, 1861; b. Dec. 7, 1816, Quincy; d. there, June 25, 1897.

William G. Sheen, from Co. I, Sept. 8, '64; brevet Major, April 1, '65; M. O. June 2, 1865.

FIRST LIEUTENANTS

William G. Sheen, 24, M.; jeweller, Quincy; Aug. 14, '62; had been in Co. H, Fourth M. V. M., 3 mos. term, 1861; trans. Oct. '63 to Co. I, vice, Mulligan, res.

John D. Reed, from Co. F, Sept. 20, '63; prom. Captain, Co. I, Sept. 6, '64.

SECOND LIEUTENANTS

Charles H. Porter, 19, S.; clerk, Quincy; Aug. 14, '62; prom. 1st Lieut. Jan. 25, '64; vide Co. A.

Oscar Persons, from Co. K, Feb. 4, '63; res. Oct. 24, 1863; took up newspaper work and for last twenty years of his life was connected with the Hudson Enterprise; d. June 26, 1901, Hudson.

Joseph A. Merrifield, from Co. F, Oct. '63; prom. 1st Lieut. May 4, '64, Co. B.

George A. Barker, from Sergt; May 4, '64; taken prisoner, Aug. 19, '64; prom. 1st Lieut. Sept. 8, '64; not mustered; M. O. June 2, 1865, as 2d Lieut.

ENLISTED MEN

Ahearn, Thomas, 27, S.; bootmaker, Quincy; Aug. 6, '62; Pris. May 21, '64; Feb. 17, '65; M. O. June 5, '65.

Alden, Albert M., 28, M.; bootmaker, Quincy; July 15, '62; dis. disa., Sept. 11, '63; later, Co. B, Sixtieth Massachusetts, 100 days.

Alden, Henry A., 19, S.; wheelwright, Quincy; July 18, '62; M. O. June 2, '65.

Armstrong, John L., 44, M.; bootmaker, Quincy; July 21, '62; trans. to Second Co., Second Batt., V. R. C.; dis. July 14, '65.

Badger, Ezra (Wagoner), 44, M.; farmer, Quincy; July 30, '62; d. Oct. 14, '62.

Bailey, Christopher T. (1st Sergt.), 30, M.; bootmaker, Weymouth; Sept. 7, '63; dis. disa., Nov. 26, '64.

Barker, George A. (Sergt.), 21, S.; clerk, Quincy; prom. 2d Lieut., May 4, '64; vide Co. D.

Barry, Benjamin, 44, S.; seaman, Quincy; July 31, '62; dis. disa., Nov. 15, '62.

Barry, Patrick H., 20, S.; painter, Boston; en. July 22, '63, in Twelfth Infty.; trans. to Thirty-ninth; wd. July 8, '64; dis. disa., Oct. 28, '64; in 1897, Adjt. Gen'l, Nebraska; lat. add., Lincoln, Neb.

Baxter, Thompson, Jr., 19, S.; student, Quincy; Aug. 12, '62; dis. disa., April 27, '65.

Becker, Ferdinand, 29, S.; shoemaker, Boston; July 22, '63; Pris. Aug. 19, '64, Weldon R. R.; d. Jan. 17, '65, Salisbury.

Bertwhistle, James F., 24, —; —, Darnestown, Md.; en. Sept. 19, '61, in Twelfth Infty.; Pris. July 1, '63; Gettysburg; paroled, when or where, not stated, and the name was carried to the Thirty-ninth; just a name and nothing more.

Brackett, Walter P., 21, S.; seaman, Quincy; July 29, '62; trans. to Navy April 22, '64; dis. from U. S. vessel, Chicopee, July 18, '65, as seaman.

Brophy, John, 31, M.; bootmaker, Quincy; July 3, '62; trans. Co. H, Second V. R. C.; Sept. 25, '63; dis. July 31, '65.

Brown, Samuel (Sergt.); wheelwright, Quincy; July 18, '62; wd. May 8, '64, Spottsylvania; M. O. June 2, '65.

Bullard, Asahel, 32, S.; yeoman, Oakham; July 13, '63; Pris. Aug. 19, '64, to March 3, '65; trans. to Thirty-second and M. O.

Burk, Walter, 35, M.; bootmaker, Quincy; Aug. 6, '62; d. Dec. 22, '63.

Burns, William H., 19, S.; boatman; July 29, '62; prom. Corp.; Pris. Aug. 19, '64, Weldon R. R.; d. Nov. 27, '64, Salisbury, N. C.

Bushnell, Charles, 28, M.; shoemaker, Abington, cr. to Roxbury; Sept. 28, '63; d. prisoner Nov. 14, '64, Salisbury, N. C.

Campbell, Allen, N. F. R., except "k. in action June 17, '64," the date is that of the first day at Petersburg.

Carteze, George, 23, S.; ship carpenter, Boston, cr. Groton; July 27, '63; recruit to the Thirteenth Infty.; trans. to Thirty-ninth, thence to the Thirty-second and M. O.

Cheatham, James B., 43, —; —, Quincy; Aug. 29, '62; dis. disa., June 26, '63.

Christian, James B., 43, M.; bootmaker, Quincy; July 30, '62; dis. disa., Jan. 24, '63.

Churchill, Thaddeus (Sergt.), 39, M.; painter, Quincy; Aug. 4, '62; dis. Oct. 18, '63, for commission, U. S. C. T.

Cleverly, George F., 29, M.; bootmaker, Quincy; July 31, '62; dis. disa., Oct. 2, '63; had been in Co. H, Fourth M. V. M., 3 mos. term, 1861.

Coffin, Paul G., 36, M.; July 29, '62; M. O. June 2, '65.

Colburn, William E., 38, M.; teamster, Quincy; prom. Corp.; Pris. Aug. 19, '64; d. Feb. 18, '65, Salisbury, N. C.

Collier, George W., 30, M.; bootmaker, Quincy; July 31, '62; dis. disa., Jan. 5, '63.

Collins, Michael, 44, M.; bootmaker, Quincy; Aug. 2, '62; M. O. June 2, '65.

Cotter, John, 21, S.; seaman, Barnstable; recruit to Twelfth Infty.; trans. to Thirty-ninth, thence to Thirty-second and M. O.

Cowper, John, 25, S.; laborer, Charleston; July 27, '63; recruit to Twelfth Infty.; trans. to Thirty-ninth, thence to Thirty-second and M. O.

Crane, Seth, 41, M.; laborer, Quincy; July 29, '62; d. Dec. 22, '63.

Curtis, Albert (Mus.), 21, S.; bootmaker, Abington; Aug. 13, '62; trans. March 13, '65, V. R. C.; M. O. May 31, '65.

Curtis, Henry (Sergt.), 34, M.; bootmaker, Quincy; July 29, '62; Pris. Aug. 19, '64; M. O. June 2, '65.

Daley, Daniel, 29, M.; ledgeman, Quincy; Aug. 6, '62; dis. disa., Aug. 23, '63.

Daley, Garrett, 39, M.; ledgeman, Quincy; Aug. 1, '62; d. April 5, '65.

Damon, Edward, Jr., ledgeman, Quincy; Aug. 2, '62; Pris. Aug. 19, '64, Weldon R. R.; d. Jan. 3, '65, Salisbury, N. C.; had been in Co. H, Fourth M. V. M., 3 mos. term, 1861.

Darren, George W., 29, M.; machinist, Boston; Nov. 14, '63; recruit to Twelfth Infty.; trans. to Thirty-ninth, thence to Thirty-second and M. O.

DeForrest, Samuel D., b. June 16, 1845; 20, S.; farmer, Quincy; July 15, '62; Pris. Aug. 14, '64, to Feb. 28, '65; M. O. July 18, '65; stationary engineer; 1913, Quincy.

Derby, Alden, 20, —; shoemaker, No. Bridgewater; Feb. 24, '62; recruit to Thirty-ninth; prom. Corp.; Pris. Aug. 19, '64; N. F. R.

Derry, Barden B., 26, M.; boatman, Quincy; wd. May 8, '64; 1st Sergt. March 1, '65; M. O. June 2, '65.

Dickerman, Charles C., 22, W.; clerk, Quincy; Aug. 2, '62; prom. Corp.; Pris. Aug. 19, '64; d. Jan. 28, '65, Salisbury, N. C.

Donley, James, 18, S.; laborer, Quincy; Aug. 1, '62; d. Feb. 1, '65.

Dooner, John, 27, M.; teamster, Quincy; July 29, '62; dis., disa. March 1, '63.

Doyle, Thomas, 40, —; —, Buffalo, N. Y.; June 7, '64; Pris. Aug. 19, '64; trans. to Thirty-second and M. O.

Drury, Charles A., 23, S.; bootmaker, Concord; July 14, 62; recruit to Twelfth Infty.; trans. to Thirty-ninth, thence to Thirty-second and M. O.

Dunn, Arthur, 25, M.; bootmaker, Quincy; July 15, '62; Pris.; d. Jan. 28, '64, Belle Isle, Richmond, Va.

Durgin, Jonathan, 40, M.; teamster, Quincy; July 31, '62; wd. May 8, '64, Laurel Hill; d. Pris. Jan. 5, '65, Salisbury.

Ela, Elisha P. C., 26, M.; stonecutter, Quincy; Aug. 1, '62; k. May 8, '64, Spottsylvania.

Euderle, Joseph L. (Corp.), 20, S.; blacksmith, Quincy; Aug. 6, '62; wd. May 10, '64; M. O. June 3, '65, S. O. W. D.; had been in Co. H, Fourth M. V. M., as Enderly, 3 mos. term, 1861.

Fineran, Patrick (Mus.), 18, S.; farmer, Quincy; July 18, '62; prom. Sergt.; M. O. June 2, '65.

Forbes, James E., 25, S.; stonecutter, Quincy; Aug. 6, '62; Pris. Aug. 19, '64; M. O. June 2, '65.

Fowler, Theodore W., 42, M.; bootmaker, Quincy; July 29, '62; M. O. May 30, '65.

Freeman, John C., 22, S.; clerk, Southbridge; recruit to Twelfth Infty.; trans. to Thirty-ninth; Pris.; d. Florence, S. C., Feb. 18, '65.

French, Joseph T., 38, M.; clerk, Quincy; Aug. 1, '62; N. F. R.

Garvere, Patrick, 44, M.; stonecutter, Quincy; July 31, '62; M. O. June 2, '62.

Gavin, Patrick H. (Corp.), 18, S.; farmer, Quincy; July 18, '62; wd. May 12, '64; trans. V. R. C., Feb. 3, '65; dis. from Co. A, Eighteenth V. R. C., June 2, '65.

Gifford, Charles E., 18, S.; laborer, Florida; Aug. 22, '62; M. O. June 2, '65.

Gould, Samuel, 18, S.; laborer, Florida; Aug. 22, '64; d. April 11, '65, Long Island, N. Y.

Green, John F., 31, M.; seaman, Marblehead; July 10, '63; Pris.; d. Dec. 15, '64, Salisbury, N. C.

Groves, George D., 27, M.; bootmaker, Quincy; Aug. 5, '62; des. Sept. 14, '62.

Hanson, Hans C., 28, S.; sailor, Ashland; July 21, '63; recruit to Twelfth Infty.; recorded as trans. to the Thirty-ninth, June 25, '64, but he had died the preceding 14th of April, Andersonville, Ga.

Harrington, John, 25, M.; shoemaker, Concord; July 14, '63; recruit to Twelfth Infty.; trans. to Thirty-ninth, thence to Thirty-second and M. O.

Hayden, Joseph W., 43, M.; bootmaker, Quincy; July 29, '62; dis. disa., June 2, '63; later in Tenth Battery.

Hayden, Josiah, Jr., 38, M.; bootmaker, Quincy; July 29, '62; M. O. June 2, '65.

Hayden, William, 18, S.; stonecutter, Gloucester; Aug. 13, '62; Pris. Aug. 19, '64; d. Dec. 31, '64, Salisbury, N. C.

Haynes, Joseph P. (Corp.), 40, M.; bootmaker, Quincy; July 15, '62; Pris., June 7, '64; dis. May 22, '65.

Hazleton, Benjamin L., 22, S.; farmer, Boston; Nov. 7, '63; recruit to Twelfth Infty.; trans. to Thirty-ninth, thence trans. to V. R. C.; N. F. R.

Hersey, George W., 31, M.; painter, Quincy; Aug. 31, '62; trans. Navy, April 22, '64; dis., June 7, '65.

Hill, John, Jr., 24, S.; currier, Quincy; Aug. 7, '62; M. O. June 2, '65.

Hobbs, John J., 38, M.; bootmaker, Quincy; Aug. 31, '62; dis. disa., April 3, '63.

Horgan, Cornelius, 33, M.; bootmaker, Quincy; July 25, '62; des. April 28, '63.

Howley, Thomas, 44, M.; bootmaker, Quincy; Aug. 21, '62; dis. disa., June 2, '63.

Howley, Thomas, Jr., 18, S.; bootmaker, Quincy; July 31, '62; absent at M. O., sick; N. F. R.

Hughes, James, 42, M.; bootmaker, Quincy; July 29, '62; d. May 13, '64.

Huntress, Elijah, 19, S.; farmer, Quincy; Aug. 24, '62; wd. May 10, '64; dis. on account of wds., May 8, '65.

Huntress, Truman H., 21, M.; teamster, Quincy; Aug. 4, '62; M. O. June 2, '65; 1913, Brockton.

Kanily, Daniel, 27, M.; bootmaker, Quincy; Aug. 6, '62; Pris. Aug. 19, '64; wd. April 1, '65, Five Forks; M. O. June 2, '65.

Keep, William J., 19, S.; paper maker, Duxbury; March 14, '62; recruit to Twelfth Infty.; trans. to Thirty-ninth; Pris. Aug. 19, '64; d. March 19, '65.

Kelly, James, 43, M.; bootmaker, Quincy; July 26, '62; M. O. May 18, '65.

Kelly, John, 19, M.; farmer, Quincy; July 19, '62; d. a prisoner, July 2, '64, Richmond, Va.

Kingsbury, Charles G., 27, S.; bootmaker, Medway; Jan. 16, '65; d. May 30, '65.

Kittridge, Josiah N., 24, M.; bootmaker, Quincy; July 31, '62; d. Oct. 23, '64, Quincy.

Leavitt, Charles F., 19, S.; stonecutter, Quincy; Aug. 19, '62; prom. Sergt.; M. O. June 2, '65.

Littlefield, Henry B., 21, S.; farmer, Holliston; July 14, '63; recruit to Thirteenth Infty.; trans. to Thirty-ninth; trans. March 13, '65, V. R. C.

Lunt, Theodore H., 35, M.; stone cutter, Quincy; Aug. 6, '62; Pris. Aug. 19, '64; d. Oct. 23, '64, Annapolis, Md.

Luzarder, Joseph M., 19, S.; bootmaker, Quincy; July 22, '62; k. Aug. 18, '64, Weldon R. R.

Luzarder, Moses, 23, S.; bootmaker, Quincy; July 23, '62; dis. disa., Jan. 26, '64; later Co. B, Sixtieth Massachusetts, 100 days.

McCarthy, John, 44, M.; bootmaker, Quincy; July 19, '62; wd. Aug. 18, '64; M. O. June 2, '65.

McGlone, Michael, 27, M.; stone cutter, Quincy; Aug. 4, '62; d. May 12, '64, Belle Plain, Va.

Mahan, Patrick, 37, M.; laborer, Boston; July 29, '63; recruit to Thirteenth Infty.; trans. to Thirty-ninth, thence to the Thirty-second and M. O.

Mahoney, James, 38, M.; bootmaker, Quincy; July 29, '62; wd. May 8, '64; trans. Nov. 3, '64, to Eighty-second Co., Second Batt., V. R. C.; M. O. June 28, '65.

Marsden, Joseph, 35, S.; yeoman, Charlton; July 14, '62; recruit to Twelfth Infty.; trans. to Thirty-ninth; d. Aug. 28, '64, Bristol, Penn.

Miller, Charles H., 19, M.; clerk, Quincy; Aug. 29, '62; dis. March 12, '64, S. O. W. D.

Miller, George L., 44, M.; stonecutter, Quincy; July 29, '62; dis. disa., Feb. 4, '63.

Moran, Patrick, 35, M.; bootmaker, Quincy; July 19, '62; Pris. Aug. 19, '64; M. O. June 7, '65.

Moriarty, John, 24, S.; farmer, Quincy; July 15, '62; M. O. June 3, '65.

Morrison, Sylvander H., 19, S.; ledgeman, Quincy; July 26, '62; M. O. June 2, '65.

Moynihan, John, 21, M.; laborer, Boston; July 22, '63; recruit to the Thirteenth Infty.; trans. to Thirty-ninth, thence to Thirty-second and M. O.

Murray, George H., 24, M.; cabinet maker, Boston; Aug. 2, '62; recruit to Thirteenth Infty.; re-en. Jan. 4, '64; trans. to Thirty-ninth; wd. May 28, '64; trans. to Thirty-second and M. O.

Murray, Michael A., 27, M.; mason, Boston; July 9, '63; recruit to Twelfth Infty.; trans. to Thirty-ninth, thence to Thirty-second and M. O.

Nelson, John, 24, S.; porter, Worcester, July 25, '63; recruit to Twelfth Infty.; trans. to Thirty-ninth, thence to Thirty-second and M. O.

Newcomb, Harrison G. O., 32, M.; boot-trimmer, Quincy; July 31, '62; dis. disa., Feb. 11, '63.

Newcomb, Henry A. (Corp.), 39, M.; trader, Quincy; July 29, '62; d. Dec. 23, '64, a prisoner in Salisbury, N. C.

Newcomb, Isaac T., 44, M.; bootmaker, Quincy; July 30, '62; dis. disa., Feb. 11, '63.

Nightingale, Frederick, 22, S.; teamster, Quincy; Aug. 4, '62; dis. disa., Dec. 17, '62.

Nightingale, Samuel (Corp.), 23, S.; clerk, Quincy; July 29, '62; dis. disa., Aug. 19, '64.

O'Brien, Timothy, 37, M.; bootmaker, Quincy; July 31, '62; wd. May 10, '64; dis. June 15, '65.

Parrott, Albert, 18, S.; boatman, Quincy; July 29, '62; M. O. June 2, '65.

Parrott, Luther H., 22, M.; seaman, Quincy; July 29, '62; trans. to Navy April 22, '64; dis. June 12, '65.

Peck, George E., 21, S.; farmer, Acton; July 18, '63; recruit to Twelfth Infty.; trans. to Thirty-ninth, thence to Thirty-second and M. O.

Percival, George P., 32, M.; bootmaker, Quincy; July 31, '62; wd. May 10, '64; M. O. June 2, '65.

Perkins, Charles H., 20, M.; clerk, Quincy; July 31, '62; prom. 2d Lieut. Sept. 8, '64; vide Co. B.

Perry, Samuel N., 40, M.; carpenter, Quincy; Aug. 6, '62; d., a prisoner, March 31, '64, Andersonville, Ga., grave 274.

Pierce, Eli, 43, S.; bootmaker, Quincy; July 26, '62; Pris. Aug. 14, '64; d. April 3, '65.

Roach, Maurice, 29, M.; bootmaker, Quincy; July 29, '62; dis. at Tuton General Hospital, Delaware, May 31, '65.

Rodgers, Horace C., 19, S.; student, Quincy; Aug. 1, '62; ab. at M. O. June 2, '65, detached duty.

Russ, George W., 39, M.; bootmaker, Quincy; July 31, '62; wd. Aug. 18, '64; M. O. June 2, '65.

Russell, George A., 24, S.; seaman, Quincy; July 29, '62; trans. Sept. 26, '63, to V. R. C.; as he re-en. Aug. 25, '64, in Co. E, Ninth V. R. C., he must have been dis. at some date in his first enlistment.

Sargent, George, 34, M.; farmer, Foxboro; July 11, '63; recruit to Twelfth Infty.; trans. to Thirty-ninth; M. O. May 15, '65.

Savill, George W., 31, M.; stonecutter, Quincy; Aug. 7, '62; d. a prisoner Dec. 4, '64, Salisbury, N. C.

Shavlin, Hugh, 18, S.; ledgeman, Quincy; July 30, '62; Pris. Aug. 19, '64, to March 3, '65; M. O. June 30, '64.

Sheehan, Jerry, 20, M.; teamster, Quincy; July 30, '62; Pris. Aug. 19, '64; M. O. June 2, '65.

Simonds or Simons, William (Corp.), 44, M.; stonecutter, Quincy; Aug. 2, '62; wd. May 8, '64; trans. Co. E, Sixteenth Reg't, V. R. C.; M. O. July 5, '65.

Slattery, Edward, 29, M.; laborer, East Weymouth; July 17, '63; recruit to Twelfth Infty.; trans. to Thirty-ninth; dis. disa., Dec. 24, '64.

Sweet, John, 19, S.; painter, Shelburne; June 13, '64; recruit to Thirteenth Infty.; trans. to Thirty-ninth; des. July 29, '64.

Taylor, Marcus, 20, S.; farmer, Quincy; July 26, '62; M. O. June 2, '65.

Thayer, John J. H., 29, M.; engineer, Quincy; July 23, '62; dis. disa., March 2, '65.

Thomas, Erasmus, 34, S.; stonecutter, Quincy; Aug. 2, '62; prom. Corp.; Pris. Aug. 19, '64; d. March 14, '65.

Trask, George W. (Corp.), 21, M.; stonecutter, Quincy; July 29, '62; wd. May 8, '64; M. O. June 8, '65.

Walsh, Michael, 30, S.; laborer, Worcester; July 26, '65; recruit to Twelfth Infty.; trans. to Thirty-ninth, thence to Thirty-second and M. O.

Ware, Henry A., 18, —; —, Quincy; Aug. 8, '62; N. F. R.

Watts, George H., 24, S.; porter, Boston; June 26, '61; en. Twelfth Infty.; re-en. Jan. 5, '64; trans. to Thirty-ninth, thence to Thirty-second and M. O.

Wellman, John H., 31, S.; shoemaker, Attleborough; July 14, '62; recruit to Twelfth Infty.; trans. to Thirty-ninth, thence to Thirty-second and M. O.

Willett, George A., 19, S.; boatman, Quincy; Aug. 2, '62; dis. disa., Jan. 31, '63.

Williams, John (1st Sergt.), 24, M.; bootmaker, Quincy; July 15, '62; dis. disa., Nov. 20, '64; had been in Co. E, Fourth M. V. M., 3 mos. term, 1861.

Williams, William, 21, S.; seaman, Boston; April 28, '63; recruit to Thirteenth Infty.; trans. to Thirty-ninth, thence to Thirty-second and M. O.

Wood, Thomas, 32, M.; bootmaker, Quincy; July 30, '62; k. June 19, '64, Petersburg.

Young, William J., b. Sept. 8, 1837; 24, M.; seaman, Quincy; July 26, '62; M. O. June 2, '65; seaman, Quincy.

A Panel from the Old Soldiers' Monument, Somerville.
The first erected in Massachusetts.

COMPANY E

Somerville

CAPTAIN

Frederick R. Kinsley, b. July 30, 1829, Croydon; 33, S.; brickmaker, Somerville; Aug. 15, '62; Major June 13, '64; Pris. Aug. 19, '64, to March, '65; Colonel June 7, '65; M. O. as Captain June 2, '65; was 2d Lieut., Co. I, Fifth M. V. M., 3 mos. term; vide F. & S.

Charles W. Hanson, Sept. 8, '64; not mustered; dis. disa. as 1st Lieut. April 22, 1865.

Lieut. H. F. Felch commanded the Company on its return.

FIRST LIEUTENANTS

Joseph J. Giles, b. March 24, 1842; 20, S.; painter, Somerville; Aug. 15, '62; in 1863 for 11 mos. A. D. C. to Military Governor, Washington; dis. disa., Aug. 23, '64; had been in Co. I, Fifth M. V. M., 3 mos. term, 1861; 1913, real estate and insurance, Somerville.

Henry F. Felch, from Co. F, Sept. 15, 1864; on resignation of Captain Nelson, Co. A, Lieut. Felch was trans. as Acting Captain; 1913, Natick.

SECOND LIEUTENANTS

Willard C. Kinsley, 29, S.; brickmaker, Somerville; Aug. 9, '62; 1st Lieut. Nov. 13, '62; vide Co. H.

T. Cordis Clarke, from Sergeant Major, Nov. 13, '62; trans. to Co. B, Nov. 12, '63.

Charles W. Hanson, trans. from Co. H Nov., '63; prom. 1st Lieut. Co. C.

Isaac F. R. Hosea, from Co. C, Dec., '63; prom. 1st Lieut. Jan. 15, '65; not mustered; M. O. June 2, '65.

ENLISTED MEN

Abbott, Jesse B., 25, M.; carpenter, Somerville; Aug. 12, '62; M. O. May 16, '65; d. Cambridge, Feb. 18, 73.

Allen, James M., 18, S.; brickmaker, Somerville; Aug. 12, '62; Pris. Aug. 19, '64, Weldon R. R.; d. Nov. 23, '64, Salisbury, N. C.

Amsden, Julius A., 27, S.; bootmaker, Ware; cr. to Brookfield; July 13, '63; recruit to Twelfth Infty.; trans. to Thirty-ninth; M. O. June 25, '65.

Arnold, William J., 18, S.; teamster, Somerville; Aug. 12, '62; wd. May 8, '64, Laurel Hill; M. O. May 20, '65; d. Ashland, 1905.

Baker, William A. (Corp.), 25, M.; hospital attendant, Somerville; Aug. 12, '62; dis. disa., Oct. 26, '63; d. Cambridge March 25, 1897.

Bartlett, William H., 21, M.; calker, Beverly; July 10, '63; recruit to Twelfth Infty.; trans. to Thirty-ninth; Pris. Aug. 19, '64; d. Nov. 18, '64, Salisbury, N. C.

Bean, George W. (Corp.), 23, M.; artist, Somerville; Aug. 12, '62; Pris. Oct. 11, '63, for 17 mos.; M. O. May 12, '65; Somerville police force; 1912, Cambridge.

Belding, Charles H., 22, S.; provisions, Somerville; Aug. 12, '62; trans. March 31, '64, V. R. C.; dis. Oct. 3, '64; provision dealer; 1913, Malden.

Benz, August, 21, S.; sausage-maker, Somerville; Aug. 15, '62; d. Oct. 5, '64, on transport Utica, James River.

Bledden, Thomas G., 38, S.; So. Reading, cr. to Chelmsford; Aug. 13, '64; trans. to 32 and M. O.

Bodge, George A., 18, S.; teamster, Somerville; Aug. 12, '62; prom. Corp., Sergt. and 1st Sergt.; prom. 2d Lieut. April 3, '65; M. O. June 2, '65, as 1st Sergt.; never ill nor had a furlough; Somerville police force; d. Nov. 4, 1899.

Bodge, George W., 44, S.; carpenter, Chelsea, cr. Weymouth; Jan. 7, '65; trans. to Thirty-second and M. O. Bolton, John T., 20, S.; clerk, Somerville; Aug. 12, '62; on det. Serv. Ordnance Dept.; M. O. June 2, '65; d. Mexico, April 23, 1885.

Boynton, William F., 30, M.; painter, Somerville; March 29, '64; dis. disa., Co. D, Jan. 12, '65; had been in Co. D, Fifth M. V. M., 9 mos. term, 1862-3; d. Aug. 29, 1892, Somerville.

Bradley, George C., 23, S.; sailor, Boston; July 27, '63; recruit to Twelfth Infty.; trans. to Thirty-ninth, thence to Thirty-second and M. O.

Brotchie, James, 18, S.; painter, Somerville; Aug. 12, '62; M. O. June 2, '65; many years Somerville employee; 1912, Cambridge.

Brown, James, 20, S.; b. April 19, 1829; laborer, Boston; July 23, '63; recruit to Co. D, Twelfth Infty.; trans. to Thirty-ninth; Pris. Aug. 19, '64; trans. to Thirty-second and M. O.

Bucknam, Davis P. (Corp.), 25, M.; mason, Somerville; Aug. 12, '62; dis. disa., June 18, '63; d. July 10, 1910, Somerville.

Byrnes, John, 31, M.; teamster, Somerville; Aug. 12, '62; trans. Feb. 15, '64, V. R. C.; dis. July 3, '65; Boston elevated; 1913, Somerville.

Canfield, John B., 35, M.; carpenter, Somerville; Aug. 12, '62; Pris. Aug. 19, '64, to March 3, '65; M. O. June 14, '65; d. Nov. 12, 1897.

Carr, William M., 22, M.; ropemaker, Somerville; Aug. 12, '62; dis. disa., Dec. 9, '62; had been in Co. I, Fifth M. V. M., 3 mos. term, 1861; d. Chelsea, 1893.

Carter, Charles L., 20, S.; driver, Boston; June 26, '61, in Twelfth Infty.; for some reason, not given, was trans. to Thirty-ninth; Pris. Aug. 19, '64; d. Feb. 9, '65, Salisbury, N. C.

Champney, Lewis C., 23, M.; moulder, Adams; July 14, '63; recruit to Twelfth Infty.; trans. to Thirty-ninth, thence to Thirty-second and M. O. Clark, Gustavus A., b. April 16, 1830; 25, S.; hospital attendant, Somerville; Aug. 12, '62; Corp. May 23, '63; M. O. June 1, '65; eighteen years Boston P. O.; 1913, Somerville.

Clemmens, James, 20, S.; Fall River, cr. Falmouth; seaman, July 28, '63; recruit to Thirteenth Infty., Co. D; trans. to Thirty-ninth, thence to Thirty-second and M. O.

Cole, Chandler G., 44, M.; sawyer, Somerville; Aug. 12, '62; wd. Aug. 18, '64; M. O. June 2, '65; d.

Coles, Ambrose W., 28, M.; painter, Somerville; Aug. 12, '62; lost left arm Feb. 7, '65, Hatcher's Run, Va.; dis. May 16, '65; d. 1882, Somerville.

Collett, Herbert, 26, M.; painter, Somerville; Aug. 12, '62; dis. disa., Feb. 8, '63; d. Philadelphia since 1899.

Conner, Thomas, 36, M.; bootmaker, Somerville; Aug. 12, '62; dis., disa. March 12, '63; d.

Creedon, John, 18, S.; seaman, Philadelphia; en. April 20, '64, Co. F, Twelfth Infty.; trans. to Thirty-ninth; "Supposed to have joined the Rebels," says the State House Record, but whether from the Twelfth or Thirty-ninth, not stated.

Crosby, Elkanah (Corp.), 24, S.; trunkmaker, Somerville; Aug. 12, '62; prom. Sergt. March 1, '65; M. O. June 2, '65; had been in Co. I, Fifth M. V. M., 3 mos. term; 1912, Somerville.

Crowley, Daniel (Mus.), 21, S.; machinist, Somerville; Aug. 20, '62; M. O. June 2, '65; 1912, Somerville.

Cutter, George, 27, M.; teamster, Somerville; Aug. 12, '62; des. June 3, '63; later seen in N. Y. Cav. Reg't.

Dailey, Ebenezer W., 40, M.; carpenter, Marlborough; Jan. 2, '64; recruit to Thirteenth Infty.; trans. to Thirty-ninth, thence to V. R. C. March 15, '65; dis. disa., June 13, '65, from Co. G, Sixteenth V. R. C.

Davis, Amos F., 19, S.; trader, Somerville; Aug. 12, '62; det. Serv. Ambulance Corps; M. O. June 2, '65; 1913, Dorchester. Dodge, Albert H., 29, M.; carpenter, Somerville; Aug. 12, '62; des. Sept. 18, '64; from Nova Scotia; d.

Dodge, William H., carpenter, Somerville; Aug. 12, '62; M. O. May 18, '65; brother of Albert; d. 1896.

Dusseault, John H. (1st Sergt.), 22, S.; carver, Somerville; Aug. 12, '62; prom. 2d Lieut. Oct. 20, '63; vide Co. H.

Dyer, Jonathan C., 24, S.; —, Somerville; Aug. 12, '62; trans. to Navy April 22, '64; dis. from Naval Hospital, Norfolk, Va., Aug. 20, '64; d. 1903, Somerville.

Edlefson, Charles E., 19, S.; grocer, Somerville; Aug. 12, '64; dis., disa. Feb. 26, '63; d. Dec. 24, 1891, Somerville.

Emerson, Samuel, 36, M.; teamster, Somerville; Aug. 12, '62; M. O. June 5, '65; police force, Boston; d.

Fairchild, Willard C., b. Sept. 23, 1832; 28, M.; teamster, Somerville, Aug. 12, '62; wd. slightly May 8, 10, and 12, '64; in right arm, Aug. 18, '64, Weldon R. R.; trans. Co. H, Third Reg't., V. R. C.; 1913, Fitchburg.

Farrar, George A. (Wagoner), 38, M.; teamster, Somerville; Aug. 14, '62; wd. June 18, '64; dis. disa., July 29, '65; Worcester; d. June 27, 1901, Somerville.

Fay, Walter, 34, —; —, Somerville; Aug. 15, '62; trans. Aug. 1, '63; V. R. C.; dis. disa., Jan. 9,'64; d. Sept. 25, 1904, Somerville.

Felker, Samuel O., 35, S.; cabinet-maker, Somerville; Aug. 12, '62; k. as Corp. May 10, '64, Spottsylvania.

Fellows, Charles C, 34, S.; blacksmith, Somerville; Aug. 12, '62; det. Serv.; M. O. June 2, '65; d. Sept. 11, 1897.

Fitcham, Charles E. (Corp.), 20, S.; clerk, Somerville; Aug. 12, '62; trans. Sept. 23, '64, Seventy-fifth Co., 2d Batt. V. R. C.; dis. Aug. 10, '65, Hartford, Conn.; d.

Flinsky, Leon, 27, S.; watchmaker, Raynham; Aug. 5, '63; recruit to Thirteenth Infty.; trans. to Thirty-ninth; ab. sick in Hosp., "supposed to have deserted," but his name is carried to the Thirty-second.

Flood, Thomas, 33, M.; laborer, Easton; Oct. 16, '63; recruit to Twelfth Infty.; though his name is brought to the Thirty-ninth, he had des. May 31, '65; a name, but no man.

Fuller, John E., 18, S.; gardener, Somerville; Aug. 12, '62; wd. June 18, '64; dis. disa., Feb. 12, '65; police force, Somerville; 1912, retired.

Gilcrease, Elijah H., 30, M.; carpenter, Somerville; Aug. 12, '62; dis. disa., April 22, '63; d. Feb. 18, 1888, Somerville.

Glines, Frederick A., 18, S.; mail clerk, Somerville; Aug. 12, '62; prom. Corp. July 1, '64; Pris. Aug. 19, '64; d. Jan. 6, '65, Salisbury, N. C.

Goodhue, Levi K., 28, M.; carpenter, Beverly; recruit to Twelfth Infty.; trans. to Thirty-ninth, thence to Thirty-second and M. O.

Gorham, David, 26, M.; hospital attendant, Somerville; Aug. 12, '62; prom. Corp.; d. a prisoner Dec. 11, '64, Salisbury, N. C.

Graham, William F. C., 24, M.; cabinet-maker, Somerville; Aug. 12, '62; ab. sick after May 19, '63, supposed to have deserted; from Nova Scotia.

Grant, Edward L., 29, M.; teamster, Somerville; Aug. 12, '62; det. Serv. Ordnance Dept.; M. O. June 2, '63; d. Feb. 5, 1911, Somerville.

Gray, Dexter, 24, S.; hospital attendant, Somerville; Aug. 12, '62; prom. Corp.; wd. Aug. 18, '64; dis. disa., May 17, '65, from General Hospital, Whitehall, Va.; d.

Hadley, Eugene B., 34, M.; engineer, Somerville; Aug. 12, '62; k. Feb. 6, '65, Hatcher's Run.

Hafford, John, 18, S.; butcher, Somerville; Aug. 12, '62; dis. disa., June 20, '63; d. Nov. 15, 1905.

Hagan, Patrick, 43, M.; trader, Somerville; Aug. 13, '62; dis. disa., April 13, '63; claimed to have served in Crimean War; d.

Hale, Edward M., b. March 31, 1841; (Sergt.) 21, S.; clerk, Somerville; Aug. 12, '62; absent on detached service at office of Adjutant General, Washington; M. O. June 2, '65, as absent; bookkeeper and accountant; 1913, Passaic, N. J.

Hanley, John H., 30, M.; trader, Somerville; Aug. 12, '62; dis. disa., Aug. 12, '63; d. Somerville.

Harburn, William M., 18, S.; —, Somerville; Aug. 12, '62; k. Aug. 18, '64, Weldon R. R.

Harlow, George R., 24, S.; hospital attendant, Somerville; Aug. 12, '62; wd. May 10, '64, also Aug. 19, '64; dis. disa., March 17, '65; lat. add. Chattanooga, Tenn.

Haskell, William J., 20, S.; farmer, Otis; July 13, '63; recruit to Twelfth Infty.; trans. to Thirty-ninth, thence to Thirty-second and M. O.

Hatch, George H., 18, S.; baker, Somerville; Aug. 12, '62; d. Feb. 1, '65, a prisoner, Salisbury, N. C.

Hill, George A., b. March 6, 1842; 20, S.; carpenter, Somerville; Aug. 12, '62; dis. disa., April 29, '63; drug business, later real estate and fire insurance; 1913, Springfield.

Horgan, Patrick D., 19, S.; hostler, Somerville; Aug. 12, '62; Pris. Aug. 19, '64, to May 20, '65; M. O. June 2, '65; d.

Horton, John E., 32, M.; milkman, Somerville; Aug. 12, '62; prom. Corp.; July 1, '64; d. Dec. 10, '64, a prisoner, Andersonville, Ga. His diary freely drawn upon in this history.

Howard, William L., 28, S.; shoemaker, Lynn; July 13, '63; recruit to Twelfth Infty.; trans. to Thirty-ninth; Pris. Aug. 19, '64; dis. as Corp. May 26, '65.

Howe, Henry E., 19, S.; milkman, Somerville; Aug. 12, '62; d. Nov. 22, '63, a prisoner, Richmond, Va.

Hutter, John, 34, S.; shoemaker, Abington; June 26, '61; in Twelfth Infty.; re-en. Jan 5, '64; trans. to Thirty-ninth, thence to Thirty-second and M. O.

Hyde, Richard J. (Sergt.), 20, S.; brass tubemaker, Somerville; Aug. 12, '62; d. Aug. 13, '64, a prisoner, Andersonville, Ga.; had been in Co. I, Fifth M. V. M., 3 mos. term, 1861.

Hyde, Thomas L., 23, S.; butcher, Somerville; Aug. 12, '62; wd. May 8, '64; dis. disa., March 9, '65; last heard from in N. Y. city in 1905.

Jones, Charles G., 29, M.; carriage-smith, Somerville; Aug. 12, '62; d. a prisoner Nov. 23, '64, Salisbury, N. C.

Johnson, Mortimer, 19, S.; farmer, Sudbury; July 16, '61; in Thirteenth Infty. and re-en. Feb. 19, '64; trans. to Thirty-ninth; dis. Jan. 5, '65, O. W. D.

Jordan, John F., 18, S.; farmer, Boston; Oct. 16, '63, recruit to Twelfth Infty.; trans. to Thirty-ninth, thence to Thirty-second and M. O.

Kelly, Thomas P., b. Sept. 11, 1842, So. Boston, 18, S.; glass cutter, Somerville; Aug. 12, '62; dis. disa., Oct. 27, '63; glass cutter; Jun. and Sen. Vice Com'der, G. A. R. Post; 1913, Medford.

Kendrick, David, 43, M.; watchmaker, Somerville; Aug. 12, '62; Pris. Aug. 19, '64; d. Annapolis, Md., March 15, '65.

Kennedy, John, 28, M.; Aug. 12, '62; blacksmith, Somerville; Pris. Aug. 19, '64, escaped, recaptured, finally came back; M. O. as Sergt., June 2, '65; d. S. H. Chelsea, Jul. 24, 1898.

Kenneston, E. F., 19, S.; baker, Somerville; Aug. 12, '62; dis. disa., April 21, '63.; d. soon after the war.

Kinmings, Francis M., 19, S.; shoemaker, Bolton; July 16, '61; in Thirteenth Infty.; re-en. Feb. 19, '64; trans. to Thirty-ninth and dis. as Corp., no date.

Ladd, Edward, 22, —; —, Boston; July 22, '61, in Twelfth Infty.; re-en. Feb. 20, '64; trans. to Thirty-ninth; Pris. Aug. 19, '64; drowned in the Potomac River April 23, '65, though his name was carried over to the Thirty-second.

Levins, Morris, 26, M.; cook, Boston; en. Jan. 6, '62, in Thirteenth Infty.; trans. to Thirty-ninth and was M. O. Jan. 5, '65, ex. of s.

Locke, John F., b. March 27, 1844; 18, S.; clerk, Somerville; Aug. 12, '62; Pris. Aug. 19, '64; M. O. May 26, '65; studied in Meadville, Penn.; Harvard Divinity School, 1870; Unitarian clergyman, 25 years, in Stowe; Boston's Y. M. C. U.; Castine, Me.; and Wolfboro, N. H.; since Dec. 10, 1894, Shelf Dep't, Boston Public Library; Locke was detained in Richmond till after the Rebel Evacuation and was the first to hang out a Union flag; 1913, Dorchester.

Lovett, Washington, 23, S.; currier, Somerville; d. July 14, '64, Annapolis, Md.; had been prisoner.

McCarthy, John, 24, M.; laborer, Somerville; Aug. 12, '62; trans. to Co. F, Fourteenth V. R. C.; dis. May 15, '65; d. Nov. 2, 1907, Somerville.

McDonald, George F., 18, M.; Seaman, Framingham; June 28, '63; recruit to Thirteenth Infty.; trans. to Thirty-ninth, thence to Thirty-second and M. O.

McGurdy, Alexander, 38, M.; glass worker, Somerville; Aug. 12, '62; trans. Sept. 12, '62, to Co. F, Fourteenth V. R. C.; dis. July 15, '65; d.

McJunkin, Samuel, 21, S. (Mus.); hostler, Somerville; Aug. 14, '62; M. O. June 2, '65; d. May 9, 1887, Somerville.

McNall, George, 28, M.; glass worker, Somerville; Aug. 2, '62; M. O. June 12, '65; d.

McQuade, John, 42, M.; laborer, Somerville; Aug. 12, '62; dis. disa., Jan. 23, '63; d.

Merrett, James H. (Mus.), 29, —; —, Somerville; Aug. 20, '62; dis. disa., Dec. 6, '62.

Merritt, John S., 37, M.; laborer, Somerville; Aug. 12, '62; det. Serv. Construction Corps; M. O. June 2, '65; d.

Mills, Edwin (Sergt.), 21, S.; plumber, Somerville; Aug. 12, '62; prom. Sergt. Major, Sept. '63.

Moran, James, 18, S.; glass worker, Somerville; Aug. 12, '62; prom. Corp.; d. Aug. 7, '65.

Murray, Thomas, 22, S.; blacksmith, Worcester; July 28, '63; recruit to Thirteenth Infty.; trans. as deserter to Thirty-ninth and as such carried to the Thirty-second.

Myers, George, 21, S.; carpenter, Somerville; Aug. 12, '62; wd. May 23, '64, North Anna River, Va.; dis. as Sergt., March 2, '65, disa.; d. Dec. 30, 1896, Florida.

Newell, James H. (Mus.), 29, M.; machinist, Somerville; Aug. 20, '62; dis. disa., Dec. 13, '62; had been in Co. F, Fifth M. V. M., 3 mos. term, 1861; d. Jan. 4, 1893, Jamaica Plain.

Northey, George A., 29, S.; baker, Somerville; Aug. 12, '62; wd. and taken pris., May 8, '64; dis. disa., March 6, '65; d. Sept. 4, 1902, Malden.

O'Brien, Daniel, 19, S.; shoemaker, Boston; June 26, '61, in Twelfth Infty. and, for some unstated reason, trans. to the Thirty-ninth; at the time was in Haddington Hosp., Philadelphia; N. F. R.

O'Brien, Thomas; no data except "Sept. 20, '64," as enlistment, and trans. to Thirty-second.

Odiorne, William, 26, M.; laborer, Somerville; Aug. 12, '62; wd. May 13, '64; M. O. June 2, '65; d.

Oliver, Francis J., 18, S.; trader, Somerville; Aug. 14, '62; Pris. Oct. 11, '63; d. Oct. 10, '64, Andersonville, Ga.; grave, 1059.

Oliver, Judson W. (Sergt.), 30, M.; currier, Somerville; Aug. 12, '62; M. O. June 2, '65; had been in Co. I, Fifth M. V. M., 3 mos. term, 1861; 36 years in the Police Dep't of Somerville; d. April 7, 1908.

O'Neil, Henry, 40, M.; glass worker, Somerville; Aug. 14, '62; dis. disa., May 15, '63; d.

O'Sullivan, John, 43, M.; laborer, Somerville; Aug. 12, '62; wd. June 18, '64; M. O. June 2, '65; d. Nov. 19, 1875, Cambridge.

Otta, Antone, 37, M.; civil engineer, Beverly; July 29, '63; d. of wds., July 18, '64, Alexandria, Va.

Paine, Jeremiah T., 28, S.; carpenter, Somerville; Aug. 15, '62; d. Oct. 13, '63, Washington, D. C.

Palmer, William D., 31, M.; plumber, Somerville; Aug. 12, '62; k. as Sergt. May 8, '64, Spottsylvania. Parkhurst, Melville C. (Corp), 20, S.; grocer, Somerville; Aug. 12, '62; prom. from Sergt. to 2d Lieut. Sept. 8, '64; vid. Co. B.

Perry, Gideon W., b. Jan. 6, 1840; 22, S.; hosp. attendant, Somerville; Aug. 12, '62; in Aug., '64, detailed as pioneer; M. O. June 2, '65; farmer; 1913, West Fairlee, Vt.

Phillips, Albert W., 43, M.; teamster, No. Bridgewater; Jan. 4, '64, in Twelfth Infty.; trans. to Thirty-ninth; d. a prisoner, Nov. 26, '64, Salisbury, N. C.

Pinkham, Horace W., 25, S.; carpenter, Somerville; Aug. 14, '62; dis. disa., Dec. 9, '62; d.

Powers, Martin, O., 21, M.; farmer, Medford; July 14, '63; in Twelfth Infty.; ab. on detached duty, he was carried as such to the Thirty-second and M. O.

Powers, Robert, 40, M.; laborer, Somerville,; Aug. 12, '62; k. May 10, '64, Spottsylvania, Va.

Randall, George W., 25, S.; Machinist, Charleston; July 16, '63; in Twelfth Infty.; trans. to Thirty-ninth, thence to Thirty-second and M. O.

Richards, Henry, 32, S.; bookkeeper, Amesbury; July 29, '63, in Thirteenth Infty.; trans. to Thirty-ninth, thence to Thirty-second and M. O.

Richardson, Henry C., 18, S.; mechanic, Boston; July 8, '61; in Twelfth Infty.; re-en. Feb. 16, '64; trans. to Thirty-ninth, thence to Thirty-second and M. O.

Riley, John, 2d, 20, M.; baker, Falmouth; July 28, '63, in Thirteenth Infty.; trans. to Thirty-ninth; Pris. Aug. 19, '64; trans. to Thirty-second and M. O.

Roberts, John S., 23, S.; bookkeeper, Somerville; Aug. 13, '62; State House rolls say, "Missing since Aug. 19, '64"; Lieut. Dusseault says he was k. while carrying the Brigade Colors on that disastrous day.

Rollins, Samuel P., 18, S.; baker, Somerville; Aug. 12, '62; d. Nov. 22, '62, Offutt's Crossroads, Md. Shaw, Henry, 20, S.; paper hanger, Somerville; Aug. 12, '62; det. Serv. Hosp.; M. O. June 2, '65; 1912, Somerville.

Shaw, John B., 23, S.; paper hanger, Somerville; Aug. 12, '62; M. O. June 2, '65; 1912, Somerville.

Shaw, Thomas P., 28, M.; yeoman, Warren; July 1, '63, in Twelfth Infty.; trans. to Thirty-ninth; Pris. Aug. 19, '64; trans. to Thirty-second and M. O.

Skehan, John, 23, S.; laborer, Somerville; Aug. 12, '62; dis. disa., Feb. 8, '65.

Smith, Albert H., 21, S.; farmer, Florida; Aug. 22, '64; M. O. June 2, '65.

Smith, Addison, 39, M.; cordwainer, Somerville; Aug. 12, '62; trans. July 1, '63, to V. R. C.; dis. disa., March 17, '64, David's Island, N. Y. Harbor; d. June 25, 1895.

Smith, Sidney N., 27, M.; mechanic, Winchendon; July 20, '63; in Twelfth Infty.; trans. to Thirty-ninth; M. O. May 22, '65.

Smith, William M., 22, S.; farmer, Florida; July 14, '63, in Twelfth Infty.; trans. to Thirty-ninth, thence to Thirty-second and M. O.

Stevens, Leslie, b. Aug. 9, 1846, Walpole; (Corp.) 18, S.; moulder, Somerville; Aug. 14, '62; dis. disa., Jan. 25, '63; iron moulder, sewing machine agent, teacher of boxing and breeder of St. Bernard dogs; Q. M., Post 94, G. A. R.; 1913, Canton.

Stickney, Herman C., 21, S.; farmer, Somerville; Aug. 13, '62; special duty; dis. disa., April 22, '63; 1912, Somerville.

Thomas, William H., 32, M.; gentleman, Somerville; Aug. 12, '62; prom. Sergt.; M. O. June 2, '65.

Thompson, Frank W., 18, S.; farmer, Somerville; Aug. 12, '62; Pris. Aug. 19, '64; d. Jan. 10, '65, Florence, S. C.

Ulrich, Lewis, 30, S.; laborer, Chatham; July 27, '63, in Thirteenth Infty.; trans. to Thirty-ninth; Pris. Aug. 19, '64; trans. to Thirty-second and M. O.

Van Cleff, John S., 35, S.; sailor, Boston; July 25, '63; in Twelfth Infty.; trans. to Thirty-ninth; d. a prisoner Feb. 1, '65, Salisbury, N. C.

Van de Sands, George (Corp.), 18, S.; clerk, Somerville; Aug. 12, '62; prom. Sergt.; dis. Aug. 23, '63, O. W. D. for commission, Tenth U. S. C. T.; d.

Webster, Henry K., 28, M.; clerk, Lawrence; July 16, '62, in Twelfth Infty.; trans. to Thirty-ninth; Pris. Aug. 19, '64; M. O. May 15, '65.

Wentworth, Alonzo P., 33, M.; laborer, Charleston; July 9, '63; in Twelfth Infty.; trans. to Thirty-ninth; M. O. May 18, '65.

Whitmore, Joseph W., 28, M.; carpenter, Somerville; Aug. 12, '62; Pris. Oct. 10, '63; supposed to have died in Rebel Prison.

Wilcutt, William C., 30, S.; laborer, Somerville; Aug. 13, '62; des. Sept. 9, '62; had been in Co. F, Fifth M. V. M. 3 mos. term, 1861; later in Co. K, Fifty-ninth Infty. from which he deserted; Willcut seemed a fitting name.

Williams, John, 32, —; seaman, Boston; July 29, '63, in Thirteenth Infty.; trans. to Thirty-ninth and was dis. disa., Aug. 7, '64.

Wilton, George T., 28, S.; boatman, Conway; Aug. 1, '63; in Twelfth Infty.; trans. to Thirty-ninth and was wd. May 5, '64, Wilderness; dis. disa., Aug. 18, '64.

Woodward, Elbridge G., 23, M.; farmer, Colrain; Aug. 1, '63; trans. to V. R. C., March 21, '65; des. from 22d Co. Second Batt. V. R. C., June 28, '65.

Wright, Robert, 23, —; boiler maker, Ashfield; July 26, '63, in Twelfth Infty.; trans. to Thirty-ninth, thence to Thirty-second and M. O.

COMPANY F

Taunton

CAPTAIN

Joseph J. Cooper, 34, M.; nailer, Taunton; Aug. 22, '62; wd. Feb. 7, '65, Hatcher's Run, Va.; bvt. Major, April 1, '65; M. O. June 2, '65; b. May 8, 1828, Preston, England; came to America, when three years old; as a boy, worked in Taunton Cotton mill; as a young man, worked at tack making; in Pittsburg, Penn., from 1854 to beginning of the Civil War; after the war, engaged in the nail business in Bridgewater and continued the same for years; later he followed the same business in Taunton, retiring several years ago; from boyhood, he was interested in the Fire Department, being an active member of the Taunton force for many years, and then Ass't Engineer; was a lifelong member of the Baptist Church; a life member of the Old Colony Historical Society, his interest continued to the end; Lieut. James E. Seaver, secretary of the Society pays the Major this tribute, "Always an honest man! A man with the strongest convictions which he held to the last, if he believed them to be right; a good friend, an excellent neighbor, a good citizen and a brave soldier"; he died August 22, 1912.

FIRST LIEUTENANT

Isaac D. Paul, 38, S.; dresser, Taunton; Aug. 22, '62; k. May 8, '64, Spottsylvania; a member of the Masonic Order, Confederate Masons carried his body to the rear and buried it with Masonic Rites; had been a corporal in Co. G, Fourth M. V. M., 3 mos. service; before the war, had been Supt. in the Whittaker Cotton Manufacturing Co. For a time, Post 55 of Taunton bore his name.

SECOND LIEUTENANT

John D. Reed, 35, S.; grocer, Taunton; Aug. 22, '62; prom. 1st Lieut. Sept. 20, '63; vide Co. I.

Joseph A. Merrifield, from Sergt. Major, Sept. 20, '63; trans. to Co. D, Oct. '63.

Henry F. Felch from Co. I, Oct. 25, '63; wd. Aug. 18, '64; prom. 1st Lieut. Sept. 15, '64, Co. E.

ENLISTED MEN

Adams, George F., 24, M.; nailer, Taunton; Aug. 22, '62; M. O. June 2, '65.

Alexander, William, 21, S.; laborer, Boston; July 27, '63, in Twelfth Infty.; trans. to Thirty-ninth, thence to Thirty-second and M. O.

Anthony, Sylvanus, 28, M.; farmer, Uxbridge; July 5, '63; in Twelfth Infty.; trans. to Thirty-ninth, thence to Thirty-second and M. O.

Austin, Charles B., 33, M.; Aug. 22, '62; Pris. May 10, '64, to May 10, '65; M. O. June 2, '65.

Babbitt, Charles E., 20, M.; tailor, Taunton; Aug. 22, '62; k. May 8, '64, Alsop's Farm.

Babbitt, Frank S., b. Dec. 22, 1843; 18, S.; tailor, Taunton; Aug. 25, '62; trans. to U. S. Signal Corps, Sept. 1, '63; served in Army of the Potomac; 1865 to 1889, manufacturing machinery; 1882-'83, Representative in General Court; 1887, Alderman, Taunton; 1888-'93 inclusive, Bristol Co. Commissioner; 1891-'93 inclusive, Mayor of Taunton; 1894-'97, Administrator of Estates; 1897-1900 inclusive, Chief of Police; 1901 to date, Probation Officer, Massachusetts Superior Court; 1913, Taunton.

Babbitt, George H., Jr., b. Sept. 7, 1841; (Sergt.) 20, S.; auctioneer, Taunton; Aug. 22, '62; M. O. June 2, '65; auctioneer and commission merchant; 1871-'72, Rep. General Court; later was Coroner, Deputy Sheriff, Justice of the Peace, Constable, Ass't U. S. Marshal, Enumerator, etc.; d. Dec. 9, 1877.

Barker, Orville A., b. June 17, 1840, 22, S.; apothecary, Taunton; Aug. 22, '62; prom. Corp.; prom. Hosp. Steward, Oct. 13, '62; vide F. & S.

Barnes, Charles A., 27, S.; bookkeeper, Taunton; Dec. 28, '63; d. July 15, '64, Taunton.

Barnes, William L., 35, M.; painter, Roxbury; July 15, '63, in Twelfth Infty.; trans. to Thirty-ninth; dis. disa., April 22, '65.

Barnum, George D., 29, S.; bootmaker, Boston, cr. to Holliston; July 14, '63, in Twelfth Infty.; trans. to Thirty-ninth, thence to Thirty-second and M. O.

Barrows, George L., 18, S.; shoemaker, Taunton; Aug. 22, '62; trans. Co. F, Twenty-fourth V. R. C., March 13, '65; dis. June 28, '65.

Betagh, James, 35, M.; laborer, Taunton; Aug. 22, '62; Corp., Jan. 1, '64; wd. May 10, '65; Pris. Aug. 19, '64, to May 16, '65; M. O. June 2, '65.

Boardman, Alfred, 24, S.; shoemaker, Taunton; Aug. 22, '62; trans. to U. S. Navy, April 19, '64; dis. July 31, '65.

Borden, Clark P., 20, S.; harness maker, Fall River; Aug. 22, '62; wd. May 8, '64; M. O. June 2, '65.

Braddock, William, 26, M.; knife cutter, Chatham; Oct. 1, '63, in Twelfth Infty.; M. O. May 15, '65.

Brewster, Charles W. (Corp.), 19, S.; clerk, Taunton; Aug. 22, '62; dis. March 31, '65.

Briggs, Preserved, 26, M.; wheelwright, Taunton; Aug. 22, '62; M. O. June 2, '65.

Brizzee, Lorenzo, 29, M.; farmer, Deerfield; July 16, '63, in Twelfth Infty.; trans. to Thirty-ninth, thence to Thirty-second and M. O.; name also found, Brizzer and Brizzie.

Brooks, Freelove, 29, M.; armorer, Springfield; July 11, '63, in Twelfth Infty.; trans. to Thirty-ninth, thence to Thirty-second and M. O.

Brunn, John, 25, S.; shoemaker, Roxbury; Sept. 23, '63, in Twelfth Infty.; trans. to Thirty-ninth, thence as prisoner of war to Thirty-second and M. O.

Burt, Henry A., 25, S.; machinist, Taunton; Aug. 22, '62; wd. May 16, '64; M. O. June 2, '65.

Carney, John, 22, S.; shovel maker, Acton; July 23, '63; in Twelfth Infty.; trans. to Thirty-ninth, thence to Thirty-second and M. O.

Cochran, Matthew, 28, M.; sailor, Marblehead; July 10, '63, in Twelfth Infty.; trans. to Thirty-ninth; wd., time and place not given; dis. disa., June 7, '65.

Cole, Charles H., 19, S.; hostler, Taunton; Aug. 22, '62; M. O. June 2, '65.

Conway, Patrick, 28, S.; farmer, New York, cr. to Truro; Oct. 5, '63, in Twelfth Infty.; trans. to Thirty-ninth; Pris. Aug. 19, '64; dis. June 13, '65.

Cotter, Edward A., 22, S.; shoemaker, Dorchester; June 26, '61, in Twelfth Infty.; re-en. Jan. 5, '64; trans. to Thirty-ninth; dis. disa., April 3, '65.

Crooker, Lucius (Sergt.), 23, S.; clerk, Bridgewater; Aug. 22, '62; dis. Dec. 22, '63, for commission, U. S. C. T.; vide Seventy-seventh Infty. and Tenth H. Arty.; reporting in New Orleans he was commissioned 1st Lieut. and ordered to Ft. St. Philip and made Post Adjutant; later became Provost Marshal in N. O., remaining there till Reg't was M. O. Later still was secretary of U. S. Consul at Panama; he died several years ago.

Cummings, John A., 25, —; —, Taunton; Aug. 22, '62; des. Aug. 29, '62.

Daniels, George M., 32, M.; mason, Adams; July 14, '63, in Twelfth Infty.; trans. to Thirty-ninth; wd., no time or place stated; trans. to Thirty-second and M. O.

Day, John, 32, S.; fisherman, Gloucester; July 22, '63, in Twelfth Infty.; trans. to Thirty-ninth; Pris. Aug. 19, '64; d. from wds. Oct. 28, '64.

Dean, Anson J., 18, S.; machinist, Taunton; Aug. 22, '62; Corp., March 1, '65; wd. June 18, '64, and March 31, '65; M. O. May 25, '65.

Dean, Erastus L., 18, S.; machinist, Taunton; Aug. 22, '62; k. May 8, '64, Spottsylvania.

Dean, William E., 24, S.; Aug. 22, '62; Pris. Aug. 19, '64, to March 2, '65; M. O. June 2, '65.

Delphin, Joseph, Jr., 19, S.; carpenter, Taunton; Aug. 22, '63; M. O. June 2, '65.

Doherty, William (Sergt.), 33, M.; laborer, Taunton; Aug. 22, '62; Pris., Aug. 19, '64, to May 16, '65; M. O. June 2, '65.

Dunbar, Robert, 28, S.; plasterer, Boston; July 27, '63; in Twelfth Infty.; trans. to Thirty-ninth; wd. Aug. 19, '64; des. March 2, '65.

Elms, Cyrus O., 35, M.; carpenter, Taunton; Aug. 22, '62; wd., Aug. 19, '64; trans. Feb. 25, '65, to Co. A, Tenth V. R. C.; dis. May 26, '65.

Ensminger, John, 22, S.; farmer, Stockbridge; July 15, '63; in Twelfth Infty.; trans. to Thirty-ninth; M. O. May 31, '65.

Findell, Adolphus, 44, —; —, Taunton; Aug. 3, '63; though given on the State House rolls as trans. from the Thirteenth Infty., his name does not appear in that regiment, nor in the Twelfth; dis. disa., Sept. 26, '64.

Gay, Abraham S., 34, M.; shoemaker, Natick; March 17, '62, in Thirteenth Infty.; trans. to Thirty-ninth; M. O. March 17, '65, ex. of s.

Gay, George W., 19, S.; stitcher, Taunton; Aug. 22, '62; Pris. Aug. 19, '64; M. O. June 2, '65.

Grover, Hartson C., 27, S.; blacksmith, Canaan, Me., cr. Methuen; July 13, '63, in Twelfth Infty.; trans. to Thirty-ninth thence to Co. A, Ninth V. R. C.; dis. July 22, '65.

Gushee, Sacuel M., 17, —; —, Taunton; Aug. 22, '62; N. F. R.

Hall, Benjamin J., 18, S.; printer, Taunton; Aug. 22, '62; prom. Corp. July 1, '64; Pris.; d. Dec. 6, '64, Salisbury.

Hall, Daniel, b. Nov. 27, 1839; 23, —; —, Boxford; Nov. 21, '62, in Washington, D. C.; trans. Aug. 1, '63, U. S. Signal Corps; served in Dep't, N. C., Dept. of Shenandoah, Georgetown, D. C.; dis. as Sergt. July 5, '65; says he was in the Navy, '61 and '62; through the treachery of a Lieutenant, he and twelve others were prisoners of war ten months; rolls say M. O. in absence, June 2, '65; salesman; 1913, S. H. Togus, Me.

Hall, Eben A., 22, M.; printer, Taunton; Aug. 22, '62; Corp. Sept. 1, '63; Sergt. Feb. 1, '65; Pris. Feb. 7, '65, to April 30, '65; M. O. June 2, '65; Rep. in General Court; Executive Council with Gov. Butler; publisher of Greenfield Gazette; d. New Orleans, March 17, 1900, while on Press Excursion to that vicinity.

Hall, George W., 18, S.; seaman, Boston; Aug. 23, '62, in Thirteenth Infty.; re-en. Jan. 4, '64; trans. to Thirty-ninth, thence to Thirty-second and M. O.

Hall, Rufus W., b. July 30, 1836; 34, S.; machinist, Taunton; Aug. 22, '62; Pris. May 8, '64; recaptured by Sheridan, May 9; dis. disa., April 28, '65; machinist; 52 years in Mason Machine Works, including army service and nineteen months disa. at close; 1913 (retired), Taunton.

Haniford, William, 20, S.; farmer, Chelmsford; July 11, '63, in Twelfth Infty.; trans. to Thirty-ninth, thence to Thirty-second and M. O.

Harris, Alfred B., 21, S.; clerk, Taunton; Aug. 22, '62; trans. Jan. 12, '64, U. S. Signal Corps; served in Depts. of Ohio, Va., and N. C.; taken pris. Feb. 18, '65, near Fort Anderson, N. C.; d. April 7, '65, Taunton.

Harvey, William F., 22, M.; moulder, Taunton, Aug. 22, '62; dis. disa., Jan. 2, '64.

Hathaway, James A., 18, S.; nailer, Taunton; Aug. 22, '62; Pris., Aug. 19, '64; d. Jan. 10, '65, Salisbury, N. C.

Hewett, John G., 29, M.; dresser tender, Taunton; Aug. 22, '62; dis. disa., Jan. 12, '63.

Holloway, Isaac N., 27, M.; shoemaker, Taunton; Aug. 22, '62; wd. May 10, '64, and Aug. 18, '64; dis. May 12, '65.

Horton, Horace B. (Corp.), 36, M.; mason, Taunton; Aug. 8, '62; prom. Sergt. Nov. 1, '65; wd. and prisoner, Aug. 19, '64; paroled, N. F. R.

Howland, Benjamin L., 21, S.; cooper, Taunton; Oct. 16, '63; in Twelfth Infty.; trans. to Thirty-ninth; Pris. Aug. 19, '64; trans. to Thirty-second and M. O.

Jewett, Jesse G., b. Oct. 9, 1840, 21, S.; clerk, Bridgewater; Aug. 22, '62; Corp. March 2, '63; dis. Jan. 2, '64, for Commission, U. S. C. T.; vide Seventy-seventh Infty. and Tenth H. Arty.; with Sergt. Crocker he reported to General Wm. Dwight, New Orleans; commissioned 1st Lieut.; sent to Fort St. Philip, serving as boarding officer, i.e., looking after contraband goods in passing vessels; later, served on staffs of Generals Hamlin, Banks, Hurlbert, Canby, Sheridan and J. W. Sherman; resigned June 7, 1866; clothing business and farming till 1871; since then with Old Colony, or N. Y., N. H. and H. R. R. to date, in Paymaster's or Treasurer's Dept.; 1913, Dorchester.

Jones, William H., 23, S.; harness maker, Chatham; July 27, '63, in Thirteenth Infty.; trans. to Thirty-ninth; Pris. Aug. 19, '64; trans. to Thirty-second and M. O.

Kane, David S., 20, S.; farmer, Bridgewater; Aug. 27, '62; wd. May 10, '64; Pris. Aug. 19, '64; M. O. July 24, '65.

Kellar, Balthaser, 24, M.; clothier, Littleton; Nov. 5, '63, in Thirteenth Infty.; trans. to Thirty-ninth, thence to Thirty-second and M. O.

Kelly, William, 21, S.; mule-dresser, Taunton; Aug. 29, '62; dis. disa., March 4, '63.

Kelly, William B., 23, S.; painter, Taunton; wd. Aug. 18, '64; d. Aug. 30, '64, Philadelphia.

King, Edward, b. June 6, 1843, 19, S.; clerk, Taunton; Aug. 22, '62; on detached duty, the most of his service; M. O. June 2, '65; in National Banks and manufacturing companies, in Taunton or Newcastle, Penn.; 1913, New Castle.

Knapp, George L. (Corp.), 36, M.; carpenter, Taunton; Aug. 22, '62; dis. disa., June 3, '64.

Knapp, Lorenzo S., 29, M.; farmer, Richmond; July 15, '62; in Twelfth Infty.; trans. to Thirty-ninth, thence to Thirty-second and M. O.

Laahy, Jeremiah, 42, M.; laborer, Taunton; Aug. 22, '62; wd. May 8, '64; dis. disa., Dec. 3, '64.

Lane, Henry A., 27, S.; coppersmith, Taunton; Aug. 22, '62; Corp. March 2, '63; Sergt. Jan. 1, '64; wd. June 19, '64; M. O. June 8, '65.

Lawler, James A., 20, S.; farmer, Taunton; Aug. 22, '62; wd. May 10, '64; Pris., Aug. 19, '64, to March 2, '65; M. O. June 13, '65.

Leonard, Henry F., 34, M.; tinner, Taunton; Aug. 22, '62; M. O. June 2, '65.

Leonard, William E., 24, M.; moulder, Taunton; Aug. 22, '62; M. O. June 2, '65.

Lincoln, Daniel, 35, M.; carpenter, Taunton; Aug. 22, '62; d. May 10, '64, Laurel Hill, Va., from wds. rec'd on the Eighth, Alsop's Farm.

McClearance, Archibald, 43, M.; weaver, Taunton; Aug. 22, '62; dis. disa., June 18, '63.

McFarland, Samuel G., 18, M.; clerk, Winchester; July 21, '62; in Twelfth Infty.; trans. to Thirty-ninth, thence to Thirty-second and M. O.

Makepeace, Norman G., 23, M.; shoemaker, Taunton; Aug. 22, '62; wd. May 5, '64; M. O. June 20, '65.

Mason, William W., 35, M.; wheelwright, Taunton; Aug. 22, '62; Corp. Oct. 29, '62; M. O. June 2, '65.

Mitchell, Edward, Jr., 19, S.; clerk, Bridgewater; Aug. 22, '62; dis. disa., Oct. 13, '63.

Mitchell, Nathan, 21, M.; clerk, Bridgewater; Aug. 22, '62; d. Sept. 27, '62, Edwards Ferry, Md.

Monroe, Charles E., 21, S.; apothecary, Taunton; Aug. 22, '62; dis. for prom. hospital steward, U. S. A., Feb. 17, '63; March 14, '64, prom. 1st Lieut. and assistant surgeon, One Hundred and Seventy-fourth Ohio Vols.; M. O. June 28, '65.

Naylor, Abraham C., 23, M.; machinist, Taunton; Aug. 22, '62; M. O. June 2, '65.

Nelson, William, 44, M.; dresser, Taunton; Aug. 22, '62; Pris. May 8, '64, recaptured by Sheridan May 9; wd. Aug. 18, '64; dis. disa., April 18, '65.

Nichols, William L., 21, S.; blacksmith, Taunton; Aug. 22, '62; Corp. Dec. 1, '64; wd. Feb. 7, '65; M. O. May 27, '65.

Packer, States, 30, M.; laborer, Taunton; Aug. 22, '62; d. a prisoner Jan. 4, '65, Salisbury, N. C.

Paull, Dyer S., 34, M.; teamster, Taunton; Aug. 22, '65; dis. disa., Nov. 18, '64.

Paull, Thomas W., 21, S.; nailer, Taunton; Aug. 22, '62; Pris. Aug. 19, '64, to March 13, '65; M. O. June 2, '65.

Pearson, Charles E., 28, —; —, Taunton; Corp. Nov. 1, '63; M. O. June 2, '65.

Phillips, Dexter M., 24, M.; farmer, Pittsfield; July 4, '62, in Twelfth Infty.; trans. to Thirty-ninth; Pris. Aug. 19, '64; trans. to Thirty-second and M. O.

Pierce, Charles A., 25, S.; carpenter, Taunton; Aug. 22, '62; Corp. Jan. 16, '64; dis. disa., Oct. 22, '64.

Quimby, Ira B., 33, M.; carpenter, Boston; Aug. 26, '62; dis. Feb. 2, '64, for prom. U. S. C. T.

Rand, William L., 25, S.; farmer, Nahant; June 26, '61; in Twelfth Infty.; re-en. Jan. 5, '64; trans. to Thirty-ninth; prom. Corp.; k. March 31, '65, Hatcher's Run.

Reynolds, William H. (Mus.), 19, S.; clerk, Taunton; Aug. 22, '62; dis. May 18, '65.

Riley, James, 33, M.; laborer, Taunton; Aug. 25, '62; trans. to Co. E, Ninth V. R. C.; dis. June 26, '65.

Rocket, James, 19, S.; nailer, Taunton; Aug. 22, '62; dis. disa., March 4, '63.

Rogers, Eugene S., 26, S.; shoemaker, Natick; March 17, '62; in Thirteenth Infty.; trans. to Thirty-ninth; dis. 17, '65, ex. of s.

Russell, Nathan, 28, M.; carpenter, Marlborough; Jan. 2, '64; in Thirteenth Infty.; trans. to Thirty-ninth; dis. May 13, '65.

Shaw, George W., Jr., 22, S.; —, West Brookfield; July 13, '63; in Twelfth Infty.; trans. to Thirty-ninth, thence to Thirty-second and M. O.

Sherburne, Benjamin F., 20, S.; machinist, Taunton; Aug. 22, '62; des. July 9, '63.

Skinner, Fernando C., 21, S.; shovel-maker, Taunton; Aug. 22, '62; wd. May 8, '64; Pris. Aug. 19, '64, to May 16, '65; M. O. June 2, '65.

Smith, Edwin H. C., 18, S.; shoemaker, Taunton; Aug. 22, '62; wd. May 10, '64; Pris. Aug. 19, '64, to March 2, '65; M. O. June 6, '65.

Smith, George T., 20, S.; farmer, Wayland; July 16, '61; in Thirteenth Infty.; re-en. Feb. 17, '64; trans. to Thirty-ninth; dis. disa., Oct. 17, '64.

Smith, James, 38, M.; mechanic, Taunton; Aug. 22, '62; Pris. Aug. 19, '64, to Oct. 9, '64; dis. May 12, '65.

Snow, Charles H., 18, S.; farmer, Taunton; Aug. 21, '62; M. O. June 3, '65.

Sproal, Arthur H. (Corp.), 19, S.; clerk, Taunton; Aug. 22, '62; M. O. May 18, '65.

Stall, John M., 40, S.; Aug. 22, '62; farmer, Taunton; wd. May 8, '64; dis. Dec. 13, '64.

Staples, Benjamin F., 22, S.; clerk, Taunton; Aug. 22, '62; ab. sick at M. O.; N. F. R.

Sullivan, Daniel, 23, M.; laborer, Dorchester; Aug. 4, '63, in Thirteenth Infty.; trans. to Thirty-ninth; though ab. under arrest, and as such was carried to the Thirty-second.

Taylor, George W. (Wagoner), 34, M.; teamster, Taunton; Aug. 22, '62; dis. disa., Feb. 1, '64.

Terry, Apollos P., 22, S.; cooper, Taunton; Aug. 26, '62; Pris. Aug. 19, '64, to Sept. 12, '64; M. O. June 13, '65.

Thayer, Edgar S. (1st Sergt.), 23, M.; farmer, Taunton; Aug. 22, '62; dis. Oct. 22, '63, for commission as Captain, Co. H, Seventh U. S. C. T.

Thayer, Henry F., 29, M.; metal-worker, Taunton; Aug. 22, '62; trans. Feb. 15, '64, Co. H, 1st V. R. C.

Thomas, Charles, 34, M.; moulder, Taunton; Aug. 12, '62; d. a prisoner, Florence, S. C., Oct. —, '64.

Thomas, Charles S. (Corp.), 23, S.; farmer, Raynham; Aug. 22, '62; M. O. June 2, '65.

Tighe, Terrance, 39, M.; laborer, Taunton; Aug. 22, '62; trans. Oct. 27, '63, to Co. A, Twentieth V. R. C.; dis. June 28, '65.

Tinkham, Herbert, 21, S.; clerk, Taunton; Aug. 22, '62; June 2, '65.

Tisdale, Samuel L., 24, S.; marine, Taunton; Aug. 22, '62; trans. Navy May 4, '64; dis. July 15, '65.

Titus, George L., 20, S.; carpenter, Taunton; Aug. 22, '62; wd. May 8, '64; Pris. Aug. 19, '64, to May 16, '65; M. O. June 2, '65.

Townsend, Percival J. (Corp.), 23, S.; clerk, Taunton; Aug. 22, '62; no M. O.

Turner, George, 37, S.; laborer, Taunton; Aug. 22, '62; dis. disa., March 4, '63.

Walsh, Harold, 19, M.; machinist, Taunton; Aug. 22, '62; des. July 9, '63.

Walsh, William, 22, —; —, Charlestown; July 25, '63, in Thirteenth Infty.; trans. to Thirty-ninth; Pris. Aug. 19, '64, to May 16, '65; trans. to Thirty-second and M. O.

Washburn, Otis (Corp.), 31, M.; clerk, Taunton; Aug. 22, '62; Sergt. March 2, '63; dis. disa., Oct. 20, '63.

Washburn, Salmon, Jr. (Corp.), 19, S.; clerk, Taunton; Aug. 22, '62; wd. May 10, '64; M. O. May 19, '65.

Waters, Clark, 28, M.; carpenter, Boston; July 13, '63, in Twelfth Infty.; trans. to Thirty-ninth, thence to Thirty-second and M. O.

Webster, Charles C. (1st Sergt.), 25, M.; currier, Boston; June 26, '61, in Twelfth Infty.; re-en. Jan. 5, '64; trans. to Thirty-ninth; dis. O. W. D. Sept. 21, '64.

Wescott, Andrew A., 28, S.; carpenter, Taunton; Aug. 22, '62; Corp. May 6, '63; wd. May 8, '64; d. a prisoner, Richmond, June 1, '64.

Wheeler, Charles E., 23, S.; machinist, Taunton; Aug. 22, '62; wd. May 8, '64; M. O. June 2, '65.

White, Albert R., 21, M.; butcher, Taunton; Aug. 22, '62; dis. disa., Dec. 10, '62.

Whitney, Lorenzo L., 21, M.; teamster, Boston; July 13, '63, in Twelfth Infty.; trans. to Thirty-ninth, thence to Thirty-second and M. O.

Whitters, Edward, b. 1839, 23, S.; harness-maker, Taunton; Aug. 22, '62; M. O. June 2, '65; harness manufacturer; d. Oct. 12, 1913.

Williams, Reuben B. P., 23, M.; nailer, Taunton; Aug. 22, '62; d. June 26, '63, Washington.

Wilson, George W., 2d, 22, S.; brickmaker, Taunton; Aug. 22, '62; dis. disa., June 3, '64.

Wood, David (Sergt.), 34, M.; Aug. 22, '62; 1st Sergt. Oct. 22, '63; Pris. Aug. 19, '64, to April 30, '65; prom. 2d Lieut. June 7, '65; M. O. June 2, '65, as 1st Sergt.

Wood, Jesse, 26, S.; painter, Taunton; Aug. 22, '62; dis. disa., Dec. 29, '63.

Woodward, Edward M., 21, S.; machinist, Taunton; Aug. 22, '62; Corp. Nov. 1, '63; wd. May 10, '64; M. O. June 2, '65.

Woodward, George T., 20, S.; student, Taunton; Aug. 25, '62; trans. to U. S. Signal Corps Aug. 12, '63; served Dept. of Gulf; dis. July 18, '65; d. Sept. 17, '65, Taunton.

Woodward, Matthew, 38, M.; moulder, Taunton; Aug. 22, '62; chief mus. Nov. 1, '63; vid. F. & S.

Woodward, Roland P., 23, M.; machinist, Taunton; Aug. 22, '62; wd. May 8, '64; M. O. June 2, '65.

COMPANY G

Boston and South Shore

CAPTAIN

Ezra J. Trull, 20, S.; b. Sept. 13, 1842, Boston; Sept. 2, '62; Pris. Aug. 19, '64; M. O. June 2, '65; he had en. as Private in Co. A, Thirteenth Infty. and was dis. Aug. 30, '62, for prom. in the Thirty-ninth; in the firm of Chase & Trull, he was long a distiller in Charlestown; d. Charlestown, April 29, 1886; one of the best drilled men in the Regiment, after the war he enlisted as a private in the Fifth Regiment, M. V. M.; rose through the grades to its command and was at its head in the famous Bunker Hill Centennial Parade; also rose to a captaincy in the Ancient and Honorable Artillery.

FIRST LIEUTENANTS

Charles W. Thompson, —, —; Boston; Aug. 20, '62; on detached service nearly his entire term; dis. disa., May 3, '64.

William G. Sheen, from Co. I; prom. Captain Sept. 8, '64, Co. D, vice Spear, res.

Charles K. Conn, March, '65; detached as Quarter-Master, One Hundred and Fourth N. Y. Vols.; M. O. June 2, '65; d. Oct. 3, 1906.

SECOND LIEUTENANT

Charles Henry Chapman, from Sergt. Major; commissioned Aug. 30, '62; mustered Nov. 11, '62; Act. Ass't Inspector Gen'l Fourth Brigade, 2d Div. 1st A. C. until Brig. was disbanded, July 17, '63; Pris. Aug. 19, '64; prom. 1st Lieut. Sept. 6, '64, not mustered; dis. for Captaincy, Forty-first U. S. C. T., April 29, '65; commissioned Sept. 16, '64; Act. Ass't Adjt. Gen'l 2d Brig. 2d Div. 25th A. C., and Post Adjt. Edinburg, Texas, Sept. 2, '65, till disbandment of Brigade; M. O. Dec. 10, '65; 1866, manufacturer, Lambertville, N. J.; 1870 to '74, Civil Engineer in N. J. and N. E.; in Insurance Business '69 to '95, for much of the time officially connected with important fire companies; retired, 1895; since then, spending his winters in warm climates. The Lieutenant had been first Lieut. and Adjutant in the Fifth R. I. H. Arty., beginning Nov. 30, '61; dis. disa., May 14, '62.

ENLISTED MEN

Adams, Joseph (Corp.), 28, S.; seaman, Boston; Sept. 2, '62; prom. Sergt.; Pris. as Color Sergt. Aug. 19, '64; M. O. June 2, '65; d.

Bailey, Charles C. (Corp.), 21, S.; clerk, Hingham; Sept. 2, '62; "dis. Dec. 23, '63, to en. U. S. Signal Corps," thus the record reads; on the contrary, Bailey en. as hospital steward, U. S. A., but on account of his excellent penmanship served as clerk in the office of the Surgeon General till the fall of 1865.

Bailey, John W., 19, S.; farmer, Hingham; Sept. 2, '62; prom. Sergt.; M. O. June 2, '65; dead.

Bannon, James, 38, M.; boot crimper, Braintree; Sept. 2, '62; Pris. Aug. 19, '64; d. April 12, '65, Braintree.

Barney, Horace, 23, —; —, West Cambridge; Aug. 1, '62; des. Aug. —, '62.

Bates, Charles E., 24, S.; boatman, Scituate; Sept. 2, '62; wd. May 8, '64; d. Nov. 2, '64, Baltimore, Md.; dead.

Bates, Lorenzo, 21, S.; butcher, Scituate; Sept. 2, '62; trans. June 18, '64, V. R. C.; dis. from One Hundred and Tenth Co., 2d Batt. V. R. C., Sept. 2, '65; 1913, Hingham Centre.

Bird, John, 27, S.; farmer, West Boylston; July 24, '63, in Twelfth Infty.; trans. to Thirty-ninth, thence to the Thirty-second and M. O.

Blanding, Daniel W., 30, M.; shoemaker, Warren; July 14, '63, in Twelfth Infty.; trans. to Thirty-ninth, thence to Thirty-second and M. O.

Breck, Elijah F., 30, M.; lawyer, New Salem; N. H., cr. Westford; Sept. 2, '62; M. O. May 30, '65; dead.

Bright, Willard (Mus.), 19, S.; laborer, Watertown; Sept. 2, '62; Pris. Aug. 19, '64; d. March 29, '65.

Broderick, James, 35, —; —, Watertown, July 23, '62; des. Aug. —, '62.

Brooks, Albert F., 26, M.; bookkeeper, So. Reading; July 29, '61, in Thirteenth Infty.; trans. to Thirty-ninth; thence to Thirty-second and M. O.

Brown, Charles H. C., 23, M.; upholsterer, Boston; Sept. 2, '62; prom. Corp.; dis. Oct. 2, '63, for Commission, U. S. C. T.; 2d Lieut. Seventh Colored Infty.; 1st Lieut. and Adjutant Oct. 21, '64; bvt. Captain March 13, '65; M. O. Oct. 13, '66; 1913, Brookline.

Butters, Willie R., 18, S.; farmer, Reading; Dec. 28, '63, Thirteenth Infty.; trans. to Thirty-ninth; wd. March 31, '65, Hatcher's Run; trans. to Thirty-second and M. O.; 1913, Plymouth.

Carlin, Thomas B., 22, S.; printer, Barnard, Vt., cr. Brookline; Sept. 25, '63, in Twelfth Infty.; trans. to Thirty-ninth, thence to Thirty-second and M. O.

Chapman, Timothy B., 31, M.; shoemaker, So. Scituate; Sept. 2, '62; M. O. June 2, '65; 1913, Ridge Hill.

Chase, Timothy H., 27, S.; blacksmith, Charlestown; July 8, '63, in Twelfth Infty.; trans. to Thirty-ninth, thence to Thirty-second and M. O.

Child, Henry, 45, —; —, —; en. July 29, '62; des. Aug. —, '62.

Chipman, Andrew A. (1st Sergt.), 25, S.; fireworker, Salem; June 26, '61, in Twelfth Infty.; re-en. Jan. 5, '64; trans. to Thirty-ninth; dis. Aug. 23, '64, O. W. D.; later 1st Lieut. Fourth H. Arty.; M. O. June 17, '65.

Chubbuck, Eleazer, 18, M.; shoemaker, Hingham; Sept. 2, '62; M. O. June 2, '65; dead.

Churchill, James T., 21, M.; painter, Hingham; Sept. 2, '62; d. a prisoner June 24, '64, Andersonville; grave 2416.

Clapp, Caleb W., 22, S.; shoemaker, So. Scituate; Sept. 2, '62; dis. on account of wds. May 8, '64; dead.

Cochrane, George, 33, M.; oysterman, Boston; Sept. 2, '62; trans. Sept. 30, '63, Co. A, Sixth V. R. C.; M. O. June 2, '65.

Connell, John, 33, M.; farmer, Concord; Sept. 2, '62; trans. Aug. 2, '64, V. R. C.; dis. from Co. B, Sixth V. R. C.; July 3, '65; dead.

Corrigan, Thomas, 27, S.; waiter, Boston; Sept. 2, '62; M. O. June 2, '65; d. Togus, Me.

Corthell, John, b. Sept. 15, 1836; 25, M.; carpenter, So. Scituate; Sept. 2, '62; M. O. June 2, '65; provision dealer, constable and tree warden; 1913, Somerville.

Cowan, Thomas, 23, M.; clerk, Boston; Sept. 2, '62; dis. disa. Feb. 28, '63.

Creswell, John, 29, S.; boat builder, Hingham; Sept. 2, '62; M. O. June 2, '65; had served in Co. I, Fourth M. V. M., 3 mos. term; dead.

Damon, Andrew J., 19, S.; mason, Scituate; Sept. 2, '62; dis. disa., July 31, '63; dead.

Danbenmayer, Charles, 20, S.; farrier, West Cambridge; Sept. 2, '62; Pris. Aug. 19, '64, Weldon R. R.; supposed to have joined the Rebels and afterwards killed.

Day, Joshua D., 21, M.; shoemaker, Weymouth; June 26, '61, in Thirteenth Infty.; re-en. March 20, '64; trans. to Thirty-ninth; prom. Corp.; Pris. Aug. 19, '64; trans. to Thirty-second and M. O.

Dean, Warren F., 25, S.; farmer, Taunton; Sept. 23, '63, in Thirteenth Infty.; trans. to Thirty-ninth, thence to Thirty-second and M. O.

Delany, Jack M., 19, M.; printer, Worcester; Sept. 2, '62; des. July 9, '63.

Dodge, William G., 18, —; farmer, Essex; Sept. 2, '62; Pris. Aug. 19, '64; M. O. June 2, '65; 1913, Salem.

Earle, William H., 37, M.; carpenter, Melrose; Sept. 2, '62; dis. June 12, '65; had served in the Navy.

Elliot, Andrew L. (Mus.), 23, S.; shoemaker, Malden; Sept. 2, '62; M. O. June 5, '65.

Elliot, George A., 25, —; —, en. Boston; Aug. 8, '62; deserted.

Elwell, Daniel R., 22, S.; shoemaker, So. Scituate; Sept. 2, '62; Pris. Aug. 19, '64, to Feb. 24, '65; M. O. July 14, '65.

Fitzgerald, Michael A., 21, —; bootmaker, Boston; April 4, '62, in Thirteenth Infty.; Pris. Aug. 19, '64, to April 25, '65; M. O. May 17, '65.

Fitzgerald, William, 23, M.; shoemaker, Uxbridge; July 16, '63, in Twelfth Infty.; trans. to Thirty-ninth; wd. May 7, '64; Pris. Aug. 19, '64; trans. to Thirty-second and M. O.

Ford, Charles E. H., 22, S.; operative, Blackstone; Sept. 2, '62; M. O. June 2, '65.

Foster, Jacob, 21, —; —, —; Aug. 8, '62; des. Aug. —, '62.

French, Benjamin W., 18, S.; So. Scituate; Sept. 2, '62; dis. disa., Nov. 21, '62; 1913, Ridge Hill.

French, Charles E., 20, S.; shoemaker, Hingham; Sept. 2, '62; d. a prisoner May 19, '64, Salisbury, N. C.

French, Henry C. (Corp.), 26, S.; sailmaker, Hingham; Sept. 2, '62; prom. Sergt.; shot by Rebel guard Aug. 26, '64, Belle Isle, Richmond, Va.

Gardner, George D., 34, S.; painter, Hingham; Sept. 2, '62; d. Aug. 4, '65, City Point, Va.

Glines, Alvin R., 21, S.; farmer, Hingham; Sept. 2, '62; M. O. June 2, '65; 1913, No. Scituate.

Goodwin, Thomas, 23, S.; teamster, Bromfield, Me., cr. Charlestown; July 17, '63, in Twelfth Infty.; trans. to Thirty-ninth, thence to the Thirty-second and M. O.

Gorman, Michael, 22, S.; shoemaker, Lynn; Sept. 2, '62; Pris. Aug. 19, '64; d. Jan. 9, '65, Salisbury, N. C.

Hall, Samuel, 28, M.; picture-framer, Boston; Sept. 2, '62; prom. Corp.; M. O. June 2, '65; d. Oct. 3, 1912.

Ham, Henry W. (Sergt.), 27, S.; clerk, Boston; Sept. 2, '62; dis. disa., Jan. 31, '63; dead.

Hanson, Franklin K., 32, M.; shoemaker, So. Scituate; Sept. 2, '62; Pris. Aug. 19, '64; M. O. June 2, '65; dead.

Hatch, George C., 19, S.; clerk, West Cambridge; Sept. 2, '62; M. O. June 2, '65; 1913, Chicago.

Hatch, Grafton, 22, S.; carpenter, Mansfield or Marshfield; Sept. 2, '62; wd. May 5, '64; M. O. June 2, '65; dead.

Hayden, Zenas M. (Corp.), 26, M.; mechanic, Randolph; Sept. 2, '62; Pris., d. Feb. 4, '65, Salisbury, N. C.

Hayes, Edmund P., 18, S.; clerk, Westboro; March 24, '62, in Thirteenth Infty.; trans. to Thirty-ninth; wd. Aug. 18, '64; d. Sept. 15, '64, a returned prisoner, Annapolis, Md.

Haynes, Albert S., 20, S.; shoecutter, Hingham; d. of wds. June 11, '64, Hingham.

Hersey, Alfred, 29, M.; teamster, Hingham; Sept. 2, '62; M. O. June 2, '65.

Hersey, George L., 31, M.; shoemaker, Hingham; Sept. 2, '62; M. O. June 2, '65; dead.

Hersey, Henry F., 29, M.; carpenter, Hingham; Pris. Aug. 19, '64, to March 1, '65; M. O. June 2, '65; 1913, Soldiers' Home, Chelsea.

Hill, John M., 32, S.; bootmaker, Westboro; Feb. 27, '62, in Thirteenth Infty.; trans. to Thirty-ninth; dis. Feb. 17, '65, ex. of s.

Hutchins, Samuel W. (Corp.), 21, S.; plumber, Watertown; Sept. 2, '62; Pris. Aug. 19, '64, to Feb. 24, '65; M. O. June 2, '65; d. May 10, 1900, Guilford, Me.

Hyland, Albert (Wagoner), 21, —; —, Watertown; July 24, '62; des. Feb. 11, '63.

Jackson, William H., 25, M.; carpenter, Melrose; Sept. 2, '62; dis. disa., May 19, '64.

Jacobs, William H. (Corp.), 31, M.; blacksmith, Hingham; Sept. 2, '62; prom. 1st Sergt.; Pris. Aug. 19, '64, and escaped while on his way from Richmond to Salisbury; M. O. June 6, '65.

Jones, Charles S., 18, S.; clerk, Melrose; Sept. 2, '62; trans. March 31, '64, to Fiftieth Co., 2d Batt. V. R. C.; dis. June 24, '65; 1913, Chelsea.

Jones, George W., 22, M.; farmer, Randolph; Feb. 25, '64, in Twelfth Infty.; trans. to Thirty-ninth, thence to One Hundred and Seventeenth Co., 2d Batt. V. R. C., April 17, '65; dis. Oct. 12, '65.

Kennedy, John, 21, M.; cooper, Boston; en. July 29, '62; Pris. Aug. 19, '64; trans. May 5, '64, to V. R. C.

Lawless, Maurice (Mus.), 18, —; —, Malden; Sept. 2, '62; N. F. R.

Leach, Edmund C., 23, S.; blacksmith, Worcester; July 18, '63, in Twelfth Infty.; trans. to Thirty-ninth, thence to Thirty-second and M. O.

Leavitt, Henry W., 18, S.; shoemaker, Scituate; Dec. 8, '63; Pris. Aug. 19, '64; trans. to Thirty-second and M. O.

Lendall, Samuel N., 37, S.; seaman, Manchester; July 10, '63, in Twelfth Infty.; trans. to Thirty-ninth; dis. disa., Nov. 29, 64.

Leroy, Charles, 22, —; —, Hingham; Sept. 2, '62; M. O. June 2, '65; dead.

Lewis, James, 18, S.; carpenter, Boston; June 26, '61, in Twelfth Infty.; re-en. Jan. 5, '64; trans. to Thirty-ninth; wd. May 31, '64; dis. on account of wds. March 8, '65.

Lincoln, Benjamin C., 22, S.; bookkeeper, Boston; Sept. 2, '62; prom. Corp.; dis. Aug. 25, '63, for commission, U. S. C. T.; Captain Second Colored Infty.; Major, July 30, '64; d. Key West, Fla., from wds. rec'd March 6, '65, Natural Bridge, Fla.

McCann, John, 19, —; —, Belmont; Sept. 2, '62; N. F. R.

McNaughton, Michael, 36, M.; carpenter, Boston; Sept. 2, '62; trans. Jan. 5, '64, to V. R. C.; dead.

Miller, George L., 23, M.; upholsterer, Boston; Sept. 2, '62; d. Feb. 26, '63, as Corp., Poolesville, Md.

Miller, Henry F., 21, S.; shoemaker, Hingham; Sept. 2, '62; prom. Corp.; d. of wds. May 25, '64, Washington, D. C., dead.

Minard, Nelson C., 21, S.; clerk, Chelsea; Aug. 1, '62, in Thirteenth Infty.; re-en. March 31, '64; trans. to Thirty-ninth, thence to Thirty-second and M. O.

Mordo, John A., 30, M.; clerk, Boston; Sept. 2, '62; trans. to Thirty-seventh Co., 2d Batt. V. R. C.; dis. June 28, '65; dead.

Murdock, George, 19, S.; farmer, Boston; June 26, '61, in Twelfth Infty.; re-en. Jan. 1, '64; trans. to Thirty-ninth, thence to Thirty-second and M. O.

Murphy, Thomas, 30, M.; shoemaker, Roxbury; Aug. 5, '63, in Thirteenth Infty.; Pris. and d. Jan. 1, '65, Salisbury, N. C.

Neal, John S., 30, M.; shoemaker, Hingham; Sept. 2, '62; Pris. Aug. 19, '64; d. Jan. 16, '65, Salisbury, N. C.

Newcomb, Levi, 45, M.; mariner, Hingham; Sept. 2, '62; dis. disa., June 11, '63; dead.

O'Hara, Patrick, 25, —; —, Watertown; June 29, '62; des. Dec. 27, '62.

Ord, John, 33, M.; farmer, Belmont; Sept., '62; trans. March 7, '64, to Co. C, Twenty-fourth V. R. C.; dis. June 28, '65; 1913, Ridgebury, Conn.

O'Sullivan, Thomas, 20, S.; seaman, Boston; Oct. 13, '63, in Twelfth Infty.; trans. to Thirty-ninth; wd. Aug. 18, '64; trans. to Thirty-second and M. O.

Parsons, John G., 29, S.; painter, Boston; July 25, '63, in Twelfth Infty.; trans. to Thirty-ninth, thence to Thirty-second and M. O.

Penniman, John M., 19, M.; shoemaker, So. Scituate; Sept. 2, '62; prom. Sergt.; wd. March 31, '65; dis. disa., July 25, '65; dead.

Pike, Jacob F., 22, S.; farmer, Melrose; Sept. 2, '62; M. O. June 13, '65.

Pingree, Charles C. (Sergt.), 25, S.; clerk, Boston; Sept. 2, '62; M. O. June 2, '65.

Pomeroy, Alonzo, 26, M.; farmer, Roxbury; Sept. 2, '62; wd. May 5, '64; M. O. as Corp. June 2, '65; 1913, Paris, Me.

Poole, Charles N., 18, S.; shoemaker, Hingham; Sept. 2, '62; wd. May 5, '64; dis. disa., Dec. 17, '64; 1913, Pembroke.

Prouty, Benjamin W., 34, S.; farmer, So. Scituate; Sept. '62; dis. disa., Sept. 12, '64; dead.

Prouty, Elijah, 26, M.; shoemaker, Weymouth; Sept. 2, '62; d. Dec. 9, '63, Washington, D. C.

Prouty, Isaac, 44, M.; shoemaker, So. Scituate; Sept. 2, '62; trans. to Co. D, Twelfth V. R. C., Sept. 7, '63; dis. June 28, '65; dead.

Prouty, John H. (Sergt.), 23, M.; clicker, So. Scituate; Sept. 2, '62; prom. 2d Lieut. June 7, '65; M. O. as Sergt. June 2, '65; 1913, Ridge Hill.

Prouty, William, Jr., 28, M.; teamster, So. Scituate; Sept. 2, '62; M. O. June 2, '65; dead.

Roby, David F., 28, M.; mechanic, Cambridge; Sept. 2, '62; dis. disa., Jan. 31, '63; dead.

Russell, Harry H., 21, M.; cook, So. Danvers; Sept. 2, '62; M. O. June 9, '65, Washington, D. C.

Sanborn, William H., 18, S.; pedler, Boston; June 26, '61, in Twelfth Infty.; re-en. Jan. 1, '64; trans. to Thirty-ninth, thence to Thirty-second and M. O.

Shaw, Patrick J., 29, —; blacksmith, Weymouth; Dec. 10, '63; in Twelfth Infty.; trans. to Thirty-ninth; Pris. Aug. 19, '64; trans. as Corp. to Thirty-second and M. O.

Sherman, Calvin F., 17, S.; farmer, So. Scituate; Sept. '62; M. O., June 2, '65.

Short, Thomas G., 18, S.; moulder, Cambridge; Sept. 2, '62; prom. Corp.; d. as prisoner, Jan. 9, '65, Salisbury, N. C.

Simmons, Thomas, 33, M.; farmer, So. Scituate; Sept. 2, '62; d. March 3, '64, Washington, D. C.

Skeele, Milo B., 24, M.; teamster, Boston; Sept. 2, '62; M. O. June 2, '65; dead.

Skinner, John B., 40, M.; farmer, Boston; Nov. 5, '63, in Thirteenth Infty.; trans. to Thirty-ninth, thence to thirty-second and M. O.

Smith, Stratton V., 34, M.; clerk, Charlestown; July 9, '63; in Twelfth Infty.; trans. to Thirty-ninth; d. Nov. 16, '64, a prisoner, Salisbury, N. C.

Spaulding, Charles A. (Mus.), 21, S.; farmer, Boston; Sept. 2, '62; Pris. Aug. 19 '64; M. O. June 13, '65.

Spear, Edward A. F., 33, M.; shoemaker, Hingham; Sept. 2, '62; Pris. Aug. 19, '64; d. Jan. 21, '65, Salisbury, N. C.

Sprague, Seth M., 19, S.; farmer, Hingham; Sept. 2, '62; M. O. June 2, '65; 1913, So. Hingham.

Sprague, Thomas, 35, S.; farmer, Hingham; Sept. 2, '62; d. July 5, '64, Washington, D. C.

Stebbins, Thaddeus S., 32, M.; bookbinder, Melrose; Sept. 2, '62; for some reason, not stated, trans. to Thirty-second Infty.

Stetson, Warren, 25, M.; clerk, Braintree; July 17, '63; in Twelfth Infty.; trans. to Thirty-ninth; M. O. May 18, '65.

Stockwell, Alonzo G., 22, S.; farmer, Hingham; Sept. 2, '62; wd. Aug. 18, '64; dis. Sept. 1, '65, as of One Hundred and Fifth Co., Second Batt., V. R. C.; dead.

Stone, Henry D. (Corp.), 18, S.; clerk, Melrose; Sept. 2, '62; dis. disa., Sept. 30, '63; later in Co. H, Fifty-ninth Infty.; d. Togus, Me., April, 1912.

Sylvester, John Q. A., 40, M.; farmer, Randolph; Sept. 2, '62; dis. disa., Jan. 10, '63; later in Co. H, Second H. Arty.; dead.

Thayer, Noah W., 31, S.; bootmaker, Weymouth; Dec. 11, '63; in Twelfth Infty.; trans. to Thirty-ninth; d. a prisoner, Nov. 16, '64, Salisbury, N. C.

Thomas, Alpheus (Corp.), 25, M.; shoemaker, So. Scituate; Sept. 2, '62; prom. Sergt.; Second Lieut. Sept. 15, '64; vide Co. K.; had served in Co. I, Fourth M. V. M. three mos. term, 1861; dead.

Thomas, Orson C., 28; —, —; Watertown; July 15, '62; des. Aug. —, '62.

Thomas, William O., 32, M.; farmer, So. Scituate; Sept. 2, '62; M. O. June 2, '65; 1913, Hanson.

Tisdale, Charles H., 29, M.; shoemaker, Hingham; Sept. 2, '62; dis. disa., Nov. 4, '62; dead.

Torrey, Franklin J., 26, M.; butcher, Hingham; Sept. 2, '62; wd. May 8, '64; dis. disa., Dec. '65; dead.

Van Winkle, Henry M. (1st Sergt.), 22, S.; dentist, Boston; Sept. 2, '62; dis. O. W. D., June 11, '63; vide First U. S. C. T.

Warren, Daniel S., 36, W.; bootmaker, Hopkinton; July 16, '61, in Thirteenth Infty.; for some reason, not stated, he evidently had to make up time and was trans. to the Thirty-ninth, thence to the Thirty-second and M. O.

Webster, Samuel D., 16, S.; printer, Martinsburg, Va.; Feb. 28, '62, in Thirteenth Infty.; trans. as Mus. to the Thirty-ninth; dis. Feb. 28, '65, ex. of s.

Welch, Augustus W., 32, S.; painter, Roxbury; July 9, '63, in Twelfth Infty.; trans. to Thirty-ninth, thence to Thirty-second and M. O.

Weston, Charles B. (Wagoner), 34, M.; carpenter, East Fairport, Vt.; Sept. 2, '62; N. F. R.

White, George W., 23, M.; shoemaker, Scituate; Dec. 8, '63; wd. May 12, '64; trans. to Thirty-second and M. O., 1913, Randolph.

White, Jeremiah C., 23, S.; bookmaker, Boston; June 26, '61, in Twelfth Infty.; his record seems to be irregular, though he was trans. to the Thirty-ninth, thence to the Thirty-second and M. O.

Whiting, Franklin T., 21, S.; teamster, Pembroke; Sept. 2, '62; M. O. June 2, '65; 1913, No. Abington.

Whiting, George W., 22, S.; hostler, Pembroke; Sept. 2, '62; dis. disa., Feb. 8, '64; dead.

Whiting, T. D., en. July —, '62; N. F. R. save "deserted, Aug. —, '62."

Wilder, Albert, 21, S.; shoemaker, Hingham; Sept. 2, '62; d. from wds. June 1, '64, Washington, D. C.

Wilson, John, 2d, 23, —; seaman, Charlestown; July 27, '63, in Thirteenth Infty.; trans. to the Thirty-ninth, thence to the Thirty-second and M. O.

Woodbury, William H., 28, M.; lawyer, Boston; Sept. 2, '62; dis. disa., Jan. 9, '63; dead.

Young, Charles E., 32, M.; shoemaker; So. Scituate; Sept. 2, '62; prom. Corp.; wd. May 8, '64; M. O. June 1, '65; dead.

COMPANY H

Dorchester

CAPTAIN

Charles N. Hunt, 39, M.; stonecutter, Quincy; Sept. 2, '62; M. O. June 2, '65.

FIRST LIEUTENANTS

Robert Rhodes, 46, M.; contractor, Dorchester; Sept. 2, '62; res. disa., Nov. 11, '62.

Willard C. Kinsley, from Co. E, Nov. 13, '62; prom. Captain, Co. K, March 30, '64.

Luther F. Wyman, from Co. K, March 20, '64; June 16, '64, while on detached service, guarding Rebel prisoners, Rock Island, Ill., was prom. Captain in Second U. S. Vols., composed of former Confederates, Feb. 18, '65; M. O. Nov. 7, 1865; d. "out West," 1892.

SECOND LIEUTENANTS

Robert Williams, 24, S.; brittania-maker; Dorchester; Sept. 2, '62; res. disa., Feb. 2, '63; d. Ashland, Nov. 12, '94.

Charles W. Hanson, from Sergt. Major, Jan. 25, '63; trans. to Co. E as 2d Lieut.

John H. Dusseault, from Co. E, Oct. 20, '63; wd. slightly three times at Spottsylvania; severely, Aug. 18, '64, Weldon R. R.; Prom. 1st Lieut. Sept. 8, '64; not mustered; dis. from wds. Dec. 10, '64; sealer of weights and measures, Somerville; 1913, Somerville. Lt. D.'s printed account of Co. E used extensively in this book.

Charles K. Conn, from Sergt. Major Feb. 1, '65; prom. 1st Lieut. March, '65.

ENLISTED MEN

Arris, Herbert, 18, S.; milkman, Dorchester; Sept. 2, '62; wd. May 5, '64, Wilderness; M. O. June 2, '65.

Baker, Frederick, 18, S.; laborer, Roxbury, cr. Dorchester; Feb. 15, '64; k Aug. 19, '64.

Barker, Alfred H., 19, S.; teamster, Dorchester; Sept. 2, '62; d. Jan. 3, '64, Culpepper, Va.

Barker, George W., 18, S.; junk dealer, Dorchester; Aug. 31, '62; trans. Feb. 15, '64, Ninety-sixth Co., 2d Batt. V. R. C.; dis. from hospital, Baltimore, Md., Oct. 18, '64; 1913, Dorchester.

Barrett, William I., b. Sept. 13, 1839; 22, S.; painter, Dorchester; Sept. 2, '62; M. O. June 2, '65; house painting; 1913, Lynn.

Bartoll, William H., 20, S.; painter, Marblehead; July 10, '63, in Twelfth Infty.; trans. to Thirty-ninth; d. July 1, '64, Washington, D. C.

Beck, William J., 35, —; carpenter, Lynn; Sept. 2, '62; des. Aug. 28, '62, quitting before he was mustered, but such is the record.

Bergeson, Joseph, 22, S.; farmer, Boston; Dec. 4, '63; wd. May 10, '64; dis. disa., Oct. 10, '64.

Billings, George W., 31, M.; candle maker, Dorchester; Sept. 2, '62; dis. May 20, '65; 1913, Roxbury.

Bird, Joel E., 18, S.; cabinet-maker, Dorchester; Sept. 2, '62; d. Dec. 20, '63.

Blanchard, Brainard P., 18, S.; clerk, Boston; Aug. 18, '62, in Thirteenth Infty.; re-en. Jan 4, '64; trans. to Thirty-ninth; dis. Aug. 16, '64, for commission in U. S. C. T.; 1st Lieut. One Hundred and Sixteenth Colored Infty.; bvt. Captain March 13, '65; M. O. Aug. 7, '67.

Blanchard, William F., 23, S.; seaman, Boston; July 16, '61, in Thirteenth Infty.; re-en. Jan. 4, '64; trans. to Thirty-ninth; dis. Aug. 16, '64, for commission U. S. C. T.; 2d Lieut. Twenty-seventh U. S. Colored Infty.; 1st Lieut. April 6, '65; bvt. Capt. March 13, '65; M. O. Sept. 21, '65.

Bouldry, Welcome W., farmer, Raynham; 37, M.; Sept. 2, '62; d. Jan. 4, '64, Alexandria, Va.

Bowen, Edward J., 20, S.; clerk, Dorchester; Sept. 2, '62; dis. Sept. 10, '64, for commission U. S. C. T.; 1913, Central Falls, R. I.

Bradshaw, Elbridge, b. April 24, 1831; (Corp.), 31, M.; confectioner, Dorchester; Sept. 2, '62; prom. Sergt.; 2d Lieut. Jan. 7, '65; M. O. as Sergt. June 2, '65; salesman and librarian; 1913, librarian, lower hall, Boston Public Library.

Bronsdon, Frederick H., 24, S.; mechanic, Dorchester; Sept. 2, '62; M. O. May 20, '65; d. Dec. 31, 1911.

Brown, George, 27, S.; laborer, Eastham; July 27, '63; trans. to Thirty-second and M. O.

Brunel, Joseph, 18, S.; laborer, Roxbury; Feb. 9, '64; missing since Aug. 19, '64; J. H. Eames says, "Pris. and des."

Burke, Christopher, 18, S.; laborer, Dedham; July 28, '63, in Thirteenth Infty.; trans. to Thirty-ninth, thence to Thirty-second and M. O.

Carr, Bernard, 26, —; laborer, Boston; Sept. 2, '62; record says, "not mustered"; N. F. R.

Carroll, John, 42, S.; tailor, Dorchester; Sept. 2, '62; dis. disa., Dec. 19, '64.

Carter Calvin, 31, M.; farmer, Petersham; Sept. 22, '63, in Twelfth Infty.; record has, "dis. disa., Dec. 11, '63,"; why is his name carried on the rolls of the Thirty-ninth?

Chase, Andrew J., 26, S.; carpenter, Roxbury; Oct. 3, '63, in Twelfth Infty.; trans. to the Thirty-ninth, thence to Thirty-second and M. O.; this comrade was an inventor of great distinction, having devised the cold blast refrigerator cars, now in general use, enabling meats to be transferred over the entire country and across the sea, thus making him one of the world's great benefactors; he died in the Chelsea Soldiers' Home Jan. 17, 1913.

Chase, William, 21, S.; seaman, Albany, N. Y., cr. Dennis; July 25, '63, in Thirteenth Infty.; trans. to Thirty-ninth, thence to Thirty-second and M. O.

Childs, Edward J., b. Dec. 7, 1844; 19, S.; curtain fixtures, Dorchester; Sept. 2, '62; Pris. Aug. 19, '64, to Feb. 27, '65; M. O. June 9, '65; shoemaking; 1913, Natick.

Childs, Francis J., 18, S.; shoemaker, Dorchester; Sept. 2, '62; M. O. June 2, '65; 1913, Marlborough.

Claffey, John, 28, —; carder, Pittsfield; July 14, '63, in Twelfth Infty.; trans. to Thirty-ninth; M. O. May 15, '65.

Clark, William H., 16, S.; clerk, Dorchester; Sept. 2, '62; dis. May 18, '65; real name, Wm. H. Signor, vide letter, W. D., June 9, 1906; d. about 1900, Danville, Va., while superintendent of National Cemetery.

Collins, Patrick, 39, S.; laborer, Dorchester; Sept. 2, '62; d. a prisoner Nov. 18, '64, Salisbury, N. C.

Combs, Erastus N., 23, M.; farmer, Boylston; July 13, '63, in Twelfth Infty.; trans. to Thirty-ninth; des. July 15, '64.

Corcoran, George, 22, —; silk dyer, Salem; des. Aug. 29, '62.

Craig, Charles H., 22, S.; painter, Dorchester; Sept. 2, '62; wd. May 8, '64; M. O. June 2, '64; 1913, Needham.

Cram, Jesse T., 22, M.; teamster, Milton; Oct. 22, '63, in Twelfth Infty.; trans. to Thirty-ninth, thence to Co. C, Nineteenth V. R. C.; dis. Aug. 3, '65.

Dailey, Michael, 18, S.; farmer, Dorchester; Sept. 2, '62; Pris. Aug. 19, '64, to Feb. 26, '65; M. O. June 2, '65.

Damon, Charles E., 21, M.; bootmaker, Warren; July 14, '63, in Twelfth Infty.; trans. to Thirty-ninth; M. O. June 1, '65.

Dana, Dexter E., 18, S.; student, Dorchester; Sept. 2, '62; trans. Jan. 5, '64, V. R. C.; 1913, Burlington, Wis.

Davis, John, 45, M.; morocco dresser, Lynn; Sept. 2, '62; Pris. Aug. 19, '64; M. O. May 30, '65.

Dimond, John, 36, M.; stonecutter, Dorchester; Sept. 2, '62; wd. May 8, '64, Spottsylvania; dis. disa., May 15, '65.

Doody, John, 32, M.; laborer, Dorchester; Dec. 13, '63; Pris. Aug. 19, '64; d. Nov. 17, '64, Annapolis, Md.

Driscoll, James, 18, S.; curtain fixtures, Dorchester; Sept. 2, '62; d. Nov. 14, '64, Ft. Schuyler, N. Y. Harbor.

Dunn, Charles (Wagoner), 38, M.; teamster, Dorchester; Sept. 2, '62; trans. to One Hundred and Twelfth Co., Twelfth Batt., V. R. C.; dis. disa., Sept. 10, '64.

Ellis, Charles J., 24, S.; farmer, Dorchester; Sept. 2, '62; dis. disa., Feb. 5, '63.

Farren, James, 25, M.; laborer, Dorchester; Sept. 2, '62; wd. May 5, '64; Pris. Aug. 19, '64, to Feb. 26, '65; M. O. June 2, '65.

Farrington, David S., 31, S.; hostler, Dorchester; Sept. 2, '62; wd. May 8, '64; prom. Corp., Sergt., May 1, '65; M. O. June 2, '65.

Ferguson, John, 22, —; farmer, Boston; des. Aug. 29, '62.

Fink, John, 24, S.; bar keeper, Boston, cr. Worcester; July 24, '63, in Thirteenth Infty.; trans. to Thirty-ninth, thence to Thirty-second and M. O.

Fish, Isaac H., 38, M.; confectioner, Dorchester; wd. "June 3, '65," so says the roll at State House, but '64 is evidently intended; M. O. June 10, '65; 1913, Boston.

Fisher, Richard H. (1st Sergt.), 28, M.; stonecutter, Dorchester; Sept. 2, '62; wd. May 5, '64; prom. 2d Lieut. Sept. 8, '64; not mustered; dis. disa., May 21, 1865.

Fitz, Thomas D., 22, S.; printer, Dorchester; Sept. 2, '62; wd. June 22, '64; M. O. June 2, '65.

Fobes, John H., 23, S.; teamster, Dorchester; Sept. 2, '62; M. O. June 2, '65; d. Sept. 7, 1913, Neponset.

Follen, John, 18, S.; farmer, Dorchester; Sept. 2, '62; wd. May 12, '64; dis. July 8, '65; 1913, Roxbury.

French, George L., 18, S.; nail maker, Dorchester; Sept. 2, '62; d. Dec. 9, '63, Alexandria, Va.

Gammon, Randall T., 24, S.; clerk, Abington; Aug. 3, '63; d. a prisoner, Nov. 17, '64, Salisbury, N. C.

Gardner, Elisha P. F., b. Feb. 12, 1833 (Corp.), 29, M.; expressman, Dorchester; Sept. 2, '61; dis. disa., May 4, '63; later, Co. B, Second H. Arty.; expressing for many years; met his death, Jan. 28, 1913—the funny man of "Poet's Corner," Nantucket.

Geouggenheimer, Samuel, 21, S.; —, France, cr. Boston; July 21, '63, in Thirteenth Infty.; trans. to Thirty-ninth, thence to Thirty-second and M. O.

Gerrish, Timothy, 21, S.; teamster, Dorchester; Sept. 2, '62; M. O. June 14, '65.

Gline, David, 23, S.; farmer, en. Boston, cr. Taunton; Jan. 2, '64; trans. to Thirty-second and M. O.

Goodhue, Manassah C., 40, M.; blacksmith, Dorchester; Sept. 2, '62; May 18, '65.

Grover, Jeremiah O., 28, M.; farmer, Wrentham; July 15, '63, in Twelfth Infty.; trans. to Thirty-ninth, thence to Thirty-second and M. O.

Harris, Sullivan B., 28, M.; carpenter, Dorchester; Sept. 2, '62; k. June 23, '64, Petersburg.

Healey, Stephen C., 21, M.; clerk, Dorchester; Sept. 2, '62; dis. disa., Dec. 30, '62.

Henderson, Oliver F., 23, S.; sailor, Acton; July 20, '63, in Twelfth Infty.; trans. to Thirty-ninth, thence to Thirty-second and M. O.

Henry, Michael, 36, M.; mason, Dorchester; Sept. 2, '62; dis. disa., April 11, '64.

Hill, Daniel G., 26, M.; confectioner, Dorchester; Sept. 2, '62; M. O. June 2, '65.

Hill, Gilman L., 27, M.; teamster, Dorchester; Sept. 2, '62; prom. Corp.; wd. May 11, '64; M. O. June 2, '65.

Hill, Joseph, 23, M.; teamster, Dorchester; Sept. 2, '62; trans. Oct. 25, '63, to V. R. C.; dis. from Forty-sixth Co., Second Batt., Aug. 25, '65.

Holmes, George (Corp.), 40, M.; building mover, Dorchester; Sept. 2, '62; d. Aug. 6, '64; W. D. letter June 4, '69.

Holmes, Robert T., 18, M.; farmer, Dorchester; Sept. 2, '62; Pris. Aug. 19, '64; N. F. R.

Hunt, Sylvester, 23, S.; teamster, Acton; July 9, '63, in Twelfth Infty.; trans. to Thirty-ninth, thence to Thirty-second and M. O.

Jenkins, Albert, 26, M.; shoemaker, Stoneham; July 10, '61, in Thirteenth Infty.; re-en. Jan. 4, '64; trans. to Thirty-ninth, thence to Thirty-second and M. O.

Jones, David L., 18, S.; shoemaker, Boston; July 10, '61, in Thirteenth Infty.; re-en. Jan. 4, '64; trans. as Sergt. to Thirty-ninth; dis. as supernumerary, July 1, '64; later in Co. G, Fourth Cavalry.

Jones, Llewellyn, 20, S.; painter, Stoneham; July 10, '61, in Thirteenth Infty.; re-en. Jan. 4, '64; trans. as Corp. to Thirty-ninth; dis. as Supernumerary, July 1, '64.

Johnson, David, 21, S.; farmer, Natick; July 16, '63; in Twelfth Infty.; trans. to Thirty-ninth, thence to Thirty-second and M. O.

Johnson, William, 1st, 28, S.; seaman, Brighton; July 25, '63; in Thirteenth Infty.; trans. to Thirty-ninth, thence to Thirty-second and M. O.

Jordan, Thomas W. D., 18, M.; teamster, Dorchester; Sept. 2, '62; M. O. June 2, '65; d. April, 1911, S. H., Chelsea.

Kelley, Thomas, 22, S.; laborer, Dorchester; Sept. 2, '62; wd. May 8, '64; Pris. Aug. 19, '64, to Feb. 24, '65; M. O. June 13, '65; 1913, Washington, D. C.

Keniston, William H., 28, S.; teamster, Lowell; July 9, '63; in Twelfth Infty.; trans. to Thirty-ninth; Pris. Aug. 19, '64; trans. to Thirty-second and M. O.

Kerr, John, 40, S.; tailor, Boston; Sept. 2, '62; trans. to Co. B, Twenty-first Regiment, V. R. C., Sept. 16, '63; dis. July 31, '65.

Kimball, Charles W., 21, M.; clerk, Dorchester; Sept. 2, '62; trans. to V. R. C. May 5, '64.

Kimball, Eugene F., 18, M.; milkman, Dorchester; Sept. 2, '62; Pris. Aug. 19, '64, to May 1, '65; M. O. July 15, '65.

Landers, Daniel, 45, M.; laborer, Dorchester; Sept. 2, '62; dis. disa., Jan. 29, '63.

Langley, Samuel A., 18, S.; porter, Roxbury; Oct. 21, '62, in Thirteenth Infty.; trans. to Thirty-ninth; dis. Oct. 21, '64, ex. of s.

Lines, Daniel, 26, M.; laborer, Dorchester; Sept. 2, '62; wd. May 8, '64; M. O. June 2, '65; 1913, No. Billerica.

Loring, Abraham, 43, M.; carpenter, Dorchester; Sept. 2, '62; dis. disa., Dec. 29, '62.

Loring, A. A. (Corp.), 43, M.; carpenter, Dorchester; Sept. 2, '62; no M. O.

Lothrop, Alanson A. (Corp.), 24, M.; curtain fixtures, Dorchester; Sept. 2, '62; wd. May 10, '64; M. O. May 31, '65.

McCarthy, Eugene, 25, S.; hostler, Dorchester; Sept. 2, '62; Pris. Aug. 19, '64; dis. May 15, '65.

McFarland, William, 44, M.; laborer, Dorchester; Sept. 2, '62; dis. disa., Jan. 29, '63.

McGaken, Robert T., 22, S.; farmer, Dorchester; Sept. 2, '62; as Corp., wd. and missing since March 31, '65.

Makell, Charles, 32, M.; barber, Dennis; July 28, '63, in Thirteenth Infty.; trans. to Thirty-ninth; M. O. June 6, '65.

Marty, Jacob, 35, S.; farmer, Taunton; July 27, '63, in Thirteenth Infty.; trans. to Thirty-ninth, thence to Thirty-second and M. O.

Maxwell, James H., 29, M.; farmer, Monterey; July 14, '63, in Twelfth Infty.; trans. to Thirty-ninth, thence as Corp. to Thirty-second and M. O.

Millett, George C., 34, M.; farmer, Dorchester; Sept. 2, '62; Pris.; d. Nov. 15, '64, Salisbury, N. C.

Millett, John H., 34, M.; teamster, Boston; Nov. 16, '63; d. a prisoner Dec. 1, '64, Salisbury, N. C.

Monk, George W., b. Aug. 24, 1843; (Mus.), 19, S.; musician, Dorchester; Sept. 2, '62; M. O. June 10, '65; musician; 1913, Quincy.

Monk, Robert (Sergt.), 23, S.; stonecutter, Dorchester; Sept. 2, '62; Pris. Aug. 19, '64, to Feb. 26, '65; M. O. June 2, '65; his diary useful in compiling this book; d. in Quincy, Aug. 15, 1870; bur. Mt. Wollaston Cemetery with Grand Army and Masonic honors and rites.

Morrison, James H. (Sergt.), 28, M.; carriage-trimmer, Dorchester; Sept. 2, '62; prom. 1st Sergt.; 2d Lieut. Dec. 20, '64; not mustered; dis. as Sergt., June 13, 1865.

Murray, Thomas, 19, S.; cooper, Dorchester; Sept. 2, '62; Pris. Aug. 19, '64; d. March 27, '65, from injuries rec'd on R. R.

Newton, Benjamin S. (Sergt.), 28, S.; car-driver, Dorchester; Sept. 2, '62; M. O. June, '65; 1913, No. Rumford, Me.

Norton, Frank F., 28, M.; druggist, Dorchester; Sept. 2, '62; Pris. d. April 14, '64, Andersonville.

Page, Chester, S. 23, M.; stonecutter, Dorchester; Sept., '62; prom. Corp.; Sergt. Feb. 1, '64; M. O. June 2, '65.

Palmer, William, 18, S.; teamster, Boston; Sept. 2, '62; N. F. R.

Perry, Oliver H., 39, M.; teamster, Dorchester; Sept. 2, '62; M. O. June 2, '65.

Patterson, Joseph, 30, S.; mason, Dorchester; Sept. 2, '62; dis. disa., Jan. 29, '63.

Phelps, John, 31, S.; printer, Dorchester; Sept. 2, '62; d. Aug. 28, '64, from wds. rec'd May 8, '64.

Pierce, William L. G., 32, M.; apothecary, Lincoln; July 14, '63, in Twelfth Infty.; trans. to Thirty-ninth, thence to Thirty-second and M. O.

Prescott, Benjamin F., 30, M.; teamster, Dorchester; Sept. 2, '62; prom. Corp.; Pris. Aug. 19, '64, to March 3, '65; M. O. June 13, '65.

Preston, John, 25, S.; laborer, Dorchester; Sept. 2, '62; dis. disa., Jan. 29, '63.

Richards, Edward D., 30, M.; millwright, Dorchester; Sept. 2, '62; k. May 23, '64.

Richards, John, 30, M.; sailmaker, Dorchester; Sept. 2, '62; wd. May 10, '64; dis. June 1, '65.

Richardson, Charles W., 25, S.; mechanic, Dorchester; Sept. 2, '62; prom. Sergt.; d. March 28, '65.

Robie, John E., 18, S.; jig sawyer, Dorchester; Sept. 2, '62; k. Aug. 19, '64.

Rouse, Stephen N., 21, S.; carpenter, Dorchester; Sept. 2, '62; M. O. June 10, '65; d. Washington, D. C.

Russell, George S., 23, S.; iceman, Dorchester; Sept. 2, '62; dis. disa., Feb. 3, '63; d. about 1909, Pembroke.

Savil, Samuel O. (Corp.), 22, S.; wheelwright, Dorchester; Sept. 2, '62; was a prisoner for a time; M. O. June 2, '65.

Seaverns, Henry A. (Sergt.), 20, S.; machinist, Dorchester; Sept. 2, '62; 2d Lieut. March 30, '64; vide Co. K.

Shean, Patrick, 27, M.; hostler, Dorchester; Sept. 2, '62; Pris. Aug. 19, '64; M. O. May 13, '65.

Signor, W. H.; vide Wm. H. Clark.

Smith, Henry W., 27, M.; carpenter, Dorchester; Sept. 2, '62; M. O. June 2, '65; 1913, Boston.

Smith, Richard C., 36, M.; turner, Dorchester; Sept. 2, '62; dis. disa., Feb. 2, '63.

Southworth, Dallas, 18, S.; apothecary, Dorchester; Sept. 2, '62; Pris. Aug. 14, '64, to Feb. 26, '65; no M. O.

Stanley, Francis A., 32, M.; carpenter, Dorchester; Sept. 2, '62; trans. U. S. Navy April 19, '64; 1913, Holbrook.

Stone, Andrew C., 22, M.; blacksmith, Dorchester; Sept. 2, '62; k. May 5, '64.

Sumner, Franklin H., 26, M.; teamster, Dorchester; Sept. 2, '65; Pris. Aug. 19, '64; d. from wds. Feb. 25, '65.

Sumner, William S., 20, S.; carpenter, Dorchester; Sept. 2, '62; M. O. June 2, '65; d. Aug. 18, 1910, Jamaica Plain.

Sweetland, Benjamin E., 33, M.; farmer, Dorchester; Sept. 2, '62; M. O. June 2, '65.

Thomas, George N. B., 18, S.; confectioner, Dorchester; Sept. 2, '62; Pris. Aug. 19, '64; dis. May 18, '65, O. W. D., Tilton General Hosp., Delaware.

Tileston, Ebenezer (Corp.), 20, S.; clerk, Dorchester; Sept. 2, '62; d. March 12, '65, a paroled prisoner, Annapolis, Md.

Tileston, Lemuel (Corp.), 19, S.; clerk, Dorchester; Sept. 2, '62; missing after May 8, '64, N. F. R., though it is probable that he d. in rebel prison.

Toombs, Elliott L., 26, S.; boatmaker, Weymouth; des. Aug. 28, '62.

Veit, Frederick, 32, M.; bootmaker, Dorchester; Sept. 2, '62; k. May 10, '64, Spottsylvania.

Walford, Thomas, 25, S.; carpenter, Seekonk; July 28, '63, in Thirteenth Infty.; trans. to Thirty-ninth, thence to Thirty-second and M. O.

Wares, Franklin, 25, S.; painter, Huntington; July 20, '63, in Twelfth Infty.; trans. to Thirty-ninth, thence to Thirty-second and M. O.; also given as M. O. in the Thirty-ninth, June 5, '65.

Wheeler, Nathaniel J., 24, S.; laborer, Boston; July 13, '63, in Twelfth Infty.; trans. to Thirty-ninth, thence to Thirty-second and M. O.; also said to have been M. O. from the Twelfth.

Whiley, James, 19, S.; painter, Somerville; Sept. 2, '62; M. O. July 14, '65.

Whittier, Leavitt, 21, S.; marketman, Dorchester; Sept. 2, '62; wd. Aug. 18, '64; M. O. May 18, '65.

Wright, Theodore S., 24, M.; tinner, Pittsfield; July 14, '63, in Twelfth Infty.; trans. to Thirty-ninth; dis. disa., Feb. 9, '65.

Wyman, George, 32, M.; stonecutter, Dorchester; Sept. 2, '62; k. May 5, '64, Wilderness.

COMPANY I

Natick

CAPTAINS

Ephraim H. Brigham, 40, M.; Deputy Sheriff, Natick; Aug. 25, '62; dis. disa., Sept. 4, '64; d. Aug. 21, 1877.

John D. Reed, from 1st Lieut., Sept. 6, '64; M. O. June 2, 1865; was born in Taunton, Mar. 15, 1827; in grocery business in Taunton till his death, Sept. 16, 1890; a member of the Winslow Congregational Church, he was esteemed by all.

FIRST LIEUTENANTS

Simon Mulligan, 36, M.; trader, Natick; Aug. 25, '62; dis. disa., Sept. 19, '63; d. Nov. 15, 1905; b. Boston, Mar. 1, 1825, of Irish and Scotch ancestry; he was educated in the Boston Schools, going thence to Natick and there learning the shoemaker's trade; later as a sailor, he was shipwrecked on the Cape Verde Islands; later still, he was a Californian Argonaut and, at his death, was a member and director in the Society of California Pioneers of "'49"; after the war he conducted a prosperous restaurant and billiard saloon; a member of the Masonic Order, he was also prominent in the councils of Post 63, G. A. R., where his ability in dramatics and recitations was of signal service; his form and bearing readily proclaimed him a gentleman of the "Old School."

Wm. G. Sheen, temporarily from Co. D, Oct. '63; thence as 1st Lieut. to Co. G.

John D. Reed, from Co. F, Sept. 20, '63; wd. Aug. 18, '64; prom. Captain Co. I.

William H. Brown, from 2d Lieut.; M. O. June 2, 1865.

SECOND LIEUTENANTS

William H. Brown, 27, S.; cordwainer, Natick; Aug. 25, '62; 1st Lieut. Sept. 8, '64; vide Co. I; had been 1st Sergt., Co. H, Thirteenth Massachusetts Volunteers, was dis. to receive promotion in the Thirty-ninth.

Oliver P. Ricker, from Co. B, Sept. 8, '64; M. O. June 6, 1865; Adjutant Post 113, Boston.

ENLISTED MEN

Adams, James C., 21, —; —, Concord; July 16, '63; d. July 14, '64, City Point, Va.

Alexander, Edmund K., 18, S.; Aug. 25, '62; cordwainer, Natick; dis. disa., Jan. 20, '63.

Allen, William L., 24, M.; currier, Sturbridge; July 14, '63, in Twelfth Infty.; trans. to Thirty-ninth; Pris. Aug. 19, '64; paroled and captured again March 31, '65; paroled April 3, '65; M. O. June 24, '65.

Babb, Mark, 25, M.; cordwainer, Natick; Aug. 25, '62; dis. disa., Dec. 16, '62; d. Dec. 25, 1910, Natick.

Bacon, Jonathan, 43, M.; stone mason, Natick; Aug. 25, '62; d. Dec. 16, '63, Washington, D. C.

Balcom, Oscar, 19, S.; farmer, Wayland; Aug. 25, '62; M. O. June 2, '65; Cochituate.

Bangs, William W., 22, S.; merchant, Worcester; July 13, '73; wd. June 18, '64, Petersburg; d. City Point, Va., no date given.

Barnes, Charles H., b. Jan. 28, 1842; 20, S.; clerk, Boston; Aug. 25, '62; prom. Corp.; wd. May 8, '64, Alsop's Farm; M. O. June 2, '65; Dry goods; 1913, Melrose.

Beal, Jesse N., 32, M.; shoemaker, Natick; July 16, '63; trans. for unexpired time to Thirty-second and M. O.

Beals, William H., 22, S.; farmer, Natick; Aug. 25, '62; Pris. Aug. 19, '64; d. Feb. 19, Salisbury, N. C.

Bigelow, Chester O., 18, S.; musician, Dover; Feb. 14, '62, in Thirteenth Infty.; trans. to Thirty-ninth; dis. Feb. 23, '65, ex. of s.

Bispham, John D., 28, S.; trader, Natick; Aug. 25, '62; Pris. Aug. 19, '64; d. Jan. 25, '65, Salisbury, N. C.

Blenker, James J., 38, M.; clerk, Attleborough; July 28, '63; d. May 14, '65, Washington, D. C.

Boyden, Stephen A., 31, M.; cordwainer, Natick; Aug. 25, '62; prom. Corp.; dis. July 7, '63, for commission in U. S. C. T.

Braithwaik, Thomas, 27, S.; assistant surgeon, West Bridgewater; Aug. 3, '63; trans. to Thirty-second and M. O.; his name does not appear in the F. & S.

Brigham, Alfred M. (Corp.), brother of Capt.; Aug. 25, '62; prom. Sergt.; dis. Aug. 14, '63, for commission U. S. C. T.; 2d Lieut. Fourth Colored Infty.; k. June 15, '64, Petersburg.

Brookings, Alphonso W., 21, S.; cordwainer, Natick; Aug. 25, '62; dis. disa., Dec. 30, '62; later Corp. in Co. I, Thirteenth V. R. C., whence he was dis. Nov. 17, '65; d. April 29, 1883, Natick.

Brooks, William, 44, M.; morocco dresser, Natick; Aug. 25, '62; M. O. June 2, '65.

Brown, Edwin, 21, S.; cordwainer, Natick; Aug. 25, '62; prom. Sergt.; Pris. Aug. 19, '64, to March 25, '65; M. O. June 17, '65; d. Nov. 14, 1911, Nashua, N. H.

Brummett, John M., 39, M.; farmer, Wayland; Aug. 25, '62; dis. disa., Feb. 23, '63; d. March 2, 1900, Natick.

Bullens, Charles A., 23, M.; cordwainer, Natick; Aug. 25, '62; trans. to unassigned Co., 2d Batt. V. R. C.; dis. July 11, '65.

Bullens, Lowell S., 19, S.; cordwainer, Natick; Aug. 25, '62; dis. disa., Jan. 1, '63; later en. April 8, '64, U. S. Signal Corps; dis. Aug. 4, '64.

Butterfield, Charles B., 18, S.; cordwainer, Natick; Aug. 25, '62; Pris. Aug. 18, '64, to March 1, '65; M. O. July 20, '65; Cochituate.

Butterfield, John C., 44, M.; cordwainer, Natick; Aug. 25, '62; dis. disa., Feb. 11, '64.

Carhart, Henry, 18, S.; cordwainer, Natick; Aug. 25, '62; prom. Corp.; k. May 8, '64, Alsop's Farm.

Carhart, Joseph B., 27, M.; cordwainer, Natick; Aug. 25, '62; Corp. March 10, '65; M. O. June 2, '65; d. Jan. 1, 1871, Natick.

Carr, Joseph C., 34, M.; cordwainer, Natick; Aug. 25, '62; des. Sept. 5, '62.

Caswell, Perley, 44, M.; carpenter, Natick; Aug. 25, '62; M. O. June 2, '65; d. Nov. 15, 1877.

Chamberlain, Daniel O., 29, M.; Aug. 25, '62; Pris. Aug. 19, '64; d. a prisoner Feb. 27, '65, Richmond, Va.

Chase, Seth C., 30, M.; mariner, Nantucket; July 13, '64; in Twelfth Infty.; trans. to Thirty-ninth; d. a prisoner April 3, '65, Salisbury, N. C.

Choate, Edward H., 29, —; hostler, Natick; dis. disa., Dec. 17, '62.

Clough, William H. H., 21, M.; cordwainer, Natick; Aug. 25, '62; wd. May 10, '64; Pris. Aug. 19, '64; M. O. July 20, '65; 1913, Natick.

Colbath, Charles E., 18, S.; cordwainer, Natick; Aug. 25, '65; d. May 18, '65, Washington, D. C.

Colbath, George A., 41, M.; cordwainer, Natick; Aug. 25, '62; trans. Sept. 12, '63, V. R. C.; dis. disa., Dec. 18, '63, from Co. A, Sixth V. R. C.; he was a brother of Vice-President Henry Wilson; Charles was son of G. A. C.

Cole, Archibald M., 41, M.; tailor, Natick; Aug. 25, '62; Pris. Aug. 19, '64; d. Jan. 14, '65, Salisbury.

Collins, William, 22, S.; cordwainer, Natick; Aug. 25, '62; prom. Corp.; d. paroled prisoner April 6, '65.

Conant, Sherman (Corp.), 22, S.; student, Natick; Aug. 25, '62; dis. Aug. 17, '63, for commission U. S. C. T.; Captain Third Colored Infty.; Major Sept. 13, '65; M. O. Oct. 31, '65; d. Nov. 21, 1890, Natick.

Cook, Thomas, 26, M.; shoemaker, Beverly; July 10, '63, in Twelfth Infty.; trans. to Thirty-ninth; dis. disa., May 26, '65.

Cooper, Newell, 29, M.; cordwainer, Natick; Aug. 25, '62; dis. disa., Jan. 2, '63; 1913, Natick.

Cooper, Thomas, 20, —; —, Taunton; Aug. 3, '63, in Thirteenth Infty.; trans. to Thirty-ninth, thence to Thirty-second and M. O.

Critcherson, Joseph (Corp.), 37, M.; cordwainer, Natick; Aug. 25, '62; trans. Nov. 15, '63, to Fifty-eighth Co., 3d Batt., V. R. C.; dis. disa., June 7, '65; d. June 11, 1900, Natick.

Curran, Edward, 21, S.; cordwainer, Natick; Aug. 25, '62; Pris. Aug. 19, '64; M. O. June 2, '65.

Currier, Charles P. (Sergt.), 26, S.; cordwainer, Natick; Aug. 25, '62; dis. disa., March 10, '65; d. Dec. 19, 1907, Natick.

Currier, Joseph, 24, M.; cordwainer, Natick; Aug. 25, '62; wd. May 5, '64; Pris. Aug. 19, '64, to March 3, '65; dis. disa., June 20, '65; d. Feb. 27, 1869, Natick.

Dakin, Abel F. (Mus.), 29, M.; cordwainer, Natick; Aug. 25, '62; d. Dec. 20, '63, Washington.

Davis, Charles A., 35, M.; cordwainer, Natick; Aug. 25, '62; despatch-carrier for General Grant; dis. June 5, '65; d. July 12, 1897, Natick.

Davis, Frank E. (Corp.), 21, S.; clerk, Natick; Aug. 25, '62; dis. disa., Dec. 1, '62.

Drew, Charles F., 24, S.; shoemaker, Stoneham; July 10, '61, in Thirteenth Infty.; re-en. Jan. 4, '64; trans. to Thirty-ninth, thence to Thirty-second and M. O.

Dutton, Dana F., 29, M.; farmer, Sudbury; July 16, '61, in Thirteenth Infty.; trans. to Thirty-ninth, thence to Thirty-second and M. O.

Echibach, Louis, 25, S.; bookkeeper, Beverly; July 29, '63, in Thirteenth Infty.; trans. to Thirty-ninth, thence to Thirty-second and M. O.

Eckenroth, Charles H., 21, M.; brakeman, Dedham; July 28, '63, in Thirteenth Infty.; trans. to Thirty-ninth, thence to Thirty-second and M. O.

Endicott, Ingersoll B., 23, M.; clerk, Boston; July 23, '63, in Thirteenth Infty.; trans. to Thirty-ninth, thence to Thirty-second and M. O.

Esip, Francis, 21, S.; blacksmith, Natick; Aug. 25, '62; M. O. June 2, '65; d. 1909, Soldiers' Home, Togus, Me.

Evans, William, 23, S.; laborer, Brighton; July 22, '63, in Thirteenth Infty. trans. to Thirty-ninth, thence to Thirty-second and M. O.

Felch, Henry F., b. March 18, 1839; (Sergt.) 23, S.; clerk, Natick; Aug. 25, '62; was Color Sergt. till promotion; prom. 2d Lieut. Oct. 25, '63; vide Co. F.

Felch, Ira H., 18, S.; shoemaker, Natick; March 7, '62; in Thirteenth Infty.; trans. to Thirty-ninth; dis. March 7, '65, ex. of s.; d. May 8, 1910, Natick.

Felch, William F., 35, M.; cordwainer, Natick; Aug. 25, '62; prom. Corp.; wd. March 31, '65; M. O. May 18, '65; d. May 7, 1902, Plymouth.

Finn, James W., 18, S.; farmer, Natick; Aug. 25, '62; drowned Nov. 17, '62, Chesapeake & Ohio Canal.

Fiske, John E., 21, S.; hatter, Natick; Aug. 25, '62; dis. disa., Feb. 25, '63.

Fogg, George L., 33, M.; cordwainer, Natick; Aug. 25, '62; d. Nov. 23, Offutt's Cross Roads, Md.

Foley, Michael, 26, M.; currier, Stoneham; July 14, '63, in Twelfth Infty.; trans. Thirty-ninth, thence to Thirty-second and M. O.

Freeman, Charles F. (Mus.), 18, S.; cordwainer, Natick; Aug. 25, '62; June 2, '65.

Garfield, William H., b. May 20, 1843; 19, S.; cordwainer, Natick; Aug. 25, '62; M. O. June 2, '65; grocery, dry goods; hotel and livery keeper; 1913, Harding; rec'd a skin wound, in the face, at the Wilderness; at Laurel Hill, he drew his own seven days' rations and those of Butterfield as well, carrying them till his comrade showed up; after the Weldon R. R. disaster, he was one of the seven men who answered "Here" on the 20th of August; after the surrender, he traded his hat-cord with a rebel lieut. for a Dutch oven and two camp kettles, also securing from the reb. a confession that he was glad the war was over, though he wished the shoe were on the other foot; on the 25th return of the Weldon day his comrades and friends gave him a house warming in his new abode on the eastern slopes of Mt. Deliverance, Natick, his home, till 1893, when he moved to Medfield.

Gourley, Samuel, 30, S.; baker, Boston; July 13, '63, in Twelfth Infty.; Pris. Aug. 19, '64, to March 21, '65; M. O. June 5, '65.

Green, John T. B., 18, S.; teamster, Boston; July 31, '62, in Thirteenth Infty.; trans. to Thirty-ninth, thence to Thirty-second and M. O.

Griffin, Jonathan F., 39, M.; cordwainer, Natick; Aug. 25, '62; dis. disa., Nov. 21, '63; d. Feb. 7, 1902, Natick.

Hall, Benning, Jr. (1st Sergt.), 36, M.; expressman, Natick; Aug. 25, '62; dis. disa., Feb. 8, '64.

Hammond, Charles F., 28, M.; cordwainer, Natick; Aug. 25, '62; trans. to Sixty-ninth Co., Second Batt., V. R. C., dis. June 29, '65.

Hancock, Henry, b. April 22, 1839, England; 23, S.; blacksmith, Natick; Aug. 25, '62; wd. May 5, '64, Wilderness; dis. disa., Feb. 6, '65; blacksmith; 1913, So. Natick.

Hardy, Simeon, 27, M.; Aug. 25, '62; cordwainer, Natick; Pris. Aug. 18, '64, to March 1, '65; M. O. July 20, 65; d. 1885, Natick.

Hayes, Daniel, 44. M.; cordwainer, Natick; Aug. 25, '62; dis. disa., Nov. 5, '62; d. Nov. 29, 1902, Natick.

Hayward, Paul, 34, M.; farmer, Boston; July 11, '63, in Twelfth Infty.; trans. to Thirty-ninth; M. O. May 3, '65.

Hazelton, Warren, 30, —; —, Concord; July 14, '63, in Thirteenth Infty.; k. Aug. 19, '64.

Hoey, Michael, 26, M.; cordwainer, Natick; Aug. 25, '62; wd. May 8, '64; M. O. June 2, '65; d. July 17, 1872, Natick.

Hoey, Thomas, 36, M.; cordwainer, Natick; Aug. 25, '62; wd. May 12, '64; Pris. Aug. 19, '14; M. O. June 2, '65.

Howe, Ansel L., 18, S.; flagman, Natick; Aug. 25, '62; k. Aug. 18, '64, Weldon R. R.

Jennings, John E., 31, M.; shoemaker, Natick; July 25, '64; trans. to Thirty-second and M. O.

Jennison, Charles W., 30, M.; cordwainer, Natick; Aug. 25, '62; M. O. June 2, '65; d. May 17, 1902, Natick.

Jones, Nathan, 34, M.; farmer, Natick; Aug. 25, '62; dis. disa., April 1, '63; d. June 11, 1884, Natick.

Kemp, Nathan S., 20, —; shoemaker, Watertown; Aug. 2, '64; d. May 19, '65, Watertown, Mass.

King, Albert F., 22, S.; cordwainer, Boston; Aug. 25, '62; dis. disa., June 25, '63; d. Aug. 11, 1898, Seattle, Wash.

LeBarron, David J., 25, M.; cordwainer, Natick; Aug. 25, '62; M. O. June 2, '65; d. June 7, 1904, Natick.

Lilley, Richard G., 33, S.; shoemaker, Natick; June 26, '61, in Twelfth Infty.; trans. to Thirty-ninth, thence to Thirty-second and M. O.; d. April 13, 1898, Natick.

Littlefield, George H., 35, M.; cordwainer, Natick; Aug. 25, '62; k. Aug. 19, '64, Weldon R. R.

Lynch, John, 21, S.; seaman, Raynham; July 26, '63; in Thirteenth Infty.; trans. to the Thirty-ninth, thence to the Thirty-second and M. O.

McAuliffe, Samuel, b. Jan. 7, 1841; 21, S.; machinist, Agawam; July 17, '63, in Twelfth Infty.; trans. to Thirty-ninth and thence to Thirty-second and M. O.; is glad that his change from the Twelfth to the Thirty-ninth took him into such excellent company, enjoying his new comrades and officers, Capt. Reed and Lieut. Brown, very much; selling machinery in this country and abroad; Mercantile Inspector, Rochester, N. Y.; fifteen years, chief mustering officer and Inspector; two years each, Dept. N. Y. G. A. R. and Inspector General for Commander-in-chief John C. Black; 1913, Gates, N. Y.

McCaffrey, James, 37, M.; bookmaker, West Roxbury; Jan. 14, '64; trans. to Thirty-second and M. O.

McLain, Charles W., 28, M.; cordwainer, Natick; Aug. 25, '62; prom. Sergt. and 1st Sergt.; M. O. June 2, '65; d. Nov. 21, 1910, Natick.

Mann, Francis E., 20, S.; cordwainer, Natick; Aug. 25, '62; d. Nov. 23, '62, Offutt's Cross Roads, Md.

Marsh, William W., 30 M.; yeoman, Grafton; July 14, '63, in Twelfth Infty.; trans. to Thirty-ninth; wd. Aug. 18, '64; trans. to Thirty-second and M. O.

Mead, Alfred, 30, M.; cordwainer, Natick; Aug. 25, '62; M. O. June 2, '65; d. July 8, 1911, Newton.

Merrill, Franklin, 27, M.; expressman, Boston; July 13, '63, in Twelfth Infty.; trans. to Thirty-ninth, thence to Thirty-second and M. O.

Merrill, Stephen, 36, M.; teamster, Natick; Aug. 25, '62; d. from wds. March 3, '65.

Messenger, Charles W., 27, M.; farmer, Wrentham; July 15, '63; in Twelfth Infty.; trans. to Thirty-ninth; d. from wds. Sept. 20, '64.

Mills, Josiah R., 45, M.; cordwainer, Natick; Aug. 25, '62; wd. Feb. 7, '65; dis. disa., Sept. 5, '65; d. Mar. 18, 1887, Natick.

Monahan, Michael, b. May 24, 1841; 21, S.; cordwainer, Natick; Aug. 25, '62; Pris. May 8, '64, recaptured by Sheridan on the 9th; wd. June 18, '64; M. O. June 2, '65; shoemaking and farming; 1913, So. Framingham.

Morey, Raphael, 20, S.; farmer, Hopkinton; Aug. 2, '64; M. O. June 2, '65.

Moore, Charles H., 32, M.; cordwainer, Natick; Aug. 25, '62; trans. May 12, '64, to Co. H, Eighteenth V. R. C.; dis. as Corp. June 24, '65; d. Mar. 14, 1905, Natick.

Morrill, Robert W., 34, S.; yeoman, Worcester; July 11, '63, in Twelfth Infty.; trans. to Thirty-ninth, thence to Thirty-second and M. O.; 1913, West Boylston.

Morrison, Charles H., 18, S.; cordwainer, Natick; Aug. 25, '62; d. Nov. 21, '62, Offutt's Cross, Roads, Md.

Morse, Curtis, 18, S.; cordwainer, Natick; Aug. 25, '62; wd. May 24, '64; M. O. May 25, '65; d. 1909, Plymouth.

Morse, Henry M., 21, M.; blacksmith, Medway; Aug. 25, '62; dis. disa., Sept. 12, '63; d.

Morse, Horace B. (Corp.), 42, M.; farmer, Natick; Aug. 25, '62; dis. disa., May 1, '63; d. Nov. 8, 1911, Winstead, Conn.

Moulton, George W., 33, M.; cordwainer, Natick; Aug. 25, '62; wd. May 10, '64; M. O. June 2, '65; d. Feb. 8, 1907, Natick.

Moulton, Otis H., 31, M.; cordwainer, Natick; Aug. 25, '62; M. O. June 2, '65; d. April 21, 1883, Natick.

Murphy, James 19, S.; cordwainer, Natick; Aug. 25, '62; M. O. June 2, '65; d. Sept. 8, 1910, Cochituate.

Newhall, Francis E., 37, M.; cordwainer, Natick; Aug. 25, '62; d. Nov. 25, Offutt's Cross Roads, Md.

O'Brien, Cornelius, 18, S.; carpenter, Boston; Oct. 13, '63; Pris. Aug. 19, '64; d. Salisbury, N. C., after Feb. 22, '65, at which time he was in a dying condition.

O'Brien, Dennis, 21, S.; shoemaker, Natick; Jan. 7, '64; wd. May 8, '64; trans. to Thirty-second and M. O.

Parlin, William D. (Sergt.), 23, S.; trader, Natick; Aug. 25, '62; dis. June 22, '63, for commission U. S. C. T.; Captain First U. S. Colored Infty.; dis. disa., March 7, '65.

Patten, Delavan M., 22, M.; blacksmith, Springfield; July 16, '63, in Twelfth Infty.; trans. to Thirty-ninth, thence to Thirty-second and M. O.; 1913, Plainfield, N. J.

Perkins, Thomas, 29, M.; cordwainer, Natick; Aug. 25, '62; dis. disa., Dec. 21, '62.

Pierson, James M., 21, S.; cordwainer, Natick; Aug. 25, '62; wd. June 18, '64; dis. disa., Feb. 8, '65; 1913, Haverhill.

Ragan, Michael, 38, S.; laborer, Boston; Oct. 1, '63, in Twelfth Infty.; trans. to Thirty-ninth, thence to Thirty-second and M. O.

Reed, Nathan (Sergt.), 43, M.; cordwainer, Natick; Aug. 25, '62; trans. Jan. 5, '64, to V. R. C.; dis. disa., Jan. 15, '65; d. April 3, 1901, Natick.

Reynolds, George, 27, M.; bookkeeper, Boston; July 28, '63, in Thirteenth Infty.; trans. to Thirty-ninth, thence to Thirty-second and M. O.

Russell, Levi, 43, M.; cordwainer, Natick; Aug. 25, '62; trans. April 10, '64, to V. R. C.; dis. July 1, '65; May 22, 1906, Natick.

Sell, James T., 28, M.; teamster, Cambridge; June 26, '61, in Twelfth Infty.; on account of unauthorized absence, he was compelled to make up time, hence his trans. to the Thirty-ninth, thence to the Thirty-second and M. O.

Sloper, Charles W., 18, S.; hatter, Natick; Aug. 25, '62; M. O. June 2, '65.

Smith, Abial E., 30, M.; cordwainer, Sherborn; Aug. 25, '62; wd. May 12, '64; Pris. Aug. 19, '64; dis. June 14, '65; d. Aug. 25, 1871, Natick.

Spooner, Lyman A., 21, S.; cordwainer, Natick; Aug. 25, '62; prom. Sergt.; 2d Lieut. June 7, '62; M. O. as Sergt. June 2, '65; d. Dec. 28, 1894, Natick.

Stearns, Nathan D., 31, —; cordwainer, Natick; Aug. 25, '62; d. a prisoner Feb. 3, '65, Salisbury, N. C.

Stedman, Charles H., 20, S.; cordwainer, Natick; Aug. 25, '62; d. from wds. July 10, '64, Willett's Point, N. Y.

Stevens, Leonard S., 21, S.; farmer, Haverhill; Sept. 23, '63, in Twelfth Infty.; trans. to Thirty-ninth, thence to Thirty-second and M. O.

Stewart, Samuel, vide Styner, below.

Stewart, Sylvanus, 22, S.; hatter, Natick; Aug. 25, '62; prom. Corp.; wd. Aug. 18, '64; M. O. June 2, '65; d. May 16, 1906, Haverhill.

Stone, Francis C, 24, S.; cordwainer, Natick; Aug. 25, '62; d. from wds. May 19, '64, Washington, D. C.

Styner, Samuel, 24, M.; painter, Concord; July 24, '63, in Thirteenth Infty.; trans. to Thirty-ninth, thence to Thirty-second and M. O.; according to a letter from the W. D., Sept. 27, '90, the man's real name was Stewart.

Sullivan, Thomas, 1st, 22, M.; boatman, Taunton; July 24, '63, in Thirteenth Infty.; trans. to Thirty-ninth, thence to Thirty-second and M. O.

Taylor, George G., 21, M.; shoemaker, Rutland; July 13, '63, in Twelfth Infty.; trans. to Thirty-ninth; M. O. May 25, '65, though roll also states that he was trans. to Thirty-second.

Travis, Fayette E., 20, S.; cordwainer, Natick; Aug. 25, '62; Pris. Aug. 19, '64, to March 1, '65; M. O. July 20, '65; 1913, Natick.

Travis, Isaac N. (Corp.); cordwainer, Natick; Aug. 25, '62; trans. Sept. 12, '63, to V. R. C.; dis. Nov. 17, '63; d. June 9, 1905, Natick.

Tyler, Stearns C., 27, M.; cordwainer, Natick; Aug. 25, '62; dis. O. W. D. May 30, '65; d. Jan. 5, 1894, Natick.

Tyrell, George H., 19, S.; cordwainer, Natick; Aug. 25, '62; d. Dec. 18, '62, Offutt's Cross Roads, Md.

Wallace, J. William, 25, M.; printer, Natick; Aug. 25, '62; trans. March 31, '64, V. R. C.; dis. Aug. 9, '65.

Warren, Samuel P. S., 18, S.; cordwainer, Natick; Aug. 25, '62; d. Dec. 18, '62, Offutt's Cross Roads, Md.

Washburn, Romanzo M., 23, S.; clerk, Natick; Aug. 25, '62; dis. June 21, '64, O. W. D.; d. March 22, 1887, Natick.

Webster, Isaac L., 15, S.; —, Martinsburg, Va.; Feb. 11, '62, in Thirteenth Infty.; trans. as mus. to Thirty-ninth and dis. Feb. 10, '65, ex. of s.

Wentworth, George W., 29, M.; hatter, Natick; Aug. 25, '62; prom. Sergt.; M. O. June 2, '65; 1913, Haverhill.

West, John, 33, S.; carpenter, Boston; July 24, '63, in Twelfth Infty.; trans. to Thirty-ninth, thence to Thirty-second and M. O.

Wheeler, Willis M., b. Aug. 11, 1841; 21, M.; mechanic, Northbridge; July 14, '63, in Twelfth Infty.; trans. to Thirty-ninth, thence to Thirty-second and M. O.; 1913, Natick.

Whitney, Constant F., b. Aug. 12, 1836; 26, M.; cordwainer, Sherburn; Aug. 25, '62; dis. disa., March 6, '63; expressing, deacon Baptist Church nineteen years; 1913, Norwood.

Whitney, John, 40, M.; farmer, Watertown; Aug. 2, '64; M. O. June 2, '65; had been in Co. E, Sixth M. V. M., 3 mos. term, 1861.

Williams, Charles H., 28, M.; carpenter, Natick; Aug. 25, '62; Pris. Aug. 19, '64; d. March 19, '65, Wilmington, N. C.

Woodward, Caleb, 40, M.; cordwainer, Natick; Aug. 25, '62; dis. disa., Jan. 30, '63.

Woodward, Heman C, 23, M.; cordwainer, Natick; Aug. 25, '62; dis. disa., April 1, '63; d. May 2, 1883.

Wright, Lewis, 25, M.; expressman, Natick; Aug. 25, '62; M. O. June 2, '65; expressing; 1913, Natick.

COMPANY K

Woburn

CAPTAINS

John I. Richardson, b. July 12, 1818, Woburn; 44, M.; mason, Woburn; Aug. 22, '62; dis. disa., March 29, '64; d. Oct. 1, 1864, Woburn.

Willard C. Kinsley, from Co. H, Mar. 30, '64; d. April 2, 1865, from wds. rec'd Mar. 31, '65.

Luke R. Tidd, April 3, '65; not mustered; M. O. as 1st Lieut. June 2, 1865; d. Aug. 15, 1893, Woburn; his body was borne to its burial by his fellow soldiers; had been a shoe manufacturer many years; his sword, captured Aug. 19, '64, was returned to him by Sergt. Whitaker of the Tenth Georgia in 1884 and was received with great rejoicing by Co. K.

FIRST LIEUTENANTS

Luke R. Tidd, b. May 5, 1822, Woburn; 39, S.; shoe manufacturer, Woburn; Aug. 22, '62; pris. Aug. 19, '64; paroled Feb. 19, '65; Captain, April 3, '65.

SECOND LIEUTENANTS

Luther F. Wyman, b. Oct. 7, 1833, Woburn; 28, M.; shoemaker, Woburn; Aug. 22, '62; 1st Lieut. March 20, '64; vide Co. H.

Henry A. Seaverns, from Co. H, Mar. 30, '64; wd. Aug. 18, '64; 1st Lieut.; not mustered; dis. disa., Jan. 7, '64; d. Sept. 26, 1894, No. Scituate.

Alpheus Thomas, from Co. G, Sept. 15, '64; wd. Mar. 31, '65; M. O. May 16, 1865; dead.

ENLISTED MEN

Avery, Michael, b. 1832, Halifax, N. S.; 30, M.; shoemaker, Woburn; Aug. 22, '62; k. May 10, '64, Spottsylvania.

Bacon, Jonas, 19, S.; japaner, Woburn; Aug. 22, '62; Pris. Aug. 19, '64; d. Dec. 30, '64, Salisbury, N. C.

Baldwin, Michael B., b. Feb. 2, 1834, Bridgeport, Conn.; 28, M.; harness maker, Woburn; Aug. 22, '62; wd. May 10, '64; Pris. Aug. 19, '64; dis. disa., May 20, '65; d. July, 1911, Stoneham.

Bancroft, Albert, b. May 18, 1844, Woburn; 19, S.; farmer, Woburn; Aug. 22, '62; M. O. June 2, '65; d. Sept., 6, 1906.

Barrett, Albert P., b. July 14, 1844, Woburn; 18, S.; painter, Woburn; Aug. 22, '62; wd. May 10, '64; detailed for clerical duty, Div. H'quarters from July 27, '64; M. O. June 2, '65; d. April, 1909; his recollections enter largely into the earlier portions of this history.

Barrett, William T., b. June 26, 1838, Boston; 24, M.; clerk, Woburn; Aug. 22, '62; d. Jan. 29, '65, Washington, D. C.

Boutwell, Asa, b. July 12, 1836, Woburn; 26, M.; butcher, Woburn; dis. disa., May 5, '65.

Bradley, Thomas H., b. 1844, Boston; 18, S.; japaner, Woburn; Aug. 22, '62; wd. Mar. 31, '65, Gravelly Run; M. O. June 2, '65; d. Nov. 14, 1873, Woburn.

Brannagan, John, b. Dec. 9, 1842, Ireland; 21, S.; blacksmith, Woburn; Aug. 22, '62; Pris. Aug. 15, '64; d. Jan. 20, '65, Salisbury, N. C.

Brown, Alvin G., b. Aug. 14, '42, Reading; 20, S.; printer, Woburn; Aug. 22, '62; M. O. May 18, '65; 1913, Malden.

Brown, William P. (Sergt.), 21, S. clerk, Woburn; Aug. 22, '62; detailed as Division Ordnance Sergt.; M. O. June 2, '65; had served in Co. I, Fifth M. V. M., 3 mos. term, 1861; b. Durham, Nova Scotia; Aug. 20, 1840; grocer before and after the war; 1872-1890, manufacturing; clerk, State Board of Health from 1890 to death; Sec. of Thirty-ninth Regimental Ass'n and a member of the Com. on Regimental history; d. Sept. 10, 1912, Winthrop.

Bryant, Francis M., b. May 8, 1847, Woburn; 18, S.; laborer, Woburn; Aug. 22, '62; d. a prisoner, Jan. 29, '65, Salisbury, N. C.

Bush, Charles, b. July 15, 1838, Canada; 25, S.; teamster, Woburn; Feb. 27, '64; Pris. May 8, '64; recaptured next day by Sheridan; wd. April 1, '65; trans. to Thirty-second and M. O.; d. Canada.

Butler, Moses, b. Mar. 19, 1824, Kentsville, N. S.; 31, M.; currier, Woburn; Feb. 25, '64; Pris. Aug. 19, '64; d. Jan. 17, '65, Salisbury, N. C.

Cady, David, b. May 17, 1837, Bedford, N. H.; 25, S.; farmer, Woburn; Aug. 22, '62; dis. disa., June 18, '63; d. N. H.

Carpenter, Alonzo D., b. Feb. 17, 1839, St. Albans, Vt.; 32, M.; currier, Woburn; Aug. 22, '62; wd. April 4, '65, Petersburg; dis. disa., June 28, '65; 1913, Woburn.

Chase, John, b. 1840, Camplin, N. H.; 22, S.; shoemaker, Woburn; Aug. 22, '62; trans. Feb. 15, '64, V. R. C.; dis. from Co. I, Second V. R. C., July 3, 1865; "Out West."

Choate, William M., b. July 10, 1844, Lynn; (Mus.) 19, S.; photographer, Woburn; Aug. 22, '62; dis. disa., Feb. 12, '63.

Colby, Freeman E., b. Jan. 3, 1840, Henniker, N. H.; 21, S.; farmer, Woburn; Aug. 22, '62; detailed with Q. M. Dep't after the No. Anna; M. O. June 2, '65; farming and lumbering; Selectman, 8 years; School Com., 3 years; Rep. Legislature, 2 years; Justice of the Peace, 35 years; 1913, Henniker, N. H.

Colby, Newton G., b. 1843, Henniker, N. H.; 19, S.; farmer, Woburn; Aug. 22, '62; dis. disa., Dec. 29, '62; d. 1894, Henniker.

Colgate, Charles H., b. July 31, 1844, Roxbury; 19, S.; currier, Woburn; Dec. 15, '63; Pris. Aug. 19, '64, to Oct. 9, '64; trans. to Thirty-second Infty. and M. O. June 29, '65; leather business and maker of extracts; 14 years, agent of Prison Commission; Past Commander G. A. R. Post; Sec. of Massachusetts Ass'n Ex-prisoners of War; Deacon in Congregational Church, and Sec. of Thirty-ninth Regimental Ass'n at time of death; d. Feb. 8, 1913.

Conn, Charles K., b. Jan. 9, 1842, Charlestown; 20, S.; bookkeeper, Woburn; Aug. 22, '62; Corp. March 1, '63; Pris. May 8, '64; Sergt. Major, April 28, '64; vid. F. & S.

Connoly, Hugh, b. 1841, Ireland; 21, S.; currier, Woburn; Aug. 22, '62; d. Nov. 25, '62, Offutt's Cross Roads, Md.

Cronan, Jeremiah, b. 1826, Ireland; 36, M.; shoemaker, Woburn; Aug. 22, '62; des. Sept. 2, '62.

Curry, Robert, b. 1823, Ireland; 39, M.; shoemaker, Woburn; Aug. 22, '62; Pris. May 8, '64, recaptured next day; Pris. Aug. 19. '64; d. Oct. 20, '64, Salisbury, N. C.

Dean, George W., b. Oct. 11, 1842, Wilmington; 22, S.; shoemaker, Woburn; Dec. 28, '63; Pris. Aug. 19, '64; trans. to Thirty-second Infty. and M. O.; had served in Sixth Battery, Light Arty.; d. April, 1902.

Dean, Joseph G., b. Jan. 28, 1821, Woburn; 41, M.; butcher, Woburn; Aug. 22, '62; wd. Aug. 19, '64; M. O. June 2, '65; d. Hudson.

Dean, Joshua H., b. Feb. 11, 1843, Woburn; 18, S.; shoemaker, Woburn; Aug. 22, '62; Pris. Aug. 14, '64; recaptured same day; wd. Feb. 6, '65; N. F. R.; 1913, Syracuse, N. Y.

Dennett, Geo. H., b. Dec. 22, 1845, Woburn; 18, S.; clerk, Woburn; Aug. 22, '62; trans. Feb. 15, '64 to V. R. C.; at his own request trans. back Aug. 10, '64; wd. Mar. 31, '65; Sergt. Major, Feb. 1, '65; vide F. & S.

Dennett, Robert M., b. Oct. 5, 1840, Chatham, N. B.; 23, S.; —, Woburn; Dec. 21, '63; one of those detailed to bear old colors to Boston and receive new ones; as Corp. d. April 12, '65, Washington, from wds. received Mar. 31, '65; had served in Co. F, Twenty-second Massachusetts Volunteers.

Doherty, Philip, b. Jan. 1, 1845, Ireland; 18, S.; currier, Woburn; wd. and Pris. Aug. 18, '64; paroled Aug. 25, '64; M. O. May 15, '65; d. California.

Doherty, Peter, b. 1842, Ireland; 21, S.; japaner, Woburn; Aug. 22, '62; wd. May 10, '64; d. May 19, '64, Washington.

Doorley, James, b. July 21, 1823, Ireland; 33, S.; teamster, Woburn; Aug. 22, '62; wd. May 8, '64; dis. May 8, '65; d. Woburn.

Downing, Jonathan P., b. April 20, 1835, Plymouth, N. H.; 27, M.; butcher, Woburn; Aug. 22, '62; wd. May 10, '64; M. O. June 2, '65; d. Oct. 16, 1894, Woburn.

Drown, Samuel H., b. Woburn; (Corp.) 28, M.; japaner, Woburn; Aug. 22, '62; dis. disa., April 27, '63; d. Mar. 3, 1871, Woburn.

Duffy, Patrick, 22, S.; shoemaker, Stoneham; en. July 28, '62, and des. same day.

Earle, Anthony, 22, S.; clerk, Worcester; July 22, '63, in Twelfth Infty.; trans. to Thirty-ninth; dis. Jan. 5, '65, for commission as 2d Lieut. Sixty-first Infty., also 1st Lieut.; M. O. July 16, '65.

Eaton, Cyrus A., b. Dec. 13, 1824, Woburn; 38, M.; shoemaker, Woburn; Aug. 22, '62; wd. May 10, '64; d. from wds. May 29, '64.

Eaton, Parker, b. April 28, 1826, Woburn; (Corp.), 35, W.; currier, Woburn; Aug. 22, '62; M. O. June 2, '65; d. Jan. 24, 1912, Woburn.

Edgecomb, Noah, b. 1818, Saco, Me.; 43, M.; carpenter, Woburn; Aug. 22, '62; trans. Sept. 13, '63, to V. R. C.; d. Feb. 27, 1882, Woburn.

Fairbanks, Amos H., 22, M.; clerk, Roxbury; July 16, '63, in Twelfth Infty.; trans. to Thirty-ninth; trans. April 24, '65, to V. R. C.; M. O. Aug. 11, '65.

Finn, Michael, b. Jan. 7, 1846, Boston; 18, S.; baker, Woburn; Dec. 6, '63; Pris. May 8, '64; d. Oct. 3, '64, Danville, Va.

Flint, Thomas W., b. Nov. 28, 1844, Woburn; currier, Woburn; Aug. 22, '62; M. O. June 2, '65; 1913, New Haven, Conn.

Flynn, John, 30, M.; laborer, Woburn; Aug. 22, '62; des. Sept. 7, '62.

Foster, Irving, b. Sept. 3, 1841, Woburn; 20, S.; currier, Woburn; Aug. 22, '62; k. June 18, '64; Petersburg; his comrades called him "Old Honesty."

Fowle, George E., b. July 4, 1837, Reading; 25, S.; carpenter, Woburn; Aug. 22, '62; prom. Sergt.; pris. and escaped, Aug. 14, '64, Weldon R. R.; prom. 2d Lieut., Jan. 15, '65; wd. Feb. 7, '65, Hatcher's Run; dis. May 18, '65; carpenter and builder; Rep. in General Court, 1894 and '95; 1913, Woburn.

Garfield, Joseph W., b. Mar. 1, 1837, Waltham; (Mus.) 23, S.; shoemaker, Lynn; detailed as Brigade Bugler, Aug. 22, '62; M. O. June 2, '65; d. Oct. 1911, Lynn.

Garrigan, John, 29, b. 1833, Ireland; 29, M.; currier, Woburn; Aug. 22, '62; dis. disa., Oct. 26, '62; re-en. Tenth N. H.; d. Woburn.

Gilcreast, John, b. July 31, 1833, Andover; (Sergt.); 29, M.; painter, Woburn; Aug. 22, '62; 1st Sergt. May 6, '63; wd. May 10, '64; dis. on account of wds., Feb. 28, '65; d. Nov. 4, 1911, Woburn.

Gilligan, James R., 38, —; boot crimper, Weymouth; Dec. 10, '63, in Twelfth Infty.; trans. to Thirty-ninth; dis. disa., Dec. 10, '64.

Gleason, Albert, b. June 1, 1845, Woburn; 18, —; —, Rappahannock Station, Va.; Sept. 15, '63; in Thirteenth Infty.; trans. to Thirty-ninth in name; he had been wd. June 18, '64, while in the Thirteenth and his left arm was amputated; dis. May 16, '65; d. 1900, Woburn.

Harris, Otis S., b. April 12, 1844, Woburn; 18, S.; shoemaker, Woburn; Aug. 22, '62; wd. May 10, '64; M. O. June 2, '65; d. Jan. 16, 1896, Stoneham.

Hemmenway, Elbert O., 29, S.; harness maker, Pittsfield; July 14, '63; in Twelfth Infty.; trans. to Thirty-ninth; wd. May 4, '64; Pris. Dec. 11, '64; d. Jan. 1, '65, Salisbury, N. C.

Hooper, Samuel T., b. 1838, Athens, Ohio; (Corp.), 24, M.; currier, Woburn; Aug. 22, '62; Pris. Aug. 19, '62; escaped about April 12, '65; M. O. June 2, '65; d. Aug. 20, 1876, Woburn.

Hoskins, Edward, b. Nov. 4, 1846; 18, S.; laborer, Woburn; Jan. 1, '64; wd. May 10, '64; Pris. Aug. 19, '64; trans. to Thirty-second and M. O.; stationary engineer; 1913, Woburn.

Hoskins, William H., b. 1841, St. Johns, N. B.; 21, S.; cabinet maker, Woburn; Aug. 22, '62; wd. May 10, '64; d. May 30, '64.

Houghton, Edward J., b. 1843 Mobile, Ala., 19, S.; mariner, Woburn; Aug. 22, '62; trans. to U. S. Navy, April 19, '64; Houghton, from the Chicopee, was one of the party of 15 men who destroyed the Rebel Ram, Albemarle, Oct. 24, '64, at Plymouth, N. C. Two were drowned, eleven captured and Lieut. Cushing and Houghton escaped, though in different directions;

Congress voted medals of honor to all participating; July 16, '65, the day before he was to receive his well earned reward, he was killed at the Gosport, Va., Navy Yard, while trying to befriend a comrade in an altercation. The medal so highly prized is in the possession of relatives in East Boston.

Howard, Henry, b. July 17, 1826, St. Johns, N. B.; 36, M.; shoemaker, Woburn; Aug. 22, '62; dis. disa., July 6, '63; later, Co. B, Fifty-ninth Infty.; d. Sept. 3, '64, Long Island, N. Y.

Hutchins, Samuel M., 21, S.; farmer, Carlisle; July 11, '63, in Twelfth Infty.; trans. to Thirty-ninth, thence, March 15, '65, to V. R. C.; dis. disa., Feb. 15, '65.

Ingerson, Nathaniel, b. 1821, Andover; 41, M.; shoemaker, Woburn; Aug. 22, '62; dis. disa., Nov. 13, '62; d. July 1899, Reading.

Jones, William H., 31, M.; shoemaker, Woburn; Aug. 22, '62; Pris. Aug. 19, '64; M. O. June 2, '65; d. Oct. 1, 1876, Woburn.

Johnson, Charles H., b. Sept. 19, 1843; 18, S.; clerk, Woburn; Aug. 22, '62; Corp. May 9, '63; M. O. June 2, '65; currier till 1891, then appointed messenger of State Senate by Capt. J. G. B. Adams, and still (1913) holds the place; residence, Woburn.

Kingsbury, Charles H., b. Sept. 14, 1829, Billerica; 33, M.; pedler, Woburn; Aug. 22, '62; Pris. Aug. 19, '64; M. O. June 2, '65.

Lapurve, Alfred, 23, S.; seaman, Taunton; July 27, '63; Pris. Aug. 19, '64; escaped April 25, '65; trans. to Thirty-second and M. O.

Le Barron, William H., b. Oct. 4, 1845, Lexington; 19, S.; ironfounder, Woburn; Aug. 22, '62; M. O. June 2, '65; d. May 16, 1901, Woburn.

Leslie, Albert S., b. March 3, 1837, Exeter, N. H.; (Sergt.) 24, M.; shoemaker, Woburn; Aug. 22, '62; 1st Sergt. Feb. 3, '65; M. O. June 2, '65; 1913, Los Angeles, Cal.

Leslie, James Fred, b. Dec. 15, 1841; 21, S.; clerk, Woburn; wd. slightly May 8 and 10, '64; severely injured June 18, '64; Pris. Aug. 19, '64; paroled Oct. 9, '64; M. O. June 2, '65; watchmaker and cabinet-maker in U. S. Navy Yard, Charlestown; Lieut. in State Militia; assessor, almoner, Board of Overseers of the Poor; 1913, Woburn.

Libby, James C., b. 1826, Ossipee, N. H.; 36, M.; driver, Woburn; Aug. 22, '62; wd. June 19, '64, Petersburg; trans. to V. R. C.; dis. June 26, '65; d. Lawrence.

Linscott, Andrew R., b. March 6, 1844; 18, S.; clerk, Woburn; Aug. 22, '62; Corp. Nov. 30, '63; M. O. June 2, '65; teacher, alderman, rep. in General Court; 1913, Woburn.

Linscott, Charles F., b. Jan. 17, 1842, Woburn; (Corp.) 20, S.; clerk, Woburn; Aug. 22, '62; dis. May 30, '64. for promotion One Hundred and Twenty-eighth U. S. C. T.; d. 1912, Illinois.

Linscott, George W., b. May 9, 1843, Woburn; 19, S.; clerk, Woburn; Aug. 22, '62; M. O. June 2, '65; d. Boston.

Linscott, Josiah P., b. April 25, 1845, Woburn; 18, S.; mariner, Woburn; Aug. 22, '62; trans. Feb. 15, '64, to V. R. C.; dis. July 9, '65; d. Fortune Island, Nov. 24, 1876.

Lombard, Richard, b. July 24, 1828, Ireland; 33, M.; shoemaker, Woburn; Aug. 22, '62; Pris. Aug. 19, '64; paroled March 20, '65; M. O. June 2, '65; d. Boston.

McCarthy, John, b. Aug. 22, 1827, Ireland; 35, M.; shoemaker, Woburn; Aug. 22, '62; wd. May 10, '64, and Feb. 7, '65; M. O. June 2, '65; d. 1901, Togus, Me.

McCarthy, Thomas, b. Oct. 1, 1839, Boston; 24, M.; shoemaker, Woburn; Dec. 26, '63; wd. May 24, '64, No. Anna; trans. to Thirty-second, thence to V. R. C. and dis. June 25, '65.

McDevitt, William, b. Feb. 21, 1843, Woburn; (Sergt.) 19, S.; currier, Woburn; wd. May 8, '64; 2d Lieut. Sept. 15, '64, for "gallant and soldierly qualities"; vide Co. C.

McFeeley, Samuel, b. May 25, 1842; 20, S.; carpenter, Woburn; Aug. 22, '62; Corp. Feb. 16, '64; Sergt. March 13, '65, for having saved the colors at the Weldon R. R. Aug. 19, '64; he was detailed to carry the old regimental colors to the State House, Boston, and to receive the new ones; M. O. June 2, '65; d. July, 1911, Illinois.

McGoff, James, b. Dec. 24, 1838, Ireland; 25, M.; currier, Woburn; Dec. 28, '63; wd. May 10, '64; trans. to Thirty-second and M. O.; d. 1900, Woburn.

McGuire, John, 21, —; shoemaker, Conway; Aug. 4, '63, in Thirteenth Infty.; trans. to Thirty-ninth; Pris. from Aug. 14, '64, to April 10, '65; trans. to Thirty-second and M. O.

McKenna, William, b. 1819, Ireland; 23, M.; shoemaker, Woburn; Aug. 22, '62; des. May 25, '63.

Mahony, Timothy, b. Feb. 22, Cork, Ireland; (Corp.) 41, M.; shoemaker, Woburn; Pris. Aug. 19, '64; M. O. June 2, '65; d. 1902, Woburn.

Marran, Thomas, b. 1840, Ireland; (Wagoner) 24, M.; shoemaker, Woburn; Aug. 22, '62; Pris. Aug. 19, '64; d. Oct. 24, '64, Annapolis, Md.; also given Mason.

Mason, Thomas, vide Marran.

Mead, John A., b. July 4, 1842, Portland, Me.; 19, S.; student, Acton; Aug. 22, '62; Pris. Oct. 10, '63, to March 18, '64, Raccoon Ford; M. O. June 2, '64; d. Jan., 1891, Pearlington, Miss.

Moore, Rufus C., 25, M.; shoemaker, Natick; Feb. 22, '62, in Thirteenth Infty.; trans. to Thirty-ninth; dis. Feb. 22, '65, ex. of s.

Morrill, David W., 20, S.; farmer, Worcester; July 25, '63, in Twelfth Infty.; trans. to the Thirty-ninth; Pris. Aug. 19, '64; trans. to Thirty-second and M. O.

Murray, Hugh, 44, S.; farmer, Wilmington; Aug. 22, '62; trans. March 16, '64, to V. R. C.; dis. July 5, '64; d. Wilmington.

Murray, Sylvester, b. 1841, Ireland; 21, S.; shoemaker, Woburn; Aug. 22, '62; wd. May 8, '64; dis. disa., April 1, '65, from V. R. C.; d. Woburn.

Norris, Wilbur F., 28, M.; shoemaker, Natick; July 16, '61, in Thirteenth Infty.; trans. to Thirty-ninth, thence to V. R. C. April 13, '65.

O'Brien, William, b. June 14, 1832, Ireland; 29, M.; mariner, Woburn; Aug. 22, '62; wd. May 10, '64; dis. June 2, '65; d. March 14, '66, Woburn.

O'Connor, Cornelius, b. July 18, 1845, Ireland; 18, S.; currier, Woburn; Dec. 29, '63; wd. May 14, '64; trans. to V. R. C.; M. O. Aug 12, '65.

O'Donald, Edward, b. Aug., 15 1827, Ireland; 35, M.; laborer, Woburn; Aug. 22, '62; Pris. Aug. 19, '64, to March 20, '65; dis. June 2, '65; d. Woburn.

O'Donald, Owen, 33, M.; teamster, Boston; Aug. 22, '62; des. Sept. 6, '62.

O'Riley, John, b. Ireland; 35, M.; laborer, Woburn; Aug. 2, '62; trans. Jan. 9, '64, to V. R. C.; Feb. 19, '64, returned to Co. K; Pris. May 8, '64; recaptured next day; wd. June 17, '64, Petersburg; wd. April 1, '65, Five Forks; M. O. June 27, '65; d. Dec. 4, 1904.

Parker, T. Marvin, b. Feb. 25, 1838, Lebanon, Me.; (Corp.) 24, W.; clerk, Woburn; Aug. 22, '62; trans. to V. R. C.; dis. July 14, '65; salesman and bookkeeper; 1913, Woburn.

Parker, Theodore M., b. Nov. 6, 1841, Woburn; 20, S.; mason, Woburn; Aug. 22, '62; wd. Aug. 18, '64; M. O. June 2, '65; 1913, Woburn.

Parks, Charles T., b. 1825, Cambridge; 37, M.; currier, Woburn; Aug. 22, '62; dis. disa., May 2, '64; d. June 24, '70, Woburn.

Parks, Peter, Jr., b. 1829, Marblehead; 33, M.; Aug. 22, '62; Pris. Aug. 19, '62; d. Jan. 28, '65; Salisbury, N. C.

Persons, Herbert J., b. June 29, 1845, Woburn; 18, S.; clerk, Woburn; Dec. 23, '63; orderly to General Henry Baxter; trans. to Thirty-second and M. O.; also given "Pearsons"; d. Woburn.

Persons, Oscar, b. Sept. 8, 1838, Woburn; (1st Sergt.) 24, S.; silversmith, Woburn; 2d Lieut. Feb. 4, '63; vide Co. D; had been in Co. I, Fifth M. V. M., 3 mos. term, 1861.

Phillips, Charles A., 25, M.; shoemaker, Auburn; July 25, '63, in Thirteenth Infty.; trans. to Thirty-ninth, thence, Aug. 6, '64, to V. R. C.

Pollard, George F., b. 1841, Charlestown; 21, S.; clerk, Woburn; Aug. 22, '62; Corp.; missing after May 8, '64, Laurel Hill; his friends say "killed."

Poole, Rufus F., b. Feb. 23, 1839, Woburn; 23, S.; shoemaker, Woburn; Aug. 22, '62; M. O. June 2, '65; 1913, Woburn.

Ramsdell, Julius F., b. Oct. 29, 1845, Lynn; 18, S.; currier, Woburn; Dec. 13, '63; Pris. Aug. 19, '64; trans. Thirty-second Infty. and M. O.; d. Oct. 1909, Woburn.

Reddy, George H., b. Nov. 5, 1845; Boston; 18, S.; stiffening-cutter, Woburn; Dec. 26, '63; wd. May 10, '64; trans. to Thirty-second Infty. and M. O.

Reed, Moses D., b. Jan. 22, 1834, Burlington; 28, M.; shoemaker, Woburn; Aug. 22, '62; Pris. Aug. 19, '64; d. March 8, '65, Annapolis, Md.

Reger, Henry B., 26, S.; seaman, Boston; Oct. 22, '63, in Twelfth Infty.; trans. to Thirty-ninth, thence to Thirty-second and M. O.

Richardson, Albert H., b. Aug. 17, 1843, Woburn; 18, S.; diemaker, Woburn; Aug. 22, '62; wd. May 10, '64; Pris. Aug. 19, '64; M. O. June 2, '65; d. May 12, 1909, Woburn.

Richardson, Alonzo L., b. Aug. 30, 1846; 18, S.; butcher, Woburn; Dec. 29, '63; trans. to Thirty-second Infty. and M. O.; d. Nov. 23, 1909, Woburn.

Richardson, Samuel, Jr., b. May 23, 1833, Woburn; 29, M.; carpenter, Woburn; Aug. 22, '62; prom. Corp.; detailed July 25, '63, for duty at Draft

Rendezvous, Gallup's Island, Boston Harbor, till Aug. 13, '64; Pris. Aug. 19, '64, Weldon R. R.; d. March 23, '65, Parole Camp, Annapolis, Md.

Rogers, Charles, 24, M.; Oct. 22, '63, in Twelfth Infty.; wd. May 6, '64; trans. to Thirty-second Infty. and M. O.

Roland, Miles, b. 1840, Ireland; 22, S.; coachman, Woburn; Aug. 22, '62; wd. June 17, Petersburg; d. a prisoner Dec. 15, '64, Salisbury, N. C.; borne in State House as Rowland.

Sanborn, Orin, b. April 6, 1836, Exeter, N. H.; 26, M.; gaspipe-maker, Woburn; Aug. 22, '62; Corp.; May 1, '64; M. O. June 2, '65; d. May, 17, 1880, Woburn.

Sawyer, Augustus T., b. 1826, Brooks, Me.; 36, M.; printer, Woburn; Aug. 22, '62; k. May 10, '64, Laurel Hill.

Scott, Charles, b. 1833, Barnet, Vt.; 29, M.; carpenter, Woburn; Aug. 22, '62; d. a prisoner Oct. 16, '64, Salisbury, N. C.

Searles, Loring, b. March 19, 1827, New Ipswich, N. H.; 36, M.; (Corp.) shoemaker, Woburn; Aug. 22, '62; M. O. June 2, '65; d. May 14, 1902, Woburn.

Shaw, William L., 36, M.; mechanic, Lowell; July 15, '63, in Twelfth Infty.; trans. to Thirty-ninth, thence to Thirty-second and M. O.

Sheehan, John H., b. Oct. 22, 1845, Boston; 18, S.; teamster, Woburn; Aug. 22, '62; wd. May 10, '64; wd. and Pris. Aug. 19, '64; paroled March 20, '65; dis. May 25, 1865; for 45 years brakeman and conductor on Erie R. R.; in 1909, chief burgess, Borough of Matamoras, Penn.; 1913, Matamoras, Penn. Of late the name appears as Sheen.

Sheehan, Timothy, b. 1818, Ireland; 44. M.; carpenter, Woburn; Aug. 22, '62; d. March 10, '64.

Sheen, J. H., vide Sheehan.

Silver, Manual, 32, S.; seaman, Yarmouth; Jan. 28, '63, in Thirteenth Infty.; trans. to Thirty-ninth; dis. disa., Sept. 12, '64.

Smith, Frederick M., b. Sept. 19, 1839; 23, S.; trader, Woburn; Aug. 22, '62; dis. disa., Feb. 16, '65; first fifteen years photography, later mercantile life; 1913, Portland, Me.

Spokesfield, Ferdinand, b. April 16, 1844; 18, S.; farmer, Woburn; Aug. 22, '62; wd. and pris. Aug. 18, '64; M. O. June 20, '65; expressman, Boston, till 1899; City Hall watchman, Worcester, to date; 1913, Worcester.

Spontroz, Augustus, 25, S.; tailor, Boston; July 24, '63, in Thirteenth Infty.; trans. to Thirty-ninth, thence to Thirty-second and M. O.

Sprague, George A., b. Dec. 5, 1846; 18, S.; shoecutter, Woburn; Dec. 23, '63; d. Oct. 26, '64, a prisoner, Salisbury, N. C.

Staggles, William E., b. Oct. 24, 1844, Johnson, Vt.; 19, S.; barber, Woburn; Aug. 22, '62; dis. disa., May 5, '63.

Staples, Howard A., 21, —; —, Boston; Feb. 24, '62, in Thirteenth Infty.; trans. to Thirty-ninth; dis. Feb. 23, '65.

Stowers, William C., b. March 26, 1845, Woburn; 18, S.; printer, Woburn; Feb. 25, '64; trans. to Thirty-second Infty. and M. O.; d. Nov. 13, 1866, Woburn.

Tabor, Newell Z., b. May 22, 1833, Barton, Vt.; 30, M.; japaner, Woburn; Jan. 5, '64; wd. May 10, '64; trans. to Thirty-second and M. O.; had been in Co. G, Fifth M. V. M., 9 mos. term, 1862-'63; d. Dec. 23, 1900, Woburn.

Thompson, Abijah 2d, b. May 22, 1823; (Corp.) 39, M.; trader, Woburn; Aug. 22, '62; was captured at the Weldon R. R. and compelled to throw down his gun; luckily for him, he and his captors were taken in by the boys in blue; when selecting a gun from the many scattered about, he was the first to welcome back his comrade, George Fowle; Sergt. Feb. 3, '65; M. O. June 2, '65; dry goods and clothing clerk in Boston; 1913, Woburn, by far the oldest survivor of the Regiment.

Waite, Silas, b. 1846, Anson, Me.; 26, S.; farmer, Woburn; Aug. 22, '62; k. May 8, '64.

Walker, Lewis M., b. Sept. 30, 1844, Beverly; 19, S.; shoemaker, Woburn; Jan. 5, '64; wd. June 18, '64, Petersburg; d. June 30, '64, Alexandria, Va.

Warren, Benjamin F., b. Jan. 18, 1839, Woburn; 23, M.; carpenter, Woburn; Aug. 22, '62; d. Dec. 26, '63; Culpepper, Va.

Warren, William P., b. July 22, 1836, Woburn; 26, M.; shoemaker, Woburn; Aug. 22, '62; wd. May 5, '64, Wilderness; Pris. Aug. 19, '64, recaptured next day; Corp. Feb. 3, '65; M. O. June 2, 65; never missed a whole day with Regiment; 1913, Woburn.

West, Francis, 22. M.; farmer, Westford; Jan. 21, '64; d. July 25, '64, City Point, Va.

Wilson, Orville A., b. June 15, 1838, Bennington, Vt.; 24, M.; shoemaker, Woburn; Aug. 22, '62; dis. disa., Oct. 23, '63.

Wilson, James, 35, M.; hostler, Charlestown; Aug. 22, '62; dis. disa., March 4, '63; d. Dec. 20, 1890, Togus, Me.

Wolfe, Adam, 23, S.; cigar-maker, Attleborough; July 24, '63; trans. to Thirty-second Infty. and M. O.

UNASSIGNED RECRUITS

Bate, Wallace H., 23, M.; plumber, Melrose; July 16, '63; drafted man, trans. Sept. 27, '64, 102d Co., 2d Batt. V. R. C.; dis. July 14, '65.

Blanchard, Wm. F., 23, S.; seaman, Boston; trans. from Thirteenth Mass. Infty. July 16, '64, in which he had en. Jan. 4, '64; dis. Aug. 16, '64, for promotion, 2d Lieut. Co. F, Twenty-seventh U. S. C. T.; 1st Lieut. Co. A of the 27th, April 6, '65; dis. Sept. 21, '65.

Buhl, Peter, 22, S.; sailor, Boston; July 20, '63; N. F. R.

Cooley, James, 35, —; cordwainer, Natick; en. Jan. 4, '64; rejected recruit, Jan. 17, '64.

Cooley, Michael, 27, —; cordwainer, Natick; Jan. 7, '64; des. Feb. 7, '64.

Fitzgerald, James, 34, —; tailor, Charlestown; Dec. 2, '63; dis. disa., Dec. 20, '63.

Griffins, George W., 25, —; laborer, Barnstable; Jan. 29, '64; rejected recruit, Jan. 31, '64.

Hersey, Harrison D., 18, —; clerk, Chelsea; Feb. 18, '63; in Twelfth Infty.; captured May 5, '64, and held till April 28, '65; in the interval he was trans. to the Thirty-ninth; never joined; M. O. Aug. 2, '65.

Hyatt, James, 29, —; barber, Medford; Feb. 6, '64; des. April 2, '64.

Jeffers, George W., 25, M.; shoemaker, Haverhill; July 15, '63; trans. from the Twelfth Mass. Infty.; N. F. R.

Jordan, Frank, H., 18, —; blacksmith, Boston; rejected recruit, Jan. 31, '64.

Kelly, Thomas, 21, —; hostler, No. Bridgewater; Aug. 14, '63; trans. from 12th Infty.; N. F. R.

Kling, Caspar, 32, M.; cigar-maker, Weymouth; Aug. 4, '63; trans. from the 13th Infty.; N. F. R.

Murray, George, 18, —; glass-polisher, Woburn; Jan. 5, '64; rejected recruit.

Oakley, Frank, 32, S.; machinist, Truro; July 28, '63; trans. from 13th Infty.; N. F. R.

Sawyer, George, 22, S.; farmer, Medford; Feb. 17, '62; trans. from 13th Infty.; N. F. R.

Tevlin, Michael, 22, —; glass-cutter, Somerville; Nov. 28, '63; rejected recruit, Dec. 17, '63.

Wall, Richard, 29, —; ship carpenter, Medford; Jan. 14, '64; rejected recruit, Jan. 7, '64.

Williams, John, 1st, 33, S.; carpenter, Groton; July 27, '63; N. F. R.

Zindel, Adolph, 45, S.; jeweller, Hanson; Aug. 3, '63; trans. from Twelfth Infty.; N. F. R.

As a fitting postlude to this list of more than fourteen hundred names, borne by as many soldiers, brave and true, four-fifths of whom have passed within the veil, and whose final resting-places are annually remembered by their surviving comrades with loving tributes of beautiful flowers; after these more than fifty years is it not eminently fitting to enter here words of the gallant leader of the Regiment, its beloved Colonel, spoken by him on Memorial Day—

The Day of Roses and wreaths, of Laurel and leaves of love and honor and happy memories, not of sorrow or sadness or regrets. No colors half-mast for them. Glory throws the banner to the breeze. All hail, dear Comrades! You left us with a smile; we will join you with the same expression, and meanwhile will keep a festival for you and call it Memorial Day. You won in the last charge. Duty triumphed. You were given that firm faith that knows no fear. Living or dying, you cared not which, you offered your all for the Cause. The Cause was the succor of your country. You saved it. We will protect it, and with the blessing of God upon us both, we will hand it down as a home for the world to envy, and to occupy.—C. L. Peirson.

TABLE OF AGGREGATES.

(Taken, in the main, from Higginson's "Massachusetts in the Army and Navy, 1861-'65.")

	Whole No. Belonging	Killed or Died of Wds.	Died in Rebel Prisons	Died by Accident or of Disease	Deserted	Missing
F. & S.						
Officers	12	2	....	....	....	....
Enlisted Men	13	....	....	....	....	....
Co. A						
Officers	4	....	....	....	....	....
Enlisted Men	130	5	10	4	2	1
Co. B						
Officers	3	1	....	....	....	....
Enlisted Men	142	5	11	7	3	3
Co. C						
Officers	5	....	....	....	....	....
Enlisted Men	133	7	10	7	1	2
Co. D						
Officers	4	....	....	....	....	....
Enlisted Men	137	4	16	14	2	....
Co. E						
Officers	5	....	....	....	....	....
Enlisted Men	140	6	15	6	3	1

Co. F						
Officers	5	1	....	....	....	....
Enlisted Men	132	6	6	3	3	....
Co. G						
Officers	3	....	....	....	....	....
Enlisted Men	129	4	11	8	9	....
Co. H						
Officers	5	....	....	....	....	....
Enlisted Men	131	9	5	11	5	3
Co. I						
Officers	4	....	....	....	....	....
Enlisted Men	144	7	7	14	0	1
Co. K						
Officers	5	1	....	....	....	....
Enlisted Men	128	8	11	9	2	1
Unassigned recruits	21	....	....	....	2	....
	1436	66	102	83	32	12

For the sake of those who may observe that, in the several companies, there were more commissioned officers than are numbered in the foregoing list, it should be stated that the same officer frequently served in more than one company, by transferral or temporary assignment. The list has the same officer's name only once.

FOOTNOTES:

[A] DECEASED

[B] The order wherein were given the quotas of all the towns in the Commonwealth and the several conditions of enlistment.

[C] The privilege of piecing out the regular rations and of providing luxuries, not thought of by the commissary in his wildest dream, was accorded in the Thirty-ninth Regiment to Gilbert and Sumner Pullen, both natives of the State of Maine and enjoying the kinship of Second Cousins. After the war, Sumner Pullen, whose home was in Dedham, was a travelling salesman throughout his business life. He died in Dedham, Sept., 1890, aged 79 years; of Gilbert Pullen, no data subsequent to the war have been found.

[D] Reference to the records of the officers, as given in the archives of Vermont and Massachusetts, shows that Colonel Davis was commissioned August 29, 1862, and Colonel Jewett on the 26th, though the document was not issued until the 30th. Since possession is universally considered nine points of law, it would seem that the burden of evidence was on the side of the Massachusetts Colonel.

[E] It was during this strenuous night that General Briggs imparted to the Thirty-ninth men near him, acting as bodyguard, the interesting item that an old farmhouse near them was the very one in which "Old John Brown," in October, 1859, had assembled his followers and whence, during the night of the 17th, they went to the attack on Harper's Ferry. As the Kennedy farm, the place of rendezvous, was within sight of Boonsboro, it is not improbable that the morning's halt was near the historic building.

[F] John C. Robinson, one of the famous officers of the Union Army, was born in Binghamton, N. Y., April 10, 1817, left West Point 1838, a year before graduation, to study law, but returned to the army in 1839; he won distinction in the Mexican War; as Commandant of Fort McHenry, Baltimore, at the breaking out of the War, he preserved it for the Union side; from the Colonelcy of the First Michigan Infantry, he rose steadily in rank to the command of a division; he was prominent through the Seven Days' Fight, was ever in evidence from Fredericksburg to Gettysburg; he lost a leg at Spottsylvania thus retiring from service in the field; with Governor General John A. Dix, he was Lieut. Governor of the Empire State in 1873-4 and was commander-in-chief of the Grand Army of the Republic in 1877-8; in 1887 he attended annual reunion of the Thirty-ninth; he died February 18, 1897.

[G] The wounding of Private Dow was the first bloodshed in the Regiment, and in token thereof he was promoted to be a corporal. As this was the only casualty in the Regiment, during the Mine Run campaign, the death which Col. T. W. Higginson gives in his story of Massachusetts in the Army and Navy 1861-65 must be an error.

[H] Long years intervening, General Peirson recalls the existence of a certain church edifice, out Slaughter Mountain way, which in a former campaign had afforded cover for a rebel battery and that the same, issuing from its concealment, had done no little harm to the Second Massachusetts Infantry, even wounding several of his good friends. Lest it might be used thus again, and with a certain feeling of resentment as though the building had been *particeps criminis*, he suggested to the builders of the winter quarters that the siding of the house and its foundations might help out their own building schemes. "A word to the wise" was sufficient, and ere long the structure disappeared, to reappear as flooring and chimneys for Yankee comfort. The story does not end here, since many years later the officer was introduced, at the home of a Boston friend, to a Virginian lady whose mission North was the soliciting of funds for the rebuilding of the very edifice whose destruction he had suggested. The General's memory seemed defective when asked whether he responded liberally or not.

[I] John Newton, like Winfield Scott and George H. Thomas, was a native of Virginia, and was appointed thence to West Point, where he was graduated in 1842, No. 2, in a class that included Rosecrans, Pope, Seth Williams, Doubleday, Sykes and other noted Federal leaders and Longstreet, D. H. Hill, Gustavus W. Smith, McLaws and Van Dorn of the Confederates. In continuous service in the Engineer Corps, he had attained the rank of captain when the war began. He was assistant engineer in the construction of the defenses of Washington; served through the Peninsular campaign; was at Antietam, Fredericksburg, Chancellorsville and at Gettysburg and followed Reynolds as commander of the First Corps. After leaving the Army of the Potomac, he commanded a division in the Fourth Corps, under O. O. Howard, in the army of the Cumberland having a part in the campaign which culminated in the capture of Atlanta, September 1864. Later he commanded various districts in Florida until his muster-out from the volunteer service, January 1866. His subsequent life was devoted to engineering, among his most notable deeds being the removal of obstructions in Hell Gate, the narrow passage of East River, between Long Island Sound and New York Harbor. Subsequent to his resignation from the army in 1884, he became Commissioner of Public Works in New York City; at the time of his death in his seventy-second year, May 1, 1895, he was president of the Panama Railroad and of the Panama and Columbian Steamship Companies.

[J] General Morris Schaff, who was a member of General Warren's Staff, says, "Robinson, who brought up the rear of the corps, camped on the Germanna Road, the middle of his division about where Caton's Run comes down through the woods from the west." P. 97

[K] Greeley in "The American Conflict" says, "Thousands of the unnamed and unknown have evinced as fervid and as pure a patriotism, but no one surrendered more for his country's sake, or gave his life more joyfully for her deliverance, than did James S. Wadsworth."

[L] In General Schaff's "Wilderness" we may read, "The victorious Confederates could not pursue beyond the guns, or even stand there, for Sweitzer's of Griffin's, and the First Brigade of Robinson's division, under my friend, Charles L. Peirson, a gentleman, together with our rallied men, now poured such a fire into them from the east side of the field, that they fled back to their lines on the edge of the woods.... In an effort to recapture the guns—whose loss, Griffin, the commander of our West Point battery in my day, felt deeply—the Ninth Massachusetts and the Ninetieth Pennsylvania suffered frightfully, adding to the thickly lying dead in the old field." (Page 163.)

[M] James Clay Rice was born in Worthington, Mass., December 27, 1829, and was graduated from Yale in 1854; after a period spent in teaching in Natchez, Miss., he came to New York, studied law, began its practice in 1856, and thus the war found him. He enlisted as a private in the Thirty-ninth (Garabaldi Guards) New York Infantry, was soon commissioned First Lieutenant, and Adjutant, and as a Captain, was present at Bull Run. On the organization of the Forty-fourth New York, or the Ellsworth Avengers, he was made Lieutenant Colonel, later Colonel, and saw all of the active service of that regiment, winning distinction at Gettysburg. At the time of his death he was in command of the Second Brigade, Fourth (Wadsworth's) Division of the Fifth Corps. Like Sedgwick, he was shot by a sharpshooter. His last words were, "Turn me over towards the enemy; let me die with my face to the foe."

[N] It is claimed that the body of Colonel Davis was carried from the field by Corp. S. H. Mitchell, "A"; Corp. B. F. Prescott and W. S. Sumner, both of "H"; and Sergt. L. A. Spooner of Company I.

[O] November 14, 1911, when visiting the Robert E. Lee Home for Confederate Veterans in Richmond, John Maxwell, an ex-confederate, whose later days were passing in this congenial harborage, was introduced and requested to tell the Northern visitors how he blew up the Yankees. Nothing loth, the veteran in gray, holding in his hands the works of an alarm clock, told the story of his sneaking into the Union lines and, when opportunity offered, placing his infernal machine, with his time-wheel for explosion properly set, where it would do the most execution and then hastening away. His auditors, so recently from the dedication of a Massachusetts monument on the edge of the Crater, recalling an even greater explosion, were hardly in position to find any great amount of fault with his act, since "Sauce for the goose is also sauce for the gander." "Where were you, Johnnie, when the thing went off?" was a natural question from one of the hearers. "Oh, I was two miles away, making the best time possible towards the Confederacy." (Vid. R. R. Serial No. 87. p. 954).

[P] When the rails, thus heated, were grasped at their ends by several stalwart men and carried so that the red hot middle might hit a good-sized tree, the extended iron would be bent almost double. The two ends being somewhat divergent; four rails thus carried and thus applied and symmetrically placed about a tree made a very good Maltese Cross, the badge of the Fifth Corps and other army corps were wont to say when, as at the North Anna, they saw many tokens of this sort, "Well, the Fifth Corps has been here."

A. S. R.

[Q] At the last reunion, attended by Sergeant McFeeley, he gave the following version of the day's incident, stating that when the Union batteries began to play on our lines, the commander of the color guard sent him back to stop the firing and in so doing, he ran into the rebel line. At once he tried to hide behind some bushes but a Johnnie got his eye on him and ordered him to come out, which he did. Walking along in the ranks, a prisoner, he saw a reb have a stand of colors and, on account of the rain, they were done up in their case, which he recognized as one that he had mended, and he also knew the staff which had been scarred by battle as belonging, both of them, to the Thirty-ninth. Naturally McFeeley kept as near the colors as possible and their present holder, who was very happy over his proud possession, though he had only picked them out of the rut where Adams had thrown them. When Wheelock's relieving column came charging through, McFeeley stepped up to the rebel and remarked that he guessed he would hold that same flag awhile, thus saving the precious token from gracing some Confederate collection of curios.

[R] Colonel Thomas F. McCoy of Scotch-Irish lineage, was born in Mifflin County, Penn., 1819. Having served seven years in the Militia, President Polk made him a first lieutenant in the Eleventh U. S. Infantry, when the Mexican War began. Participating in the principal battles of that strife, he came home a captain. A lawyer when the Rebellion began, he offered his services to Gov. Curtin and was made deputy quartermaster general of the state. When Col. Thos. A. Zeigle of the One Hundred and Seventh Penn. died July 16, '62, on the vote of the line officers of the Regiment, he was made colonel. He had a part in all of the varied service of the One Hundred and Seventh to the end and went home a Brevet Brig. General. General Warren was particularly warm in his appreciative remarks about the colonel. Going home to Lewistown, Penn., he resumed the practice of law. Marrying May 22d, '73, Miss Margaret E. Ross of Harrisburg, he led the life of respect and responsibility, one of the most prominent citizens of his town, for nearly half a century a ruling elder in the Presbyterian church and died July 20, 1899. His son, Frank R., a West Pointer, an officer in the Tenth U. S. Infantry, was wounded at San Juan, Cuba, and is now a Captain on the General Staff, Washington. Ancestors of the Colonel were in the Colonial Wars, members of Morgan's Riflemen in the Revolution; were in the War of 1812, and through father and son, in every National war since.

[S] Many opinions exist as to what and where the Petersburg Express was. Some even aver that it was a Confederate institution. General H. L. Abbot, in his History of the First Connecticut Heavy Artillery, has the following, "To check an annoying enfilade firing from the left bank of the Appomattox, a thirteen inch sea coast mortar was mounted on a curve of the Railroad track by Company G. This novelty was widely known as the 'Petersburg Express.' The mortar, on a heavy granite foundation, since Sept. 25, 1902, has stood upon the State House grounds, Hartford, as a memorial to the First Heavies."

[T] Peter Lyle, Colonel of the Ninetieth Pennsylvania, Bvt. Brig. General, and for much of the service of the Thirty-ninth in the Fifth Corps, commander of the Brigade, was born in Philadelphia, Christmas Day, 1821. Receiving very little education from the schools, he was apprenticed to the cigar trade while yet a boy. His marked boyish predelection was love for military matters, and he drilled his boyish associates, formed into a company, till they became noted for their proficiency, accomplishing in their juvenile way wonders with their broomstick guns. When only sixteen years of age, during the absence of the officers, he commanded and paraded the City Phalanx. While still a youth he organized an independent company which he commanded until it was taken into the National Guards. In 1846 he succeeded to the command of the company which before the war had increased to a battalion, becoming a regiment in 1860 under the command of Colonel Lyle. His organization had volunteered for service in the Mexican War but, the quota being full, it did not go. At the outbreak of the Rebellion, the Regiment, as the Nineteenth Pennsylvania, volunteered and so served for three months. Reorganized in August, 1861, it was sworn in for three years as the Ninetieth Regiment, still commanded by Colonel Lyle. He never fully recovered from a wound received at Antietam. Subsequent to the war he was elected sheriff in 1867, being a Democrat in politics, serving a single term. Much that he had acquired during his term was absorbed by an agricultural venture in Maryland which, failing finally, he was thrown entirely upon the outcome of carriage making, a business to which he gave immediate attention after the discharge of the Regiment, his associate being his late Adjutant, David P. Weaver. His last public appearance in a military capacity was during the riots of 1877 when, though suffering agonies from bodily ills, he sat his saddle and discharged his duties faithfully. Soon after he declined a re-election to the command of the Regiment and died in Philadelphia, July 17, 1879. His burial was attended with all the honors due a full Brigadier General, his body having lain in state in the armory of his Regiment that he had led so long and so well; it was buried in Ivy Hill Cemetery by the side of his brother, David M. Lyle, the last Chief Engineer of the Philadelphia Volunteer Fire Department. For the foregoing facts we are indebted to Captain P. Lyle Weaver, a son of Adjutant D. P. Weaver, himself a Philadelphia journalist.—A. S. R.

[U] One of the most pleasant memories of war times is that of the almost David and Jonathan relations that existed between certain regiments. This was the case with the Thirty-ninth and the Sixteenth Maine; either one had a feeling of security if, in the hour of danger, it was supported by the other; exposed repeatedly to a common peril, in a measure, the history of one is that of both; each regiment had the highest regard and respect for the leaders of its fellow organization and for years after the war exchange of courtesies on reunion occasions was an expected event. Closely related in early history as were Maine and Massachusetts, the equal intimacy between representatives of the two states in camp and march and on the field lingers long in the minds of those who participated.

[V] Condensed from a paper prepared by Captain Charles H. Porter and read by him before the Massachusetts Military Historical Society January 11, 1886.

[W] Governour Kemble Warren was born in Cold Spring, Putnam Co., N. Y., January 8, 1830, and was graduated from West Point, No. 2, in a class of forty-four members, very few of whom, however, are known to fame, Cuvier Grover and Powell T. Wyman being the most noted among his loyal classmates and Wm. T. Magruder and Robert Ransom among the rebels. Assigned on graduation to the Topographical Engineers, he was in constant and active service till his appointment as mathematical instructor at West Point, 1859, and there the Rebellion found him. At first he was Lieut. Colonel of the Fifth (Duryea's Zouaves), N. Y. Volunteers, soon succeeding to the colonelcy; he was the last to leave the field at Big Bethel, remaining to rescue the body of Lieut. J. T. Greble, the first Regular Army officer to lose his life in the war. He helped build the forts on Federal Hill, Baltimore. He served in the Peninsular Campaign, acquiring a brigade in May, '62, and, in the subsequent months, there was very little doing by the Army of the Potomac in which he did not bear a conspicuous part. His bronze figure on Little Round Top must forever tell the story of his watchfulness and alertness at Gettysburg and the members of the Fifth Army Corps, to a man, never failed to chant his praises. The incident of his suspension from his command at Five Forks is a blot on the fame of Sheridan and made Warren's place in the hearts of his followers warmer than ever. A skillful engineer, he was constantly employed in the army up to the time of his death, which no doubt was hastened by the unfortunate occurrence of April, '65. His relations with the Thirty-ninth, after the war, were of an unusually intimate character. He died in Newport, R. I., August 8, 1882.

[X] From the history of the Fifth Army Corps, William H. Powell, pp. 863-4.

Milton Keynes UK
Ingram Content Group UK Ltd.
UKHW031044120324
439302UK00006B/601

9 789357 944229